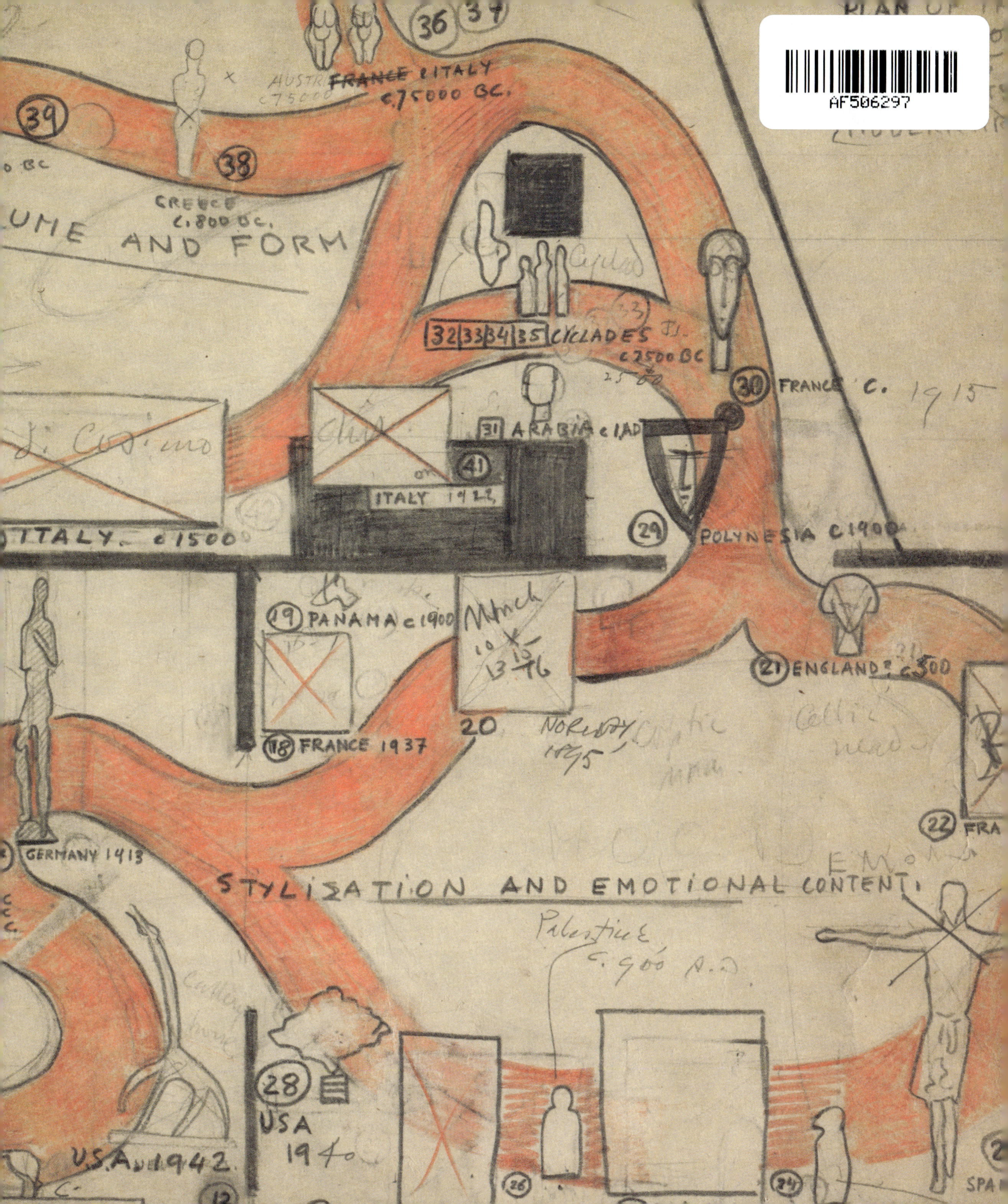
VOLUME AND FORM
STYLISATION AND EMOTIONAL CONTENT
AUSTRIA c.75000
FRANCE & ITALY c.75000 BC.
GREECE c.800 BC.
32 33 34 35 CYCLADES IS. c.2500 BC
2500
31 ARABIA c.1 AD
41 ITALY 1922
30 FRANCE c. 1915
29 POLYNESIA c.1900
ITALY. c.1500
19 PANAMA c.1900
Munch 10 13.10.76
18 FRANCE 1937
20
NORWAY 1895
21 ENGLAND c.500
22 FRA
GERMANY 1413
28 USA 1940
U.S.A. 1942.
Palestine c.900 A.D
26
24 SPA
36 37
39
38

René d'Harnoncourt
and the Art of Installation

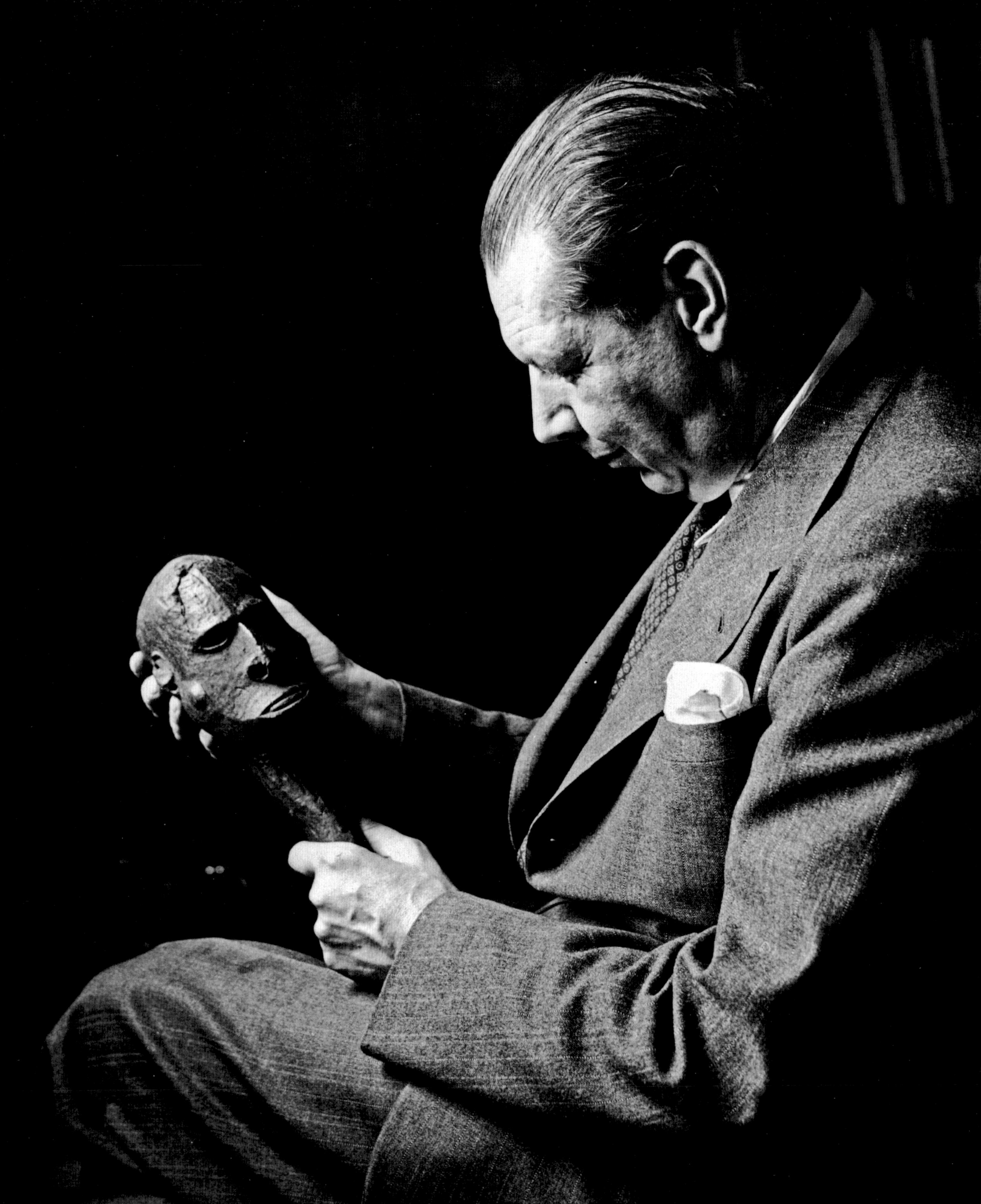

René d'Harnoncourt and the Art of Installation

Michelle Elligott

The Museum of Modern Art, New York

Contents

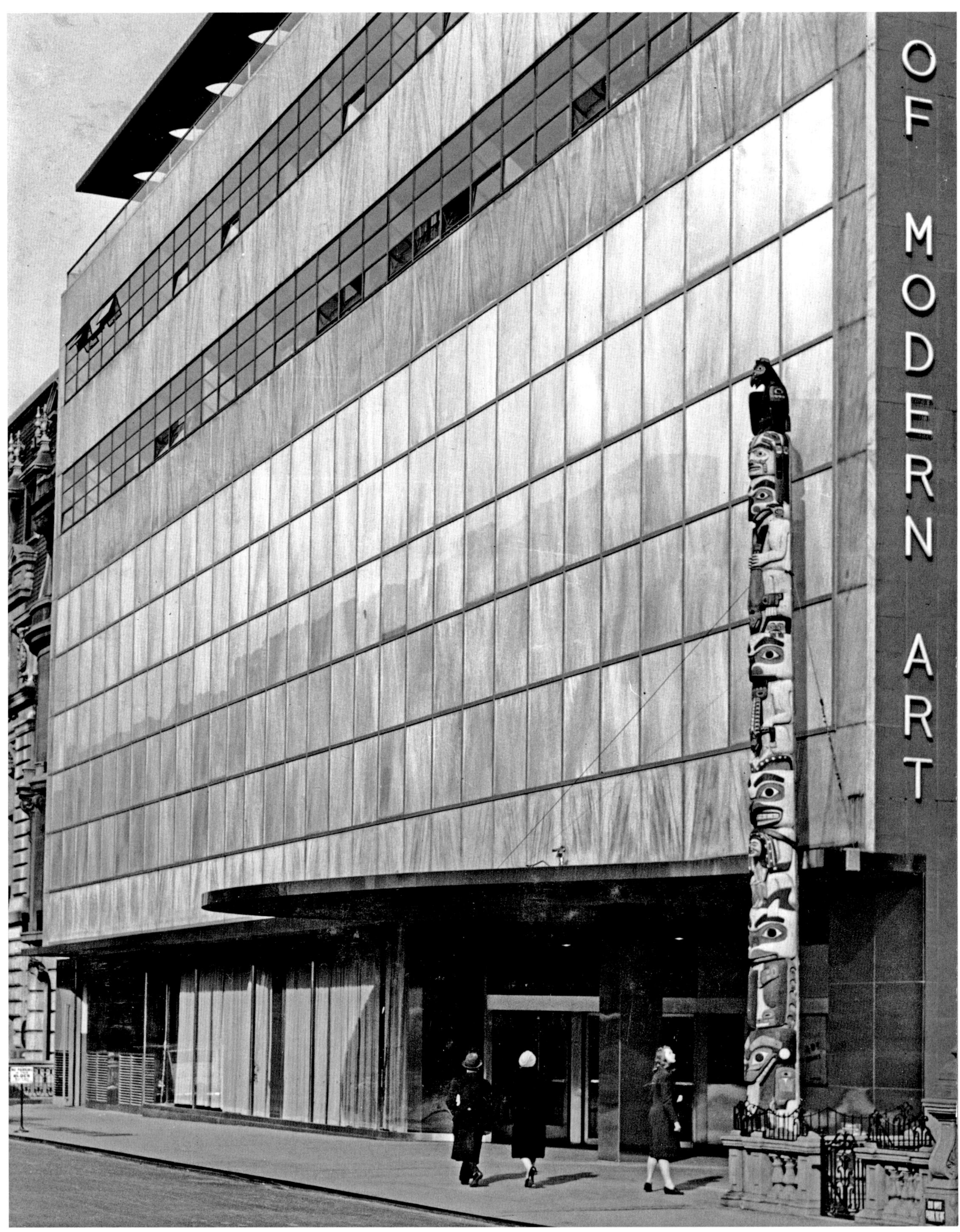

OF MODERN ART

Foreword

In 1960, toward the end of his illustrious career at MoMA, René d'Harnoncourt was the subject of a lengthy profile in the *New Yorker*. Its author described d'Harnoncourt, in the opening lines of the piece, as the "agile, gigantic, genial, hard-working, courtly, confident, aristocratic, wildly conversational, Vienna-born director and champion *installateur* of the Museum of Modern Art."

"Wildly conversational" was no exaggeration: the profile is largely taken up by the voice of its subject. Over Bloody Marys, eggs benedict, and raspberry sherbet, d'Harnoncourt recounts his colorful life story, which takes him from Austria to Mexico to the United States; from chemist to antiques dealer to curator of exhibitions of so-called primitive arts to the director of MoMA for close to two decades. As the latter—while shouldering myriad administrative responsibilities, by all accounts, with infinite tact and grace—this multitasker par excellence continued to organize and install exhibitions at MoMA and elsewhere, including the Museum of Primitive Art, of which he was also the founding vice president.

Possessing a remarkable memory, attention to detail, and draftsmanship skills (vividly on display in the pages of this book), d'Harnoncourt revolutionized the way exhibitions were conceived. He devoted an unprecedented level of analysis to the visitor's experience of art, carefully considering every aspect of its presentation. Like the author of the 1960 profile, we have to borrow the word "installateur" to describe d'Harnoncourt's role in the development of exhibitions: no title more commonly in use would adequately convey the full extent of the responsibilities he assumed and his conception of the role he created for himself. D'Harnoncourt intended to spend his retirement years on the front porch of his house in Key West, writing a book on museum-installation techniques; but just one month after taking his leave from the Museum, he was struck and killed by an intoxicated driver—a tragedy that put an end to the project, as well as to his fascinating life story.

One century after his birth in 1901, Museum archivists were busily processing his archives, arranging his papers to fully open them to researchers. D'Harnoncourt's correspondence and the hundreds of preparatory drawings they contain constitute a comprehensive record of his accomplishments and demonstrate his unique approach to installation. Michelle Elligott, who supervised these efforts, was captivated by d'Harnoncourt and became convinced that his exceptional talent for sketching, understanding, and installing art merited further scholarly attention—and indeed, its own publication. Deprived of d'Harnoncourt's own tribute to his work, we are nonetheless granted hereby the opportunity to discover his genius and insight. Building on her extensive archival research, Michelle has compiled a detailed presentation of d'Harnoncourt's life and work, relying on the words of the loquacious director himself and on the vast collection of sketches he left behind. We at the Museum are grateful for her efforts to bring attention to d'Harnoncourt's inspiring work and personality.

Glenn D. Lowry
Director, The Museum of Modern Art, New York

Opposite: Entrance to The Museum of Modern Art during the first exhibition curated by René d'Harnoncourt for MoMA, *Indian Art of the United States*, 1941

Acknowledgments

The incubation of this publication has been quite a long one, and I am very grateful to those who along the way have contributed their insights, enthusiasm, and support.

I would first like to thank several practicing exhibition designers for discussing initial ideas with me and suggesting new ways of looking at d'Harnoncourt's drawings. These include David Hollely, Lana Hum, and Wendy Evans Joseph. I am indebted to designer and curator Prem Krishnamurthy for his conversations and insights on the history of exhibition display and for sharing leads on relevant scholarship. Eminent design historian and MoMA curator Juliet Kinchen also provided invaluable expertise.

I am also appreciative of those who knew d'Harnoncourt and spoke with me about him. They include his son-in-law Joe Rishel, former MoMA curator and colleague Peter Selz, and family member Cecily Trapp. Rishel also kindly supplied an image and copyright permissions, while Trapp generously donated family photographs.

Artist Walid Raad offered wonderful encouragement in my quest to bring d'Harnoncourt's achievements to light. I am thankful for the support of colleagues at other institutions, including Claire Dienes and James Moske at the Metropolitan Museum of Art; Barbara Mathe, formerly of the American Museum of Natural History; Michele Hiltzik Beckerman at the Rockefeller Archive Center; Carla Simms at the National Archives and Records Administration; Leslie Cade from the Cleveland Museum of Art; Suz Massen from the Frick Art Reference Library; and Eri Mizukane, David McKnight, and John Pollack from the Kislak Center for Special Collections, Rare Books and Manuscripts, University of Pennsylvania Libraries.

Tod Lippy, editor of the brilliant *Esopus* magazine, deserves special mention, as he gave me the opportunity to first publish a small selection of d'Harnoncourt's drawings ten years ago. Tod's commitment to and passion for archives, in both their intrinsic and informational value, runs deep; we have been coconspirators in bringing archives to light for public consumption for more than a decade.

I am indebted to Bruce Altshuler, noted author of the canonical study on the history of exhibitions and director of the Museum Studies graduate program at New York University. Bruce shared many insights with me over the years.

This book would not exist without The Contemporary Arts Council of The Museum of Modern Art, which provided generous financial support to help defray the costs of publication. Co-Chair Tom Osborne has been particularly supportive over the years and repeatedly found delight in inquiring about the project's progress.

Of course, I owe the success of this endeavor, as well as that of the Archives, Library, and Research Collections, to Peter Reed and Glenn Lowry, who have empowered this project and program and allowed them to thrive. Kathy Fuld, Chair of the Trustee Committee on Archives, Library, and Research, is an inspiring leader.

In the Museum's Department of Publications, I am grateful to the many individuals who contributed to the creation of this volume, in particular Emily Hall, as well as Hannah Kim, Matthew Pimm, Rebecca Roberts, and Marc Sapir. I also owe gratitude to Museum Publisher Christopher Hudson for supporting this endeavor. Of course, this project would not have come to fruition without the dedicated efforts of project editor Madeleine Compagnon. Many thanks go to Miko McGinty and Rita Jules for the handsome design of this book.

I am grateful to the Imaging and Visual Resources team, led by the very able Robert Kastler, who lovingly scanned scores of delicate drawings made by d'Harnoncourt as well as photographs and documents about him. Jenny Tobias of the Library graciously facilitated interlibrary loan requests.

I absolutely would not have been able to carry out this effort without the outstanding work and cooperation of my entire team in the MoMA Archives, including in particular Michelle Harvey, with whom I have had a productive collaboration for more than two decades, as well as current and former staff: Ana Marie Cox, Megan Govin, Tom Grischkowsky, Nicole Kaack, Sofia Kofodimos, Molly Lieberman, Tellina Liu, Jonathan Lill, Courtney Lynch, Katherine Rovanpera, and Elisabeth Thomas. A very special and heartfelt thank you is owed to Christina Eliopoulos, who embraced the challenge of assisting me with research and image rights in a wonderfully upbeat and optimistic manner.

Finally, my family. My parents, Nancy and Bill, have provided me with unwavering love and support for many years, for which I am eternally grateful. My charming and loving husband, Jeff, has helped me find empowerment and confidence, encouraging me to grow professionally and to make the dream of this book a reality. I dedicate this tome to my muses, Clio Anastasia and Julian Alexander—may they always be fit to profit from whatever happy accident life brings their way.

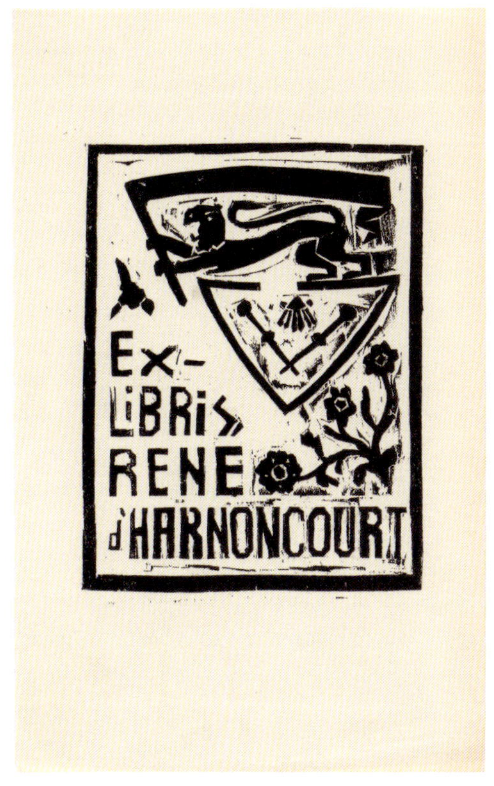

René d'Harnoncourt's bookplate, n.d.

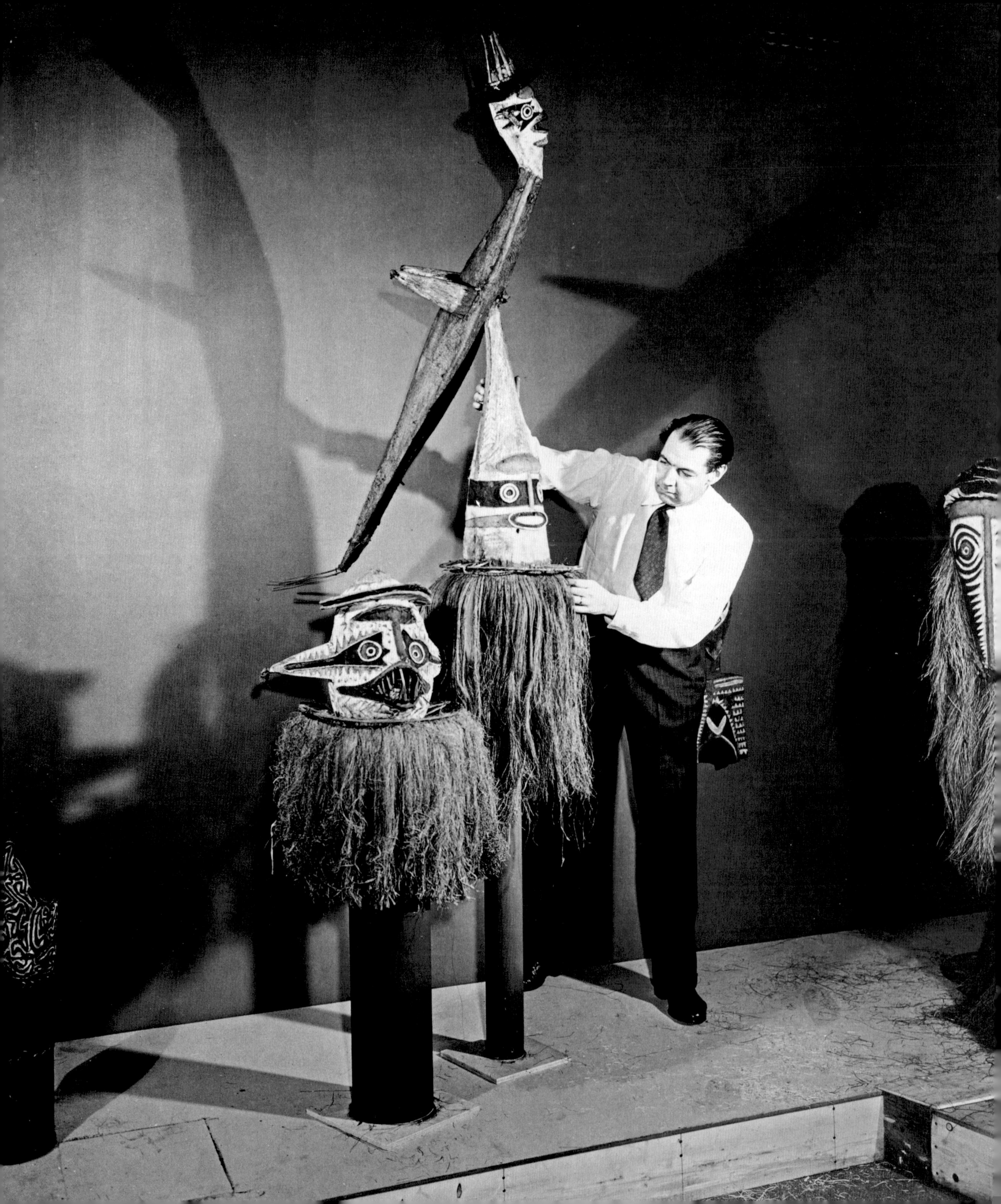

René d'Harnoncourt: *Installateur*

"Installation is terribly dangerous. It's full of terribly seductive temptations."[1]

René d'Harnoncourt

"He knew that what is of ultimate concern is *the ecstasy of the eye.*"[2]

Robert Motherwell on d'Harnoncourt

Prologue

René d'Harnoncourt was a unique specimen. Artist, collector, curator, and director of The Museum of Modern Art for two decades, he was a man of many talents, an autodidact who, rather than following the narrow path of a classically trained art historian, learned from a diverse set of experiences and direct contact with works of art and their makers in their original environments. He had an insatiable interest in and curiosity about the arts, and a respect for and delight in living artists. An Old World aristocrat, born a count, d'Harnoncourt became a true cosmopolitan of the New World.

This genial, amiable man, who stood at 6 feet 6 inches and weighed in at 230 pounds, garnered the nickname "the gentle giant." In his role at MoMA, he was, his daughter remarked, "so outgoing, so charming, so ebullient, so persuasive."[3] He seemed to find opportunity around every corner. His wife, Sarah d'Harnoncourt, characterized his philosophy of life as

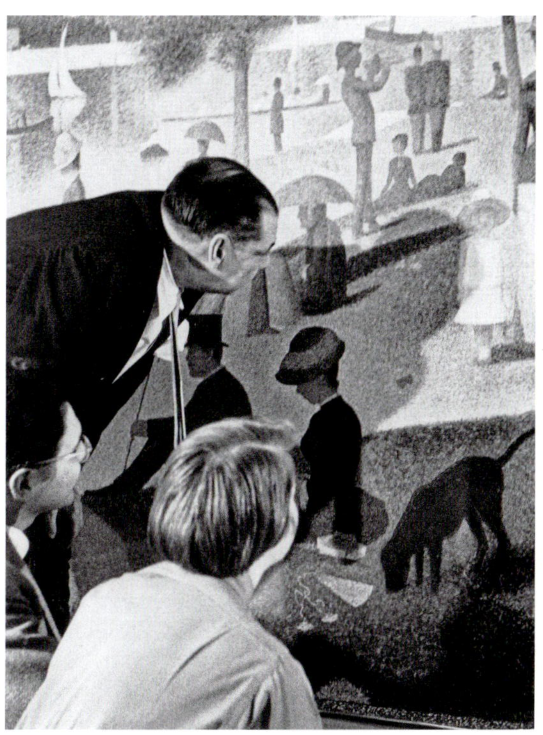

René d'Harnoncourt and others looking at Georges Seurat's painting, *A Sunday on La Grande Jatte— 1884* (1884–86), March 1958

Opposite: René d'Harnoncourt installing *Arts of the South Seas*, January 1946

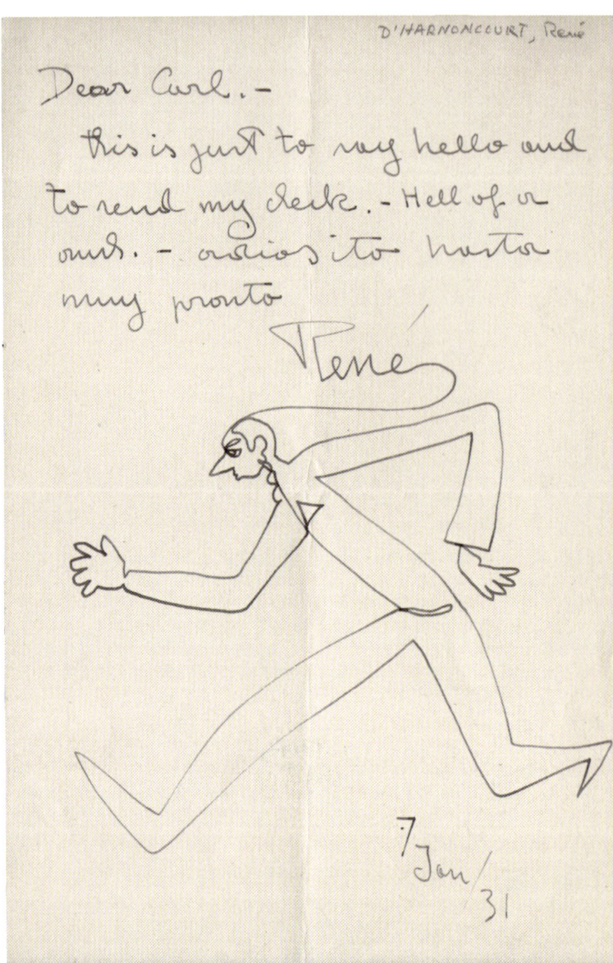

A quickly executed self-portrait by d'Harnoncourt in a letter to Carl Zigrosser, January 7, 1931. Zigrosser was the director of Weyhe Gallery, which presented d'Harnoncourt's only solo exhibition in 1932.

such: "When someone felt that everything was going wrong, R.H. always said a happy accident was sure to be on the way; the great thing was to keep yourself in shape so you would be ready to take advantage of it."[4] His seemingly boundless optimism and open-mindedness, combined with his being a humanist, polymath, and polyglot (fluent in six languages)—not to mention his well-known wonderful sense of humor—made him an ideal museum administrator, diplomat, and advocate for the arts. Or, as Nelson A. Rockefeller later remarked of his friend and collaborator, "René d'Harnoncourt was a man of love who loved people, who loved beauty, who loved life . . . Through his creative leadership as director of The Museum of Modern Art he brought joy to millions of people around the world and a cultural richness to this country—an American Renaissance."[5]

Among his numerous talents, there was one particular activity in which he truly delighted: the design and installation of museum exhibitions. MoMA's founding director Alfred H. Barr, Jr., praised d'Harnoncourt for developing "the art of installation to a point that isn't equaled anywhere in the world."[6] Beginning in the late 1920s, for several decades d'Harnoncourt devoted attention to exhibition design as a creative practice, especially during his tenure at MoMA, where he installed some two dozen shows. As his daughter stated, "He loved nothing better than installing a show and trying to make the work of art, as he would say, speak for itself."[7] Over the years, d'Harnoncourt developed a highly sophisticated installation methodology and even devised a specific nomenclature to describe his way of working, relying on his extraordinary ability to juxtapose objects and works of art to bring out contrasting and complementary styles, relationships, and affinities.

D'Harnoncourt was so passionate about the art of installation that he announced he would devote his retirement to writing a book on the subject. The book was eagerly awaited, since, as the *New York Times* pointed out in a June 1968 article announcing his retirement from MoMA, "His exhibition showmanship, one of the director's greatest accomplishments, has become internationally recognized."[8] D'Harnoncourt's desire to publish a tome about his installation practice did not rest with him alone. Several important personalities in the art world clamored for the book, including the preeminent French art dealer Louis Carré, who wrote d'Harnoncourt on the occasion of his 1958 Seurat exhibition requesting "a study of the solutions you have been able to find individually for each and every problem . . . I would also like to point to the very real need for a permanent record of your so very special work."[9]

On the occasion of d'Harnoncourt's retirement, trustee Dr. Henry Allen Moe delivered a letter to him at the Board meeting of June 13, 1968. It heralded a promise: "The facts of your accomplishments will be set forth later in what will be a book about you. The things you have done are so numerous that no letter, no readable statement, could contain them.

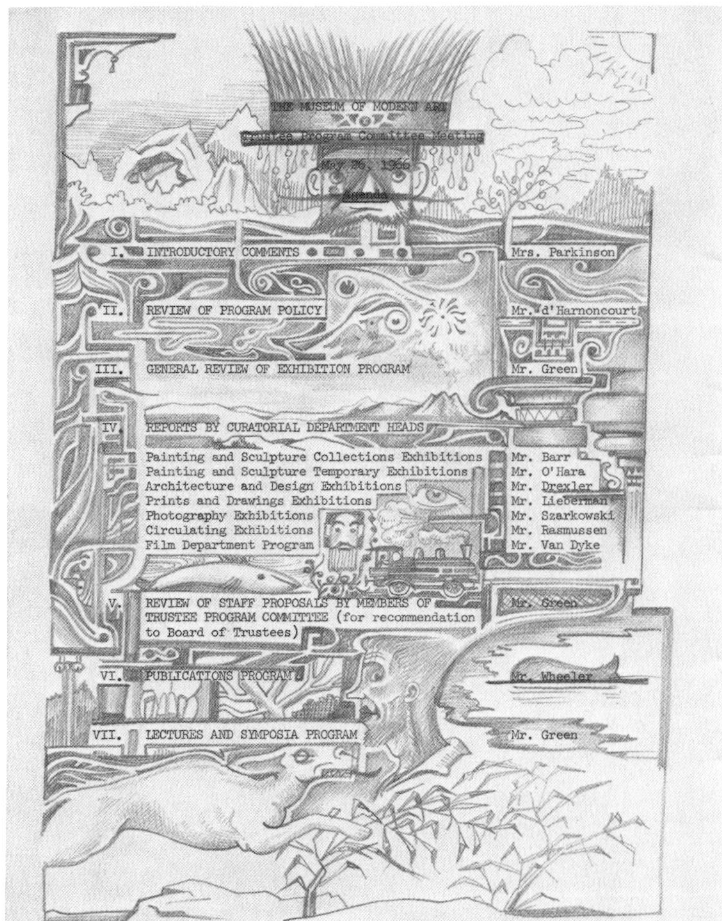

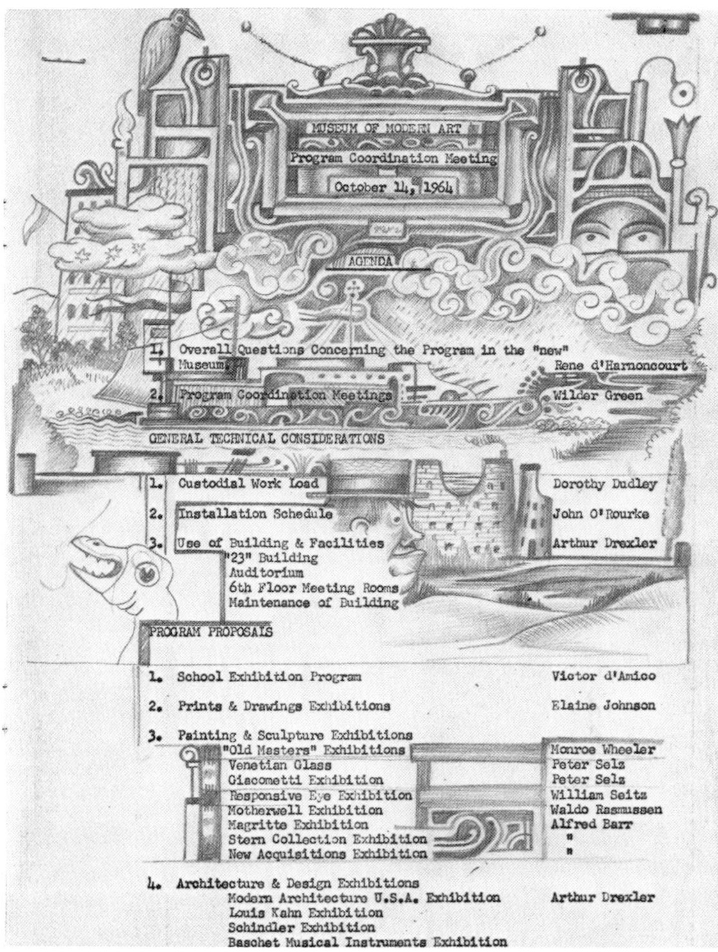

D'Harnoncourt was an inveterate doodler. A selection of his elaborate sketches, some drawn on MoMA meeting agendas, was published in a booklet entitled *d'Hoodles* in 1968, when he retired from the Museum.

There will be, in the book, some commentary; and it must also contain some of your own rich sayings. *Litera scripta manet*, as the Romans put it: that which is written endures. A great catalogue often is more important than the exhibition—in the sense that it lasts longer. The book will endeavor to set down enduringly, in one place, what has made you tick and how you tick."[10]

Unfortunately, d'Harnoncourt was not able to produce this account himself: just two months after his retirement, he was killed by an intoxicated driver.

This book endeavors to fulfill Allen Moe's appeal and introduce twenty-first-century readers to a great but little-known museum man of the twentieth century. His unique vision has left an indelible imprint on how institutions and the public think about the arts of today and yesterday, from near and far. This volume presents the fascinating story of d'Harnoncourt's life, investigates the universalist philosophy that influenced his understanding of art and thereby informed his methodology, and chronicles a dozen of his most significant and ambitious exhibitions.

European upbringing and Mexican adventures

Count René d'Harnoncourt was born in Vienna in 1901 to a titled, landowning family of French descent. Given his aristocratic background and the circumstances of his privileged childhood in Austria, no one would have predicted that he would go on to become a pioneer of museum installation and an important presence in the New York art world for decades. Yet it would be impossible to understand how d'Harnoncourt came to conceive his unique approach and methods without knowing how he himself was formed, his background, his personality, his love of adventure, and his resourcefulness.

D'Harnoncourt's interest in the arts began at an early age. While his schooling emphasized the sciences, as an adolescent he found time to collect Old Master prints; to co-found an arts club that staged the first exhibition of prints by Henri Matisse and Pablo Picasso in Graz, where his family settled in 1909; and to write poetry and plays. Pursuing a range of eclectic interests was part of d'Harnoncourt's modus operandi from his youth: as a child, he visited the Landesmuseum Joanneum in Graz, and studied its mix of collections ranging from regional Celtic antiquities and Old Master paintings to folk art, minerals, and natural history. This institution may have been the foundation of his lifelong interests in folk art and the bridging of arts and sciences.[11] At university in Vienna, d'Harnoncourt studied chemistry, writing a thesis on the creosote contents of certain soft coals of southern Yugoslavia.

In 1924, d'Harnoncourt's comfortable life was abruptly upended: with the collapse of the Austro-Hungarian empire, the family estate he had hoped to inherit was expropriated by Czechoslovakia. Faced suddenly and for the first time with the need to earn his own living, d'Harnoncourt tried to put his knowledge of the Old Masters and his connections among impoverished aristocrats to good use and sought to

René d'Harnoncourt's Mexican immigration document, 1930

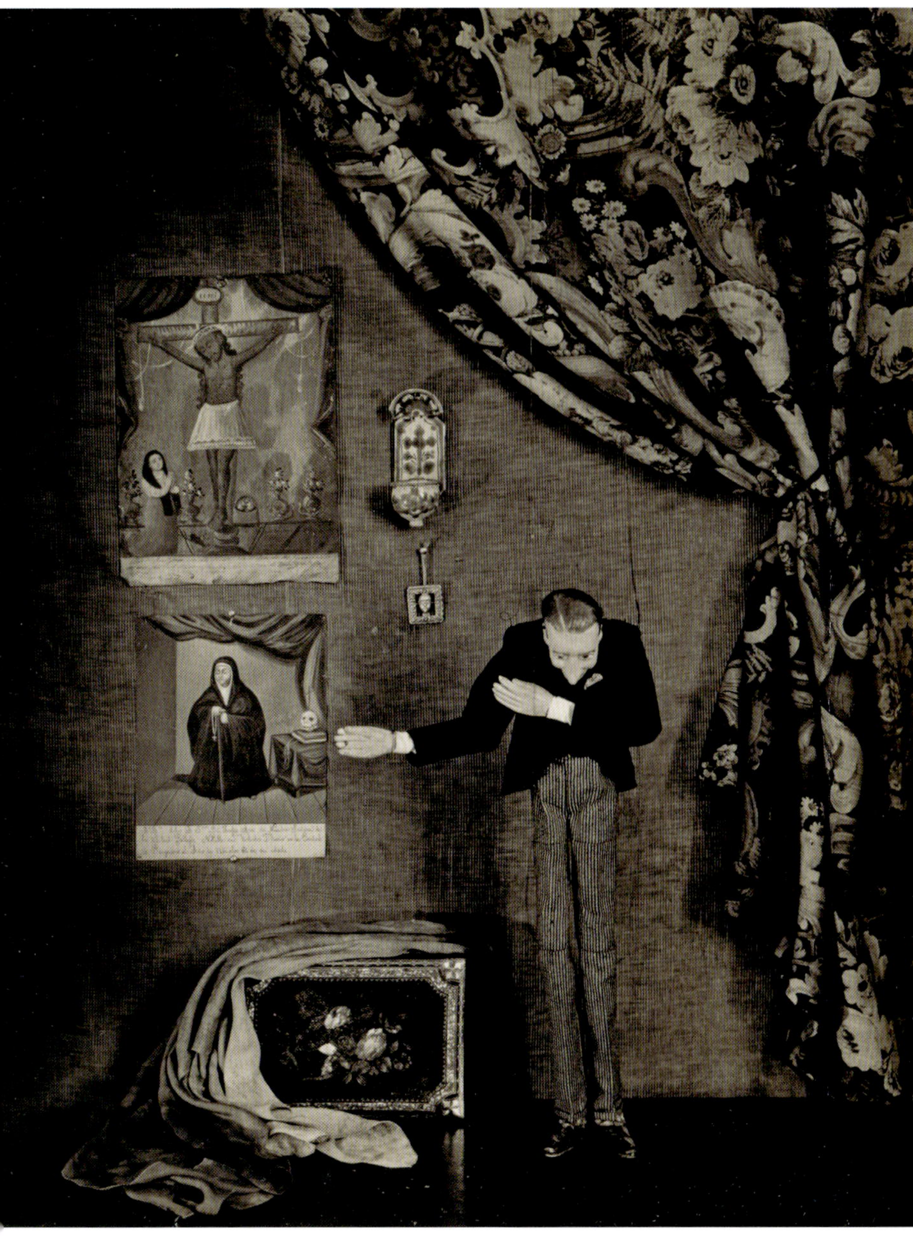

Tina Modotti. *René d'Harnoncourt Puppet*, 1929. Gelatin silver print, 9⅜ × 7 in. (23.9 × 17.8 cm)

make a living by purchasing family holdings to sell to dealers in Vienna.[12]

After a few months, d'Harnoncourt decided it would be better to be poor in a new land than in familiar territory. He set off to the New World in 1925, financing his voyage by selling a number of Old Master prints, including one by Dürer, and a manuscript by Rilke. D'Harnoncourt would have preferred to settle in the United States, but the restrictive Immigration Act of 1924 made that impossible; so he chose Mexico instead. It didn't seem to have occurred to the happy-go-lucky d'Harnoncourt, prior to his arrival, that it would be difficult for an Austrian nobleman chemist, who spoke neither Spanish nor English, to find employment there as a scientist. With this ambition set aside, he had to rely on his natural artistic talent, turning to a variety of odd jobs to make ends meet: he designed posters, sketched bullfights and portraits for the tourist trade, painted pocket-watch faces, and decorated shopwindows for department stores and pharmacies.

D'Harnoncourt had a knack for forming useful acquaintances and making himself indispensable to them—a talent that would serve him well throughout his career. He soon met several affluent Americans interested in acquiring collections of Mexican colonial objects and textiles. D'Harnoncourt saw an opportunity in this new market. Drawing on his experience in working with clients and dealers of art, he soon made contacts in commerce, assisting at first in the peddling of antique European furniture and Spanish colonial antiquities, then increasingly seeking out indigenous contemporary traditional crafts and modern art.

The most important establishment in the country at that time to carry Mexican colonial objects and textiles and nineteenth-century European items was the Mexico City arts-and-crafts showroom of the Sonora News Company, a franchise for newspapers and curios with stores in train stations throughout the country. Located in a chic part of town, on the upscale Avenida Madero, the store was managed by Frederick W. Davis, an American expatriate. D'Harnoncourt and Davis became acquainted in 1927; impressed by his discernment and taste, Davis soon invited d'Harnoncourt to enhance his store's offerings of modern Mexican art and contemporary folk art. This gave d'Harnoncourt the opportunity to travel extensively throughout the hinterland of Mexico, visiting rural areas and trekking across the countryside to visit artisan towns. He sought to collect a great diversity of objects, selecting those of superior aesthetic quality.

The 1920s were a heady time in Mexico City: as d'Harnoncourt later put it, "the nation's whole intelligentsia felt very strongly that this was a period of great social and artistic and intellectual revival."[13] He associated closely with a vibrant group of modern artists, a coterie that included Tina Modotti, Miguel Covarrubias, and Diego Rivera. In 1927, at Davis's store, he organized the first commercial exhibition in Mexico of work by the so-called Modern Mexican Muralists: Rivera, José Clemente Orozco, and Rufino Tamayo. D'Harnoncourt admired the work of the Mexican modernists, but perhaps more important for him was the discovery of pre-Columbian art that they facilitated: "In those days," he later recalled, "one could not walk into an artist's studio without tripping over a piece of just-excavated Aztec or Mayan sculpture."[14] He credited these friendships with deepening his interest in the indigenous art of Central and South America.

During these years, as he explored Mexico, d'Harnoncourt continued to develop his drawing skills. Although he received no formal training in sketching and draftsmanship, he possessed abundant natural talent, which he put to use throughout

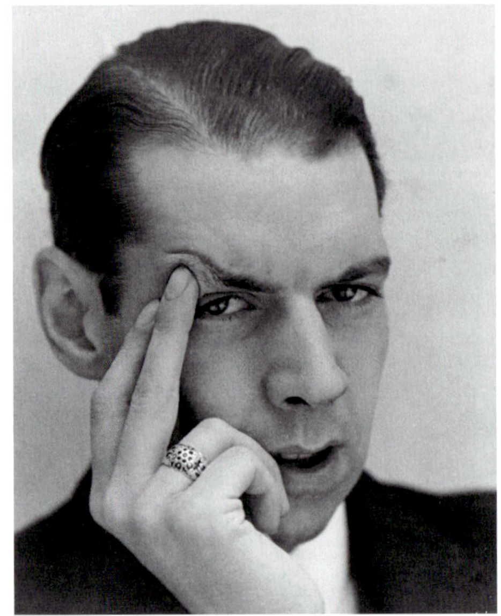

Manuel Álvarez Bravo. *René d'Harnoncourt,* 1930s. Gelatin silver print, 9¾ × 7⁹⁄₁₆ in. (24.7 × 19.3 cm)

his career. Years later, he recalled assisting Rivera, who would routinely ask whoever happened to be present as he worked to lend a hand, by putting in "quite a few nice strokes of white paint" on a fresco at the Municipal Palace in Cuernavaca.[15] In 1929, he executed a mural of the city of Cuernavaca at the house of Dwight Morrow, the US ambassador to Mexico. Morrow, a wealthy businessman and prominent diplomat, and his wife, Elizabeth, had arrived in Mexico City the previous year and promptly became clients, then friends, of d'Harnoncourt, who advised

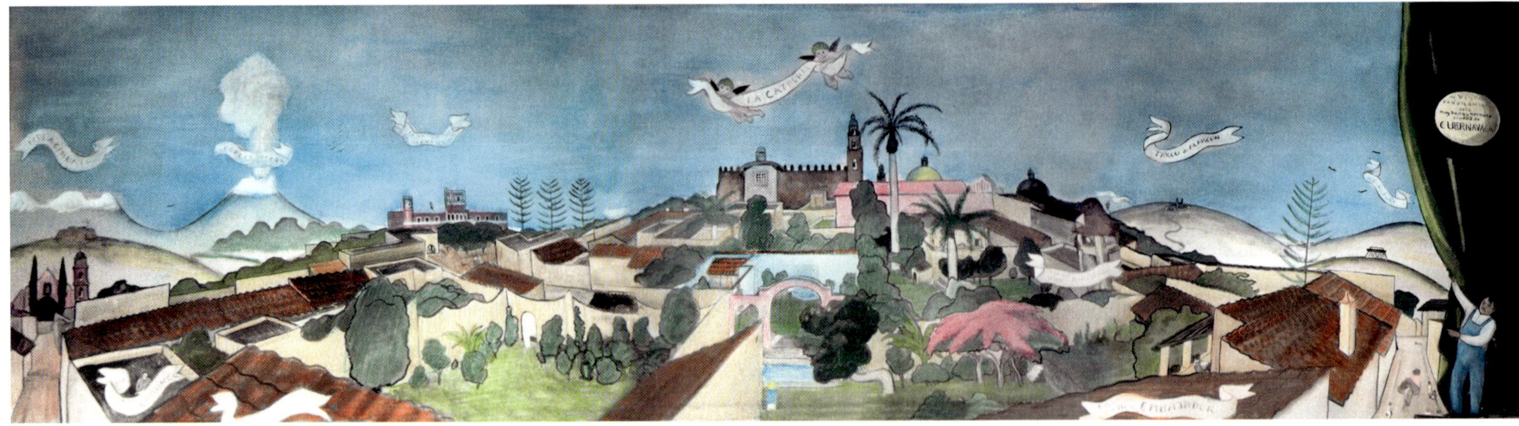

René d'Harnoncourt. Mural of Cuernavaca at the home of Dwight and Elizabeth Morrow, Casa Mañana, 1929 (now destroyed)

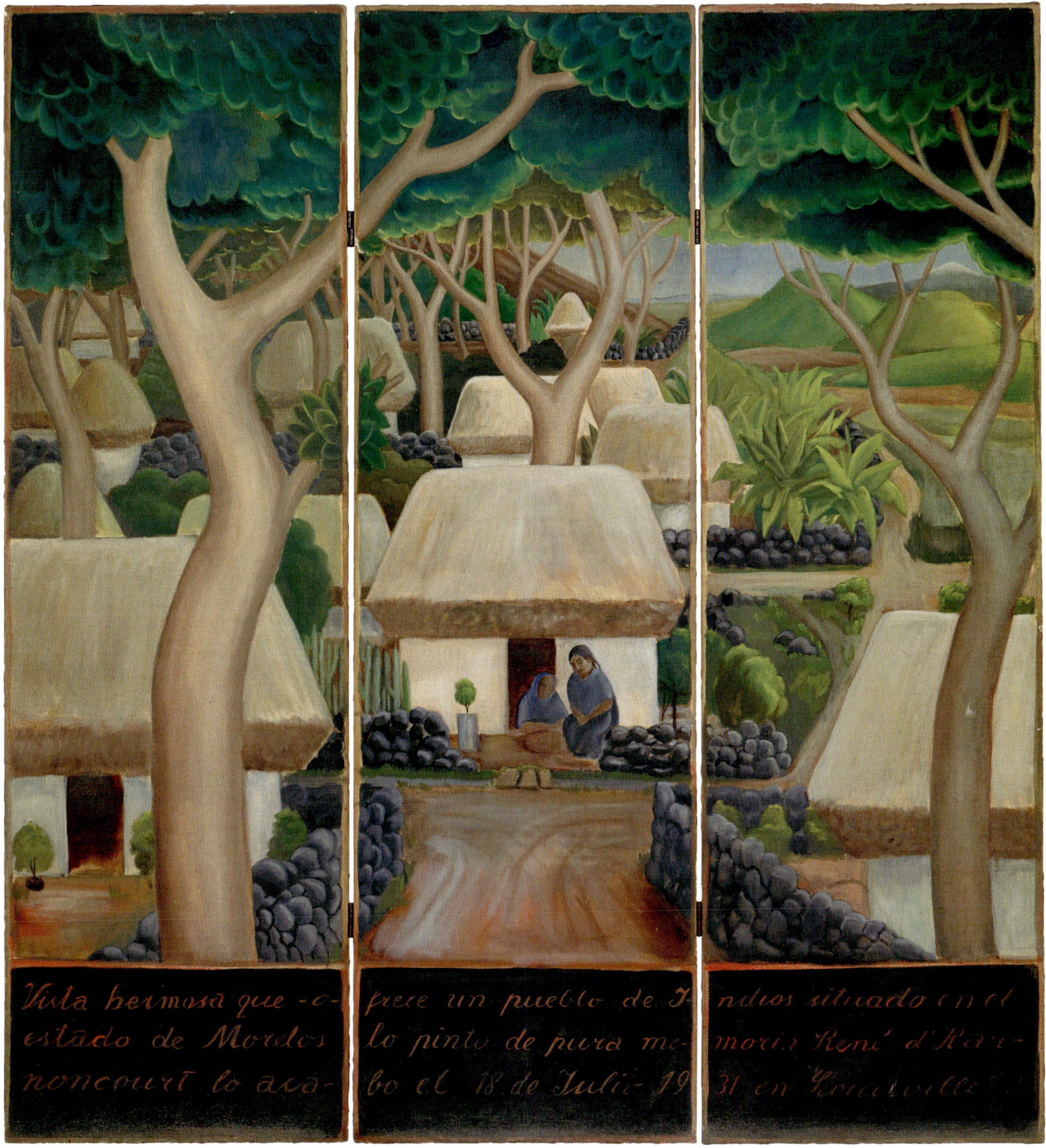

René d'Harnoncourt. Painted screen depicting a view of Miacatlán, Morelos, 1931

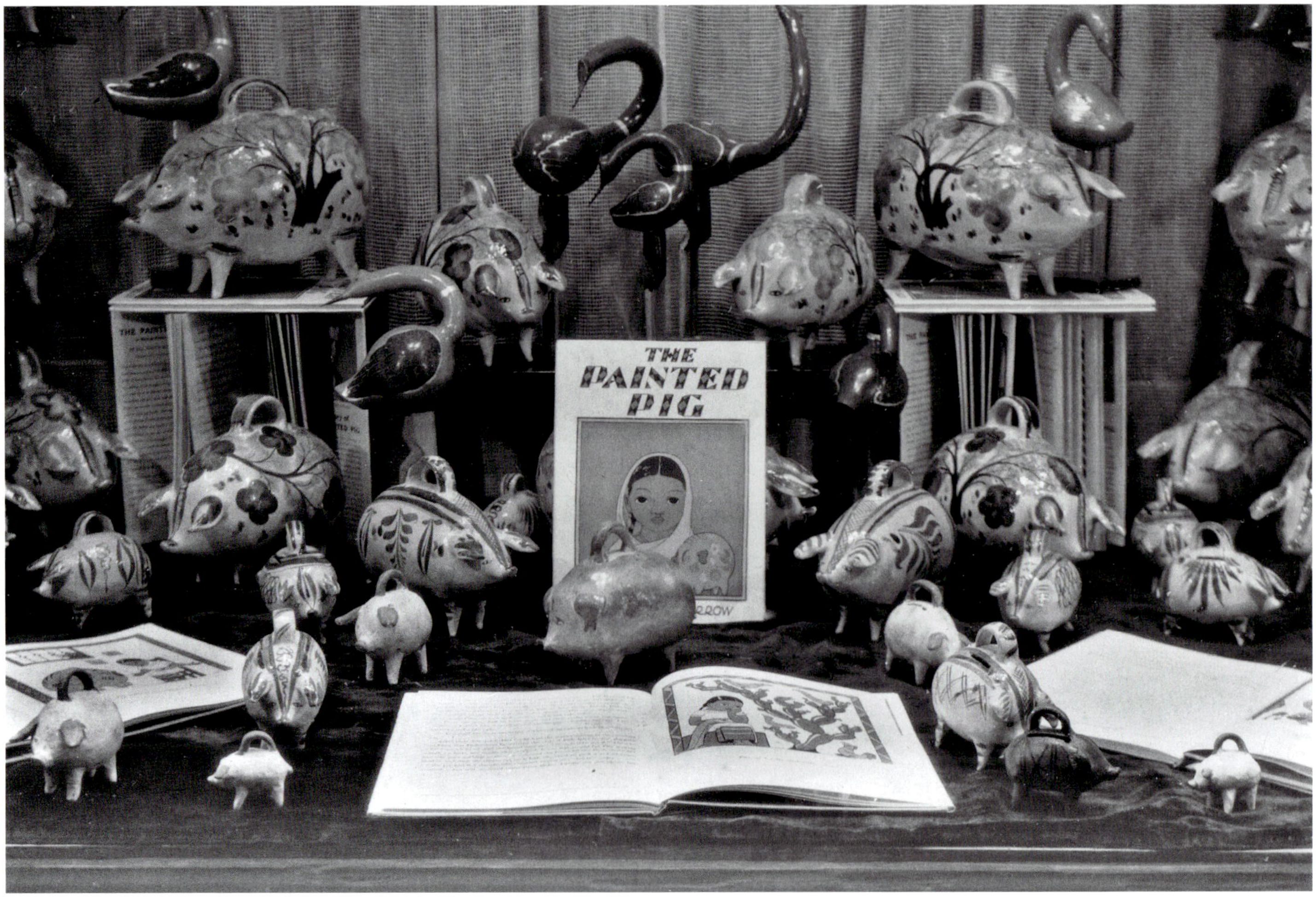

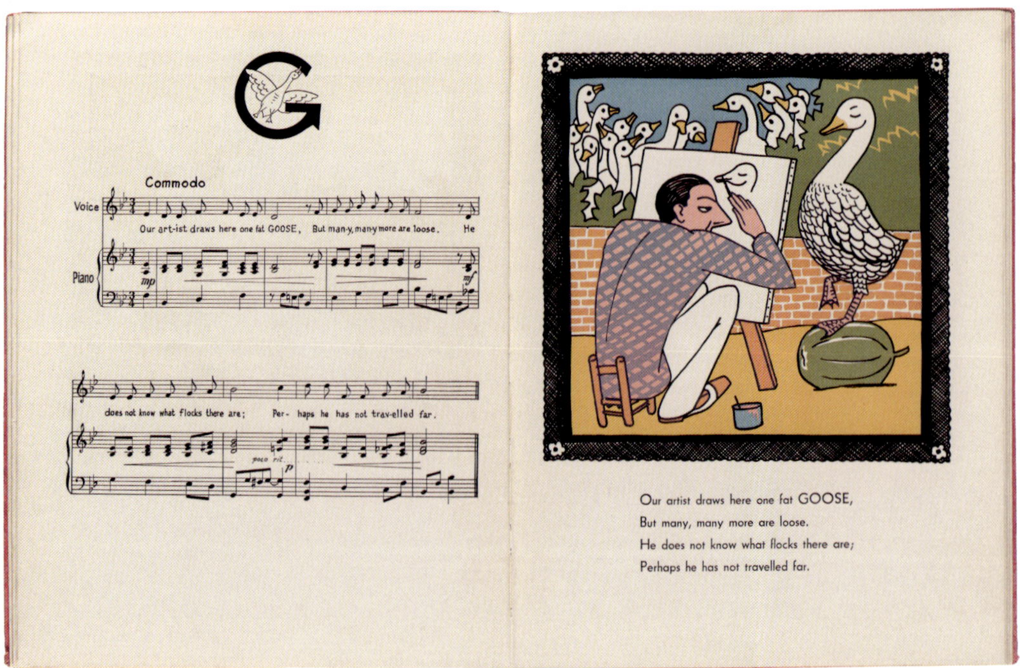

Above: Table displaying copies of *The Painted Pig: A Mexican Picture Book* (New York: Alfred A. Knopf, Inc., 1930), a children's book written by Elizabeth Morrow and illustrated by René d'Harnoncourt, surrounded by ceramic painted pigs, c. 1949

Left: Spread including music and an illustration for the letter G in the musical alphabet book *Beast, Bird, and Fish*, written by Elizabeth Morrow and René d'Harnoncourt, with music by Eberhard d'Harnoncourt (New York: Alfred A. Knopf, Inc., 1933). On the right, there is a self-portrait of d'Harnoncourt sketching a goose.

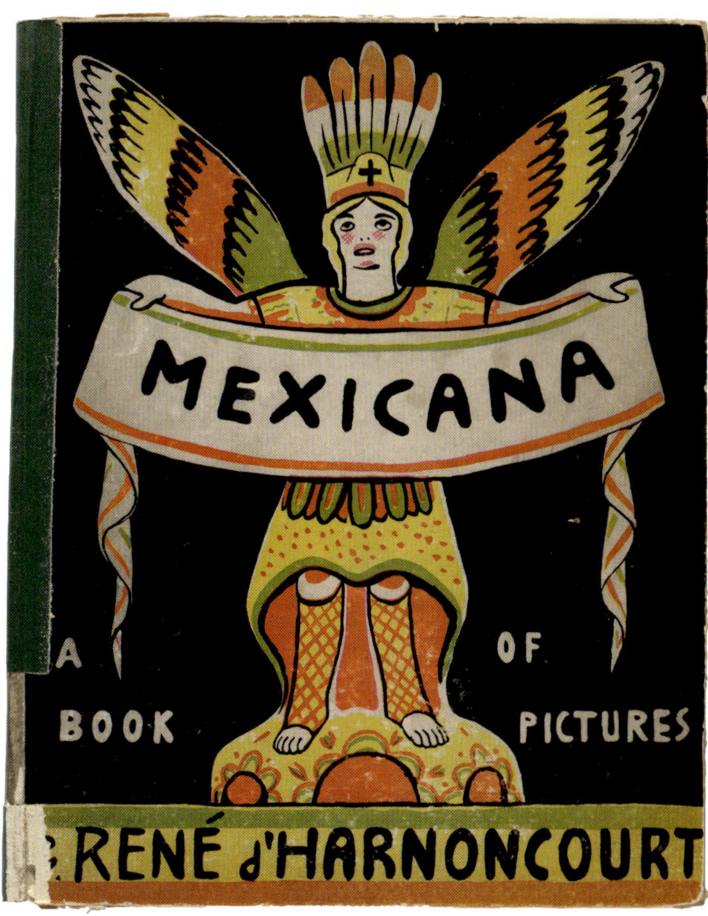

Cover of the book *Mexicana: A Book of Pictures* by René d'Harnoncourt (New York: Alfred A. Knopf, Inc., 1931)

them on assembling a collection of Mexican handicrafts and colonial art. D'Harnoncourt would also collaborate with Elizabeth Morrow on a pair of children's books, *The Painted Pig* (1930) and *Beast, Bird, Fish* (1932), and author two more books on his own (*The Hole in the Wall*, 1931, and *Mexicana: A Book of Pictures*, 1931).

According to his widow, d'Harnoncourt was emphatic about not considering himself an artist.[16] But by the early 1930s, his work was being handled by Weyhe Gallery, a professional gallery in New York that specialized in prints and drawings by modern and contemporary European, American, and Mexican artists, including Edward Hopper, Rockwell Kent, Reginald Marsh, Matisse, Orozco, Picasso, Rivera, David Alfaro Siqueiros, Tamayo, and Marguerite Zorach, among others. His one solo show at the gallery, in 1932, *Drawings by René d'Harnoncourt*, was reviewed by Edward Alden Jewell for the *New York Times*: Jewell proclaimed d'Harnoncourt to be "as romantic and versatile an artist as you will encounter anywhere today."[17]

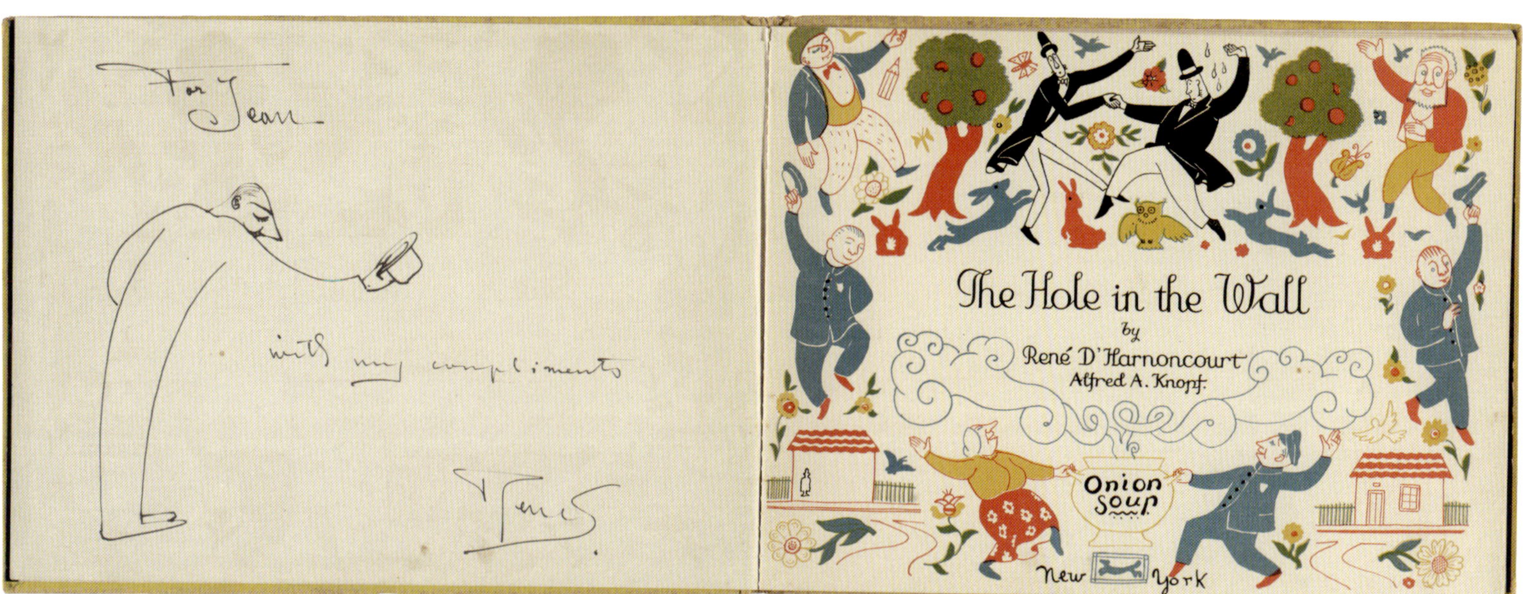

Title page of *The Hole in the Wall* (New York: Alfred A. Knopf, Inc., 1931), an illustrated children's book by René d'Harnoncourt, with personalized drawing and inscription

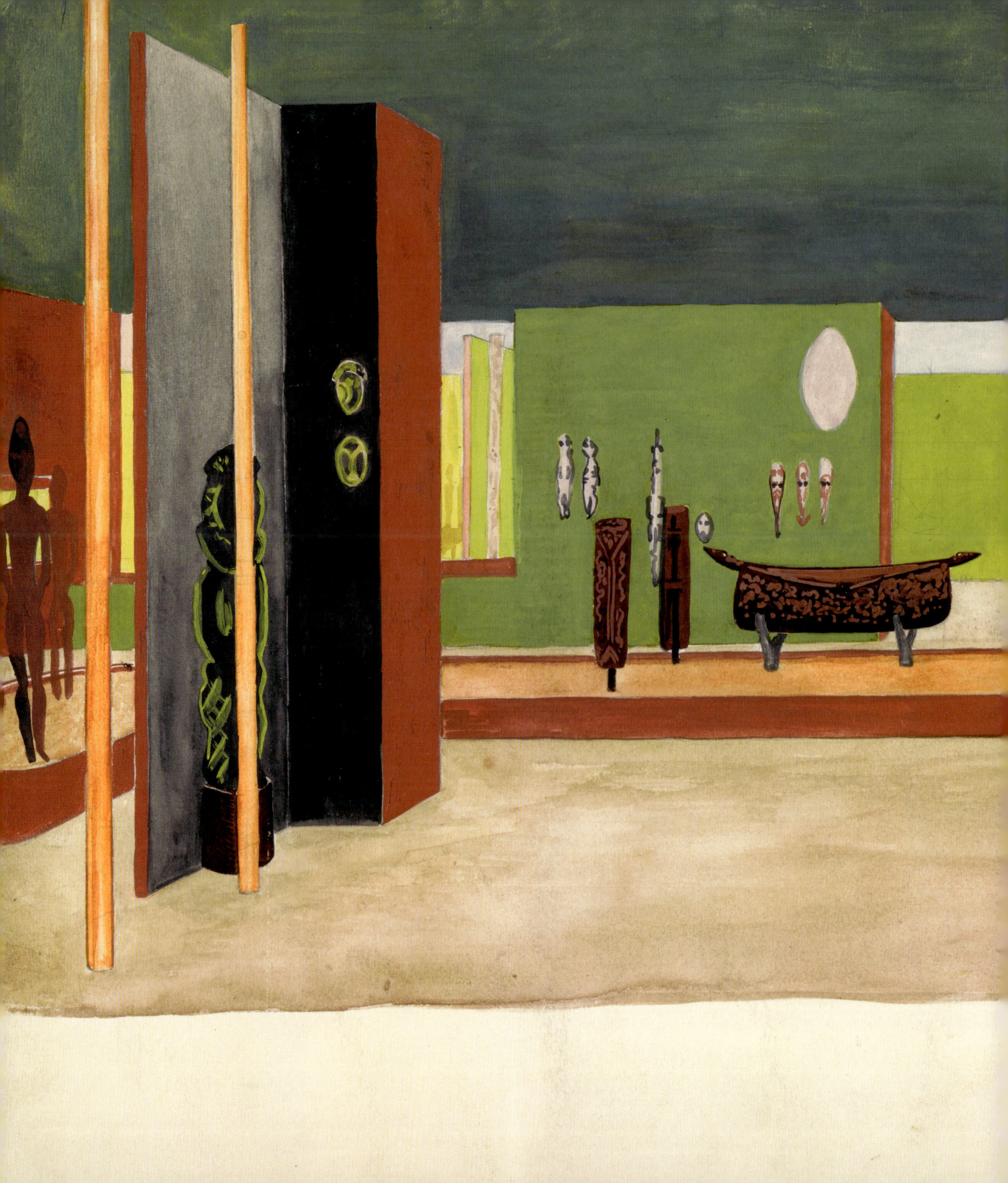

Installation Methodology

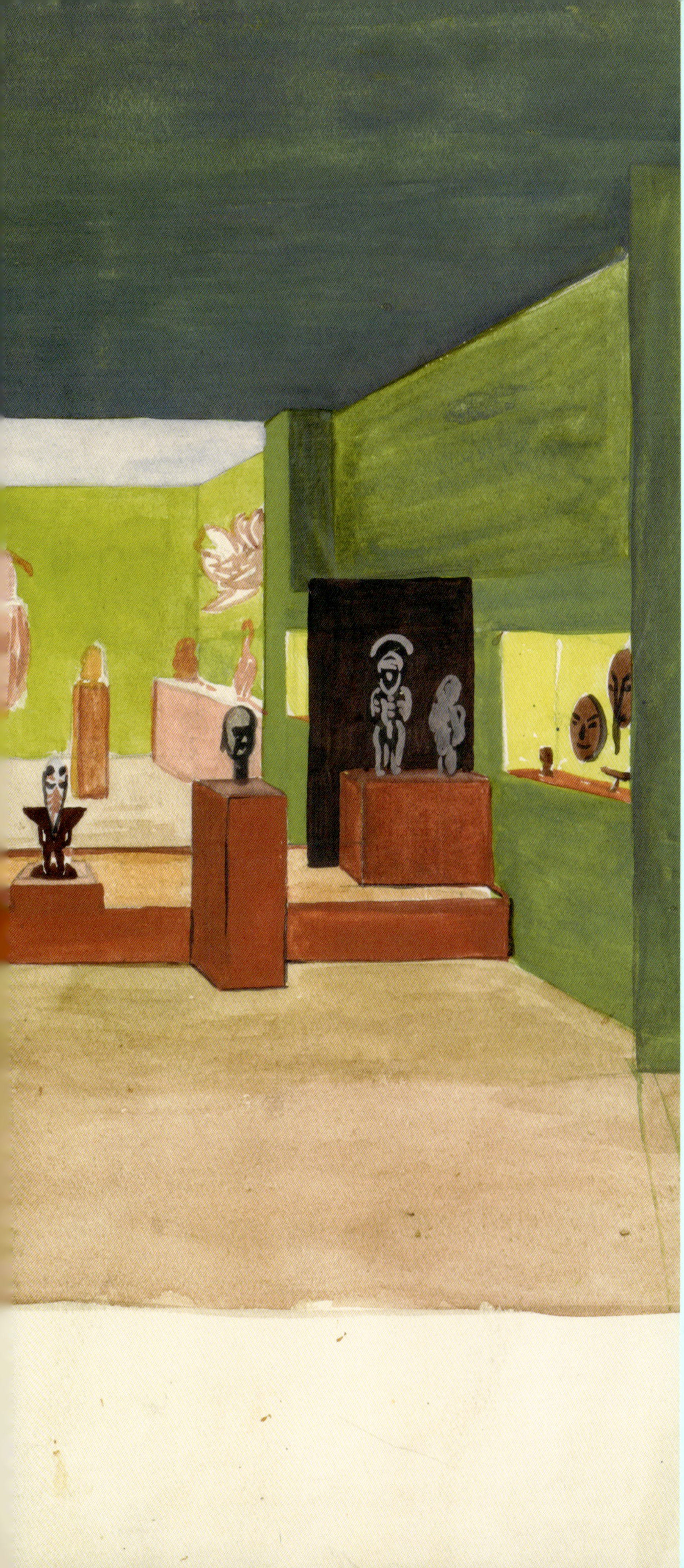

"First, after selecting and obtaining them, I made a drawing of each object, and then I made drawings of *groups* of objects, done to scale. These sketches filled two volumes. In the groups, I tried to relate the individual pieces to their cultural and artistic neighbors, rather than arrange them all by subject matter, locale, or chronology—in other words, to assemble objects that had some affinities. Then I started working on the floor plan, providing open vistas between one section and another wherever there was a close relationship between their contents, and introducing closed units only where unique local styles had developed. And I used lighting and color as symbolic aids . . . I tried to give a feeling of interlocking, so the visitor could make comparisons as he moved from one section to another."[18]

Behind this deceptively simple summary was an unprecedented level of reflection and analysis: every detail of an exhibition designed by d'Harnoncourt was carefully thought-out and deliberately planned.

Vista of the exhibition *Arts of the South Seas*, 1946. With the exception of this watercolor sketch, d'Harnoncourt used graphite, pencil, and ink to create his preparatory drawings.

Single-object studies

D'Harnoncourt's process began with single-object studies: his curatorial practice was absolutely predicated on firsthand observation and object-rooted connoisseurship. This foundational first step was the longest part of his process, often occupying him for an entire year. Drawing was d'Harnoncourt's means of absorbing information: he came to learn and know each object by making individual line drawings. As he himself explained, "A drawing forces you to concentrate on all details." "When you make a drawing of an object, you really understand it. You really get acquainted with it."[19]

While d'Harnoncourt humbly described his drawings as "simply a means of trying to find out about the things,"[20] his collaborators often commented on his impressive ability to recall. Mildred Constantine, his assistant on the 1954 exhibition *Ancient Art of the Andes* (who would go on to have a distinguished career as a curator in MoMA's Department of Architecture and Design), recounted that d'Harnoncourt was able to draw, overnight and from memory, the eighty objects they had examined the previous day.[21] Around the same time, d'Harnoncourt and Nelson Rockefeller traveled to the West Coast to view a collection of seven thousand items, from which Rockefeller purchased seventy works. On the flight back to New York, d'Harnoncourt drew a picture of each one from memory, and the pair discussed how they could be displayed in a show alongside the rest of Rockefeller's collection.[22] His colleague Monroe Wheeler, MoMA's director of exhibitions, lauded d'Harnoncourt's sketches as "an adjunct to his memory and erudition," as many opportunities "to exercise his phenomenal eye for authenticity and quality in every realm of art."[23]

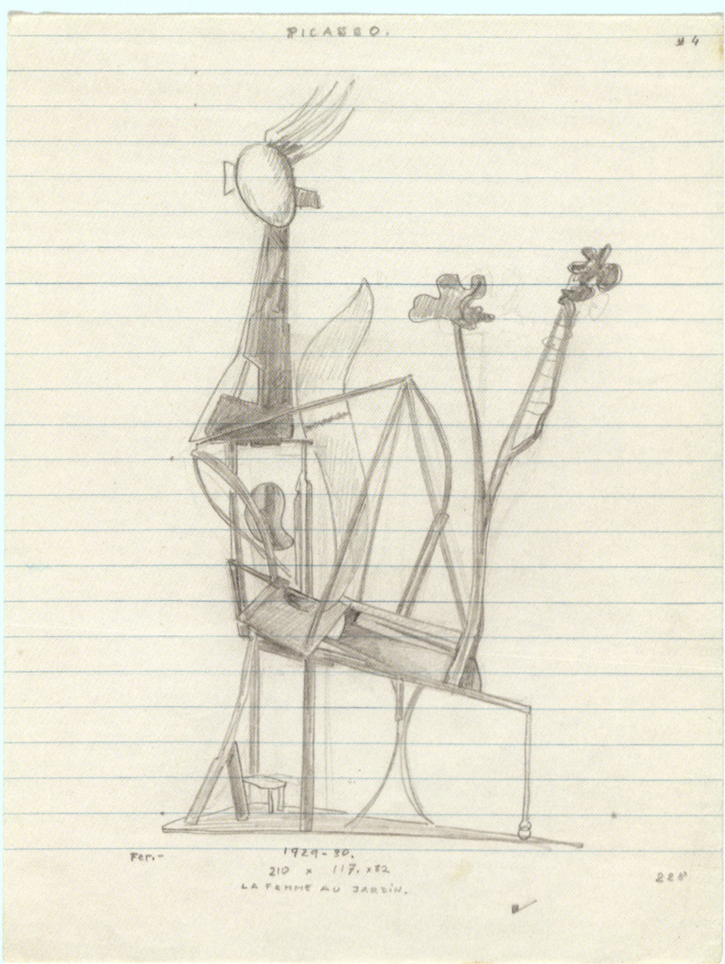

Left: Sketch of Picasso's *Femme au Jardin* (1929), 1967

Opposite and following spread: Sketches of objects included in the exhibition *Arts of the South Seas*, 1946

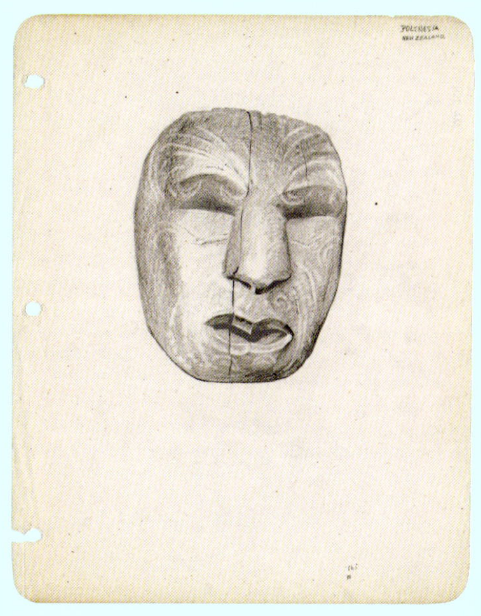
POLYNESIA
NEW ZEALAND.

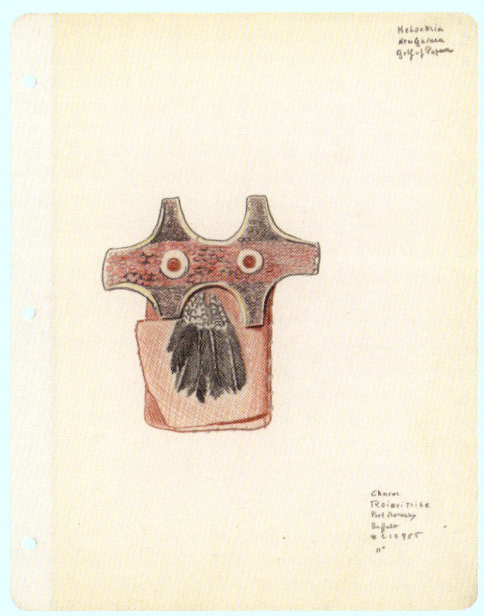
Melanesia
New Guinea
Gulf of Papua
Charm
Roiavi tribe
Port Moresby
Buffalo
610955
11"

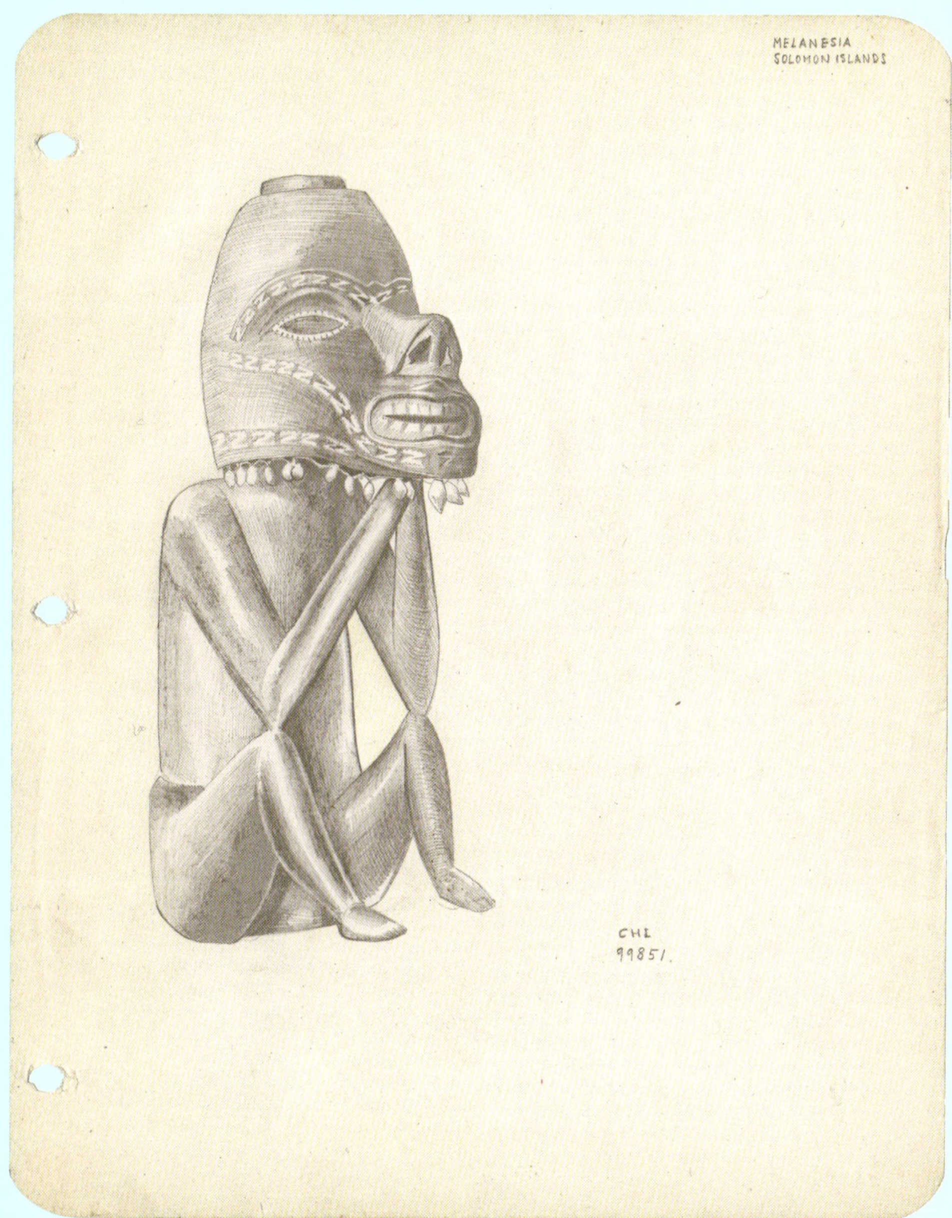
MELANESIA
SOLOMON ISLANDS
CHE
99851.

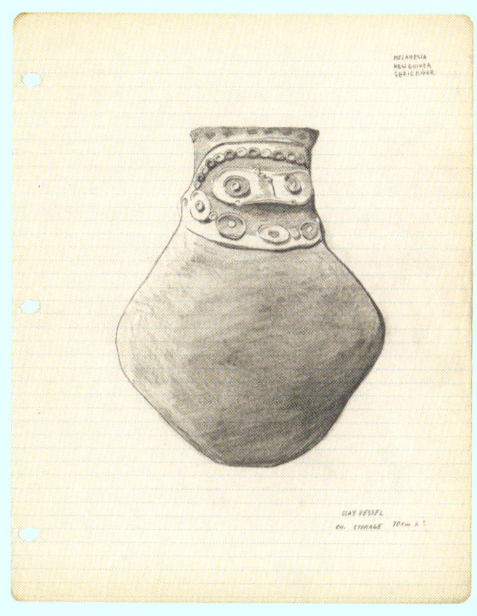
MELANESIA
NEW GUINEA
SEPIK RIVER
CLAY VESSEL
CH. STORAGE   70cm h?

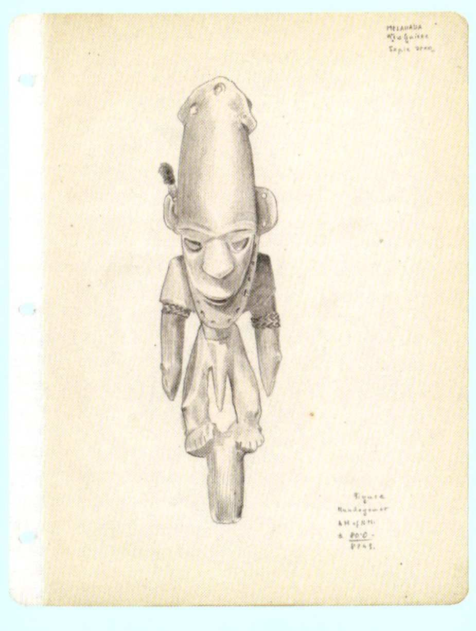
MELANESIA
New Guinea
Sepik River
Figure
Mundugumor
A.M. of N.H.
80.0
5743.

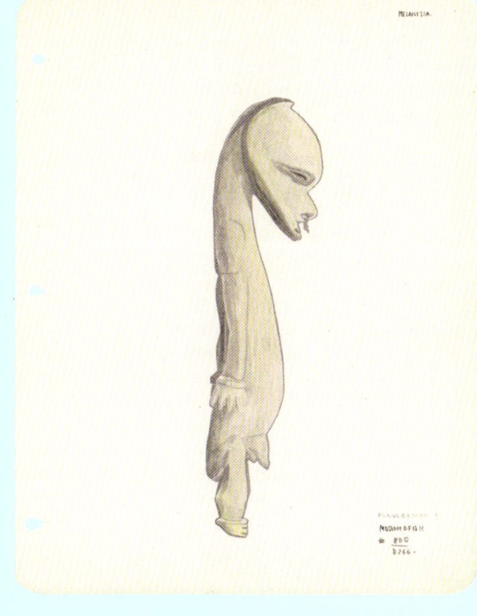
MELANESIA.
Figure charm
Museum of N.H.
80.0
5266.

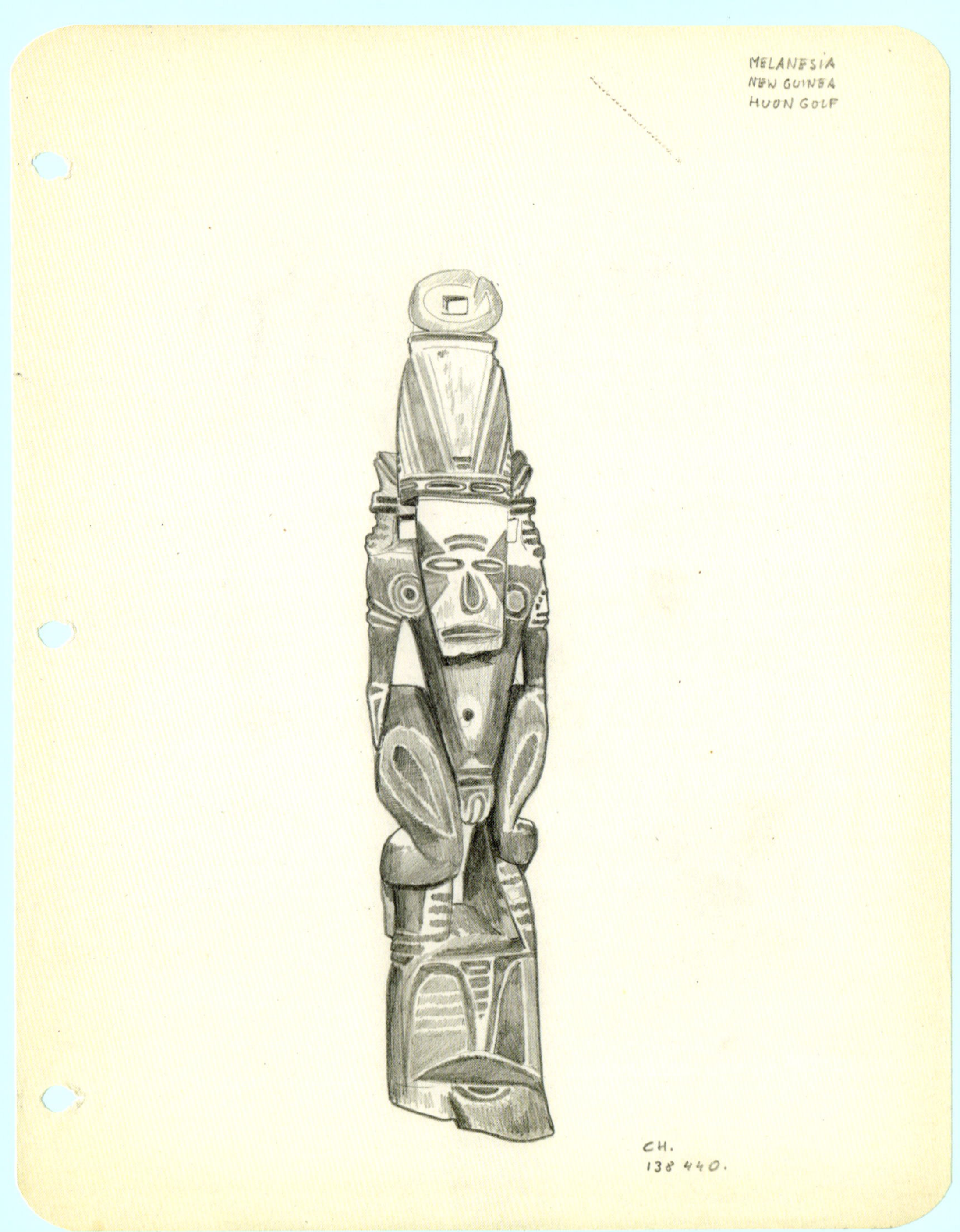

CH.
138 440.

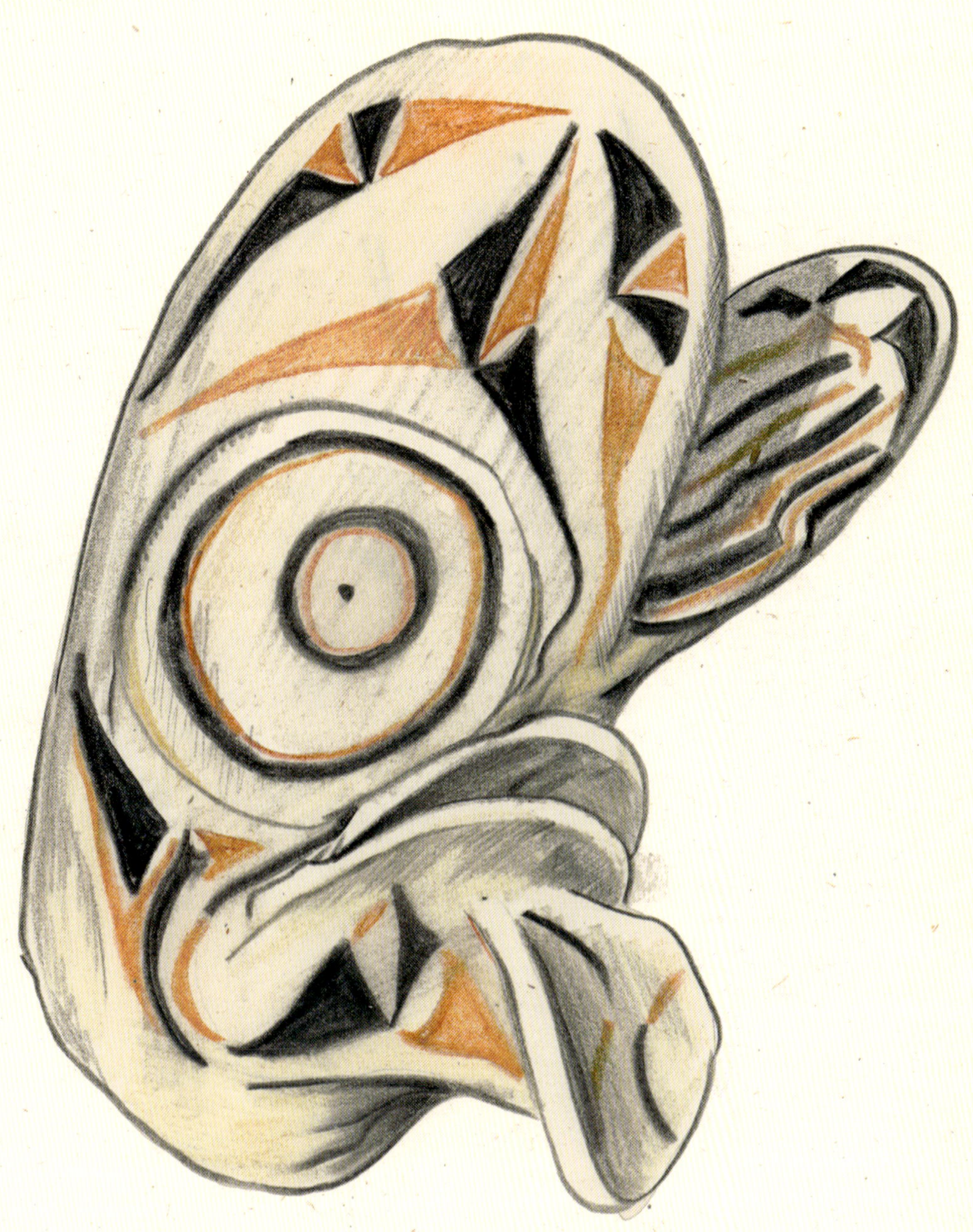

CH.
145 869.-

Curatorial beginnings: from *Mexican Arts*, 1930–32, to *Indian Art*, 1939 and 1941

In 1929, d'Harnoncourt was commissioned to curate his first large-scale exhibition. Aspiring to improve the popular conception of Mexico among Americans, Morrow approached the Mexican government to cooperate on the organization of an exhibition on the country's native art for circulation in the United States. His proposal was approved by Frederick Keppel of the Carnegie Corporation, who financed it through the American Federation of Arts. Homer Saint-Gaudens, director of Fine Arts at the Carnegie Institute in Pittsburgh, was brought on as advisor and sent to Mexico City to select a director for the exhibition. On Morrow's recommendation, he chose d'Harnoncourt.[24]

D'Harnoncourt was tasked with organizing the exhibition *Mexican Arts*, from selecting the objects to figuring out their layout in the various venues to which the exhibition would travel. He spent the year of 1930 traveling extensively throughout Mexico, assembling 1,261 items "of Mexican arts, not of arts in Mexico": he was concerned "with the presentation only of such works of art as are an expression of Mexican civilization."[25] This included both works of applied arts (metalwork, stonework, lacquer, pottery, textiles, and basketry) and the fine arts (paintings, sculpture, prints, and books). A section of the exhibition was devoted to work by important contemporary artists, including Jean Charlot, Carlos Merida, Covarrubias, Tamayo, Orozco, Rivera, and Siqueiros, several of whom were d'Harnoncourt's friends or acquaintances. The process of organizing this exhibition provided d'Harnoncourt with the unique experience of working directly with indigenous craftsmen and these artists.[26] On occasion, that could involve working with some strong artistic temperaments: the night before the opening of a preview of the exhibition at the Ministry of Education in Mexico City, Rivera, outraged by the quantity and prominence of work by Orozco, rehung the contemporary section so that his paintings occupied the whole main wall and works by other artists were relegated to the corners.[27]

The exhibition *Mexican Arts* opened to popular acclaim at the Metropolitan Museum of Art in October 1930 (see portfolio). Its success convinced the American Federation of Arts to add six additional venues to the original eight, giving d'Harnoncourt the opportunity to embark on his first travels across the United States. He thoroughly enjoyed traveling to each of those venues and meeting with local museum directors, curators, and trustees. Having made it to the US, d'Harnoncourt decided to remain: in 1933, he obtained an immigration visa, married, and settled in New York. Over the next few years, he directed a nationally broadcast radio program titled "Art in America," in collaboration with the Metropolitan and MoMA; it was on this occasion that he first met Alfred Barr.[28] Despite his lack of academic credentials, he also held faculty positions: at Sarah Lawrence College, the New School for Social Research, and as part of the Seminar for Cultural Relations with Latin America in Mexico City.[29]

In 1936, while visiting Mexico City for the Seminar for Cultural Relations, d'Harnoncourt met John Collier, the US Commissioner for Indian Affairs and a passionate champion of the rights of Native Americans, who was keen to learn how Mexico was handling the promotion of its indigenous arts and crafts. After several discussions, Collier offered d'Harnoncourt the position of assistant manager of the Indian Arts and Crafts Board (IACB), part of the Department of the Interior; a year later he was promoted to general manager, a position he would hold until 1944, when he was hired by MoMA. Created by the Indian Arts and Crafts Act of 1935, the Board was to promote the economic welfare of Native American tribes through the development of arts and crafts and the expansion of the market for such products.[30] Reporting to IACB headquarters in Washington, DC, d'Harnoncourt worked in the field, in the Dakotas and elsewhere, once again scouting the country for objects of aesthetic or cultural value. The IACB then wanted to share these with the public: in 1939, it decided to organize and present the exhibition *Indian Art in the United States and Alaska* at the San Francisco Golden Gate International Exposition. D'Harnoncourt, along with Frederic H. Douglas, curator of Indian Art at the Denver Art Museum, was charged with general oversight of the show, including the selection of objects and their installation.

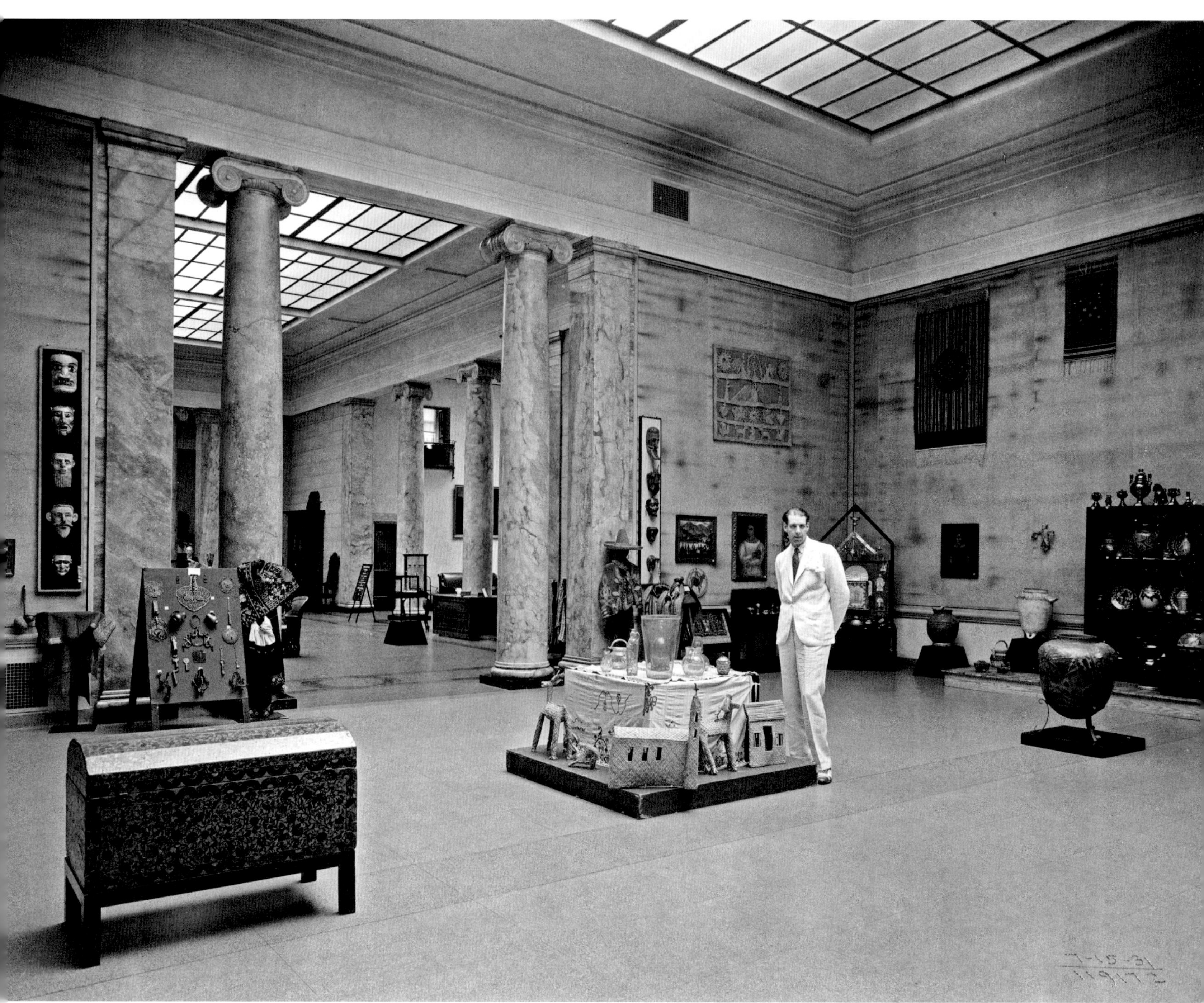

René d'Harnoncourt visiting *Mexican Arts* at the J. B. Speed Memorial
Museum, Louisville, Kentucky, 1931

Like the IACB itself, the exhibition aimed to convey an explicitly commercial message and to create a stable revenue source for craftsmen: its goal, stated on the floor plan distributed to visitors of the Exposition, was to give the living Native American artist a chance to find a new market for his products. D'Harnoncourt's prior experience working in the furniture and decorative-objects trade in Mexico meant that he was well prepared to tackle this priority: he understood how to underscore the commodity aspects of the works. During his time in Mexico, d'Harnoncourt played an important role in the revival of traditional lacquerware, resulting in great economic advantages for the native craftsmen: in 1927, noticing the decline in quality of Olinaltecan (or *rayado* style) lacquerware, he had specifically sought fine specimens of the older style of the craft, which he showed to indigenous artisans, encouraging them to adopt the traditional aesthetic, techniques, and materials found in the earlier pieces.[31] In *Indian Art*, d'Harnoncourt strove to emphasize that Indian objects could be converted for use in modern society, outside of their original context of creation and use. He was assisted in this by architect Henry Klumb (like himself, a European émigré), an expert on display and interior design. The exhibition ended with a retail operation, a "pan-Indian market of contemporary art" that included demonstrations and model homes with modern interiors adorned with Native American products. The first section was designed like a trading post on a reservation, while the second bore the trappings of a modern gift shop (which, incidentally, did much better business).[32]

The Indian Court of the International Exposition was well received, with one reviewer deeming it "the most significant exhibition of its kind ever gathered together," adding that "as a demonstration of new methods in the display and exposition of art objects the Indian show is a positive knockout, and one that might well inaugurate a new era in museum technique . . . . [The organizers] have succeeded in keeping the emphasis always on the object, placing it in settings often subtly stylized to suggest rather than describe its environment."[33] Given the success of the show, The Museum of Modern Art invited d'Harnoncourt to reprise the theme, again in conjunction with Douglas and Klumb. D'Harnoncourt's curatorial debut at MoMA went on view in January 1941, two years after the exhibition at the Golden Gate International Exposition in San Francisco (see portfolio).

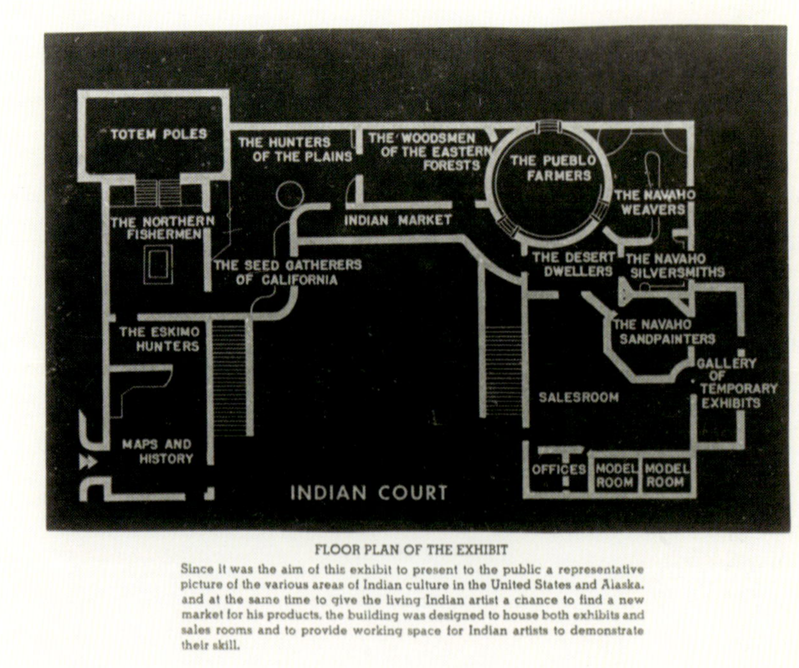

FLOOR PLAN OF THE EXHIBIT

Since it was the aim of this exhibit to present to the public a representative picture of the various areas of Indian culture in the United States and Alaska, and at the same time to give the living Indian artist a chance to find a new market for his products, the building was designed to house both exhibits and sales rooms and to provide working space for Indian artists to demonstrate their skill.

Floor plan for the exhibition *Indian Art in the United States and Alaska* at the Golden Gate International Exposition, San Francisco, California, 1939

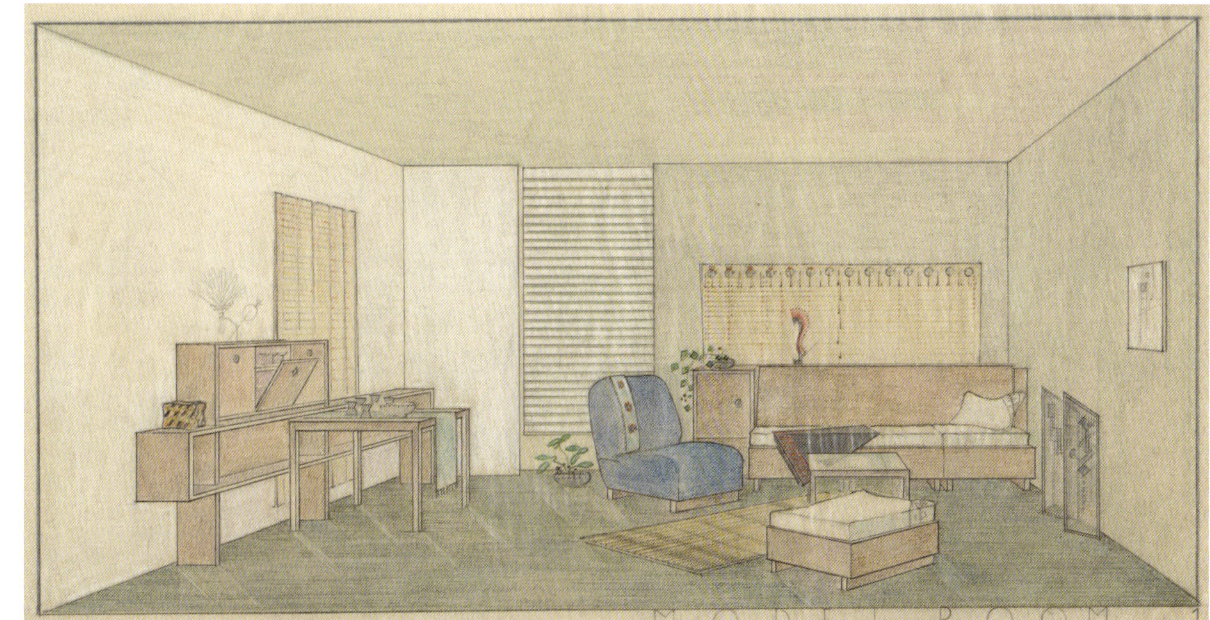

Color drawing by René d'Harnoncourt entitled "Model Room," illustrating the incorporation of Native American artifacts into modern interior design, 1938. Two model rooms based on this scheme were presented as part of the 1939 *Indian Art* exhibition at the Golden Gate International Exposition.

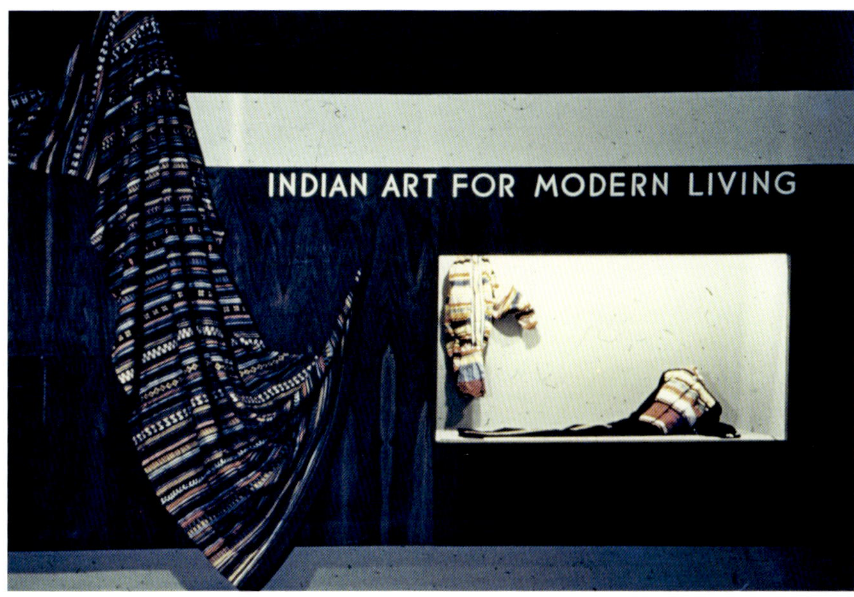

Installation view of the Modern Living section of the MoMA exhibition *Indian Art of the United States*, 1941, including, on the right, an après-ski suit designed by Fred Picard

The role of display in commerce was an important influence on exhibition design at the time,[34] something that d'Harnoncourt hinted at in his preliminary preparations for the show: in a letter to Barr, he noted the installation "should be very contemporary and Fifth Avenue in the best sense of the word."[35] Artists, architects, and designers such as Norman Bel Geddes, Salvador Dalí, and Frederick Kiesler all designed shopwindow displays in New York during the 1930s. While it is impossible to ascertain definitively whether any of these specific precedents had direct bearing on d'Harnoncourt's ideas and approach, it is clear that a general exposure to and understanding of some of these influenced his work. One reviewer of *Indian Art* noted that d'Harnoncourt had "used all the tricks known to modern advertising display" and promised "that even the general public will, if only unconsciously, appreciate this effort on its behalf."[36] Indeed, the ambition to broaden the market for Native American wares was reprised at MoMA. A section of the exhibition (which took over all three floors of the Museum) titled "Indian Art for Modern Living" presented a small group of contemporary objects recontextualized as art for the home or ornaments for the body in the modern world. D'Harnoncourt even commissioned a collaboration with Swiss fashion designer Fred Picard for a line of womenswear incorporating traditional Indian textiles.

While such maneuvers are contrary to today's emphasis on and respect for cultural specificity, it is important to underscore d'Harnoncourt's motivation: promotion, not appropriation. His universalizing approach stemmed from a tolerant, enlightened view of humanity. In line with d'Harnoncourt's work on behalf of the IACB, *Indian Art* was his most ideologically driven exhibition at MoMA. It embraced a

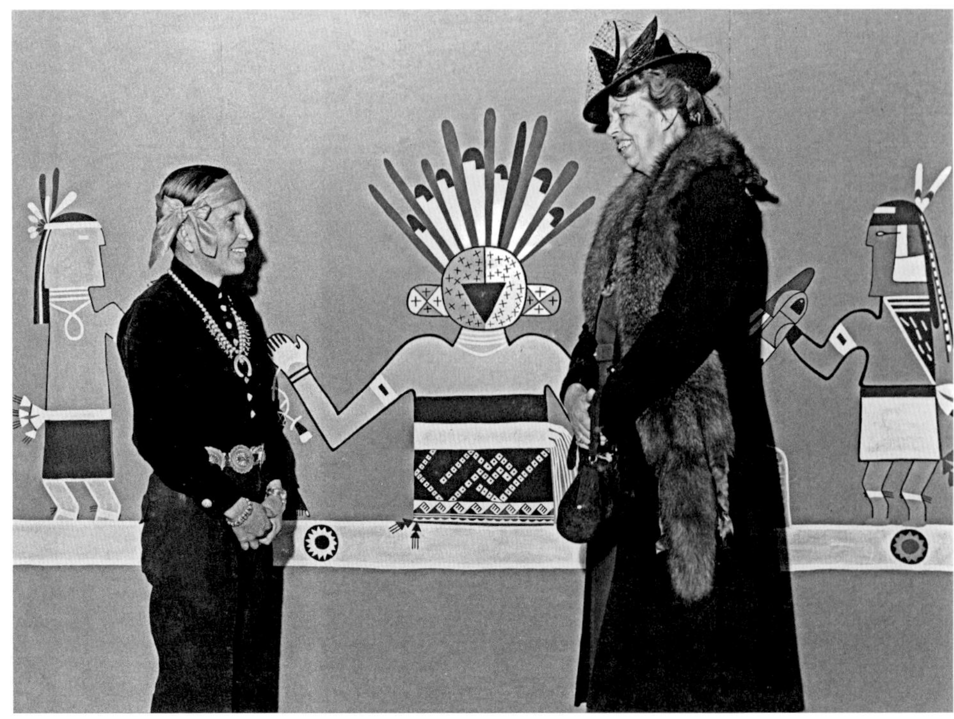

Eleanor Roosevelt and Fred Kabotie, Hopi painter, at the MoMA exhibition *Indian Art of the United States*, January 25, 1941. Behind them are reproductions of prehistoric Pueblo mural paintings from the early sixteenth century, commissioned by d'Harnoncourt.

uniquely American theme during the early years of World War II, when Americans were wary of Europe. Second, it figured into the New Deal economic policy of President Franklin Delano Roosevelt (who also promoted freedom of the arts as a touchstone of democracy), as framed by Collier: considered chiefly responsible for the "Indian New Deal," especially through the Indian Reorganization Act of 1934, Collier strove to reverse a long-standing policy of cultural assimilation of Native Americans. First Lady Eleanor Roosevelt even supported the endeavor by visiting the exhibition in person and contributing a foreword to the catalogue. In her newspaper column *My Day,* she exclaimed: "What beautiful work the Indians did . . . I am thrilled by the fact that their skill has not died out and that many of the things they make today are easily adapted to our modern life."[37]

D'Harnoncourt realized the potential impact and political implications of the presentation of *Indian Art* at MoMA, the country's preeminent institution of modern art and arbiter of aesthetic matters in contemporary society: by its very presence there, the work would gain validity not just as artifacts but also as aesthetic objects. D'Harnoncourt harbored a genuine respect for the indigenous peoples creating these objects and a deep understanding of their cultures, which he strove to communicate to the public within the exhibition itself. In his introduction to the catalogue of *Indian Art*, he explained:

> In theory, it should be possible to arrive at a satisfactory aesthetic evaluation of the art of any group without being much concerned with its cultural background. A satisfactory organization of lines, spaces, forms, shades and colors should be self-evident wherever we find it. Yet we know that increased familiarity with the background of an object not only satisfies intellectual curiosity but actually heightens appreciation of its aesthetic values.[38]

With *Indian Art*'s move to MoMA, d'Harnoncourt began to consider the needs of the public and to study different means of conveying, within the exhibition itself, as much information about the provenance of each object as was necessary to optimize the audience's appreciation of the works on display.

Groupings, done to scale

Having mastered all of the objects to be included in the exhibition, d'Harnoncourt would begin studying how to group them. An understanding of the relative size of the works is critical in designing a display, to project and anticipate their overall impact in the gallery spaces: d'Harnoncourt would render the objects to scale on a single sheet of paper, often also noting their dimensions.

D'Harnoncourt would consistently make every effort to see the objects firsthand, traveling throughout the country as well as to Europe and South America to visit works in artists' studios, in their buyers' homes, or hanging in museum exhibitions. If necessary, he would create additional drawings from the photographs published in catalogues, amassing a large personal library at home over the years.

D'Harnoncourt's daughter, Anne, fondly recalled observing her father as he used these drawings to plan an installation:

I think my father was never happier than when working on an installation. He would sit at the desk in the living room in our apartment on the Upper West Side, and have lots of little drawings, doing drawings of each object in the show—this is all very evident in the Museum's archives—just whistling away. He always whistled . . . just thinking about each object, how it fit in, where it would shine and make the most of itself, just shifting [works of art] in his mind and shifting [them] on paper.[39]

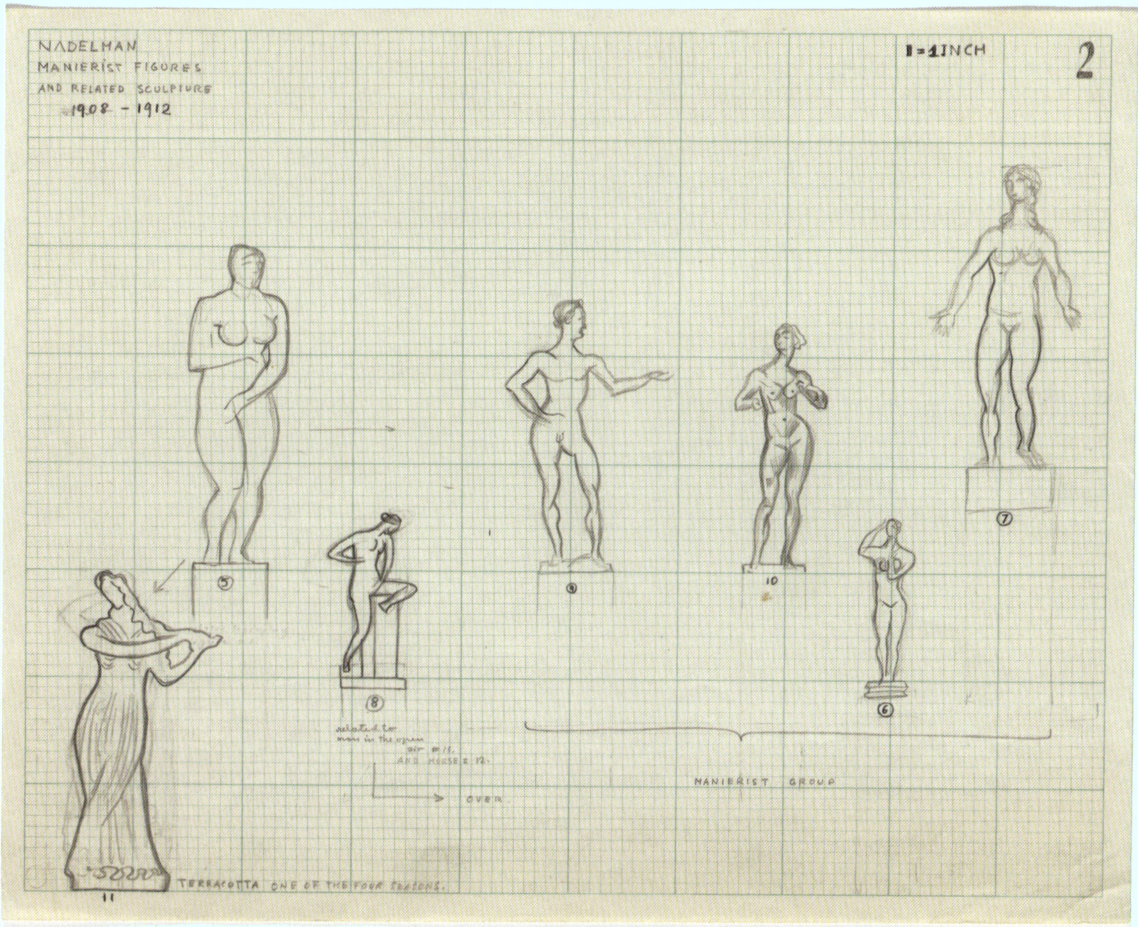

Preparatory sketch of Elie Nadelman's Mannerist figures and related sculptures, 1948

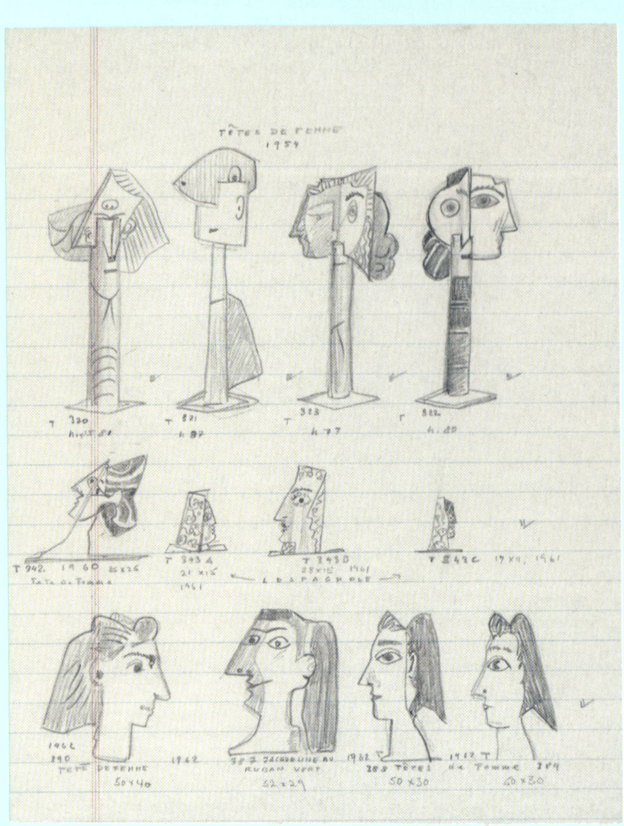
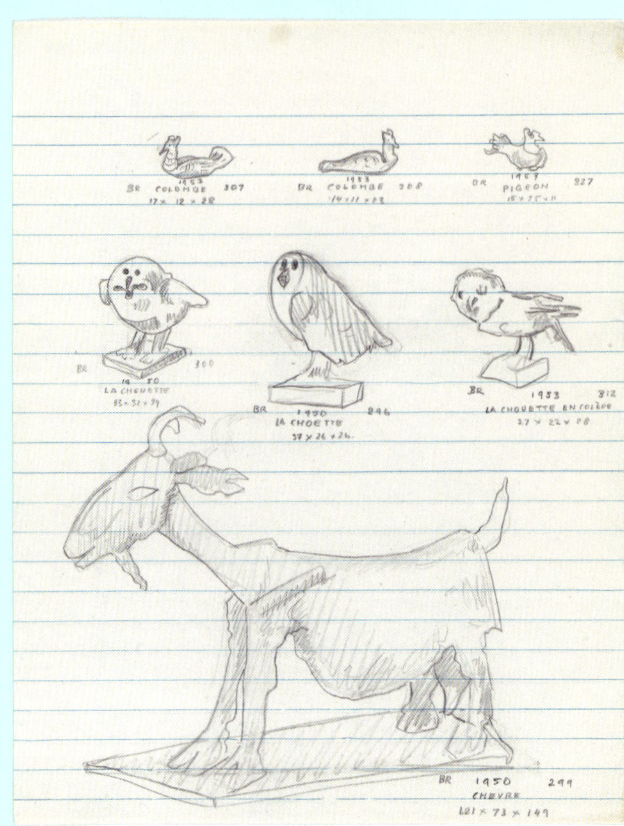
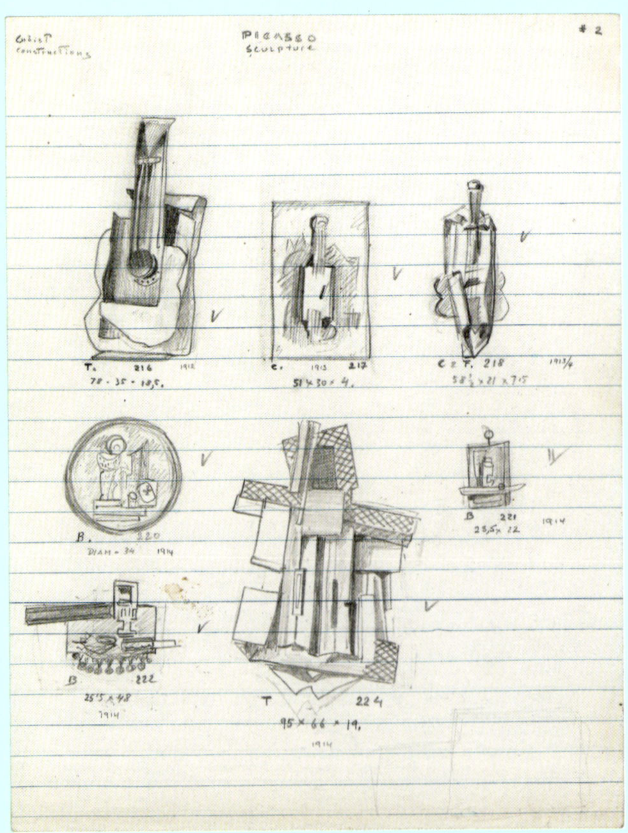
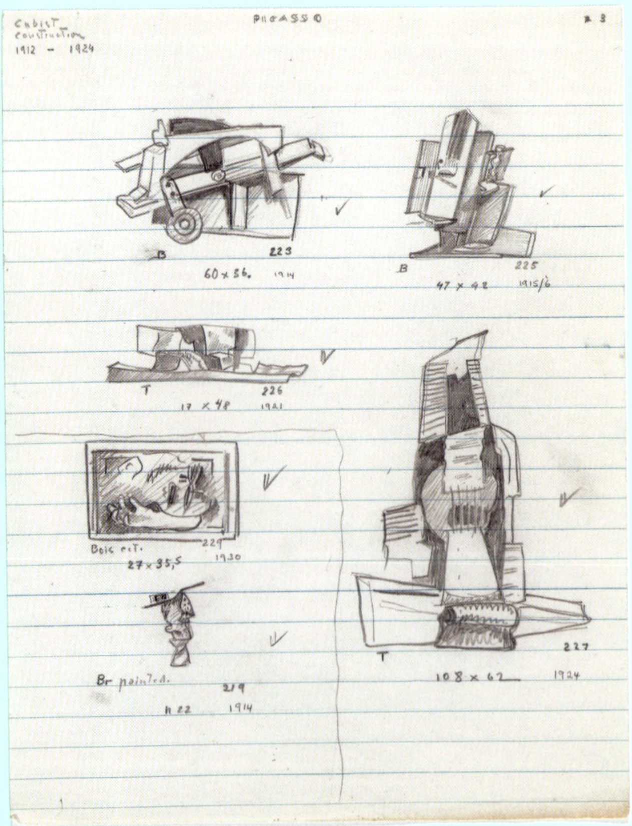

Above and opposite: Scale drawings of groups of sculptures to be presented together during the exhibition *The Sculpture of Picasso*, 1967

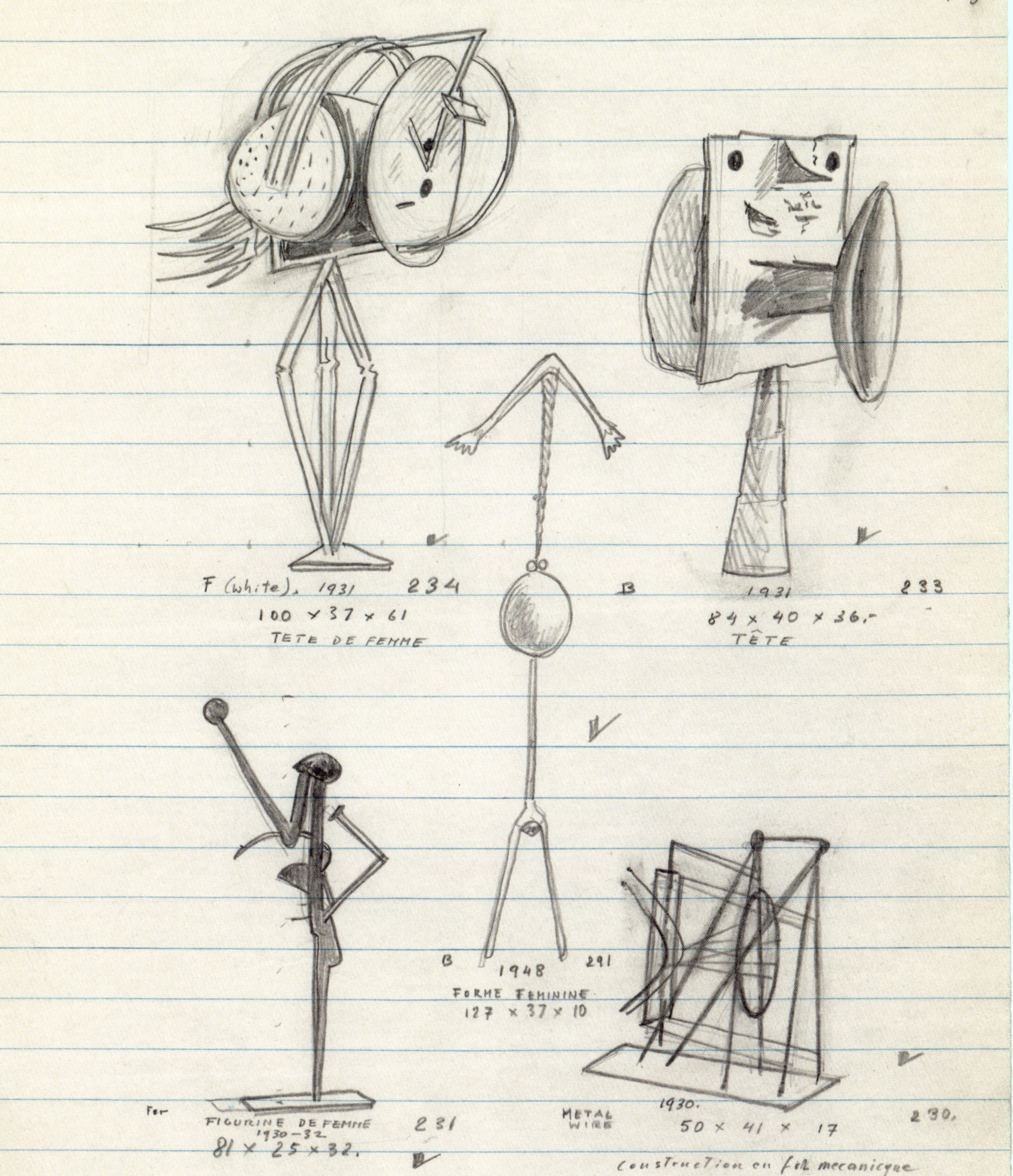

F (white), 1931   234   B   1931   233
100 × 37 × 61   84 × 40 × 36.5
TÊTE DE FEMME   TÊTE

                        B   1948   291
                        FORME FÉMININE
                        127 × 37 × 10

For   FIGURINE DE FEMME   231   METAL   1930.   230.
            1930-32   WIRE   50 × 41 × 17
       81 × 25 × 32.

                                    construction en fil mecanique

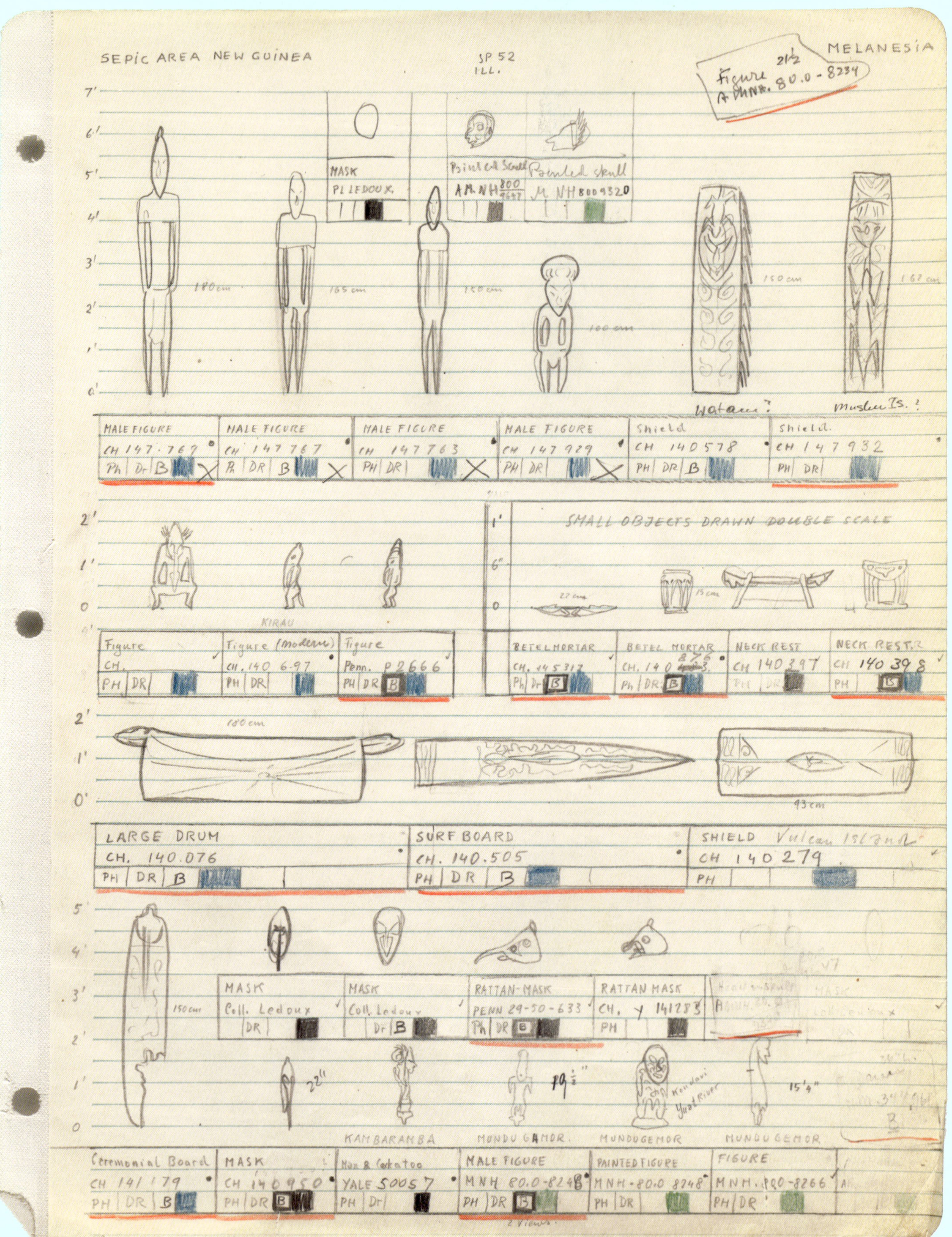

Preparatory drawing for *Arts of the South Seas*, 1946, showing groups and sequences of objects

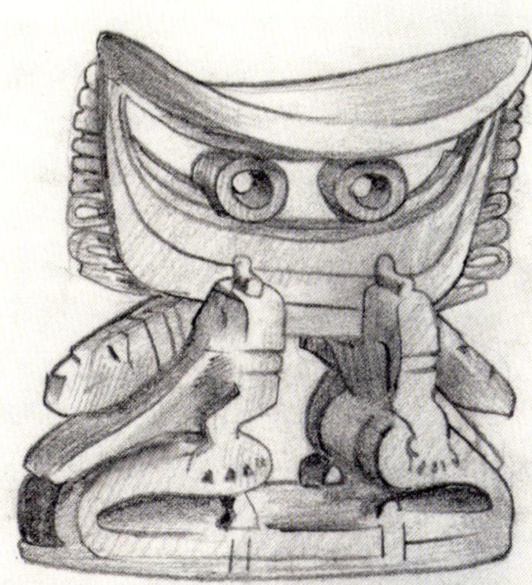

6" TAMI ISLAND
CHI M. of N.H.

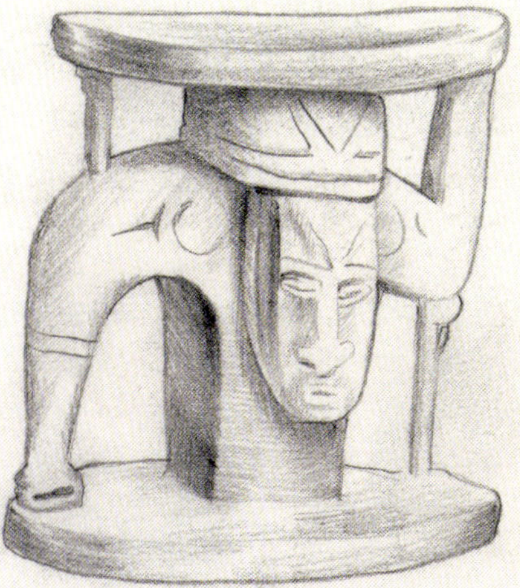

6½" TAMI ISLAND
CHI

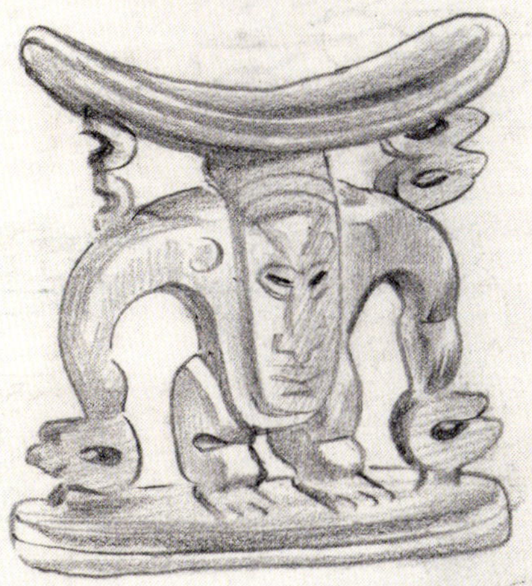

HEADREST
CHI MUS of N.H.

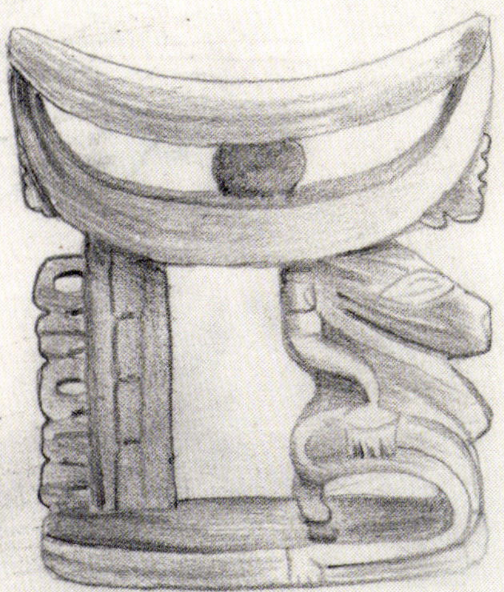

HEADREST
CHI MUS. OF N.H.

Drawings of objects included in *Arts of the South Seas*, 1946

Promoter of the "primitive": d'Harnoncourt's ascension at MoMA

In 1944, two new positions were created at MoMA specifically for d'Harnoncourt. As vice-president in charge of foreign activities, d'Harnoncourt took charge of the Museum's relations with Latin America and Europe. At the same time, he became director of its newly formed Department of Manual Industry, a complement to the Museum's Department of Industrial Design, established in 1940. In the press release announcing the creation of this department, the Museum explained that it was to be concerned with matters of design and craftsmanship in modern handmade articles. For d'Harnoncourt, this role was a natural outgrowth of the work he had undertaken at the IACB: more than a purely aesthetic exercise, the Department of Manual Industry was to "deal with the problems which affect the free function of the craftsman's skill and talent" in the rapidly modernizing postwar world. Developing manual industries was seen as a means of increasing the purchasing power of lower-income groups and of the partially disabled veterans who were returning home from the battlefronts of the Second World War.[40]

In 1946, d'Harnoncourt organized his first MoMA exhibition as a member of its staff, *Arts of the South Seas* (see portfolio). He would go on to curate and install two more exhibitions of non-Western art during his tenure at the Museum: *Ancient Art of the Andes* in 1954 and *Art of the Asmat* in 1962 (see portfolios). Throughout his career, d'Harnoncourt would be known first and foremost for his exhibitions of what was known at the time as "primitive art"—the traditional, indigenous arts of Oceania, Africa, and the Americas.[41] (In line with contemporary usage of the term, it is being used throughout this volume without the quotation marks that surround it today.) Made expressly for quotidian purposes, objects in this category differed from the "high" art with aesthetic ambitions that was typically promoted at MoMA.

In the first half of the twentieth century, so-called primitive art seemed divided between two camps: on the one hand, the anthropologists and ethnographers who would traditionally investigate such artifacts; on the other, the artists and art historians who took an increasing interest in the topic. During the 1920s and '30s, primitive art gained traction in artistic circles. Roger Fry, in his 1920 compilation of essays titled *Vision and Design*, presented entries on "The Art of the Bushman," "Negro Sculpture," and "Ancient American Art." In the 1930s and '40s, ethnographic artifacts were being displayed as artworks in museums of natural history, while in fine-art museums the exhibition of such objects drew on the contextualizing techniques characteristic of Boasian anthropological museums (for example, the life-group mode of display, which sought to depict the local and contextual meanings and functions in which the artifacts were originally created).[42] Indeed, in the early 1930s, when the Brooklyn Museum was being redefined as an art museum, Dr. Herbert J. Spinden reinstalled its ethnographic collections to highlight their aesthetic merits, defining them as masterworks of primitive art.[43] This evolution can also be seen in the selection of d'Harnoncourt to install a temporary exhibition of post-Columbian art for the 1944 reopening of the Mexican and Central American Hall of the National Museum of Natural History, for which he was acknowledged in the accompanying catalogue.

The Museum of Modern Art's attitude toward the primitive arts was established by founding director Alfred Barr. For Barr, the Museum's mission embraced both the arts of the current day as well as those of the recent or distant past, from cultures near and far, considering that these all combined to inform the thoughts and ideas of the current day.[44] In 1935, Barr conceived one of the Museum's first significant forays into primitive art, the exhibition *African Negro Art*, as part of a ten-year program of exhibitions. "This program was approved because it was evident at that time that museums in this country with ethnographical collections were little interested in the esthetic value of their material and that few museums of art were concerned with the field in even a marginal way,"[45] he explained in 1950. Under Barr's leadership, the Museum undertook this educational program of exhibitions and publications without, however, intending to build collections or take any permanent responsibility, trusting that in a few years other museums that didn't expressly focus on modern art would carry out the work.

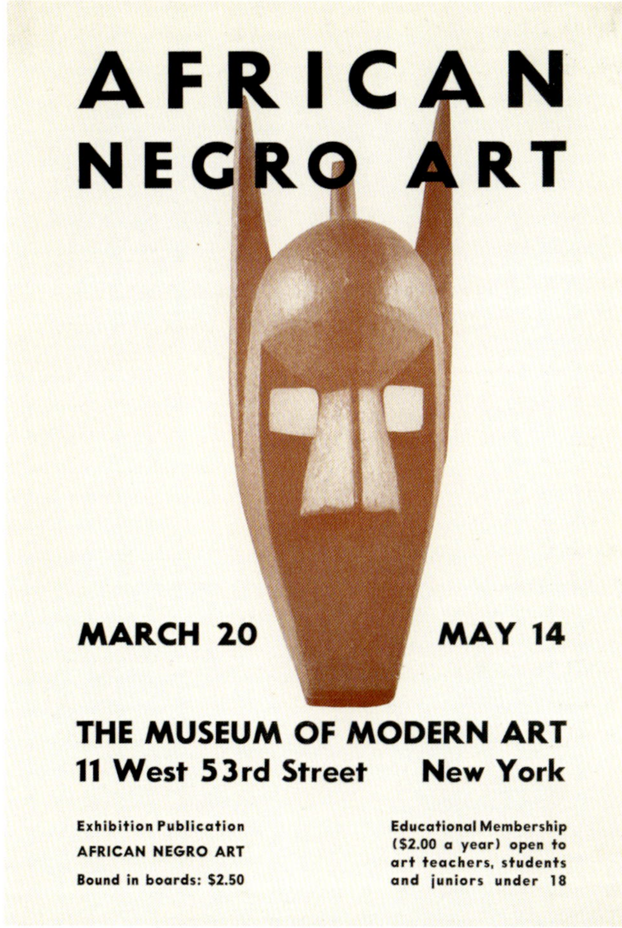

Flyer announcing the exhibition and the publication of the catalogue *African Negro Art*, March 1935

As Anne d'Harnoncourt recalled, there existed "this interaction between The Museum of Modern Art, a museum devoted to the art of its own time, and the arts of people with very different, distinct, and remote societies, cultures, and periods."[46] Exhibitions of premodern, non-Western art in the 1930s included shows on Persian frescoes, Aztec, Mayan, and Incan art, prehistoric rock pictures in Europe and Africa, and Mexican art. These exhibitions, organized under Barr's watch, emphasized the aesthetic qualities of the works; the innovative aspect of d'Harnoncourt's approach was to evoke the context, the geography, history, and function of each work, to understand the objects in depth—all the while making sure to showcase their high aesthetic value.[47]

D'Harnoncourt embraced a holistic philosophy toward the creation of art:

Every work of art from a handmade chair to the Venus of Melos is more than merely an object of aesthetic values. It is also a product of human labor and an expression of its cultural background. Therefore to appreciate a work of art thoroughly one must really consider it from all three standpoints: aesthetic values, cultural background, and production methods.[48]

His approach, a mixture of aesthetic and habitat methods of display, was also informed by two consultants who were brought on as coauthors of the publication accompanying *Arts of the South Seas*, anthropologist Ralph Linton and art historian Paul Wingert, a pioneer in the study of primitive art as an academic discipline. In the foreword to the catalogue, they explained:

An understanding of the relationship between content and form in Melanesian sculpture calls for some knowledge of the cultural background of the native artist. The growing realization in our art world that a work of art can best be appreciated in the context of its own civilization, together with the increasing interest in art shown by many scientists, holds a great promise. The collaboration among these groups should contribute greatly to our knowledge and understanding of the creative potentialities of mankind.[49]

In line with Linton and Wingert's position, d'Harnoncourt believed that because primitive art objects were made to exist within their local context, it was necessary, once they were within the museum, to convey the climatic and cultural milieus of their creation, rather than to present them as isolated aesthetic masterworks. The objective of his primitive-arts exhibitions was to emphasize the role of the objects on display as part of a whole material culture.

Circulation path

D'Harnoncourt always had a talent for grouping objects; at MoMA, this gained a deeper theoretical grounding. Beginning with *Arts of the South Seas* in 1946, d'Harnoncourt's intention became more aesthetic and art historical, setting aside the commercial, economic, and political goals of his first two exhibitions. Having drawn the individual objects selected for inclusion in an exhibition, d'Harnoncourt would begin to group them, using different rationales. Eventually, "rather than arrange them all by subject matter, locale, or chronology," criteria that he came to find too obvious or simplistic, d'Harnoncourt strove "to relate the individual pieces to their cultural and artistic neighbors—in other words, to assemble objects that had some affinities." As Monroe Wheeler explained:

> He did not bind them by mere chronology or geography, but established juxtapositions and sequences that illuminated certain universals and interrelationships between one culture and another, and inheritances from generation to generation. One of his devices was to indicate cultural and artistic kinships . . . in such a way as to stimulate the visitor to make his own comparisons.[50]

D'Harnoncourt would then consider the space, analyze the ground plan of the galleries, and roughly place the groupings in the various spaces, very conscious all the time of accommodating the visitors' needs: "You have to allow for the traffic and what people can see when other people are around them," he explained.[51] A tenet that guided d'Harnoncourt's layout was that the first item visible in a room should have a certain monumentality, whether physically or emotively. Then the circulation line through the floor plan should prepare each sequence for the next, to

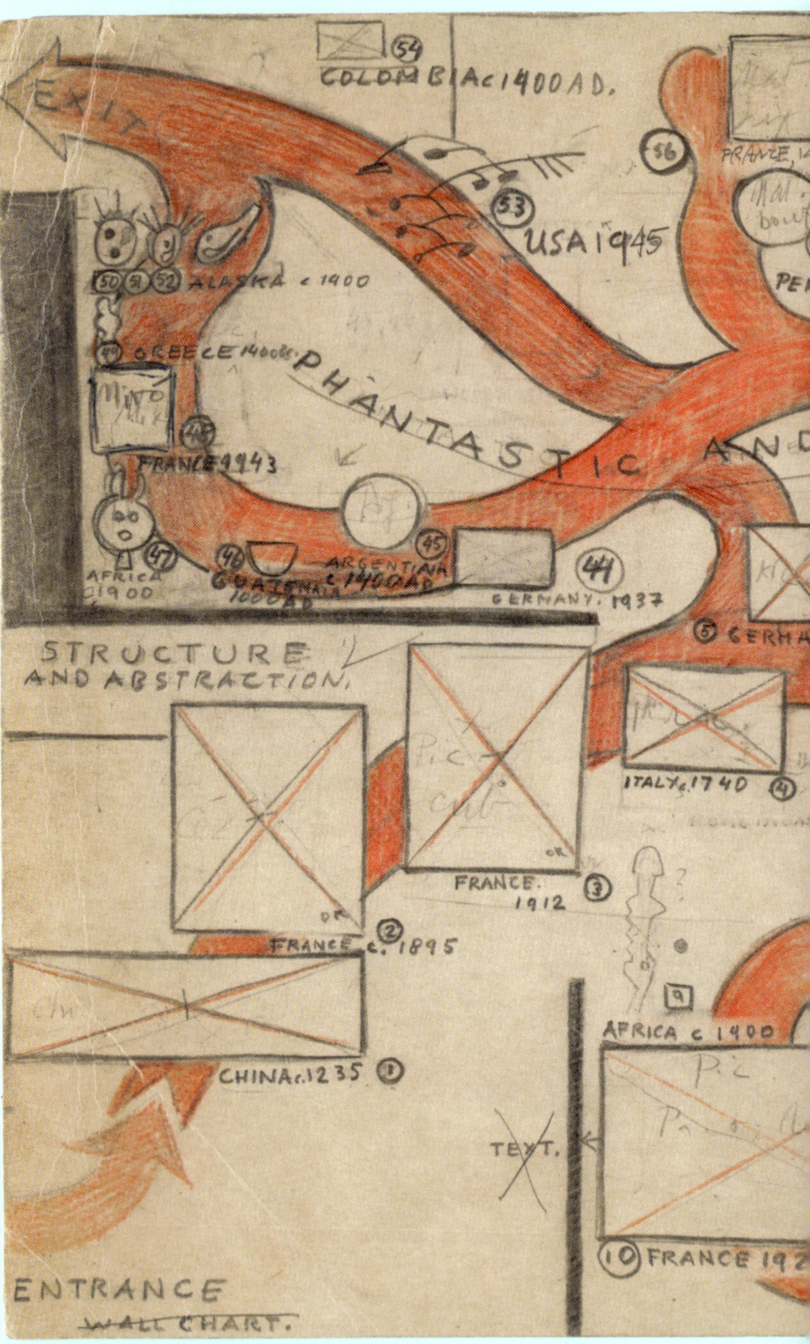

Floor plan, with circulation path, of the exhibition *Timeless Aspects of Modern Art*, 1948

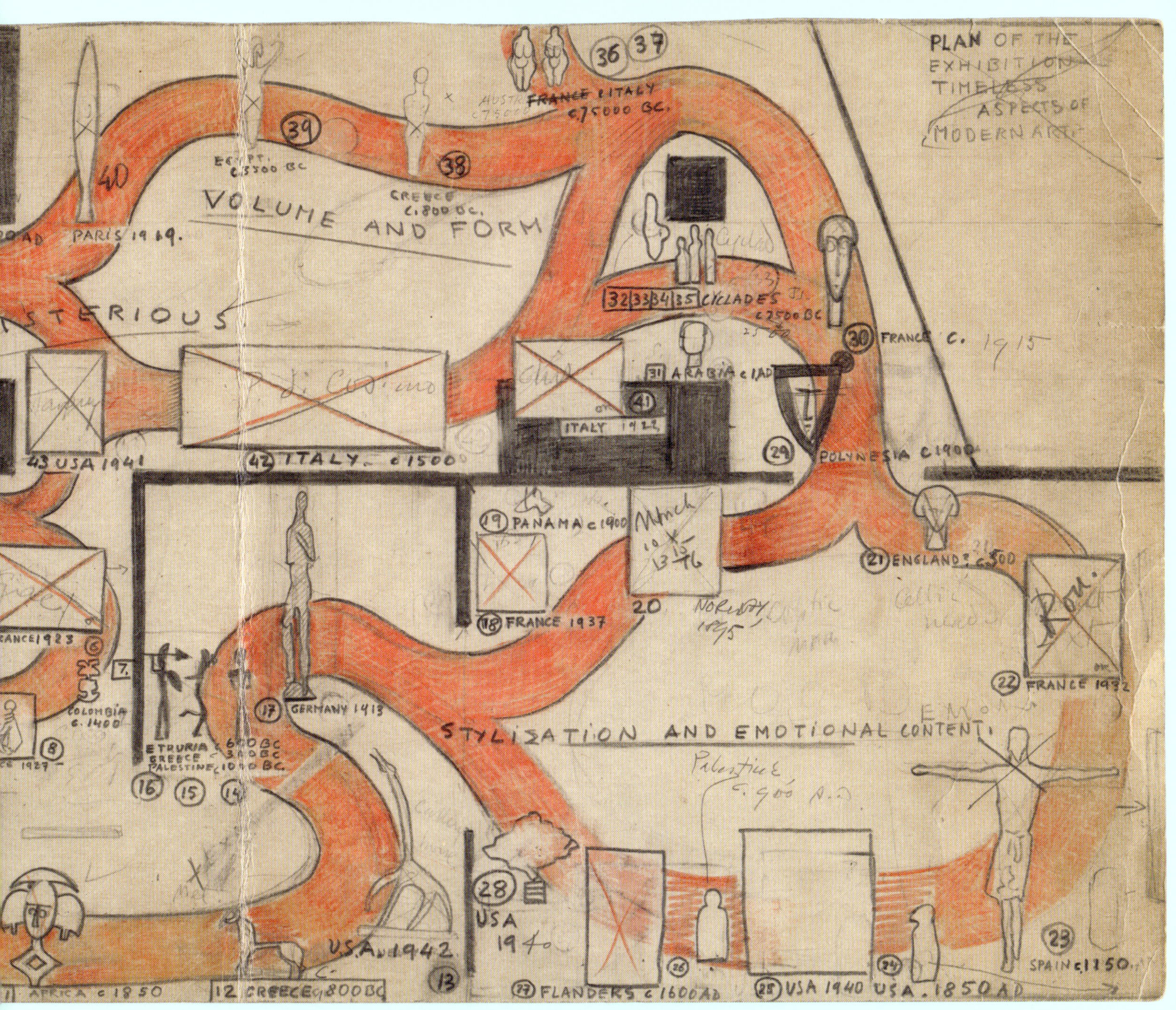

PLAN OF THE EXHIBITION
TIMELESS ASPECTS OF MODERN ART
36 37
39
38
AUSTRIA c.750
FRANCE & ITALY c.15000 BC.
EGYPT c.3500 BC
GREECE c.800 BC.
40
VOLUME AND FORM
PARIS 1969.
MYSTERIOUS
CYCLADES c.2500 BC
32 33 34 35 CYCLADES
30 FRANCE c. 1915
31 ARABIA c.1AD
41
ITALY 1422
42 ITALY c.1500
43 USA 1941
29 POLYNESIA c.1900
19 PANAMA c.1900
Munch 13-76
18 FRANCE 1937
20
NORWAY 1895
21 ENGLAND c.500
22 FRANCE 1932
FRANCE 1923
17 GERMANY 1413
COLOMBIA c.1400
8
ETRURIA 600 BC
GREECE 300 BC
PALESTINE 1000 BC
16 15 14
STYLISATION AND EMOTIONAL CONTENT
Palestine c.900 A.D.
28 USA 1940
23 SPAIN c.1150
11 AFRICA c.1850
12 GREECE 800 BC
13
27 FLANDERS c.1600 AD
USA 1942
26
24
25 USA 1940
USA 1850 AD

present a coherent unity or offer a contrast. His diagrams of the visitor's intended movement through the galleries could become highly elaborate: his sketched floor plans would include notations of the various thematic sections of the exhibitions, sometimes even miniature drawings of the works in their respective places. He thought of how to direct the visitor in a meaningful and determined order to circulate most effectively and achieve the desired effect: he understood that every exhibition has a story to tell, and part of that story is conveyed through the flow and controlled movement of the viewer.

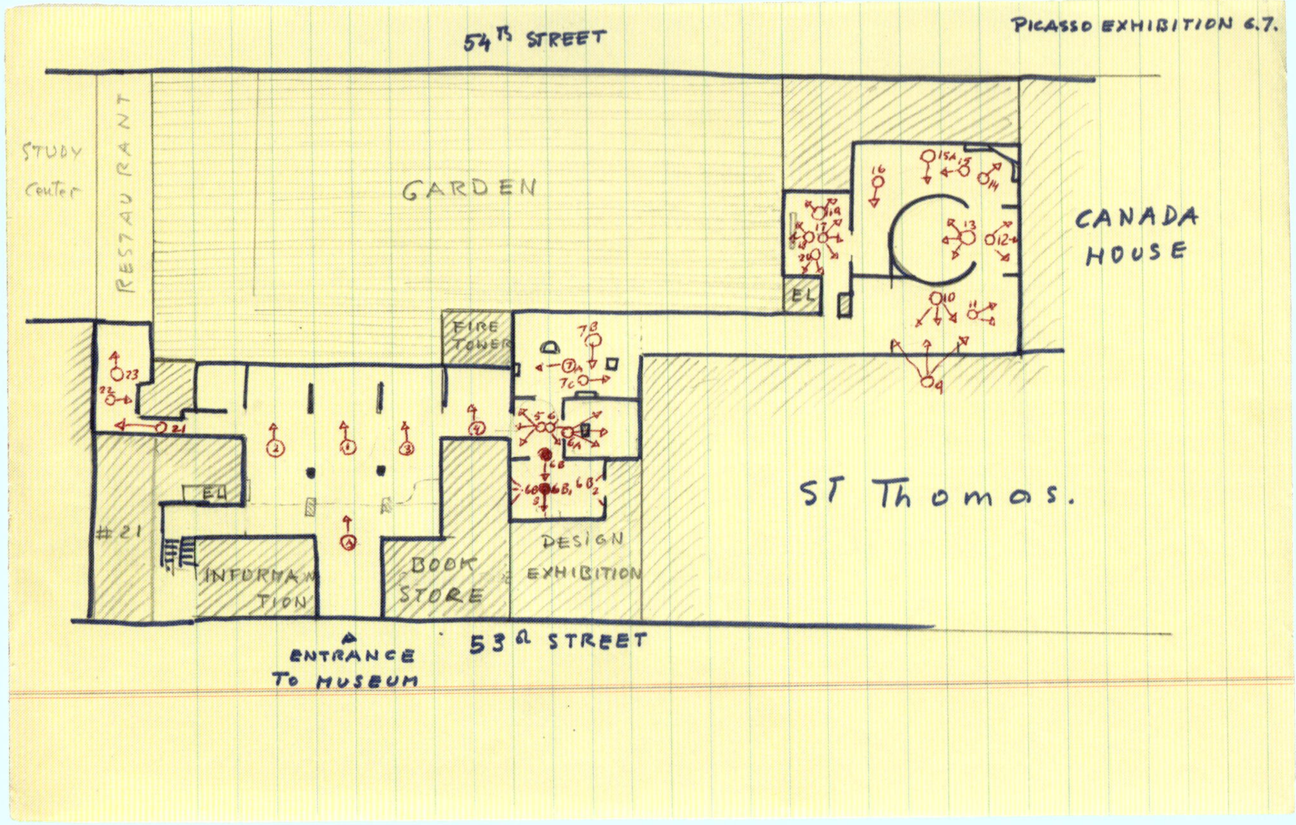

Floor plan of the exhibition *The Sculpture of Picasso*, 1967

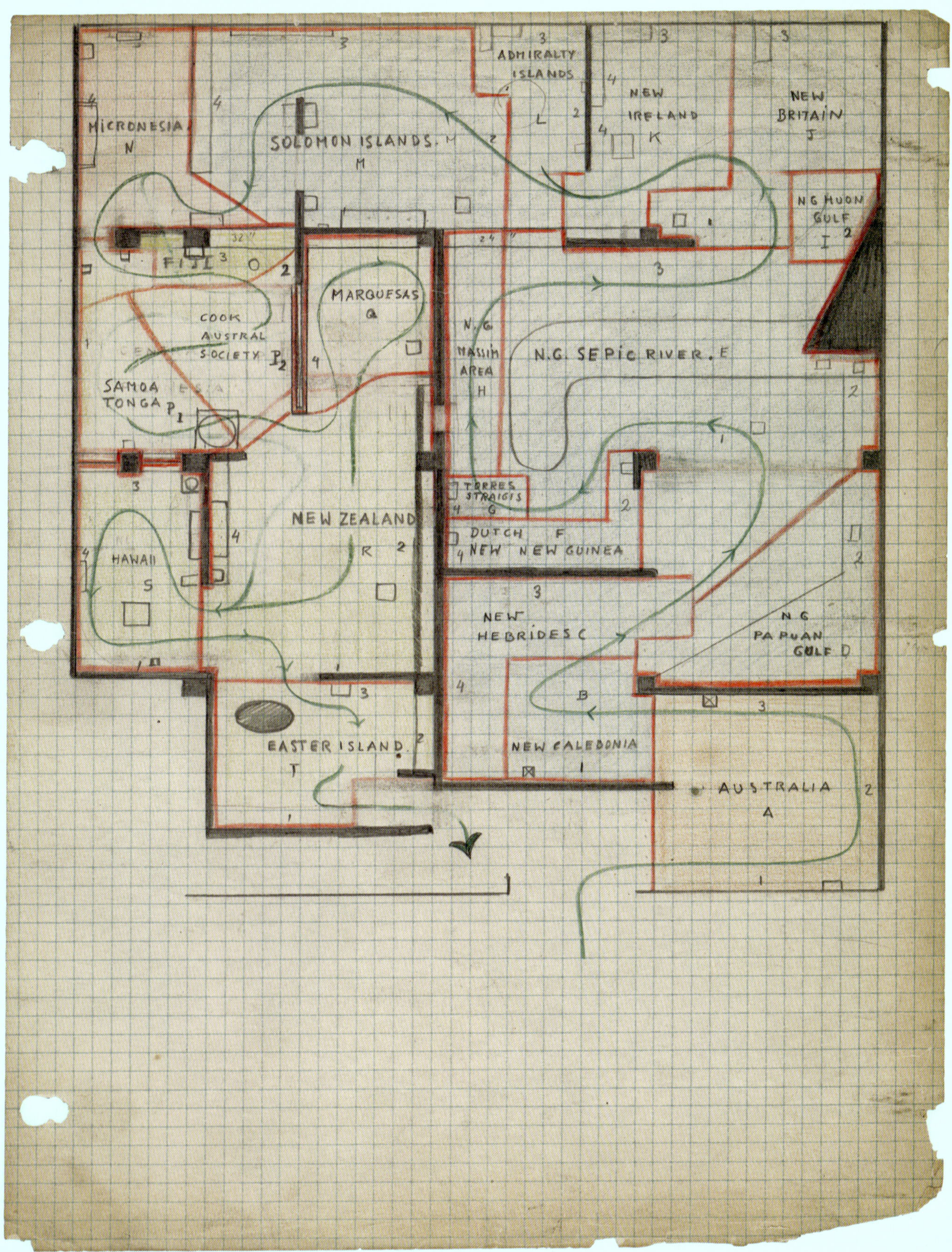

Floor plan, with circulation path, of the exhibition *Arts of the South Seas*, 1946

Over the years, d'Harnoncourt continued to draw subtle connections of affinity among non-Western art and the modern art that MoMA specialized in showing. For his 1946 exhibition on the arts of the South Seas, he identified and pointed out formal affinities between Oceanic and modern art: both drastically simplify form; their treatment of the human figure is stylized rather than realistic; and distortion is employed for emphasis. Going further, he saw the art of the South Seas as a forerunner to Expressionism and Surrealism, comparable to how African art had influenced the development of Cubism: he explained in the catalogue's foreword that artists during the later phases of Expressionism had turned to the Magic art of Oceania for inspiration, as illustrated by their shared interest in the dreamworld and the subconscious. "The affinity of this Magic art with certain contemporary movements," he added, "is not limited to concept and style but can be observed also in the choice of materials and in technique."[52] In his next exhibition of non-Western art, *Ancient Arts of the Andes* in 1954, d'Harnoncourt acknowledged that South American art had perhaps less in common with modern art than African art with Cubism or South Seas art with Surrealism, but nonetheless he emphasized the relevance of this ancient art to the art of our time. The *Times* magazine picked up on this thesis: "Like the Museum of Modern Art's other exhibitions of primitive and ancient and folk art, this one is intended to show not direct influences but certain common esthetic idioms and modes that occur and reoccur as man creates images and objects. Coincidental as the similarities to modern art and objects may be, they are provocative and entertaining."[53] According to Douglas Newton, a curator at the Museum of Primitive Art, d'Harnoncourt thought "primitive artifacts . . . *were* works of art, and that is precisely why he worried about [their] appearance. If I interpret him correctly, he believed that works of art had a universal message, and that if he could help convey that, he was conveying something about humanity, including its intellectual systems."[54]

The publication, in 1938, of Robert Goldwater's classic reader *Primitivism in Modern Painting* was a watershed moment. In this volume, Goldwater advanced his idea of "affinity," or the idea of aligning cultural objects according to their visual form, even though they may be quite different in terms of their meaning or function in their culturally specific context—a concept that clearly resonated with d'Harnoncourt, who returned to it consistently throughout his exhibitions. Goldwater wrote of affinity as a connection between children's art and modern art:

> Whether we understand it or not, and whether we approve it or not, this affinity of large sections of modern painting to children's art is one of the most striking of its characteristics. It is part of a much wider and vaguer affinity which has been generally recognized, yet never pinned down. It has been felt that modern art is in some way primitive.[55]

D'Harnoncourt's approach was greatly influenced by Goldwater, who also collaborated with d'Harnoncourt on MoMA's 1948 exhibition *Modern Art in Your Life*.

Goldwater and d'Harnoncourt joined forces with Nelson Rockefeller on another project: the Museum of Primitive Art (MPA). In 1956, d'Harnoncourt was named vice-president of Rockefeller's newly created MPA, and Goldwater was chosen as its first director. D'Harnoncourt and Rockefeller had met in 1941, when *Indian Art of the United States* was presented at MoMA; as early as 1941, Rockefeller had invited d'Harnoncourt to work for him as acting director of the Art Section of the Office of the Coordinator of Inter-American Affairs, Department of State. The pair shared a passion for indigenous arts, an interest they would cultivate together with their study of art of the ancient and native Americas, Africa, and the South Seas over the coming decades. From 1949 to 1956, d'Harnoncourt advised Rockefeller on building his collection of primitive art, which would form the core of the collection of the MPA.

Located at 15 West 54th Street (directly opposite the Museum's Abby Aldrich Rockefeller Sculpture Garden), the MPA was the fulfillment of a lifelong dream for Rockefeller and d'Harnoncourt. While establishing the Museum in 1955, d'Harnoncourt described the mission of the nascent institution, explaining that it would be dedicated to the aesthetic aspects of the indigenous arts of the two Americas,

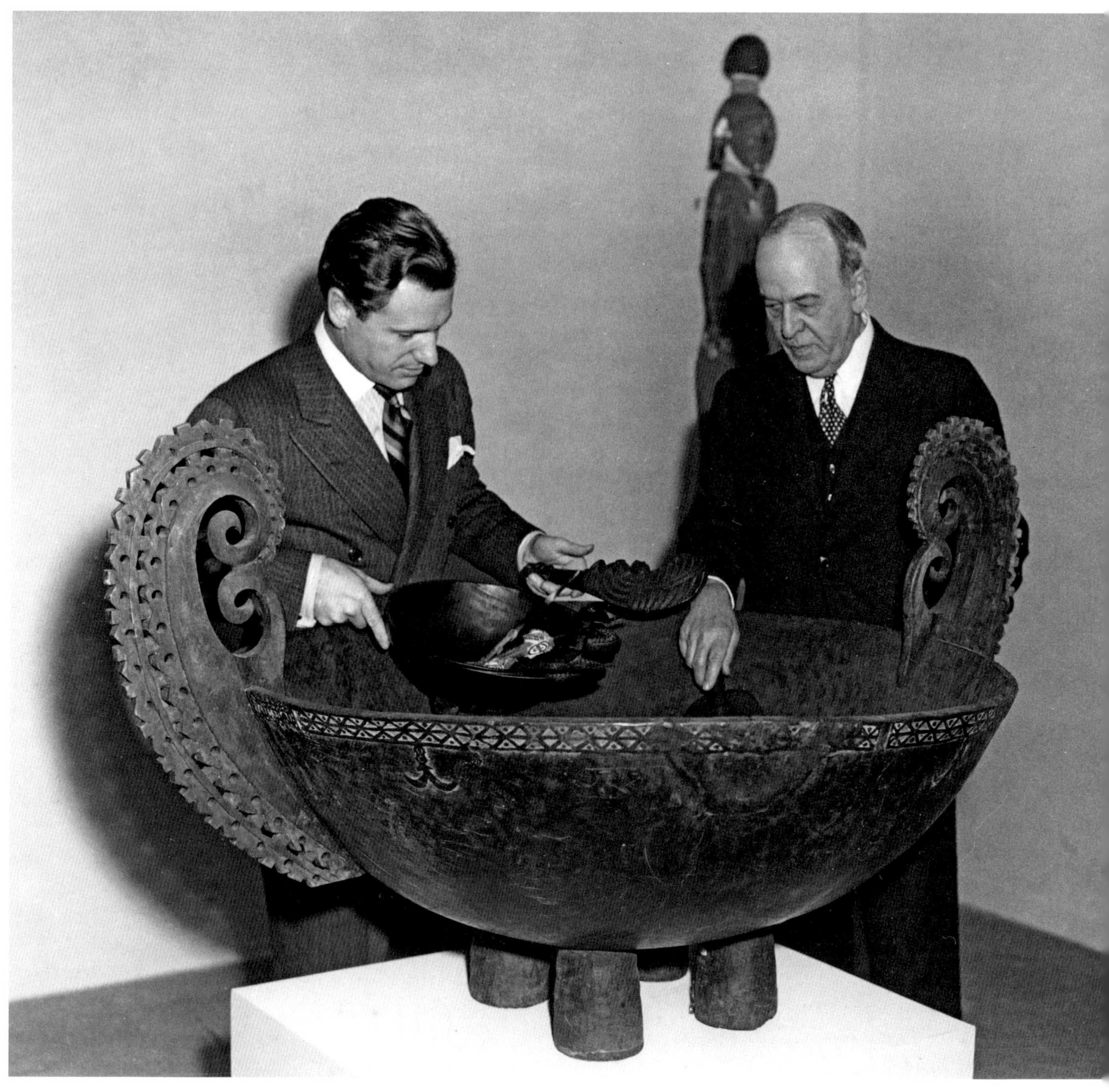

Nelson Rockefeller, MoMA's first vice-president, and Stephen C. Clark, its chairman, at the exhibition *Arts of the South Seas*, 1946

Oceania, and Africa, and to the corresponding early phases of European and Asiatic civilizations. "We have no intention to rival or duplicate the work of museums of Anthropology or Archaeology but we hope to supplement it," he specified. "By showing only objects of greatest artistic value we hope to open to the public new sources for esthetic enjoyment and at the same time to focus its attention on the merits of civilizations other than ours."[56] In 1957, d'Harnoncourt installed the opening exhibition of the Museum of Primitive Art, *Selected Works from the Collection*, followed in 1958 by *Art of Ancient Peru (Selected Works from the Collection)*. *Art of the Asmat*, organized in 1962, was a collaboration between MoMA and the MPA.

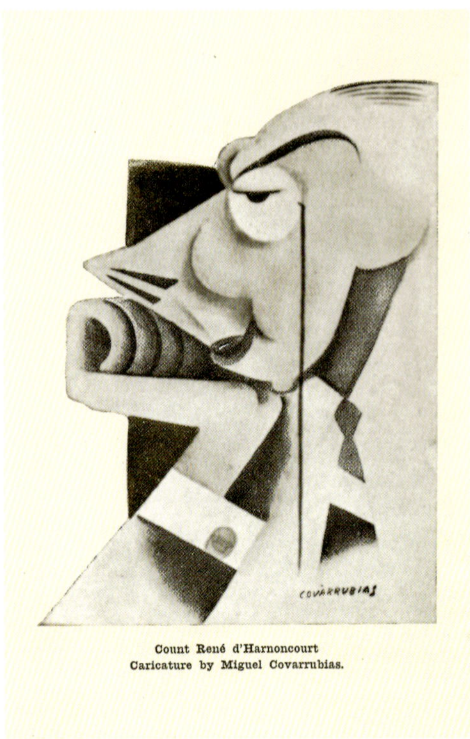

Count René d'Harnoncourt
Caricature by Miguel Covarrubias.

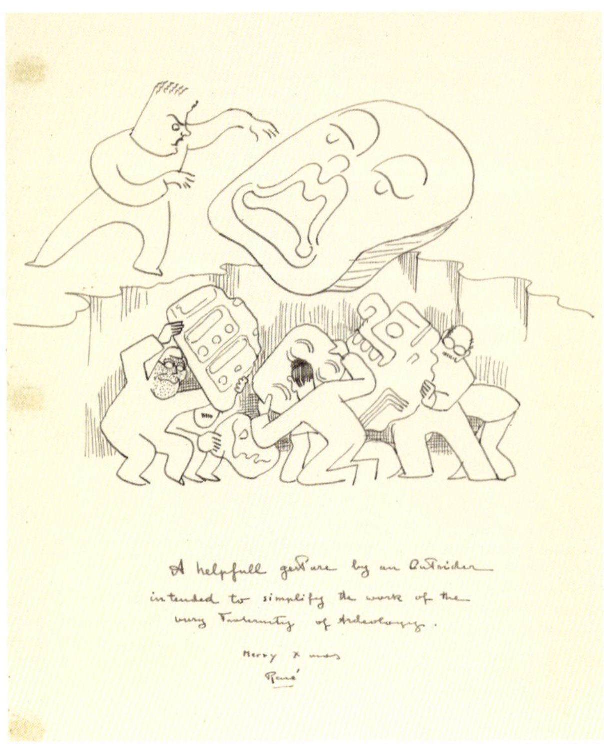

Miguel Covarrubias. Caricature of René d'Harnoncourt, published in *Domingos Mexicanos* (*Mexican Sundays*), a collection of reproductions of watercolor tableaux by René d'Harnoncourt, c. 1925–29 (Mexico City: F. W. Davis, Sonora News Co.)

René d'Harnoncourt. Sketch of Miguel Covarrubias hurling a large Olmec head onto a group of archaeologists excavating Mayan artifacts, early 1940s

Another important influence on d'Harnoncourt's conception of the primitive arts was artist Miguel Covarrubias. The two had met when Fred Davis commissioned Covarrubias to create a caricature of d'Harnoncourt: in 1928, it was included in *Domingos Mexicanos* (*Mexican Sundays*), published by Davis. D'Harnoncourt would later return the favor, drawing a caricature of Covarrubias. D'Harnoncourt and Covarrubias shared notably similar styles of drawing, both in approach, with an economy of form for expression, as well as in execution, with a masterful handling of color. D'Harnoncourt's description of his friend could apply just as well to himself:

C. had an extraordinary power of observation which enabled him to see the significant detail in every object he drew. . . . Through exhaustive study and work he acquired great factual knowledge of the ancient civilizations of the Americas. To see C.'s drawings of primitive art objects is to see these objects through the eyes of an artist and scholar. Under his sensitive eye and hand they often reveal at once a beauty and meaning difficult to discover in the original.[57]

So similar in style were their drawings that when a friend, studying a painting d'Harnoncourt had recently finished, commented, "Ah, René Covarrubias d'Harnoncourt," d'Harnoncourt agreed with a chuckle.[58]

D'Harnoncourt and Covarrubias's initial encounter in Mexico City marked the beginning of a long friendship and intellectual kinship, with d'Harnoncourt crediting Covarrubias for introducing him to the beauty and magic of pre-Columbian art. Their professional interests would intersect on multiple occasions. Covarrubias made a key contribution to the 1939 Golden Gate International Exposition in San Francisco: a cycle of six oversize mural maps titled *Pageant of the Pacific*. They included the glorious, fantastical *Art Forms of the Pacific Area,* a map of the Pacific Rim showing icons of forms of art typical of each region.[59] The map was emblematic of Covarrubias's belief in "diffusionism": thinking about the origin of forms, he came to the conclusion that part of the cultural legacy of the New World derived from contact with peoples

Miguel Covarrubias. Illustration of a Sulka Dance Mask made of a palm wood frame covered with pith, 1946. Reproduced in the exhibition catalogue *Arts of the South Seas* by Ralph Linton and Paul S. Wingert, in collaboration with René d'Harnoncourt

René d'Harnoncourt. Sketch of a Sulka Dance Mask included in *Arts of the South Seas*, 1946

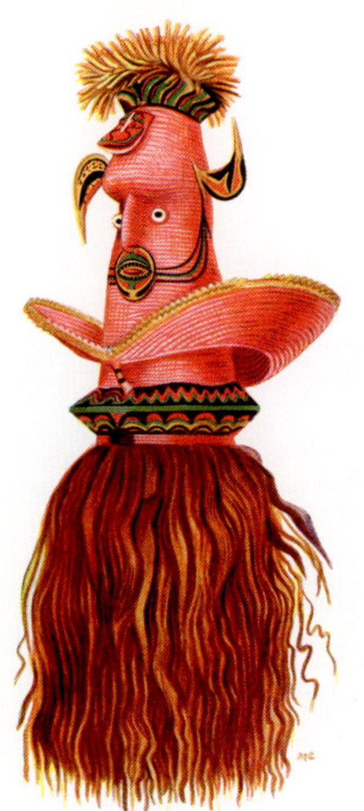

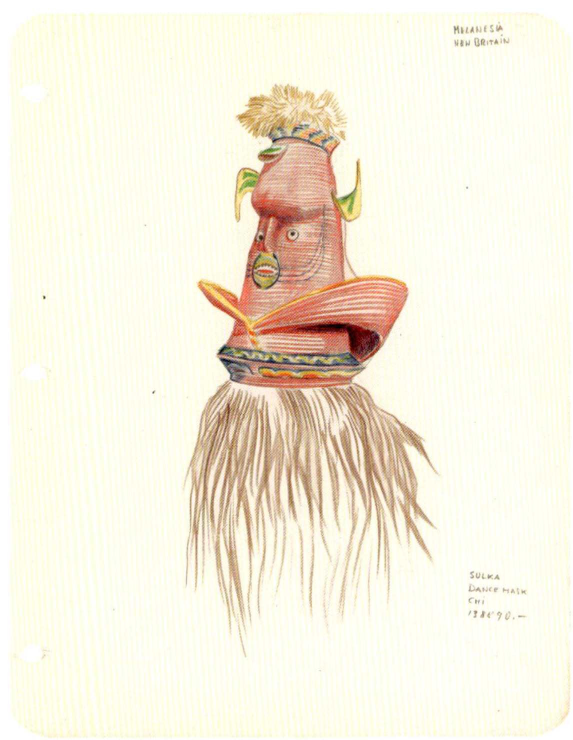

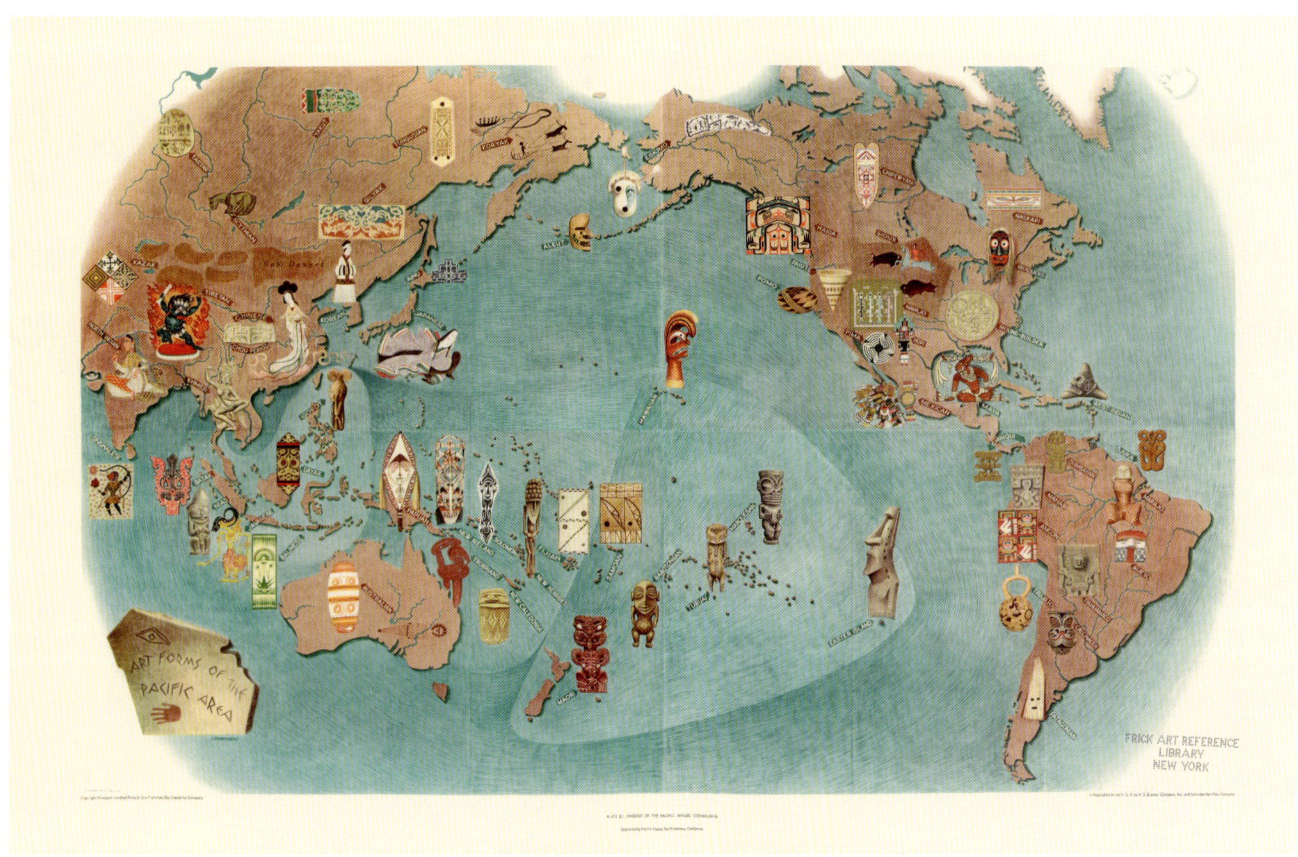

Miguel Covarrubias. *Pageant of the Pacific*, Plate III from *Art Forms of the Pacific Area* (New York: Pacific House, 1940)

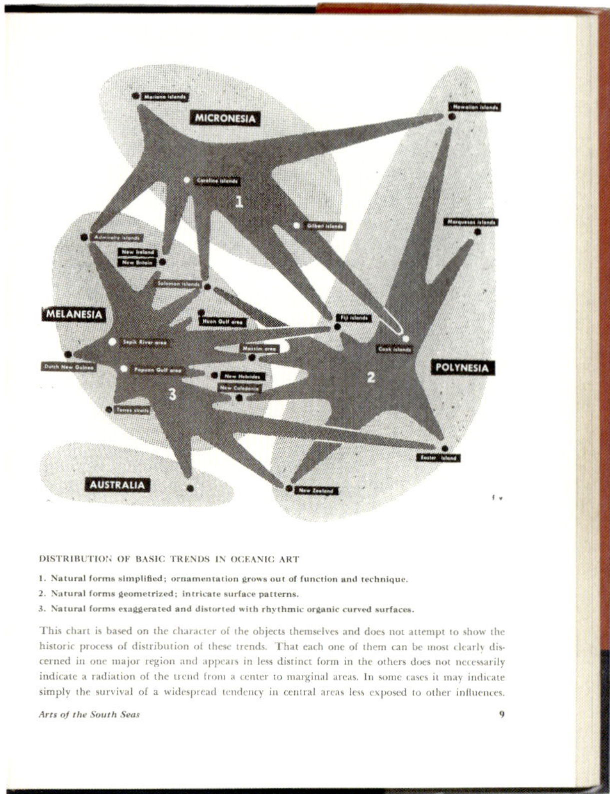

Distribution of Basic Trends in Oceanic Art, chart published on page 9 of the catalogue of the exhibition *Arts of the South Seas*, 1946

combination of typical trustee donors; artists such as Covarrubias, Marc Chagall, André Breton, Max Ernst, and Jacques Lipchitz; and anthropologists Gregory Bateson, Claude Lévi-Strauss, and Margaret Mead. There is substantial evidence to indicate that modern artists who had the opportunity to visit MoMA found inspiration in d'Harnoncourt's shows, beginning with *Indian Art* in 1941. Toward mid-century, American artists became interested in the art of the American Indian, seeking something primitive, primordial, and distinctly American.[60] *Indian Art* had a particularly profound impact on American artists associated with Abstract Expressionism: Jackson Pollock visited the exhibition multiple times, and became deeply inter-ested in the Navajo sand paintings that were created on the floor; Adolph Gottlieb and Richard Pousette-Dart's work from the period clearly resonated with the pictographs that were on display.[61] As art critic Dorothy Adlow noted in her review of *Ancient Art of the Andes*, "Modern artists have been very responsive to the natural artistic taste of tribesmen." She noticed that some present-day artists were abandoning their academic learning to imitate primitive art.[62] In an essay written in response to *Arts of the South Seas*, Barnett Newman agreed with Adlow's statement, picking up on d'Harnoncourt's notion of affinity to analyze the impetus of the art of Pacific Islanders and its shared attributes with European Surrealism and with "a new movement that has arisen here in America which shows through its works that it has, in effect, reinterpreted Oceanic art, that it has also set out on an art of magic, but that this time it is a vision-ary art, a subjective art without illusionary trap-pings."[63] Finally, artist Max Weber enjoyed visiting *Ancient Arts of the Andes* so much that he returned several times before writing a letter to d'Harnoncourt in which he expressed his "gratitude and blessings to you for the superb design of this inspiring exhibition of the undying art of a great race," as well as the wish that the exhibition—"a perfect unit and a unique exemplary masterpiece"—might become a perma-nent section of the Museum (see page 120).[64]

from the East, before European colonialism. One can surmise this thinking had some impact on d'Harnoncourt's outlook. D'Harnoncourt's interest in art from the Pacific and neighboring Bali was cer-tainly influenced by Covarrubias's knowledge of and passion for the region. In 1946, when organizing *Arts of the South Seas*, d'Harnoncourt asked his friend to serve as an official advisor and assist in the assembly and installation of the works of art. He included four drawings by Covarrubias in the *South Seas* catalogue, their style virtually indistinguishable from his own.

D'Harnoncourt's exhibits of primitive art attracted a wide and diverse audience; the dinner to celebrate the opening of *Arts of the South Seas*, for instance, brought together an eclectic group, with its bizarre

Vistas and open vistas

D'Harnoncourt possessed an uncanny ability to project himself into the space of the exhibition, elaborating on the basic two-dimensional floor plan by introducing the idea of "vistas." Treating each section of an exhibition separately, he drew perspective views, to understand each item's exact placement, its relation to neighboring works, and perhaps most importantly, its communication with objects in other sections. Today, these renderings would be done with digital tools that allow designers to visualize the visitor experience in three dimensions—after scale maquettes, we have now moved onto Photoshop and AutoCAD—but d'Harnoncourt would turn, once again, to his drawing pad. He developed these installation vistas with great care and exactitude, in many cases keying the ground plan with vista identifiers, then drawing each of the vistas to scale, often in color. In this way, he could test his installation plan, to ensure the works were grouped to their best advantage and that the visitor's visual experience would progress in a meaningful manner from group to group.

D'Harnoncourt also thought deeply about the notion of "open vistas," which he saw as a means of drawing connections between distinct (geographically or otherwise) groups to emphasize interrelationships. As he explained in 1945, when seeking to

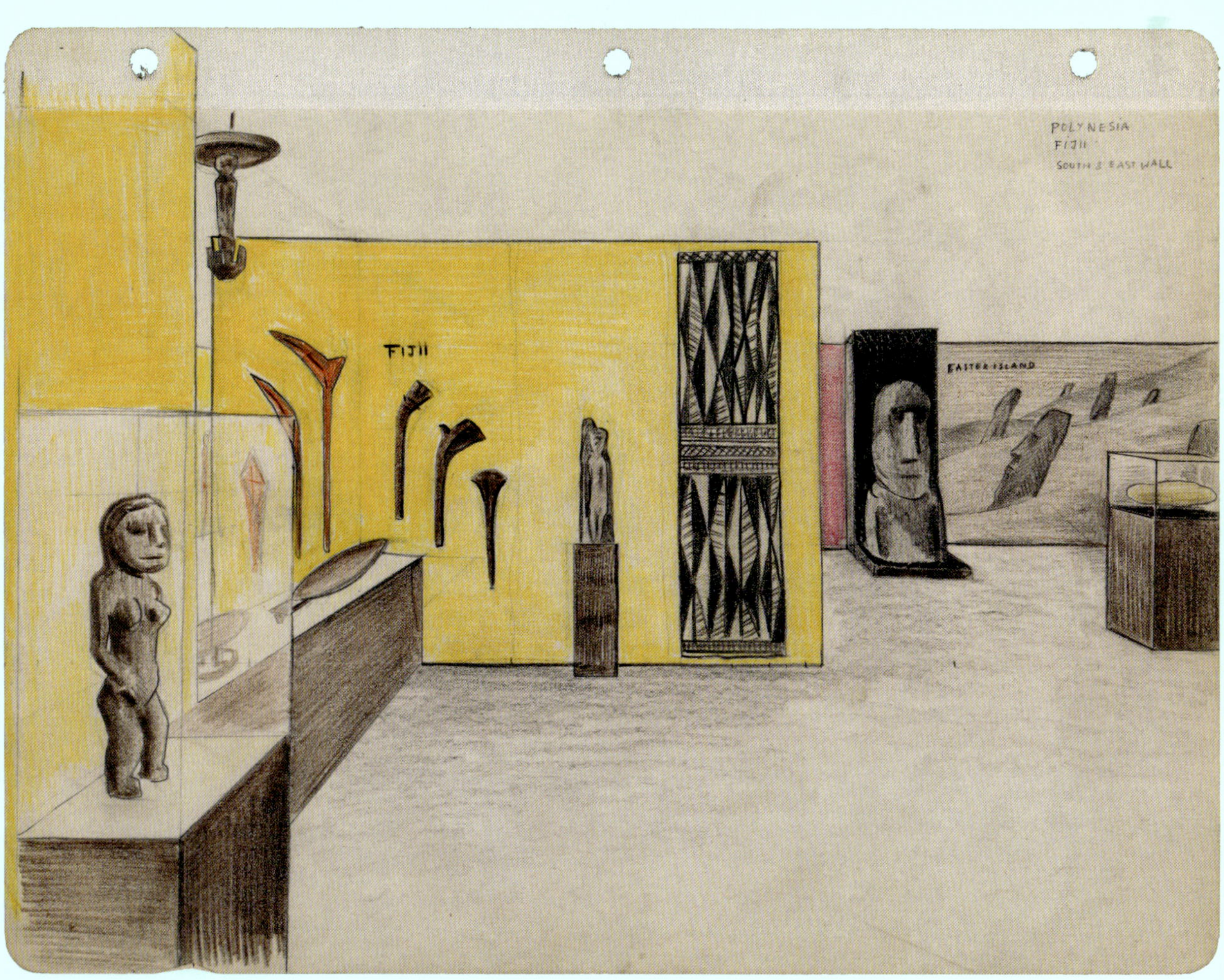

Installation vista of the Polynesia section of the exhibition *Arts of the South Seas*, 1946

obtain a grant from the Rockefeller Foundation to facilitate the research and development of a new installation style:

> Most displays so far have been organized in a purely consecutive order by which knowledge is absorbed as if from the pages of a book. This is of course an order that does not correspond to the way in which knowledge is absorbed in actual life where a person is able at any point to compare the main object of his interest with the related ones even if they are not directly in the path of his main line of progress.[65]

Aware of the inadequacy of traditional display methods to show the interrelations between objects, d'Harnoncourt developed a new method of presentation to give the visitor greater opportunities for visual comparison, founded on the recognition that the field of vision of the visitor should not to be limited to the units that are in the path of his immediate physical progress through the exhibition; "at any given point, vistas should be open to him into those sections of the exhibition that have affinities with the displays in the unit in which he stands." D'Harnoncourt wanted to avoid traditional presentations in closed exhibition units, which he said would have given a completely false picture to the visitor, since cultural characteristics and art styles extend from region to region: "The plan of the exhibition, therefore, has been designed to show the visitor open vistas from one section to another wherever there is a close relationship between the objects. Closed units are introduced only where unique local styles have developed."[66]

He further argued, "This type of installation demands a most thorough study of the subject because the placing of each piece becomes not only a matter of esthetic consideration but one of significance in establishing the chain of influences or affinities that are of scientific and educational importance."[67] In his exhibitions, d'Harnoncourt wanted visitors to be able to see from one gallery into another: the object in the center of a given space may belong to only one geographic region, but through its formal and aesthetic properties, it provided a link to another one. In his circulation diagrams, arrows would represent open views, through walls or over platforms, to connect various objects.

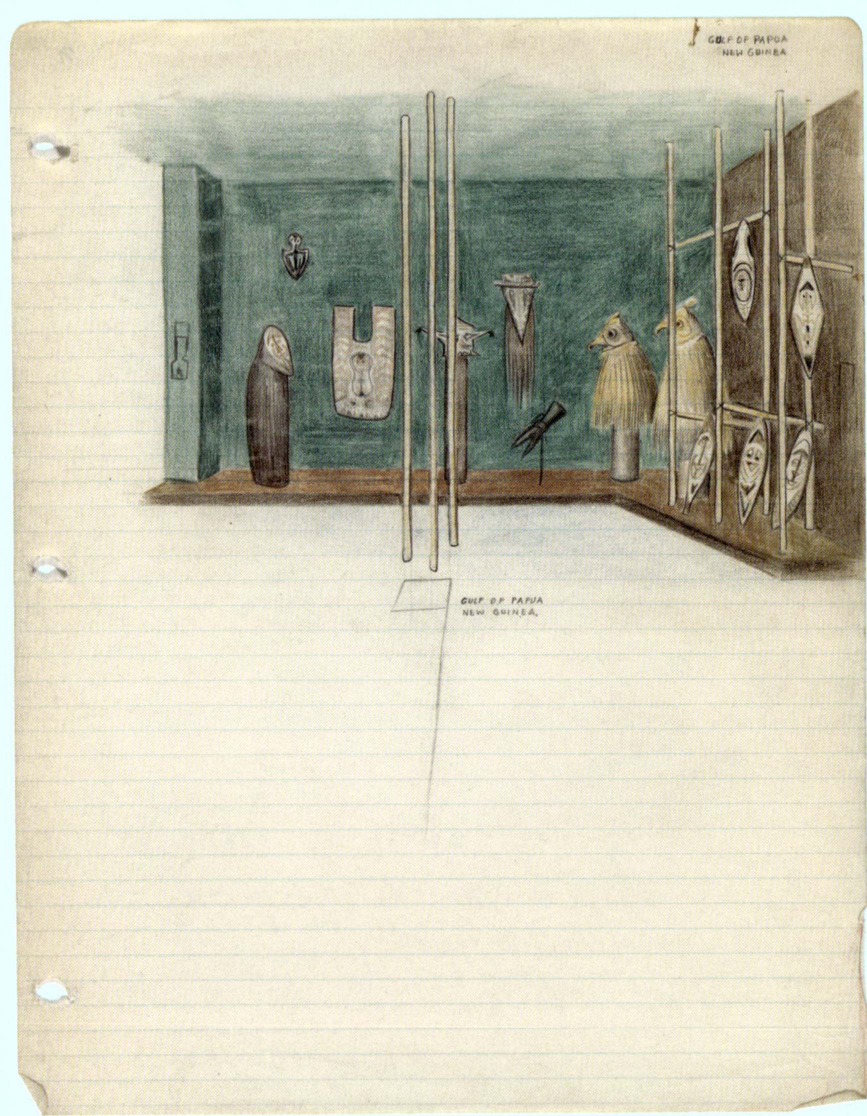

Vista of the Gulf of Papua New Guinea section of the exhibition *Arts of the South Seas*, 1946

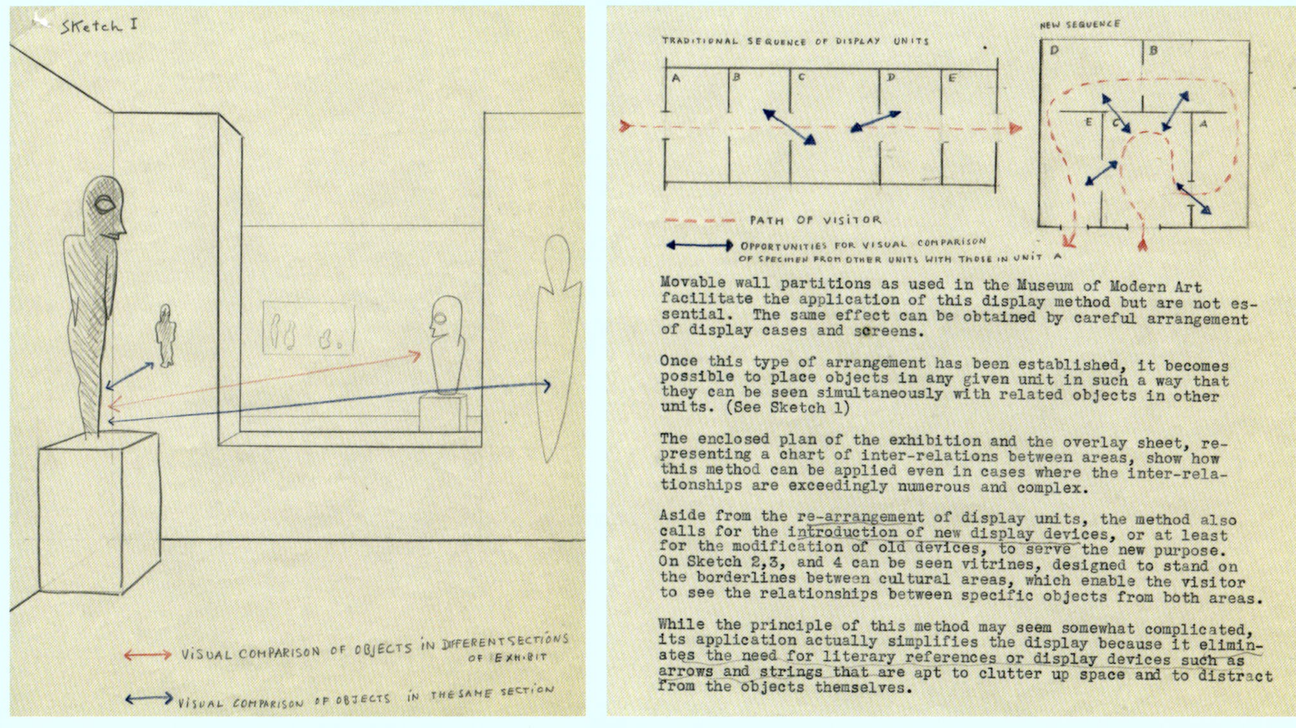

Movable wall partitions as used in the Museum of Modern Art facilitate the application of this display method but are not essential. The same effect can be obtained by careful arrangement of display cases and screens.

Once this type of arrangement has been established, it becomes possible to place objects in any given unit in such a way that they can be seen simultaneously with related objects in other units. (See Sketch 1)

The enclosed plan of the exhibition and the overlay sheet, representing a chart of inter-relations between areas, show how this method can be applied even in cases where the inter-relationships are exceedingly numerous and complex.

Aside from the re-arrangement of display units, the method also calls for the introduction of new display devices, or at least for the modification of old devices, to serve the new purpose. On Sketch 2,3, and 4 can be seen vitrines, designed to stand on the borderlines between cultural areas, which enable the visitor to see the relationships between specific objects from both areas.

While the principle of this method may seem somewhat complicated, its application actually simplifies the display because it eliminates the need for literary references or display devices such as arrows and strings that are apt to clutter up space and to distract from the objects themselves.

Illustrations from a grant proposal by René d'Harnoncourt requesting funding from the Rockefeller Foundation to develop a new display methodology, September 17, 1945

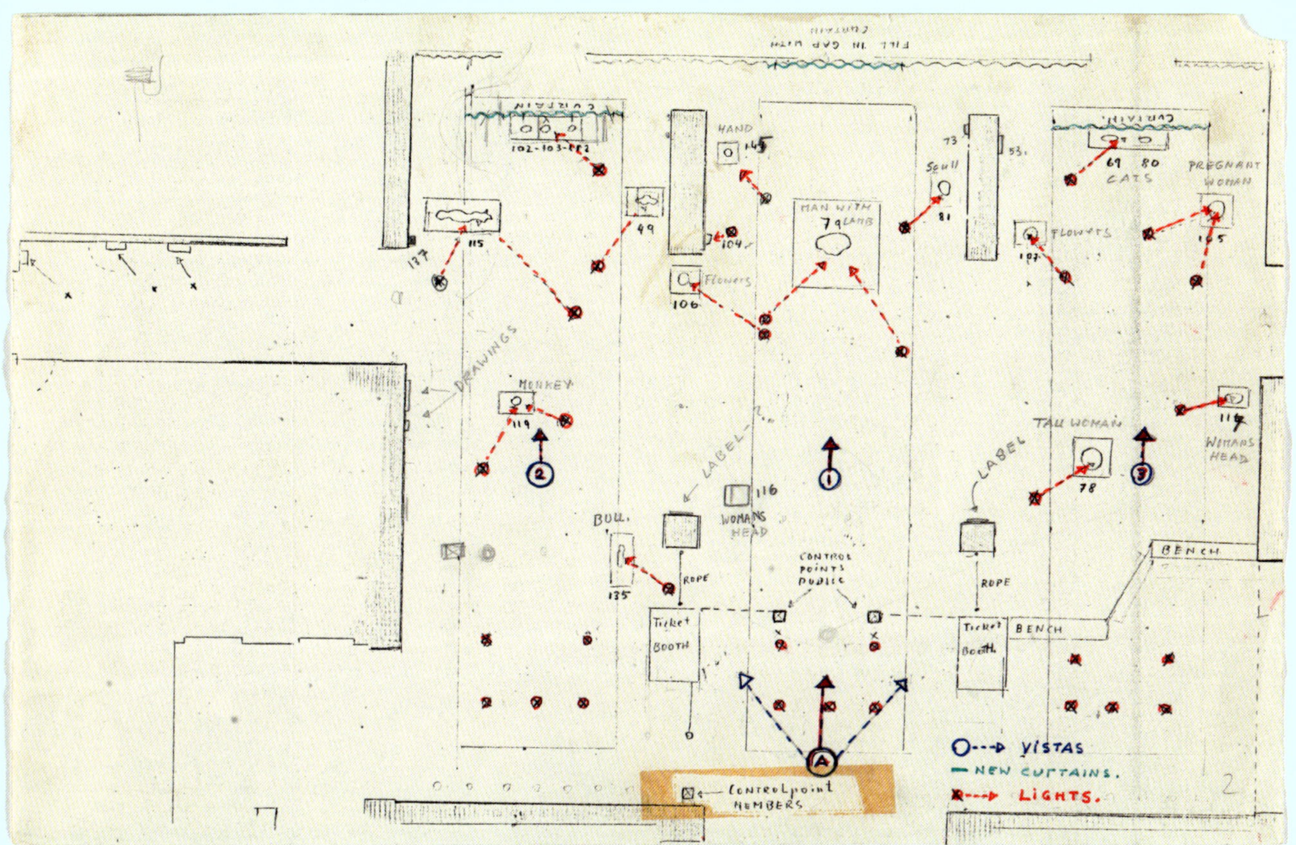

Floor plan of the exhibition *The Sculpture of Picasso*, 1967, with annotations indicating vistas and lighting

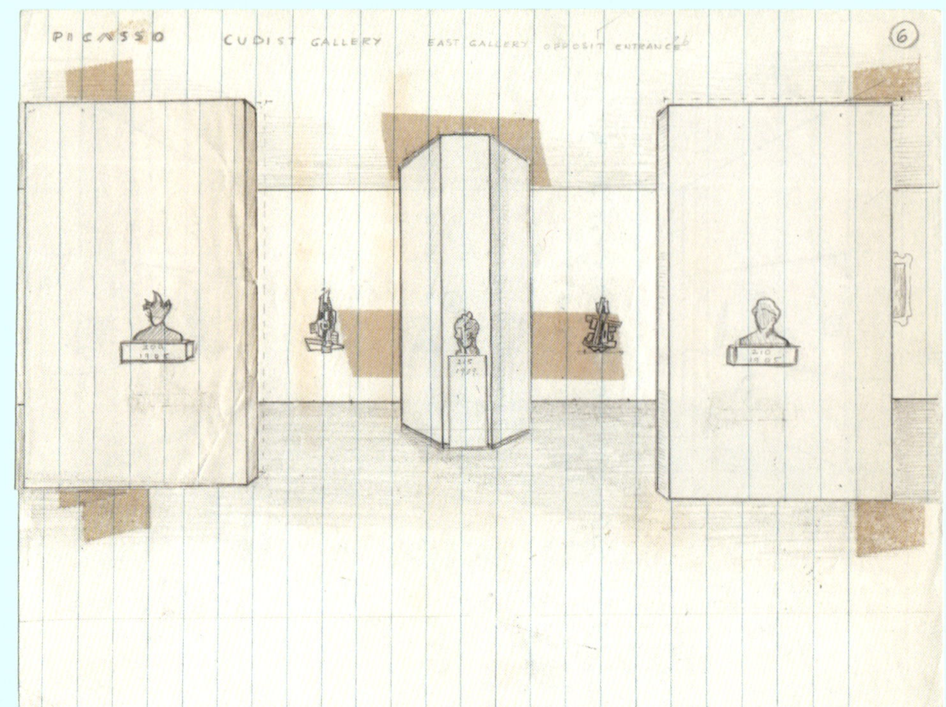

Sketch for the installation of the Cubist gallery of the exhibition *The Sculpture of Picasso*, 1967, with taped-on overlays that open to reveal the view behind the freestanding architectural elements

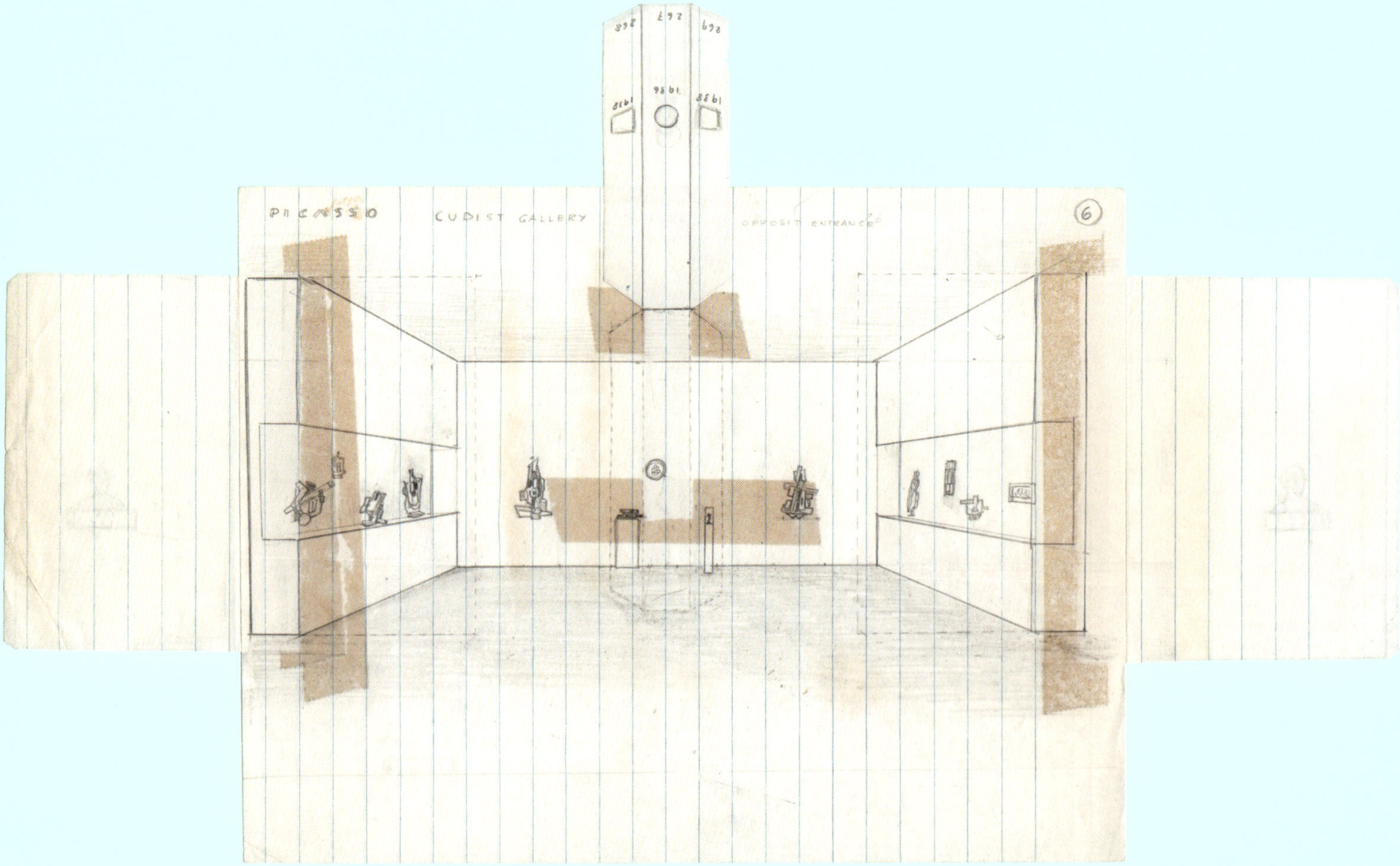

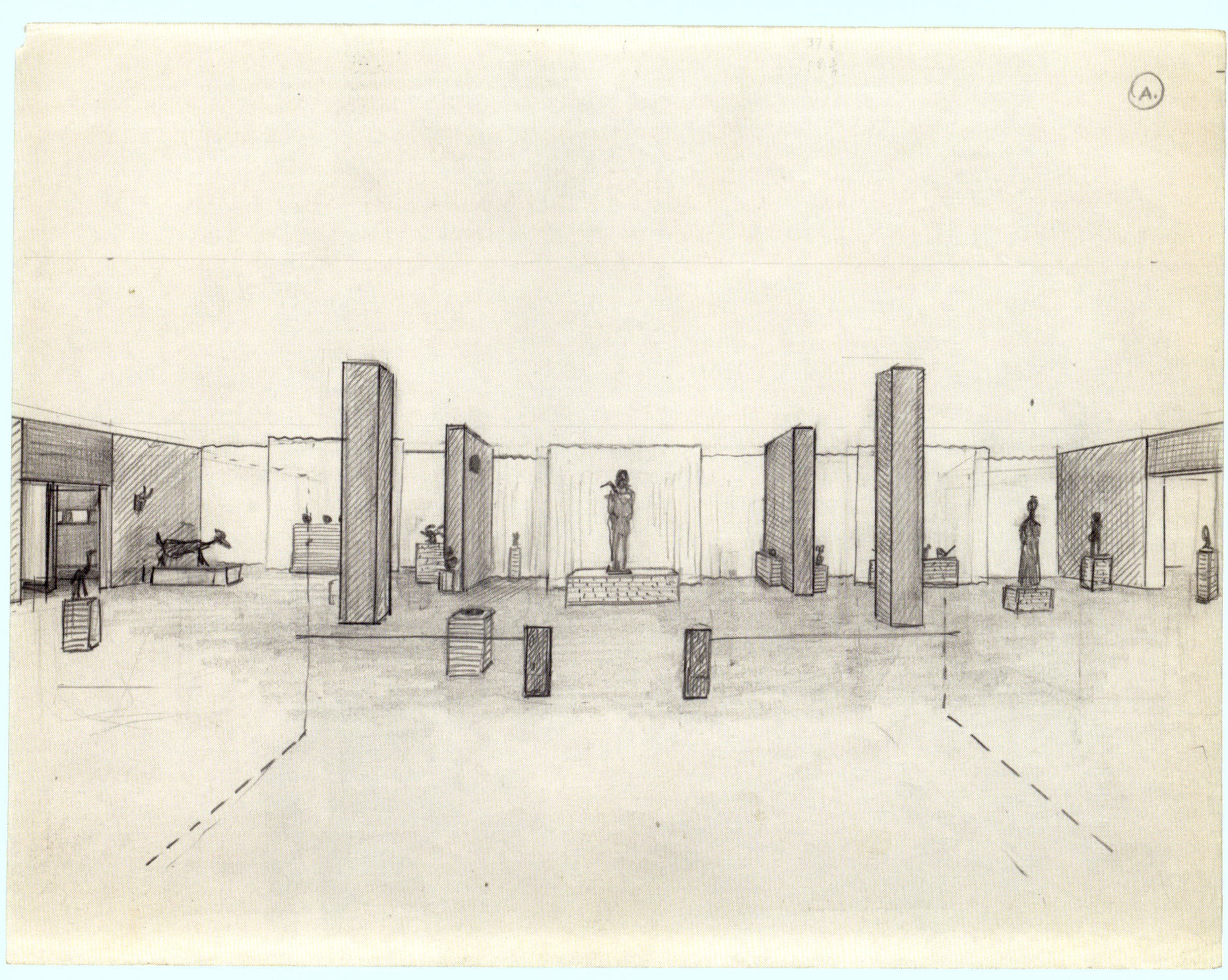

Vista of *The Sculpture of Picasso*, 1967

In 1947, d'Harnoncourt was appointed chairman of the Museum's Coordination Committee—the highest governing body of the Museum, composed of five senior staff members, which met regularly to review all matters of program, policy, and procedure for the Museum—and director of its Curatorial Departments. Given that, at this time, the Museum had no director, with this dual title d'Harnoncourt in effect assumed the responsibilities of that position.[68] In October 1949, the Board of Trustees unanimously elected d'Harnoncourt director of the Museum—a mere formality.

In 1948–49, d'Harnoncourt organized a pair of companion exhibitions to celebrate the Museum's twentieth anniversary, which provided him with an opportunity to put his imprint on the Museum's educational mission and programming. These two exhibitions, *Timeless Aspects of Modern Art* and *Modern Art in Your Life* (see portfolios), were conceived as parts of a series to elucidate the relationship of the art of our time to art from other eras and its role and function in the modern world. They were originally to be followed by a series of small exhibitions devoted to the major movements in modern art—Impressionism, Expressionism, Cubism, Abstract Art, Surrealism [realistic], Surrealism [abstract])—though these were never realized.

Both exhibitions had an unabashedly educational mission. As stated in an early proposal, the aim of *Timeless Aspects of Modern Art* was "to help the public to discover in modern art the manifestations of those constant human elements that converge the art of our time into the stream of the art of all times."[69] ("Ghastly title," d'Harnoncourt would comment ten years after it closed. "We later called it 'Modern Art, Old and New'"[70]). The exhibition brought together modern art with work from a wide range of periods and cultures. Its goal was not to trace influences, derivations, or traditions; it sought to present d'Harnoncourt's conception of affinity, or to illustrate that works of art can be related to each other in many subtle ways. For instance, d'Harnoncourt explained, "Their affinity may be based on the artists' physical pleasure in certain rhythmic movements; on their fascination with clean-cut, mathematical order; on their desire to perceive and render the inner structure of things; on religious emotion, and many other factors."[71]

D'Harnoncourt wanted to emphasize the close relationships and affinities among works from different eras and regions, "to act as a reminder that such 'modern' means of expression as exaggeration, distortion and abstraction have been used by artists since the very beginning of civilization."[72] The argument was not only to show that modern art was similar in spirit and technique to older art, but also to illustrate d'Harnoncourt's conception of affinities among works of art across time and space. (Here d'Harnoncourt was again indebted to Covarrubias, for he certainly must have had in mind his mural for the Golden Gate Exposition.) Interestingly, this language is identical to that used by d'Harnoncourt in his justification of *Arts of the South Seas.* This idea was

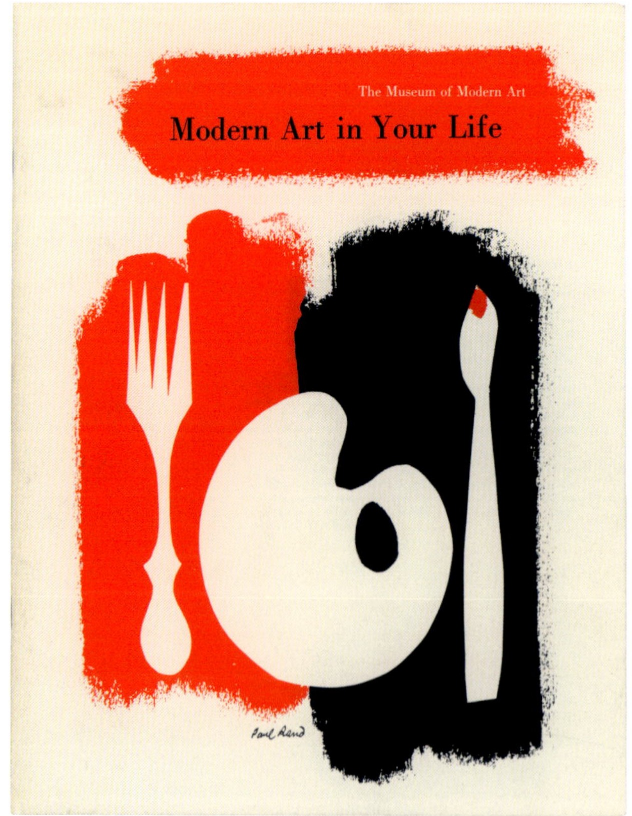

Paul Rand. Design for the cover of the catalogue of the exhibition *Modern Art in Your Life*, by Robert Goldwater in collaboration with René d'Harnoncourt, 1949

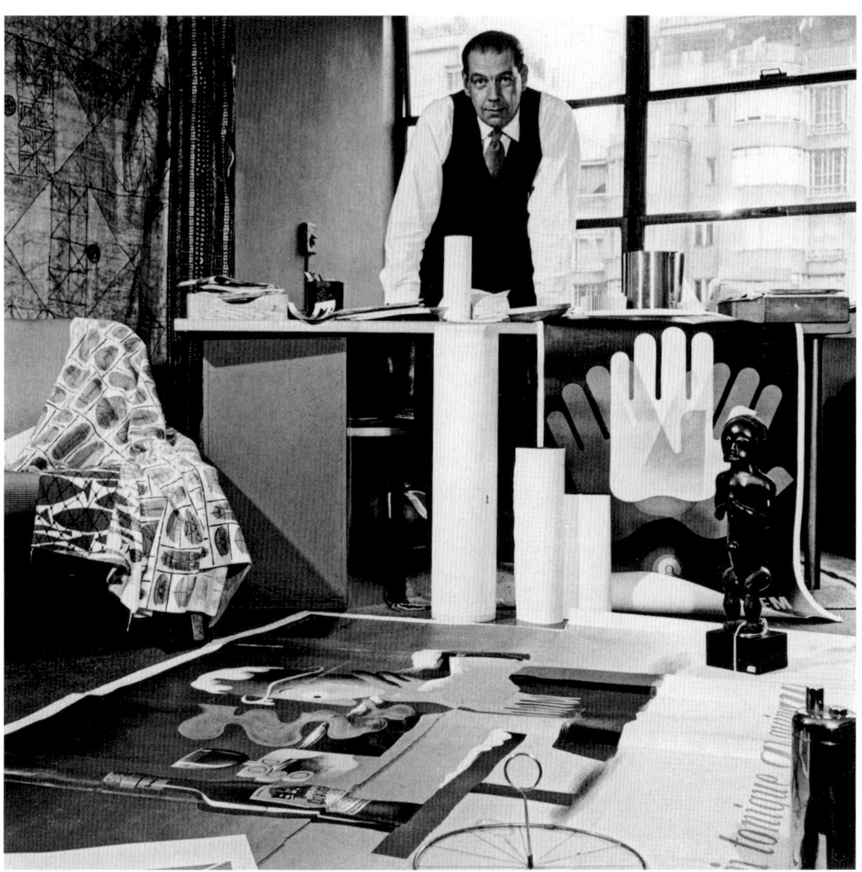

René d'Harnoncourt during the installation of the exhibition *Modern Art in Your Life,* 1949

further elaborated by the deployment of a quote by Picasso from 1923, written on the entry wall label to *Timeless Aspects*: "To me there is no past or future in art. If a work of art cannot live always in the present it must not be considered at all."[73]

With *Modern Art in Your* Life, which opened a year after *Timeless Aspects*, d'Harnoncourt once again set out to demonstrate the existence of affinities across art forms, focusing now on the relationship of fine art to the applied arts. As Howard Devree put it in his *New York Times* review, it was "less an art exhibition than a demonstration of a thesis which should not need demonstration, but which apparently does need to be reiterated at intervals—that modern art is not an orphan stepchild of the life of our time nor a product of spontaneous combustion. The exhibition does not attempt to prove that we should like modern art . . . but simply to demonstrate that it is not an isolated phenomenon of our time; rather that it is a definitely integrated part of that life which has influenced us all through adaptation in practical quotidian forms."[74]

This effort to underscore that modern art had already permeated modern living was likely a result of growing concern in certain circles that modern art was at best frivolous and a hoax, at worst part of a communist plot. While the Museum, from its early days, battled to educate the public about the merits of modern art, this mission reached a new level of urgency with the onset of the Cold War. Throughout the 1940s and '50s, Barr routinely defended modern artists against Senator George Dondero, the Joseph McCarthy of the visual arts. In May 1948, as he was planning *Timeless Aspects*, d'Harnoncourt delivered a speech in defense of modern art, underscoring the need for freedom of artistic style, later expanding it into an article.[75] He argued that modern art does not have a single, collective style, precisely because it reflects contemporary society, which enjoys freedoms and the ability to question, unlike eras of the past when a society held in common a singular, cohesive worldview.

Installation devices: ways to reconfigure a space

D'Harnoncourt was not shy about altering the interior spaces of the galleries of the Museum, and often completely changed their size and shape to create that "feeling of interlocking, so the visitor could make comparisons as he moved from one section to another."[76] He would transform spaces, using modular galleries; moveable, removable, staggered, or partial height walls; and, in the case of *Art of the Asmat*, even a purpose-built pavilion—all instruments in his tool kit to achieve the desired circulation and experience. He also devised new methods of reconfiguring a space, such as replacing full-height walls with mid-height partitions and double-sided, counter-height open vitrines.

All flexible internal walls in the building could be removed and replaced to adjust the spaces to d'Harnoncourt's specification. This was a novelty for museum practice, only achievable due to the design and construction in 1939 of MoMA's International Style building designed by Philip Goodwin and Edward Durrell Stone. Of course, today, the malleability of exhibition spaces is de rigueur, with the frequent changing of placement of walls.

In documents entitled "Installation Notes" or "List of Installation Devices," d'Harnoncourt would include such varied formats as photomurals or large reproductions, painted silhouettes, wires to suspend objects, signs, fish nets for partitions, flat figures, and casts of stone figures. He might use pedestals, cases, platforms, or columns and poles to display objects, or suspend them from boards.[77] He even suspended boomerangs on nearly invisible fishing

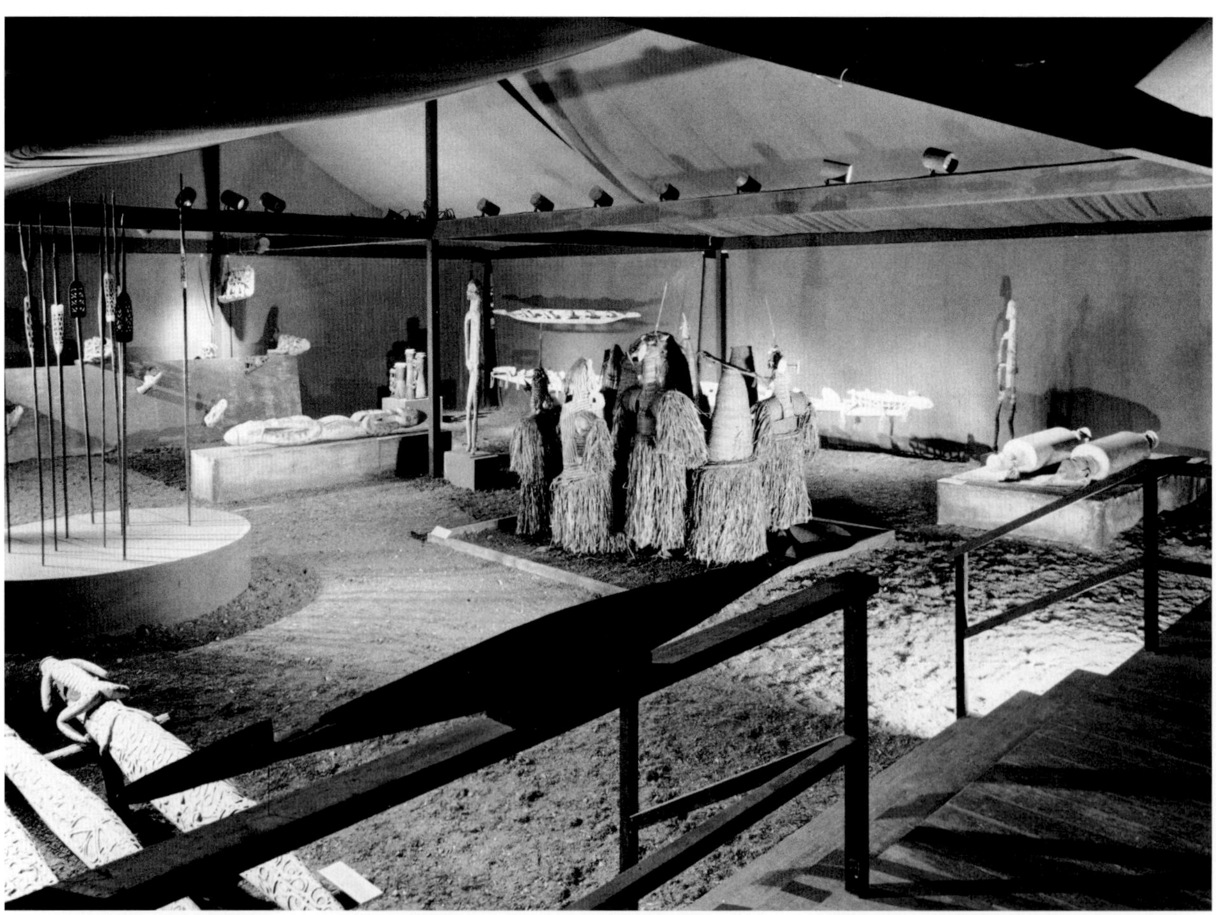

View of the pavilion designed for the exhibition *Art of the Asmat*, 1962, by Arthur Drexler, MoMA's chief curator of Architecture and Design, and the architect Guster Henschell, based on a scheme developed by d'Harnoncourt

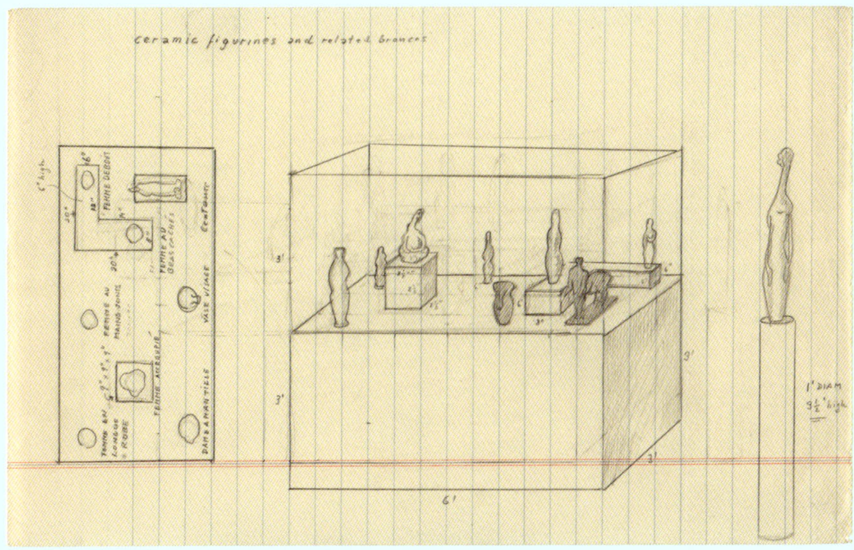

Preparatory drawing of a vitrine containing ceramic figurines and related bronzes for the exhibition *The Sculpture of Picasso*, 1967

line, so they appeared to be in flight (see page 87, upper right).

Cases and vitrines were useful in creating vistas, in that they could be designed in such a way as to stand on the borderlines between cultural areas. D'Harnoncourt personally designed the casework and vitrines for his exhibitions (which would often travel with the works once the exhibition was moved to another venue), even calculating their dimensions. He created a novel, innovative approach to an exhibition cabinet: one with a low, front panel of glass, but no top. Therefore, the items were not enclosed; there was only a low transparent barrier between the viewer and object, making the direct contemplation of the work that much more engaging. (Unfortunately, due to heightened environmental and security concerns, this is an approach that would not be entertained today).

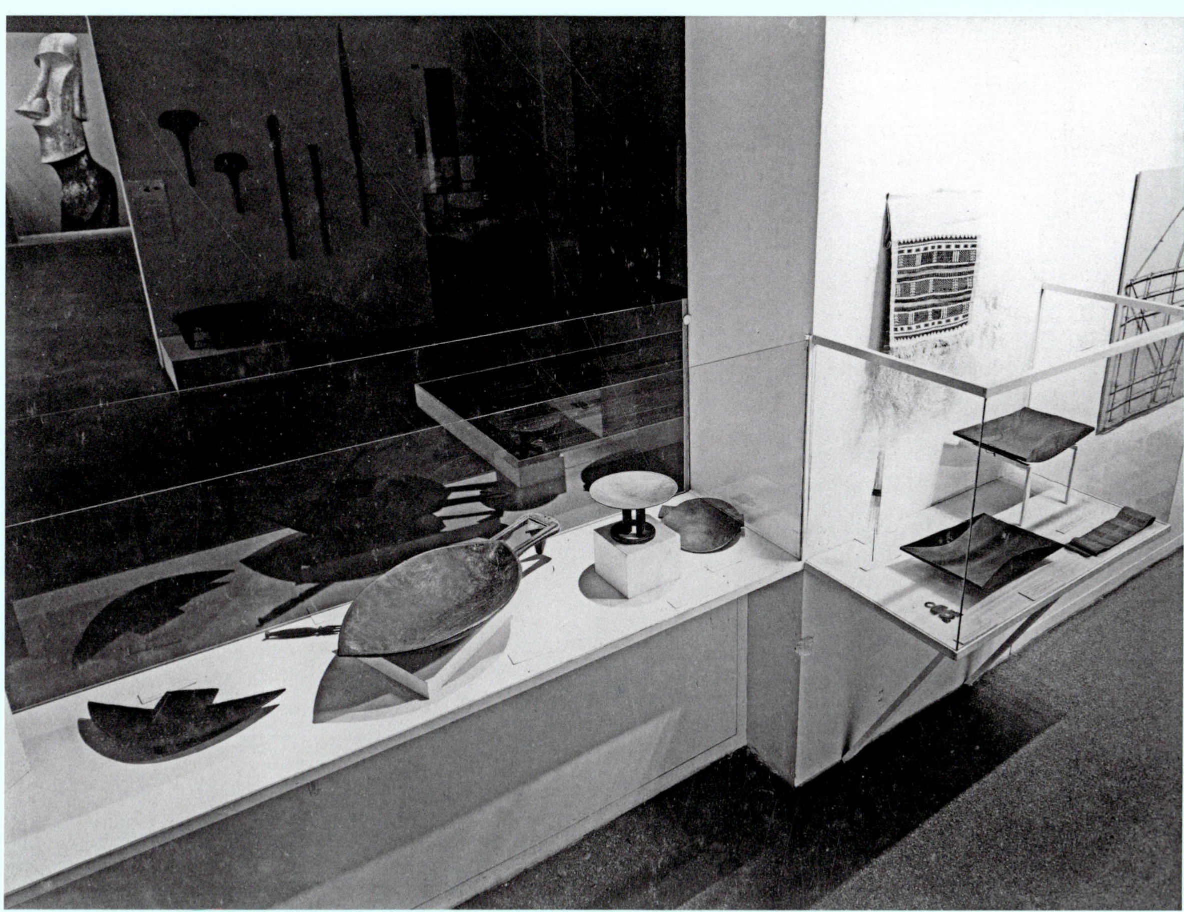

Open vitrine, consisting of front and side panels of glass without an enclosure on the top, designed by d'Harnoncourt for the exhibition *Arts of the South Seas*, 1946

D'Harnoncourt's work could be extremely subtle: when he revealed to an interviewer that twenty thousand pounds of bricks were required to create the pedestals used in *The Sculpture of Picasso*, his final and most complex installation at MoMA, his interlocutor admitted that she hadn't noticed them. D'Harnoncourt was delighted, declaring that was proof of their perfection.[78]

When d'Harnoncourt could not secure the actual works themselves, he successfully deployed photographic reproduction murals in their place. For instance, a major sculptural group could not be included in *The Sculpture of Picasso*: *The Bathers,* owned by Nelson Rockefeller, had been previously committed to another MoMA exhibition. Instead, d'Harnoncourt installed a large photomural of *The Bathers*, flanked by two groups of similar works— four bronze figures and five flat-wood assemblages similar to those from which *The Bathers* were cast, endowing the entire grouping with a sense of completeness.

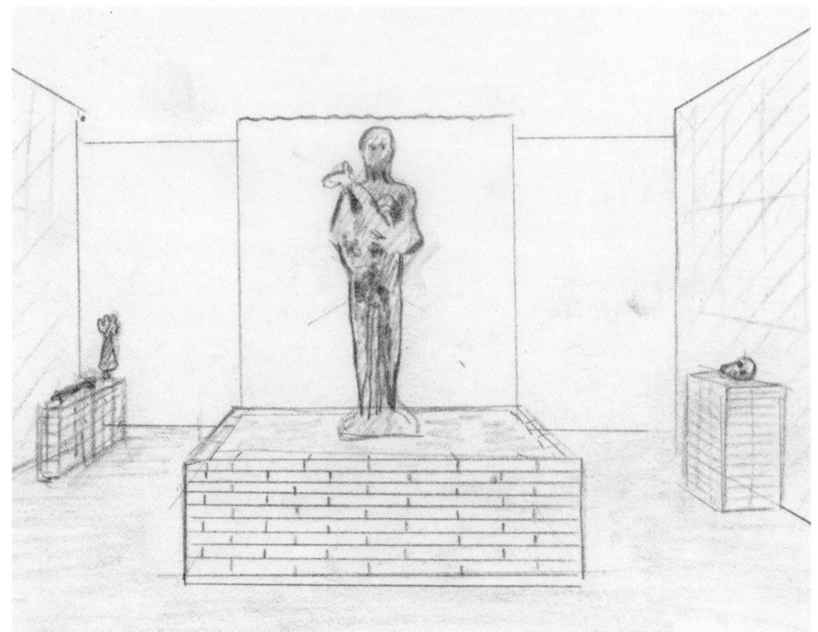

Vista of the exhibition *The Sculpture of Picasso*, 1967, showing the brick pedestal designed by d'Harnoncourt

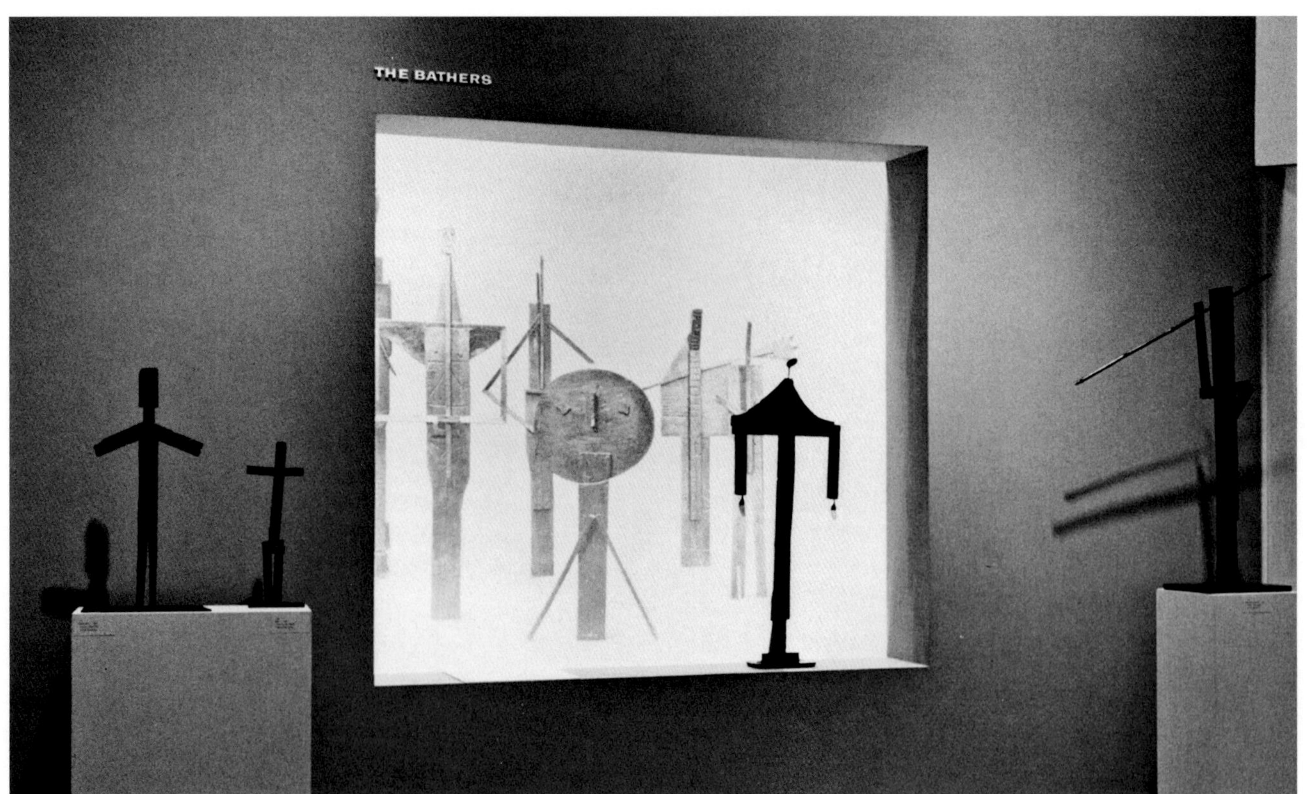

Installation view of the exhibition *The Sculpture of Picasso*, 1968, showing a work installed in front of a photo reproduction of related works

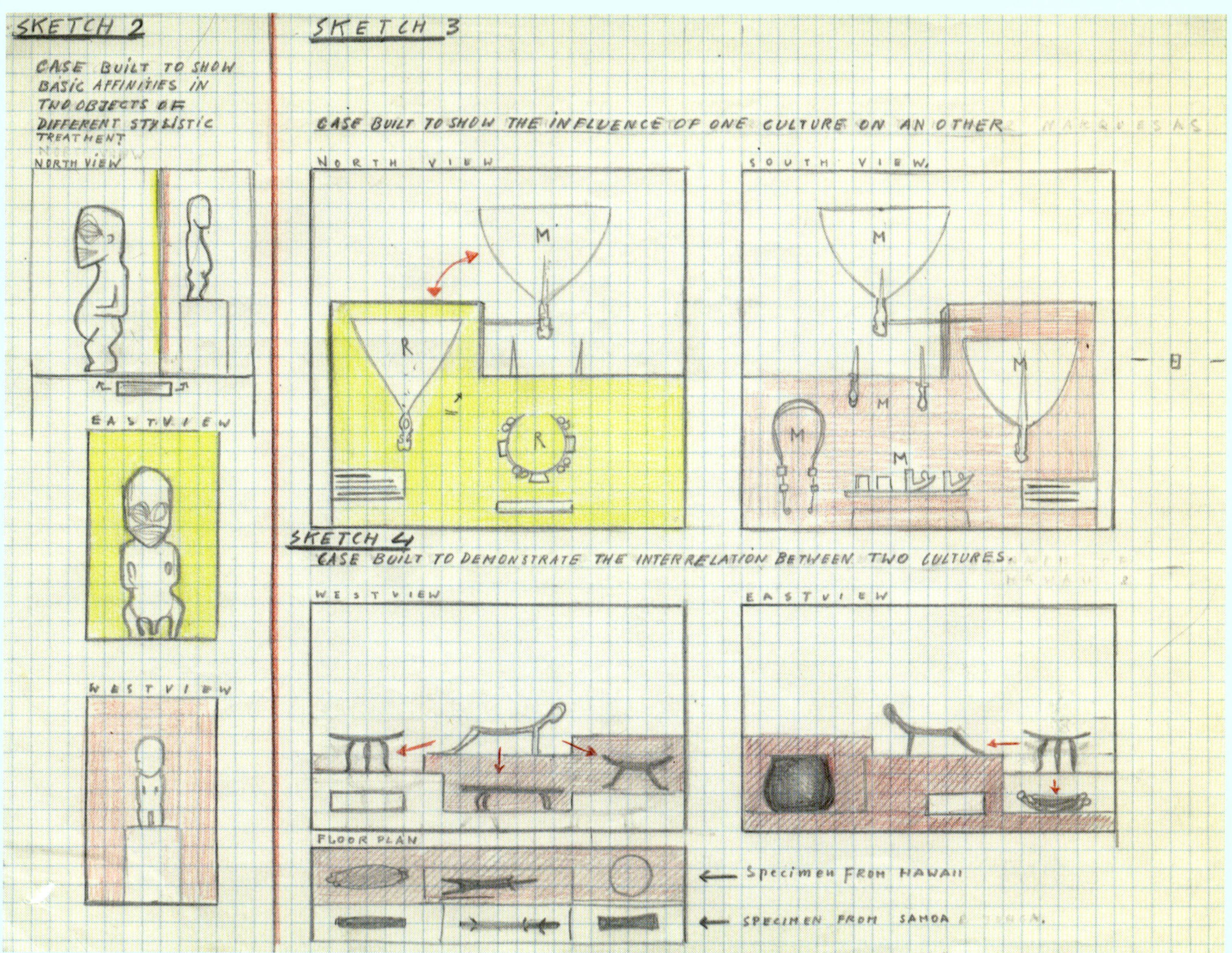

Sketches of different types of cases to be used according to an exhibition's thesis. Illustrations from a grant proposal by René d'Harnoncourt requesting funding from the Rockefeller Foundation to develop a new display methodology, September 17, 1945

Studying the most effective means of communicating an argument to the public within an exhibition was a constant subject of reflection for d'Harnoncourt. Toward the end of his career, he would state, "In installing [a] show I am trying to make the damned things speak to you through every visual means . . . display, lighting, color . . . but what I am still puzzling over is where do I need words. . . . I have always believed in putting statements on the walls whenever they are needed to increase people's understanding but it requires real judgment to know just how far to go with words."[79]

While organizing *Timeless Aspects of Modern Art,* d'Harnoncourt struggled with a "conflict which is ever present in so-called educational exhibitions where the work of art is surrounded by arrows, markers and extensive captions which, while contributing to the visitor's knowledge, actually destroy the most important function of the work of art, which is to speak spontaneously for itself."[80] D'Harnoncourt believed that literary devices, such as captions or guidebooks, were poor substitutes for visual comparison. He preferred to avoid presenting an idea in the gallery space itself, considering that the power of an original work of art is diminished if it is displayed as merely the illustration of an idea. He elected to use limited didactic materials, generally opting for simple identifying labels, to focus instead on revealing the inherent qualities of the works and communicating a message through their sequencing. When more information (text, informational graphics, and maps) was required, it appeared on walls in introductory galleries, ideally at a slight remove from the main observation point of the works of art, as in the entryway to *Timeless Aspects* (see page 109).

During *Modern Art in Your Life*, d'Harnoncourt was able to study the use of reproductions in an exhibition with an explicitly didactic premise. In the original proposed conception of the anniversary shows, the intention was that a quarter of the main gallery on the third floor be populated with reproductions—d'Harnoncourt's early drawings show an antechamber with a central, freestanding screen showing reproductions of works of art, in front of a curved wall adorned with photographs of everyday objects—and models, accompanied by captions, to provide an explicit statement of the thesis. The rest of the floor would then display original works of art (see page 112). D'Harnoncourt ultimately deemed this approach too much like a textbook and worried the relationship between fine and applied art would be read as simplistic and forgettable. Abandoning that approach, he made the comparison more striking by using real objects instead of photographs, and by bringing the sections of the exhibition together, with the fine art at the center and the applied arts as constellations surrounding the central gallery.

In this, he adopted the attitude prescribed by Barr in his influential *What Is Modern Painting?* (1943):

> The best words can do is give you some information, point out a few things you might overlook, and if, to begin with, you feel that you don't like modern painting anyway, words may possibly help you to change your mind. But in the end you must look at these works of art with your own eyes and heart and head. This may not be easy, but most people who make the effort find their lives enriched.[81]

In 1936, Barr had deployed a complex system of didactics in his iconic exhibition *Cubism and Abstract Art*. A diagram, presented on the cover of the exhibition catalogue, sought to track the lineage and evolution of modern art, through a series of cross-pollinations, in its march toward abstraction. Barr's intention to educate viewers was underscored in the galleries by charts that indicated each section—for example, Analytical Cubism or Futurism. He also employed flowcharts, arrows, wall labels, and other devices to convey information—precisely the tactics d'Harnoncourt would over time try to avoid. Ultimately, this attitude was something that Barr particularly appreciated about d'Harnoncourt, stating that:

> He has an enormous talent as an arranger of shows, with great taste in his own field, and an interest in, and a responsiveness to, the things he doesn't know about at first hand. . . . He makes things look good, but he is not afraid to impose a real, intellectual, subtly posed didacticism. He depends less on labels than on what you see and the sequence in which you see it.[82]

Installation devices: color and lighting

D'Harnoncourt recognized the power of wall color and lighting to influence the impression of an exhibition. In his exhibits of primitive art, he employed color to suggest the various topographic environments of the creators—yellow evoked areas with sandy beaches, deep green for those who inhabited the jungle, for instance. He would develop a color wheel to study the balance of complimentary shades, specifying in his drawings the color to be used on ceilings, walls, and installation devices. For exhibits of modern art, d'Harnoncourt carefully selected colors to provide a backdrop that would complement the works while also allowing them to stand out. His preparation notes for *The Sculpture of Picasso*, for instance, included a list indicating a specific shade for each individual wall of each room (dark warm grey, brick red, light blue gray); he also collected fabric swatches for curtain fabrics and fabrics for cloth covers for cases and blocks.

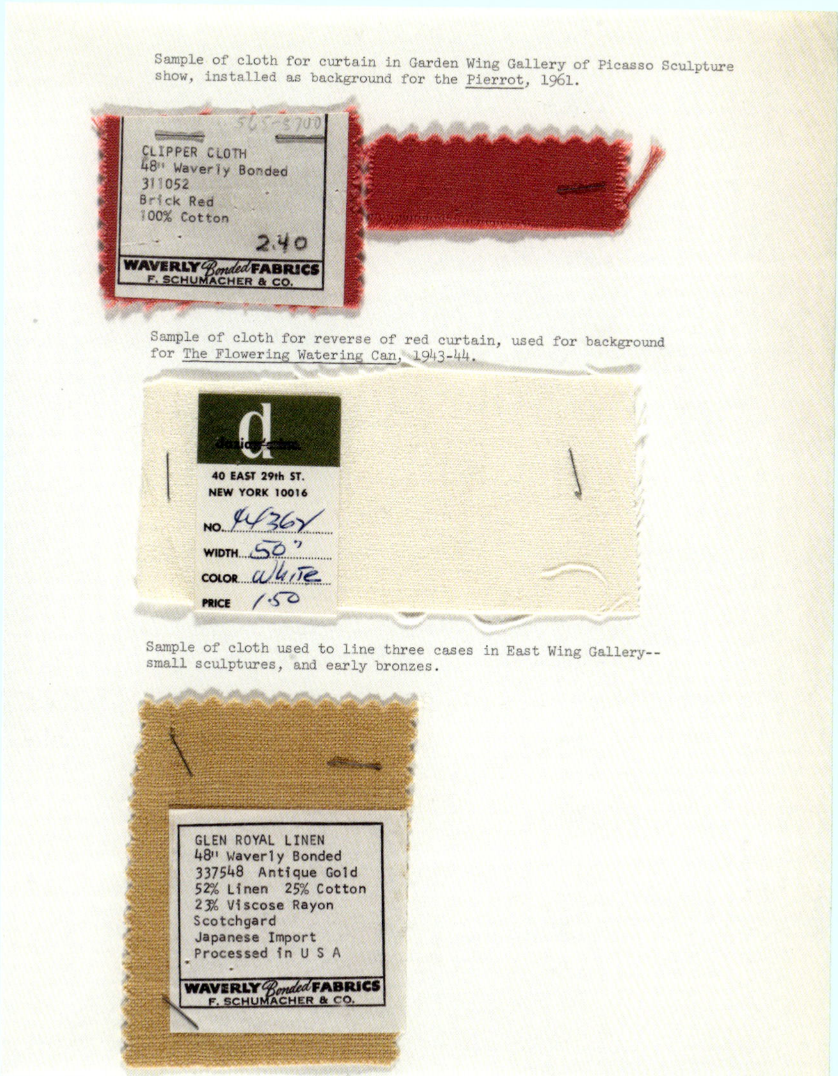

Fabric samples for the exhibition *The Sculpture of Picasso*, 1967 (see page 152 for the related vista).

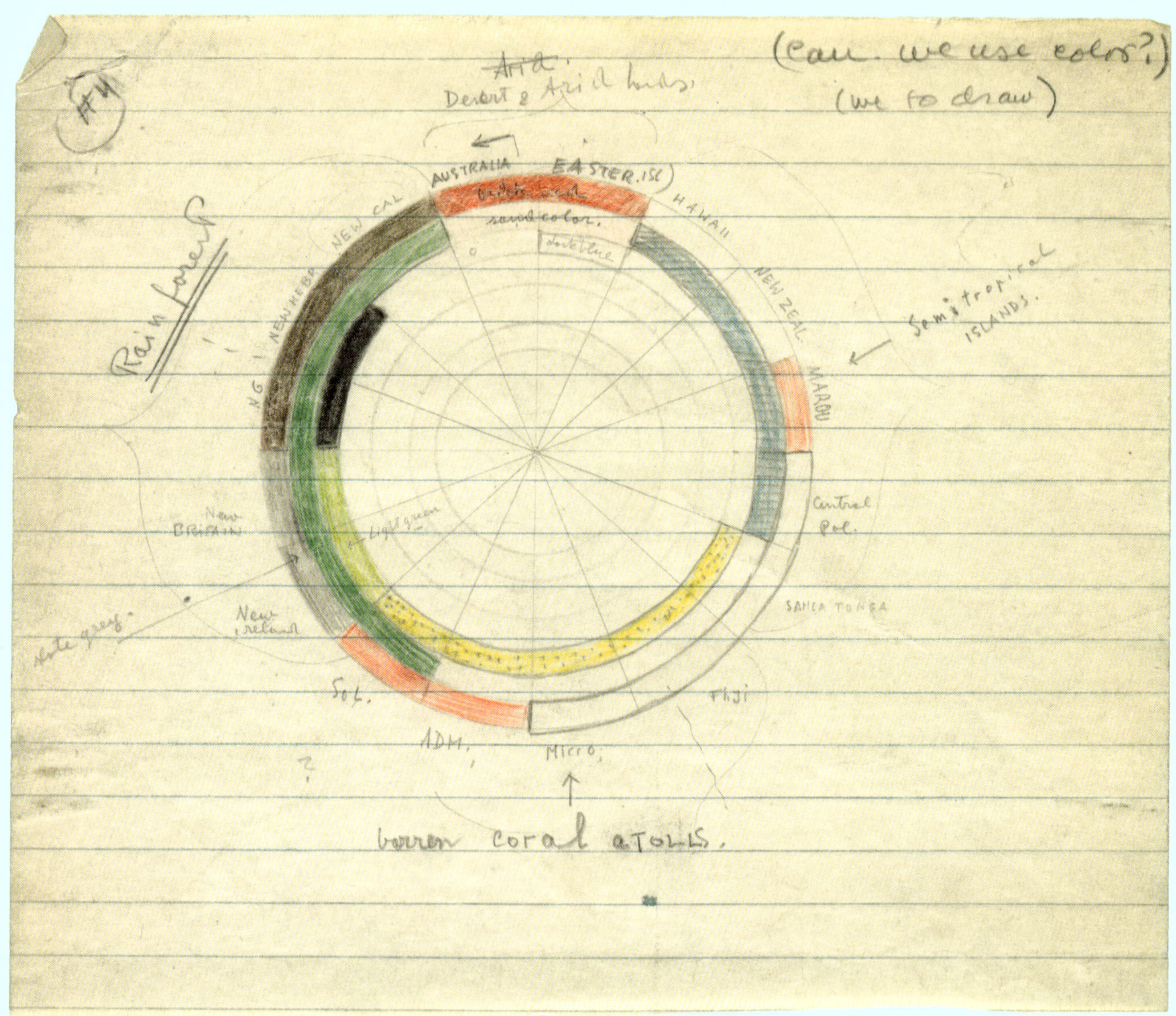

Preparatory color study for the exhibition *Arts of the South Seas*, 1946

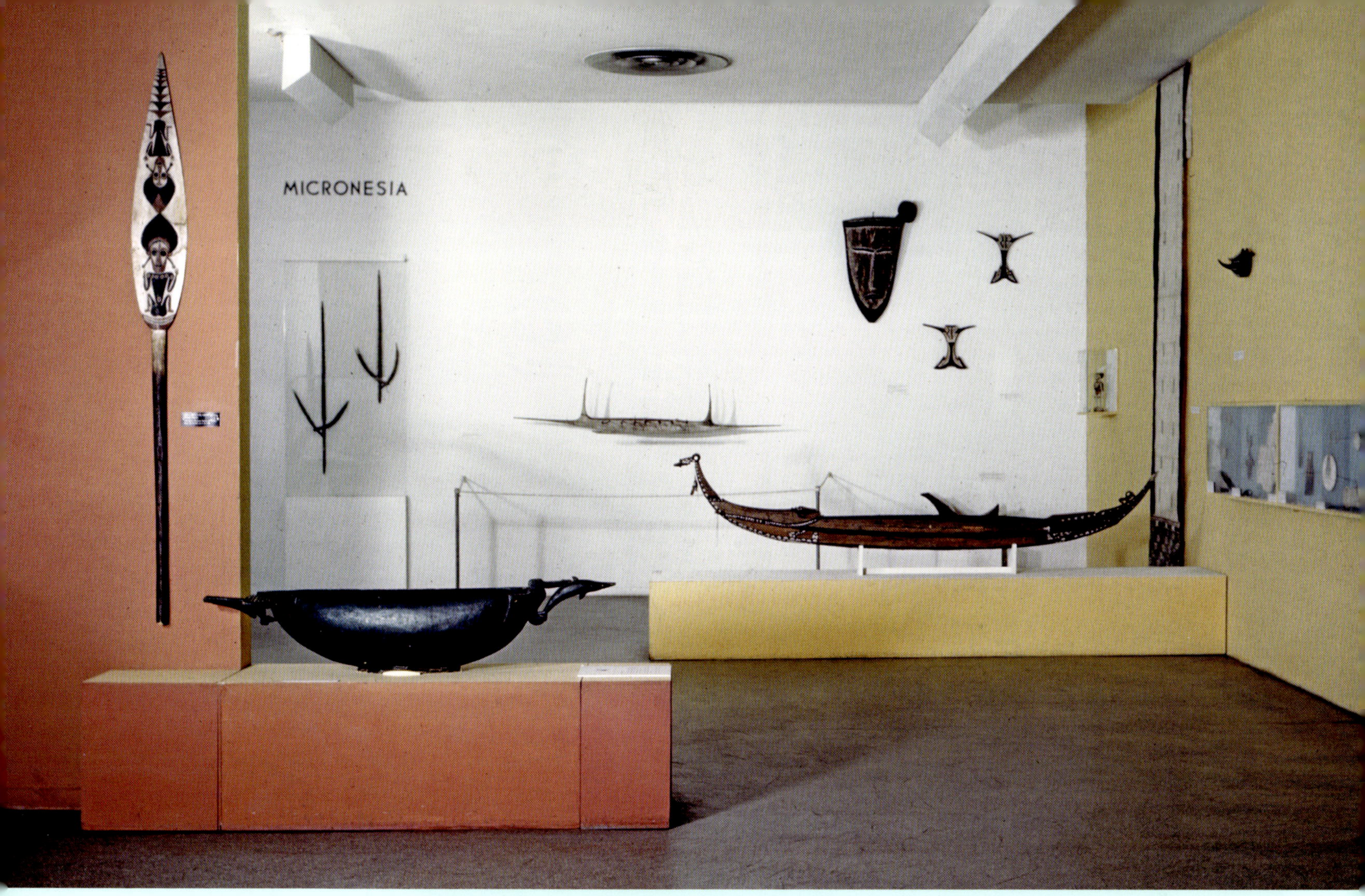

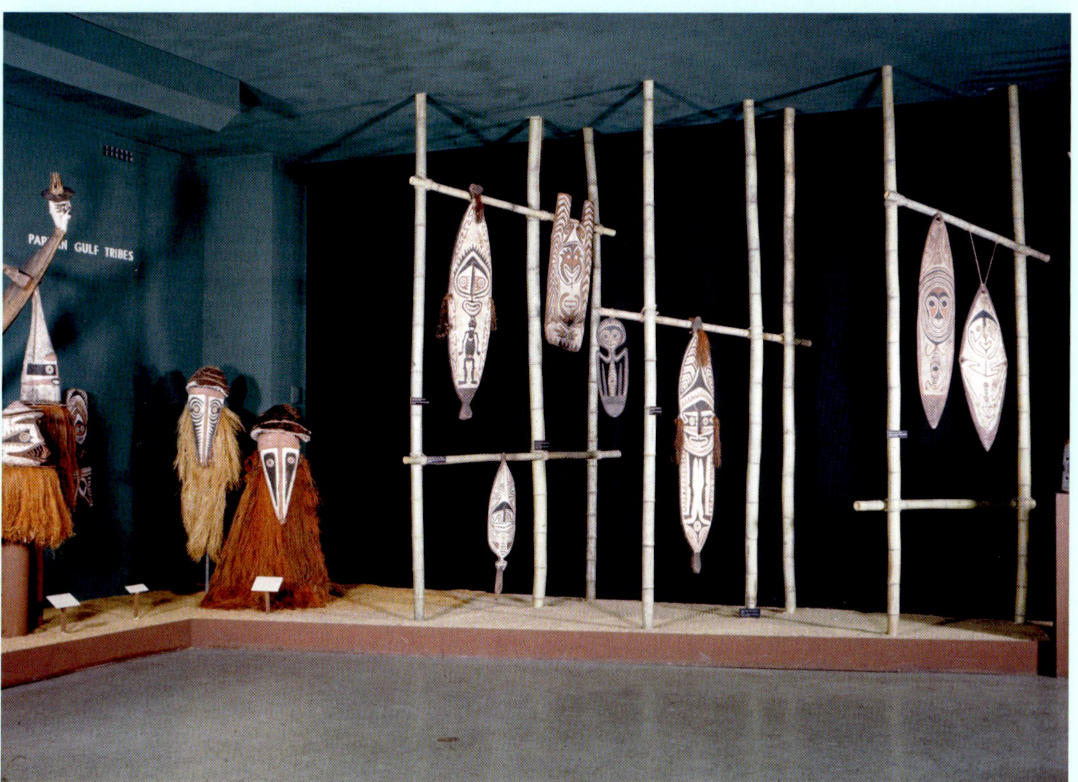

Installation views of the exhibition
Arts of the South Seas, 1946

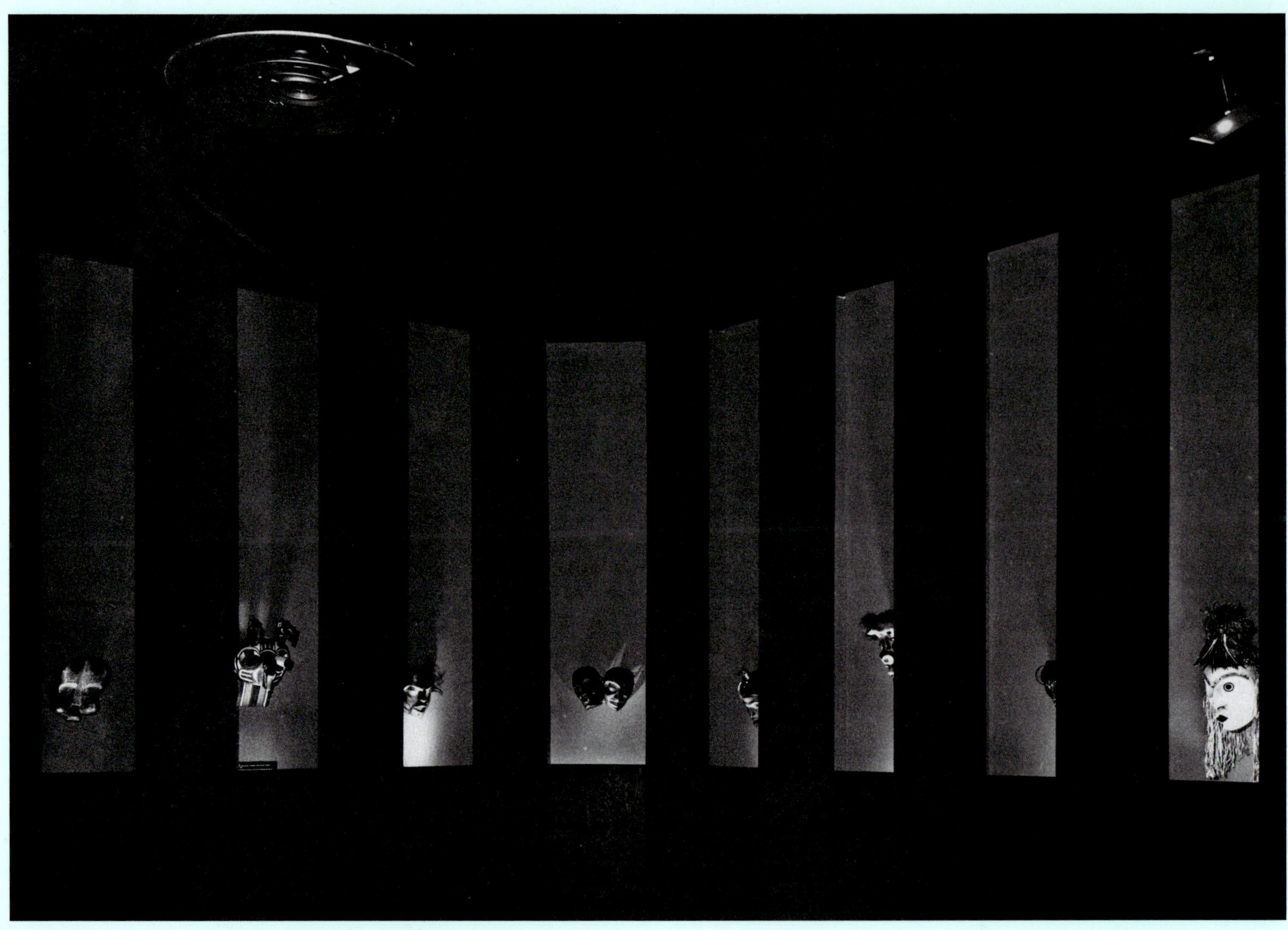

Above and opposite: Installation views of the exhibitions *Indian Art of the United States*, 1941, and *Modern Art in Your Life*, 1949, showing d'Harnoncourt's dramatic use of lighting

In a similar way, d'Harnoncourt exploited the possibilities of light, taking a cue from theatrical lighting design. Given his intimate knowledge of both the formal properties of the work and its context, he was able to employ the subtleties of dramatic lighting to great effect. D'Harnoncourt would often strive to illuminate the objects included in a manner that would evoke their original context: masks used during ceremonies performed around campfires were presented in a semi-darkened room, displayed in niches lit from below, for example; or a Spanish Gothic cross, originally lit by candlelight in a darkened church or cathedral, was lit dramatically from below (see page 103).

Reviewers often pointed out the theatrical nature of d'Harnoncourt's installations, calling them "intricate and often—if you choose to consider it so—'theatrical,'" or "as exciting as a good movie."[83] But from the beginning, they acknowledged that these techniques were

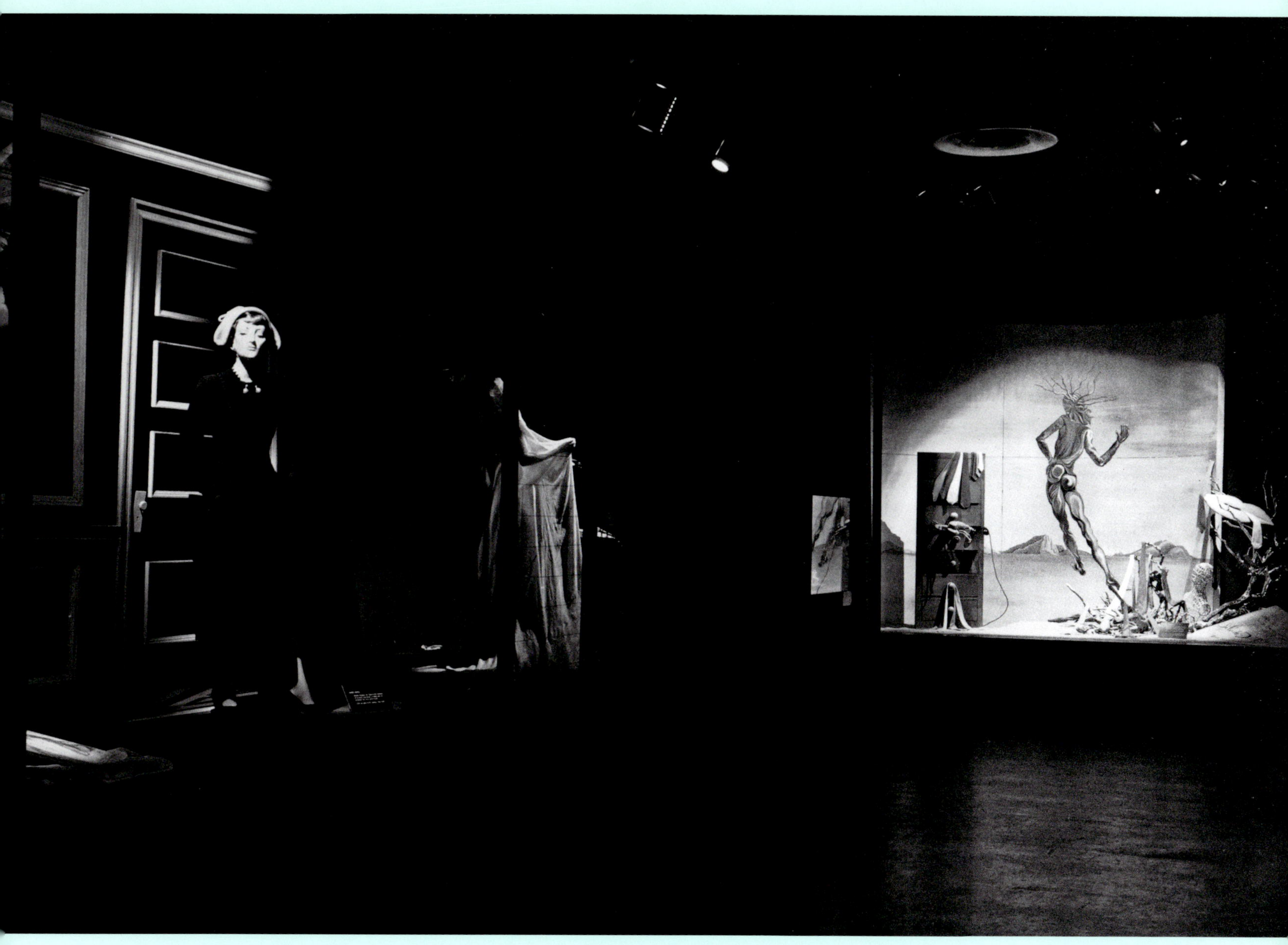

judiciously applied and commended d'Harnoncourt for using them to establish a helpful atmosphere. The *New York Times*'s Edward Alden Jewell noted of *Arts of the South Seas*, d'Harnoncourt's first exhibition after joining the MoMA staff: "I suspect that the Museum of Modern Art, with its acutely developed sense of 'theater,' could make almost anything look striking. But there is substance to justify the present high-powered dramatization."[84]

Director d'Harnoncourt, 1949–68

In the 1950s and '60s, increasingly busy with the responsibilities associated with his position as director, d'Harnoncourt continued to find time to pursue his installation practice, working regularly on monographic exhibitions of works by modern artists. He tended to gravitate toward sculpture exhibitions, possibly because of his specialization in three-dimensional primitive art and artifacts. These allowed him to refine his thinking on installation and to move away from the more dramatic register of his primitive art and didactic exhibitions toward more subtle installations.

His first monographic show, *Naum Gabo and Antoine Pevsner* (1948; see portfolio) was the only one for which he both acted as curator and installed the works. After that, he tended to work on exhibition designs in collaboration with curators, designing the installation after they had conceptualized the thesis of the show and selected the works to be presented. This was the case for *Elie Nadelman* (1948); *Seurat Paintings and Drawings* (1958); *Jean Arp: A Retrospective* (1958); *Rodin* (1963); and *The Sculpture of Picasso* (1967–68) (see portfolios).

D'Harnoncourt enjoyed working in a collaborative manner, a task to which he was temperamentally well suited. Peter Selz, a curator who worked under d'Harnoncourt (including, in 1963, as curator of the Rodin exhibition), recalled that d'Harnoncourt was a generous mentor. On occasion, d'Harnoncourt would lend his discerning eye to assist Selz with a challenging installation. When Selz was struggling with the installation of his 1964 exhibition of the work of Max Beckmann, which included six of the nine huge triptychs produced by the artist, d'Harnoncourt offered the ingenious solution of creating a hexagonal gallery in the middle of the floor to unite them into a single, cohesive display.[85]

D'Harnoncourt was far from being the first member of the MoMA staff to critically consider installation-design practices; in fact, this reflection began with the Museum's opening. Alfred Barr, though often (mis-)identified as the strict formalist who christened the "white cube," endowed the Museum's inaugural show with walls that were in fact not white, but covered with a beige monk's cloth. Galleries were often graced with overstuffed couches and potted plants, possibly with the idea of putting

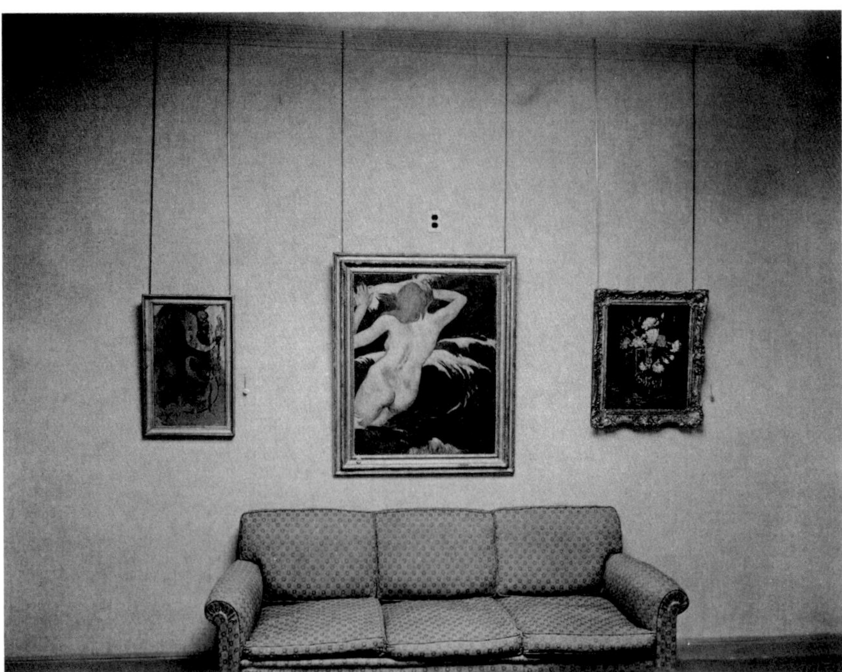

Installation view of MoMA's inaugural exhibition, *Cézanne, Gauguin, Seurat, van Gogh* (November 7–December 7, 1929)

visitors at ease by replicating a domestic environment. Barr dispensed with the tradition of hanging works in the age-old salon style, with works of different sizes filling the entire surface of a wall. Instead, works were hung at eye level, with ample space afforded to each picture, rather than "skied." They were arranged scientifically, to assert formal development or chronological progression and over time Barr experimented more with asymmetry in his hanging. The dominant installation style at the Museum during the 1930s featured white walls and a clean and spare style, similar to that employed earlier in German modern-art venues such as the Kronprinzenpalais and increasingly adopted by museums and commercial art galleries in international avant-garde circles. The idea of a white "neutral" container dominated, which allowed for a flexibility in the presentation of the works and emphasized the autonomy of the works of art, which were presented as timeless, universal objects.[86]

Over the course of the 1940s and '50s, installation was increasingly conceived of at MoMA not as a singular task, performed in a vacuum, but as a role for dedicated professionals. Several established designers and architects were enlisted to design shows, often to highly dramatic effect. These included Philip Johnson, Herbert Bayer, Paul Rudolf, Mies van der Rohe, Ivan Chermayeff, Charles and Ray Eames, Finn Juhl, Alexander Girard, Bernard Rudofsky, and George Nelson. D'Harnoncourt was likely influenced by the dramatic techniques employed by Bayer, the influential Bauhaus student, teacher, and proponent, who designed the highly acclaimed MoMA exhibitions *Bauhaus 1919–1928* (1938–39) and *Road to Victory* (1942). Bayer's installation work was guided by his "Field of Vision" ideas, according to which he positioned works not on a single static plane, but rather at different angles so that the viewer could take in multiple surfaces with a single glance, an idea that d'Harnoncourt reprised in his own installations. He also used novel display devices such as suspending items on strings from the ceiling or mounting panels on poles—all techniques d'Harnoncourt would later employ.

The work of artist, architect, and theater designer Frederick J. Kiesler was likely another influence on

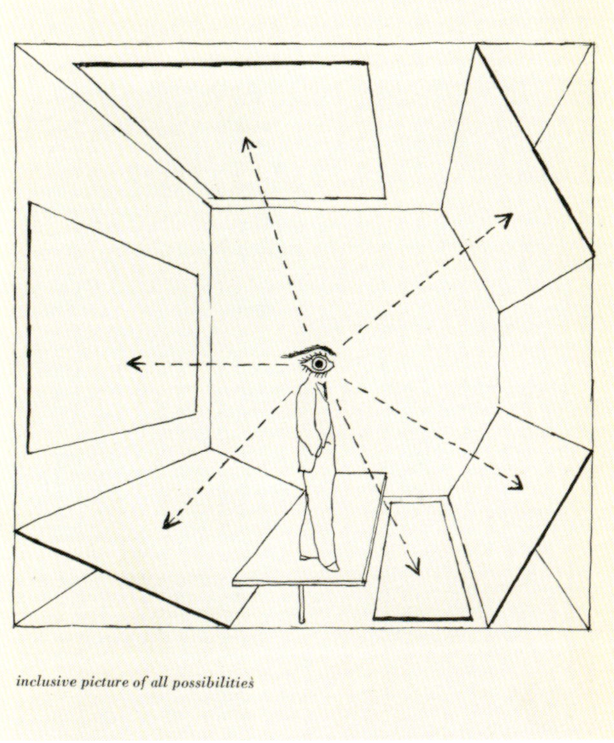

Diagram illustrating Herbert Bayer's article "Fundamentals of Exhibitions Design," published in *PM* (December 1939–January 1940)

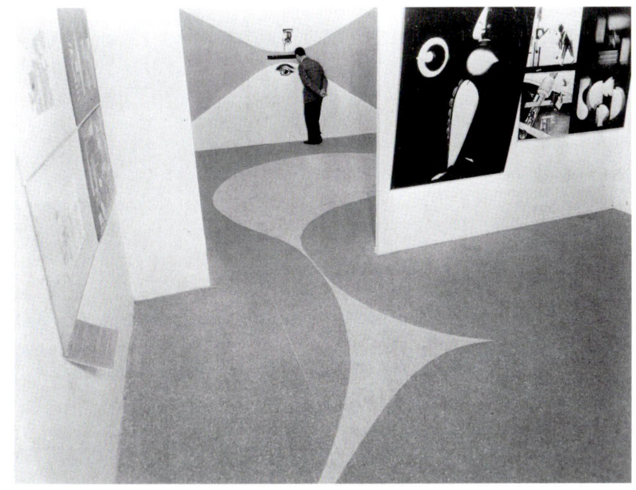

Herbert Bayer looking through a peephole at revolving mechanical robots wearing costumes from Oskar Schlemmer's *Triadic Ballet*, part of the exhibition *Bauhaus: 1919–1928* (1939)

d'Harnoncourt. The two compatriots may have met in Vienna, where they had artistic acquaintances in common, around 1924: that year, Kiesler arranged the first public screening of Fernand Léger's *Ballet Mécanique,* a landmark in the history of experimental filmmaking, which d'Harnoncourt may have attended. Later, in New York, the two were definitely acquainted.[87] D'Harnoncourt would certainly have seen Kiesler's radical installations in New York, notably the legendary abstract gallery he designed in 1942 for Peggy Guggenheim's Art of This Century gallery.

One more source of inspiration for d'Harnoncourt was the photographer Edward Steichen, director of the Museum's Department of Photography from 1947 to 1962, during which time he organized more than sixty exhibitions. In 1961, when installing a large retrospective exhibition of Steichen's work, d'Harnoncourt made sure to acknowledge his talents as *installateur*, focusing on three innovative exhibitions

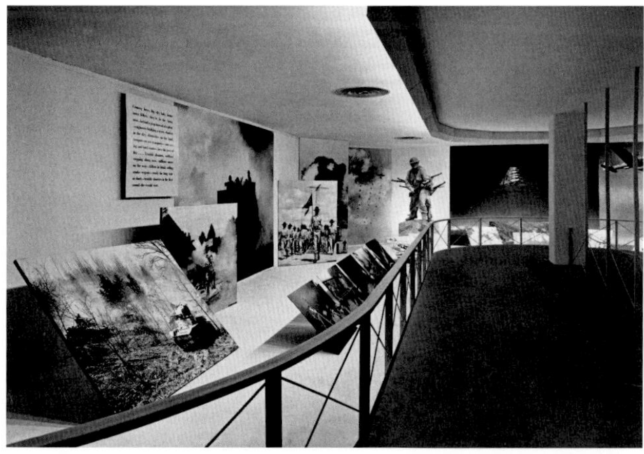

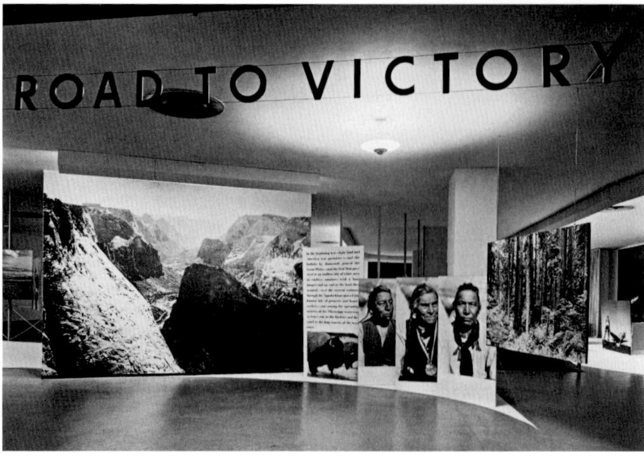

Installation views of the exhibition *Road to Victory*, designed by Herbert Bayer (1942)

assembled by Steichen during the photographer's fifteen-year tenure: *Road to Victory* (designed by Bayer, 1942), *Power in the Pacific* (1945), and *The Family of Man* (1955). Alongside three hundred and fifty prints spanning the entirety of Steichen's career, he included a scale model and a photo-enlargement of a crowd scene from *The Family of Man*, as well as six dramatic installation photographs of each of the three exhibitions. The wall text introducing this section emphasized that Steichen had created a new concept of photographic exhibition, in which the carefully thought-out relationships between the individual photographs in content, imagery, space, and scale serve to convey an overall message, emphasizing photography as a social force as well as an art form.[88] By including the practice of exhibition organization and arrangement in this presentation of Steichen's artistic work, d'Harnoncourt (identified in the press release as himself an expert in the field of exhibition techniques) was making a bold statement about the significance of installation, indicating that he considered it a valid creative practice in its own right.[89]

In 1967, as he was preparing to retire, d'Harnoncourt quizzed a reporter, "Did you know that there is simply no book in existence on museum installations? Isn't that incredible?"[90] Although d'Harnoncourt lamented the dearth of published studies on the subject of exhibition design and installation, this was in fact not the case. A brief survey of contemporary literature shows that several tomes on exhibition and display techniques had been published during d'Harnoncourt's lifetime, many of which reference specific examples from MoMA.[91] Indeed, a few of these works were even in the holdings of the Museum's library during his tenure there.

D'Harnoncourt recognized the high stakes of his vocation. To triumph over the challenges it presents, an installer must possess certain qualities. He asserted:

> Installation is terribly dangerous. It's full of terribly seductive temptations. You mustn't just make things look desirable—dramatization for its own sake must be avoided. Your job is to help the visitor see for himself and judge for himself what the object has to

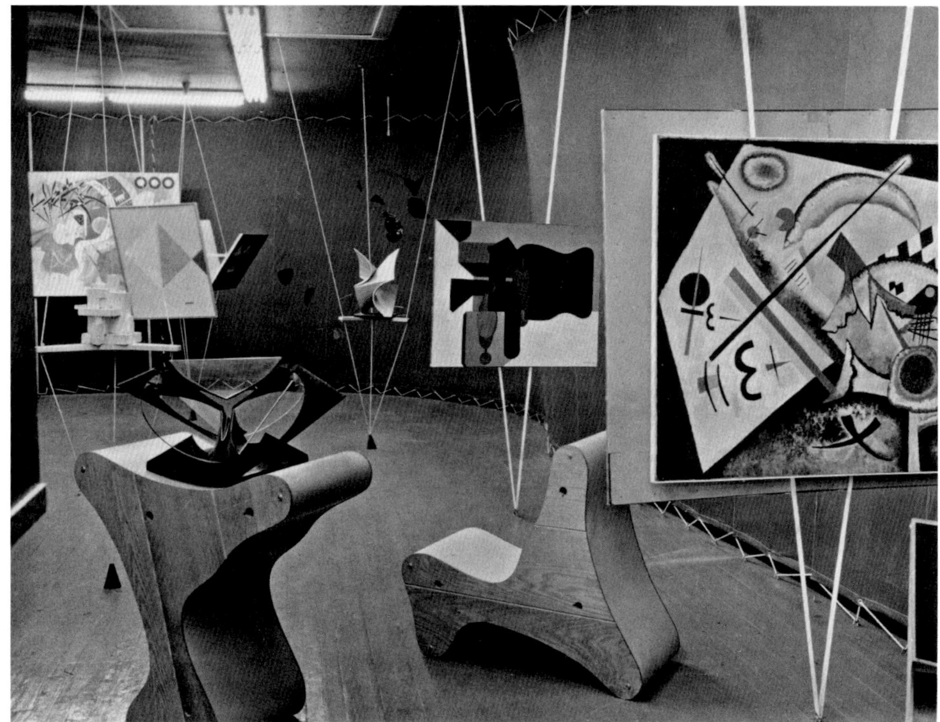

Abstract Gallery at Peggy Guggenheim's Art of This Century, New York, designed by Frederick Kiesler, 1942

1. The History of Installation
   A. The work of the Art in the Church and on the Square
   B. The Early Collections
   C. The Museum
   D. New Public Art
2. The Ethics of Installation
   A. Responsibility: public, artist, work
   B. Period Consciousness
   C. Performing Art calls for humility particularly because of importance of presentation
2½. The Responsibility for the preservation of the object
3. The One Man Show
   A. Record work—role of the artists and museum man
   B. Retrospective—the chronology problem
4. The Group Show
5. Prints and Drawings
6. Film—Photography
7. Architecture and Design: competition between object and exhibition design
8. Happenings, environments, etc.
9. Ethno art
10. The travelling show

Preliminary ideas for the contents of d'Harnoncourt's book on installation, according to Mordechai Omer

offer. The power the guy has who does the installation! . . . There is no such thing as a neutral installation . . . Installation is a very complicated and exciting subject, and it requires humility.[92]

There is evidence to suggest that d'Harnoncourt intended to devote a portion of his planned book on installation to the requisite personality traits of the installer. Deprived of the volume by its author's untimely death, MoMA commissioned scholar Mordechai Omer to develop a manuscript describing his methodology.[93] According to Omer, d'Harnoncourt had already delineated his ideas for the contents of his proposed publication. Although there is no original documentation of this in d'Harnoncourt's papers, Omer's unpublished manuscript includes an outline of the proposed contents, which contains a section dedicated to the "Ethics of Installation," stressing the installer's responsibility to the public, the artist, and the work, as well as a requisite "Period Consciousness" and, once again, humility.[94]

It is important to note that d'Harnoncourt possessed this quality in abundance and, as a result, was universally beloved. He was consistently described as genial, tactful, and considerate, possessing a mixture of understanding, kindness, and very real self-effacement: a "fundamentally selfless person with a very strong character," he knew how to put people, and artifacts, at ease.[95] Part of his success as a high-powered museum administrator and organizer of exhibitions can be related to his theory of affinity, which he applied not only to connections among artifacts and works of art, but also to relationships among human beings. He drew the parallel himself in a teaching portfolio he prepared for the Museum in 1950:

> Understanding affinities in art is not unlike understanding affinities between people. All of us are familiar with the experience of meeting persons who remind us strongly of someone we have known before. Such experience can be based on likeness of features or ways of thinking and acting. If similarities are the result of actual kinship or similarity of environment, they can help us gain a better understanding of our subject, whether it be a person or a work of art; if they are accidental, they are irrelevant and can become misleading. There are no cut and dried rules by which superficial likeness can be differentiated from true affinity, but an exploring eye and a keen interest will go a long way toward providing the experience necessary to sound judgment.[96]

Along with this exploring eye and keen interest, it is this humility that stands out as the leading characteristic of the art installer in d'Harnoncourt's conception of that role. On the occasion of his final exhibition, *The Sculpture of Picasso*, he spoke at length about his ideas of installation design. He concluded that "the most important thing about installation is that preparing an exhibition is serving the artist and an installation is no good if the installation impinges or becomes more important than the works of art. The whole purpose of displaying something is, in a sense, to help the communication between the work of art and the public, and the only good installation is one where people forget the installation and remember the work of art."[97]

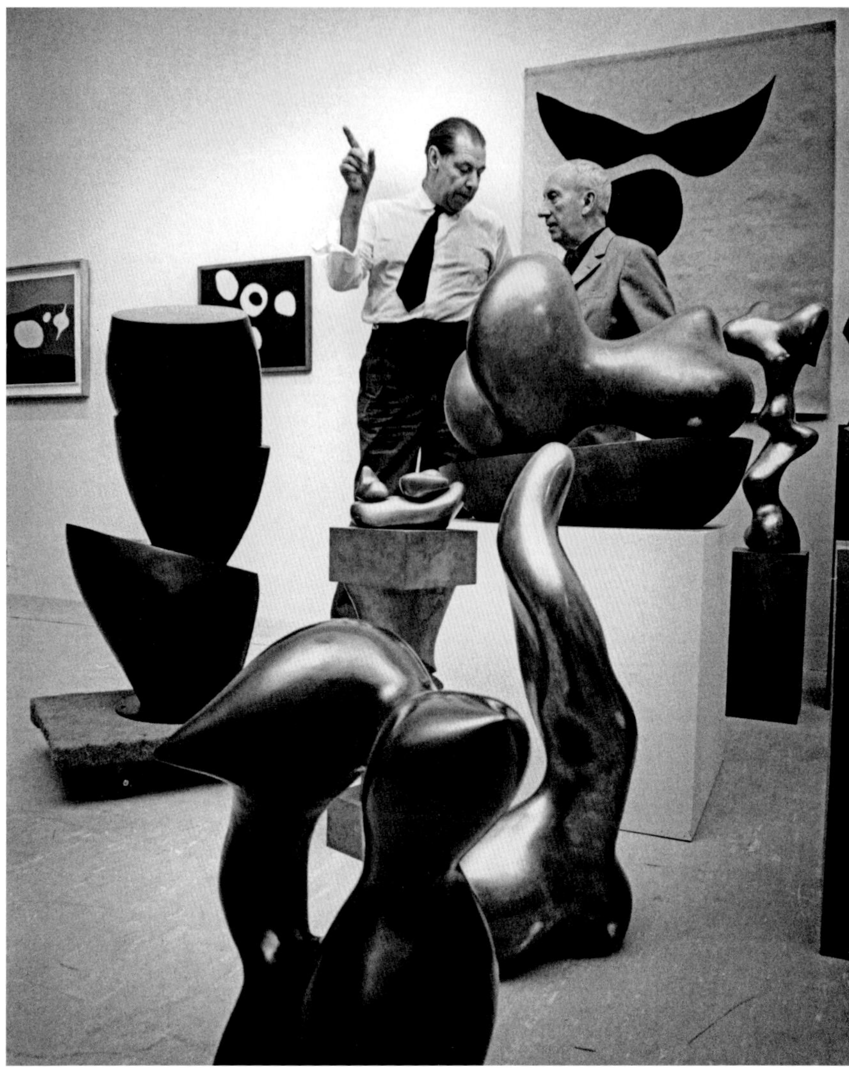

René d'Harnoncourt and Jean Arp during the installation of the exhibition *Jean Arp: A Retrospective*, October 1958

D'Harnoncourt's unique background, his auto-didacticism, his cosmopolitanism, his experiences in the mainstream of modern art, and his devotion to the arts at the peripheries all combined to make him one of the most extraordinary museum men of the twentieth century and an inspiration for the twenty-first. Drawing upon a vast and diverging confluence of experiences, he epitomized the ideal spokesperson for the arts in the mid-twentieth century and foresaw the pluralistic, globalized situation of today. As he wrote in 1948, "Yesterday's image of one unified civilization [has been replaced by] a pattern in which many elements, while retaining their own

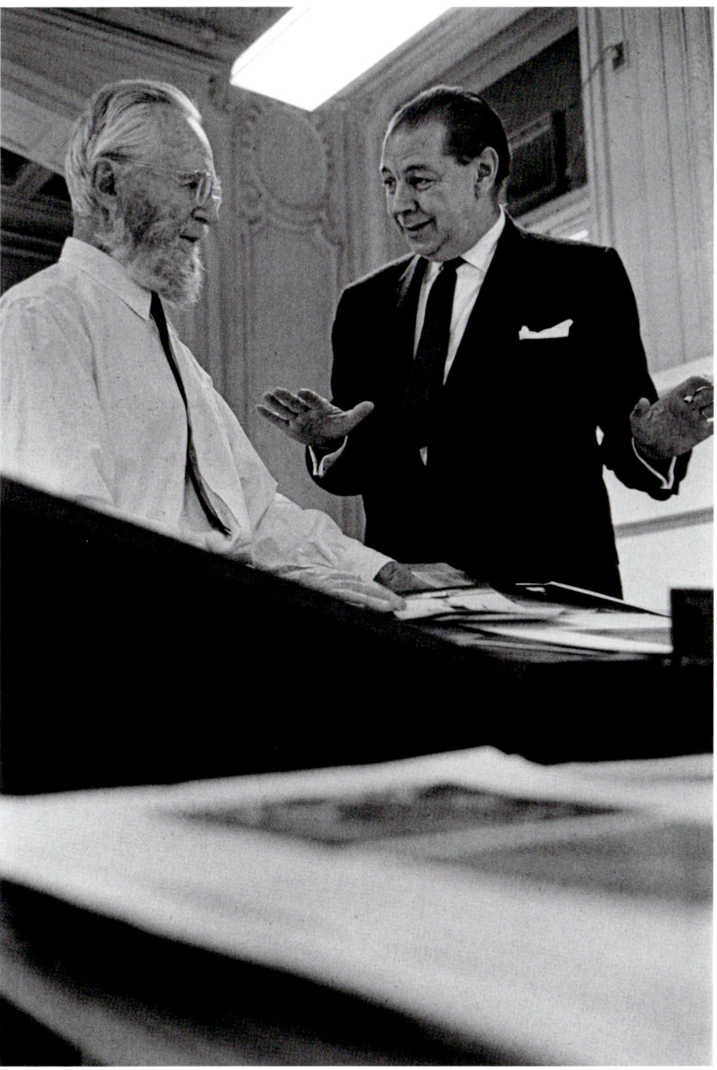

René d'Harnoncourt with Edward Steichen, preparing for the exhibition *Steichen the Photographer*, 1961

individual qualities, join to form a new entity. . . . I believe a good name for such a society is a democracy, and I also believe that modern art in its infinite variety and ceaseless exploration is its foremost symbol."[98] In reflecting on d'Harnoncourt's life upon his death, Robert Goldwater stated, "He truly believed that the forms of art, properly studied, are a language of communication among peoples, teaching an unspoken appreciation of diversity and common humanity."[99]

, THURSDAY, JUNE 27, 1968

HEAD OF MUSEUM RECALLS CAREER

D'Harnoncourt, of Modern Art, Will Retire Sunday

By SANKA KNOX

René d'Harnoncourt, who will retire Sunday as director of the Museum of Modern Art, looked back yesterday at his 19 years in the post as "the nicest thing that ever happened to me."

A big man with buoyant tread, Mr. d'Harnoncourt is 6 feet 6 inches tall, 67 years old and the possessor of an undiminished zest for plotting programs. His exhibition showmanship, one of the director's greatest accomplishments, has become internationally recognized.

In honor of Mr. d'Harnoncourt and of Alfred H. Barr Jr. and Monroe Wheeler, who retired last year, fellowships will be established by the museum.

Genesis of Programs

A great library of paintings, sculpture, graphic arts and published material for the use of fellows is in the Lillie P. Bliss Internatinal Study Center, which was opened last month. The center is in the former home of the Whitney Museum of American Art on 54th Street between Fifth Avenue and Avenue of the Americas.

Plans for the center were announced in 1949, the year Mr. d'Harnoncourt took over the directorship. "Our programs always developed in discussion; we've had very strong department heads and trustees, too."

According to a museum source, however, Mr. d'Harnoncourt was the moving spirit in the origination of many programs. "Our international program, for example." the source said, "was largely René's, and also the concept for the study center."

Mr. d'Harnoncourt said Mr. Barr, the museum's first director and then director of collections, "set the pace and standards." He continued: "And, we attracted powerful and devoted friends as trustees. We found out how much people cared about the museum after that terrible fire in 1958," the director said.

Four paintings were damaged in the fire and two by Monet were destroyed. The art loss was put at under $300,000.

Mr. d'Harnoncourt gave two reasons for the growth and success of the museum: "The collaborative spirit of those engaged in forming policy and the sensitivity of the museum to the needs of the times."

In his long career in the art field, he has made an enormous collection of friends, many of whom became friends of the museum.

Book on Installation

Mr. d'Harnoncourt is working on the first book to be published on museum installation techniques. "I'll get along with it on the front porch of my house at Key West," he said.

Mr. d'Harnoncourt will divide his time between Florida and New York. "I'm still on and National Council on the Arts and vice president of the Museum of Primitive Art. And, as an honorary trustee of this museum, I plan to attend meetings," he said.

The retiring director, who will be replaced by Bates Lowry, said he didn't hold a "job." "I participated in the development of a phenomenal institution," he asserted. Membership rose from 8,500 to about 36,000 since 1949.

Mr. d'Harnoncourt joined the Modern Museum's staff in 1944, and three years later became director of curatorial departments. He designed, among other shows, the spectacular "Art of the South Seas," "Ancient Art of the Andes" and the recent exhibition, "The Sculpture of Picasso."

The *New York Times* devoted an article to René d'Harnoncourt's career at MoMA and retirement plans on June 27, 1968.

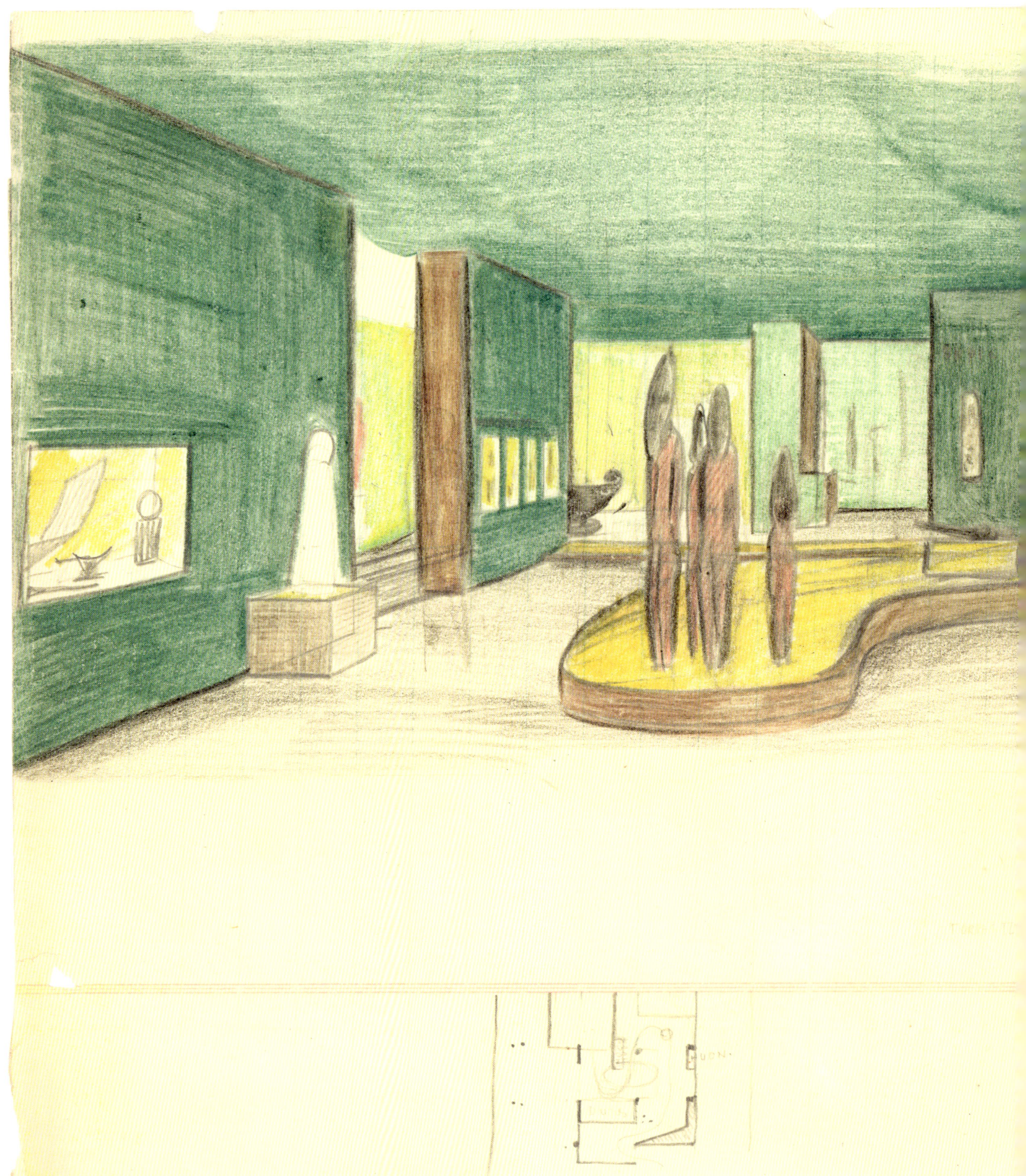

Exhibition Portfolios

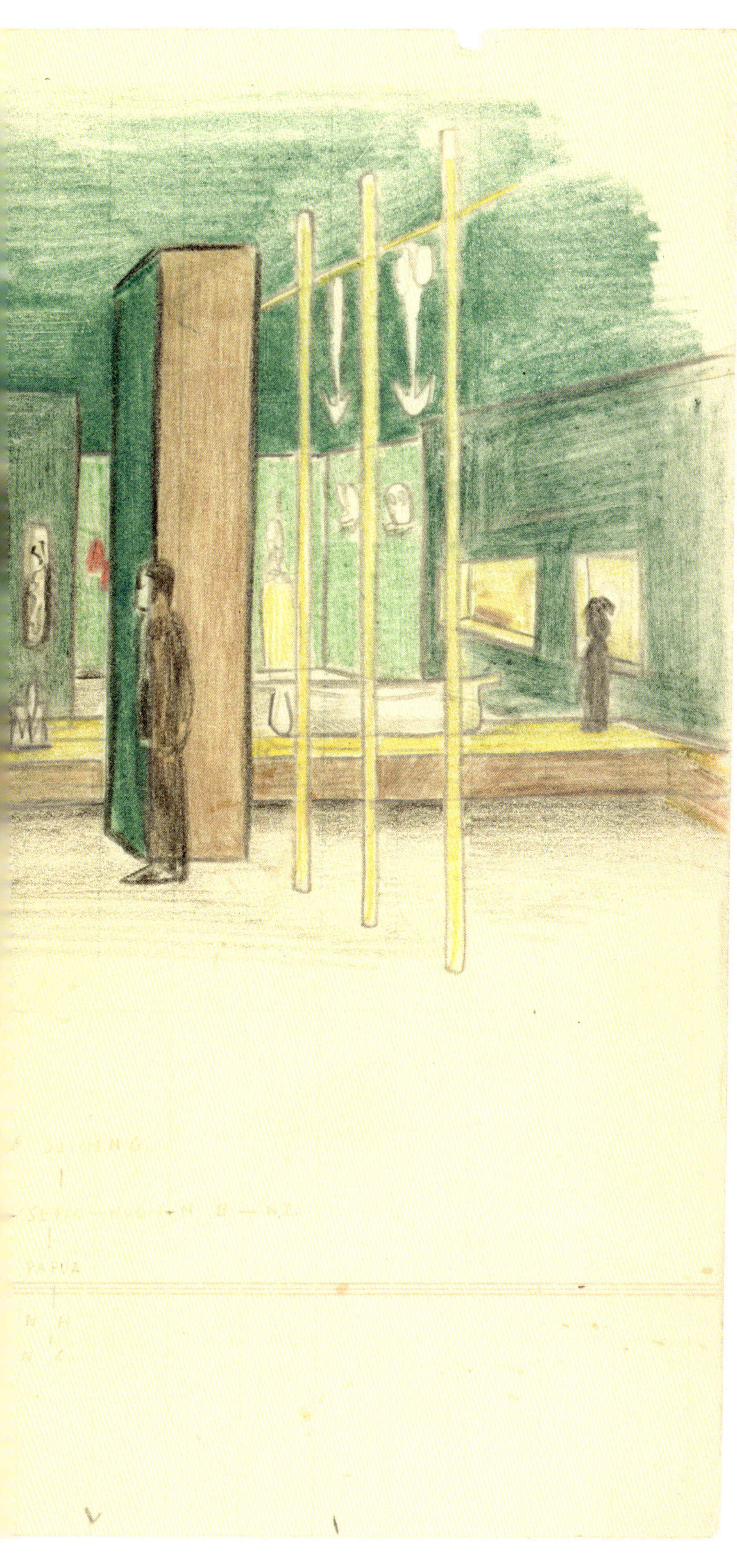

Installation vista of the exhibition
Arts of the South Seas, 1946

Mexican Arts: An Exhibition Organized for and Circulated by the American Federation of Arts

CURATOR: René d'Harnoncourt
NUMBER OF WORKS: 510
CIRCULATING VENUES:

The Metropolitan Museum of Art, New York, New York:
October 13–November 9, 1930

Museum of Fine Arts, Boston, Massachusetts: November 25–
December 15, 1930

Carnegie Institute, Pittsburgh, Pennsylvania: January 7–
February 4, 1931

The Cleveland Museum of Art, Cleveland, Ohio:
February 18–March 11, 1931

The Corcoran Gallery, Washington, DC: April 1–April 22, 1931

Milwaukee Art Institute, Milwaukee, Wisconsin: May 13–June 3, 1931

The J. B. Speed Memorial Museum, Louisville, Kentucky: June 24–
July 15, 1931

Pan-American Round Table, San Antonio, Texas:
August 12–September 2, 1931

Los Angeles Museum, Los Angeles, California: October 1–
October 20, 1931

University of New Mexico, Albuquerque, New Mexico:
November 8–November 25, 1931

Art Institute of Chicago, Chicago, Illinois:
December 22, 1931–January 15, 1932

St. Louis Art Museum, St. Louis, Missouri: February 4–
February 24, 1932

The Museum of Fine Arts, Houston, Texas: March 20, 1932–
April 15, 1932

Women's Club, El Paso, Texas: May 10—June 1, 1932

PUBLICATION: René d'Harnoncourt, *Mexican Arts: Catalogue of an Exhibition Organized for and Circulated by the American Federation of Arts* (Washington, DC: American Federation of Arts, 1930)

After a preview in July 1930 of the painting section at the Ministry of Education in Mexico City, the exhibition *Mexican Arts* opened at the Metropolitan Museum of Art in October. D'Harnoncourt arranged the show into three thematic groupings—popular art, colonial-era decorative art, and modern art—and used differing installation styles for each. The first two sections, consisting of historical and folk art, displayed a jumble of objects on the walls and on the multi-tiered tables and platforms, evoking a bazaar or *mercado*. The more restrained modern section consisted of paintings and sculpture, absent of three-dimensional artifacts; but there was still a sense of saturation, as the paintings were hung in the salon style.

The exhibition circulated for two years, to fourteen venues, and it hit a nerve. At the Met, there was friction. Director Edward Robinson, a specialist in classical Greek art, emphasized at the press opening that the Met staff was not very knowledgeable about the subject of the exhibition—almost as a way of distancing the institution from it. The article for the museum's *Bulletin* was signed by an outsider, d'Harnoncourt, rather than an internal curator. According to d'Harnoncourt, the discomfort of the institution pointed to its lack of experience with handling both popular and contemporary art.[1]

Nonetheless, the exhibition garnered widespread critical acclaim. It broke attendance records at the Met, where it was visited by more than twenty-five thousand people. This initial success led the American Federation of Arts to add six additional venues to the tour from the original eight. In a harbinger of what was to come, the young director of the new Museum of Modern Art, Alfred Barr, visited the exhibition: he later stated that the show "was much admired, particularly by museum people who were impressed as much by the installation as the art. I was one of them."[2]

Illustration of a table displaying toys,
c. 1930

Tentative floorplan for the exhibition,
c. 1930

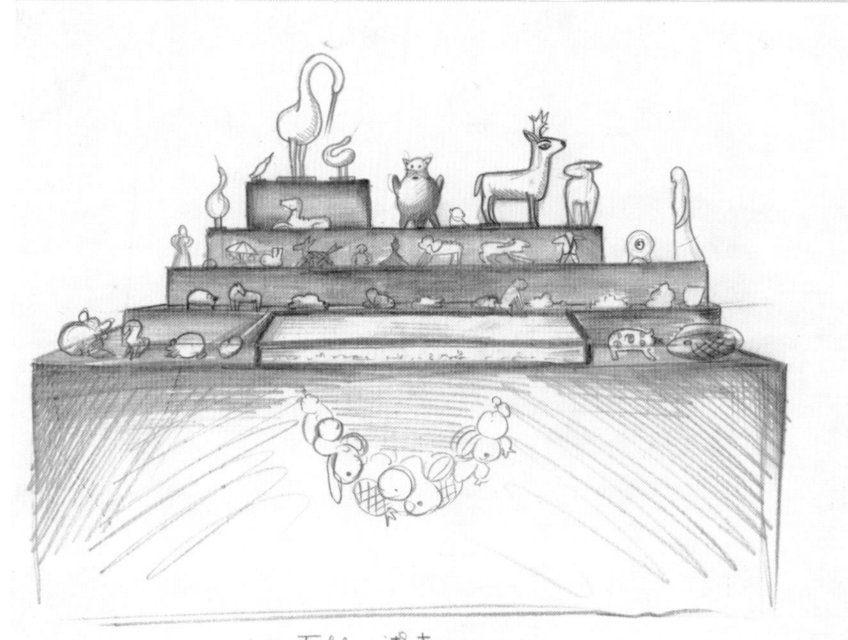

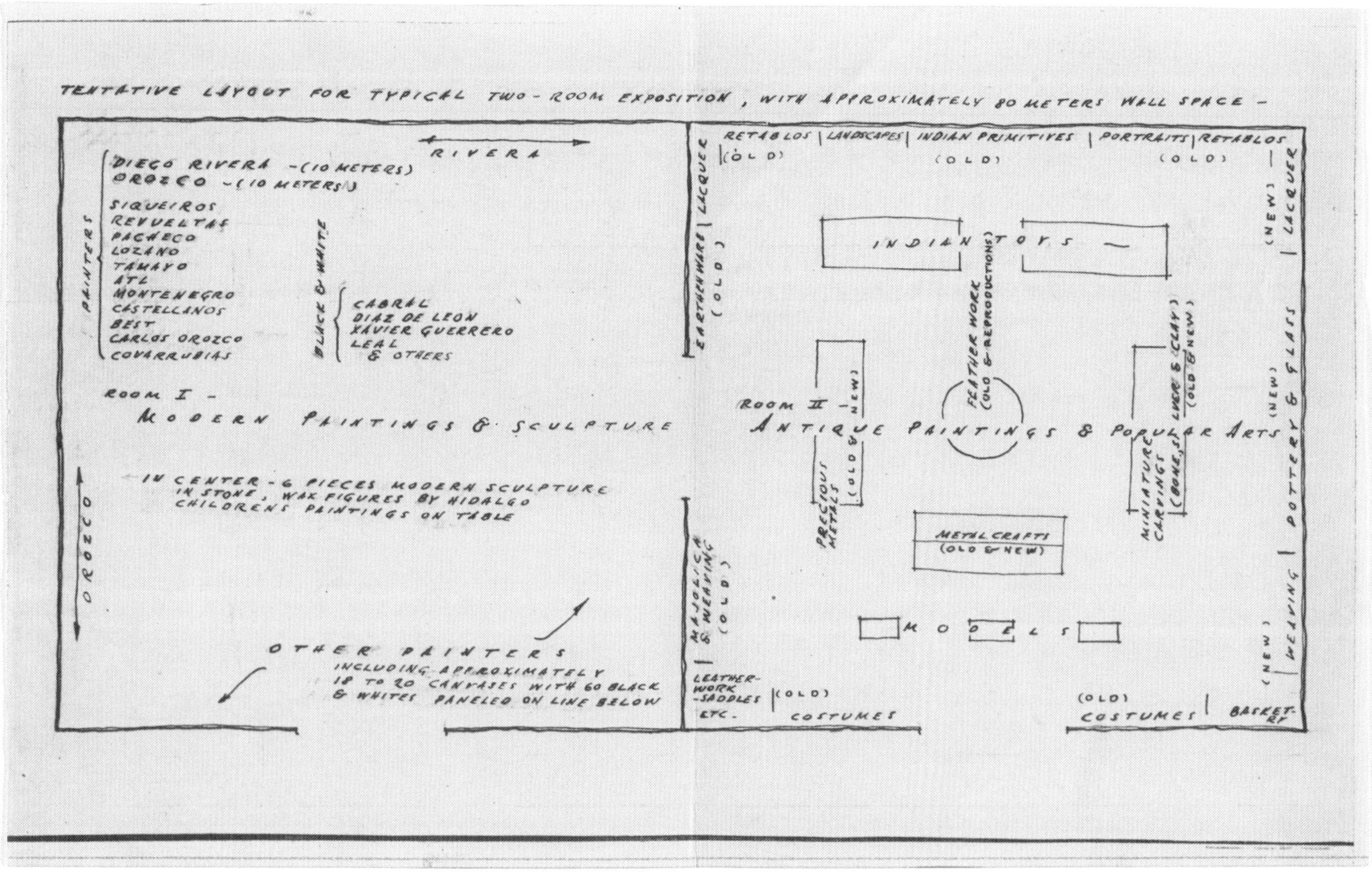

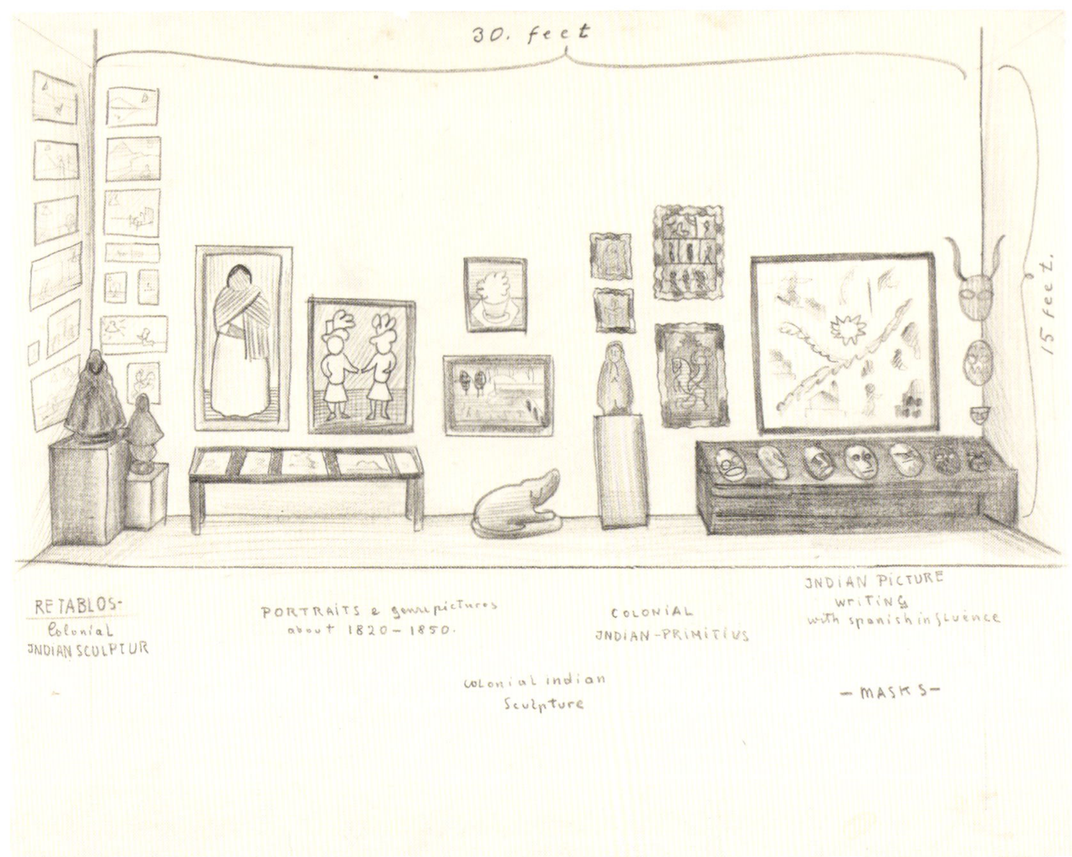

Preparatory sketch for the exhibition
Mexican Arts, c. 1930

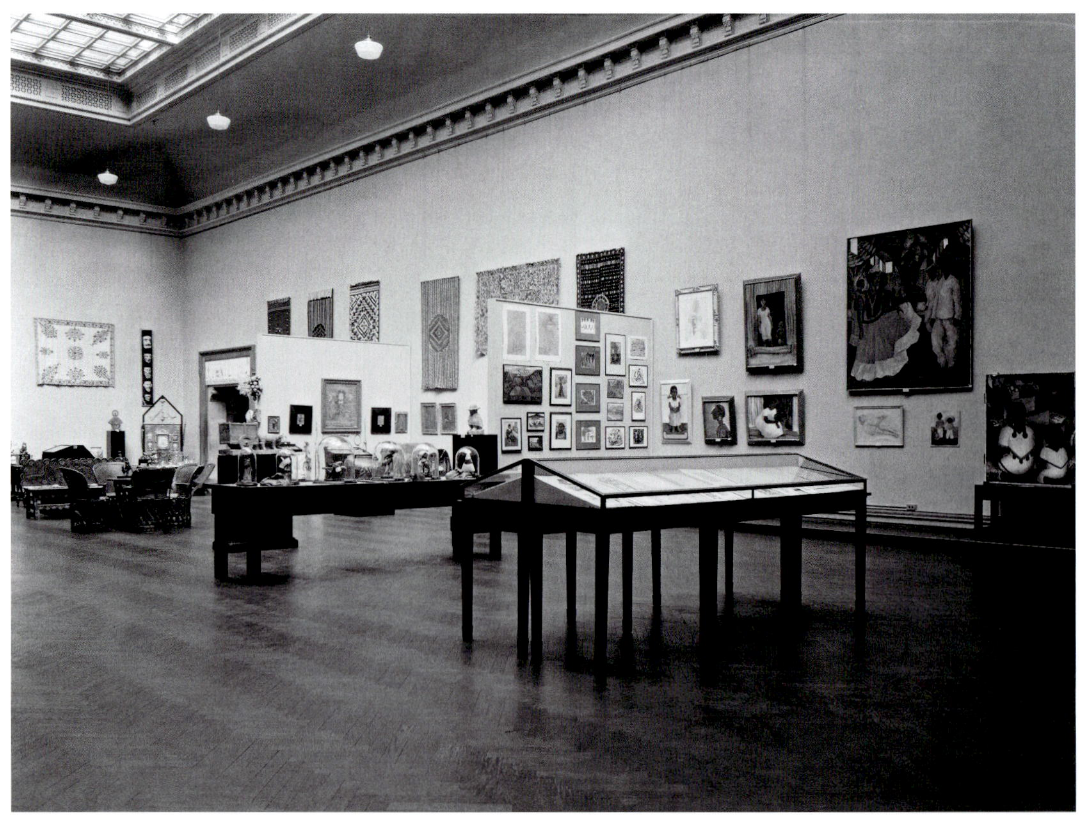

Left and opposite: Installation views of
Mexican Arts at the Metropolitan
Museum of Art, 1930

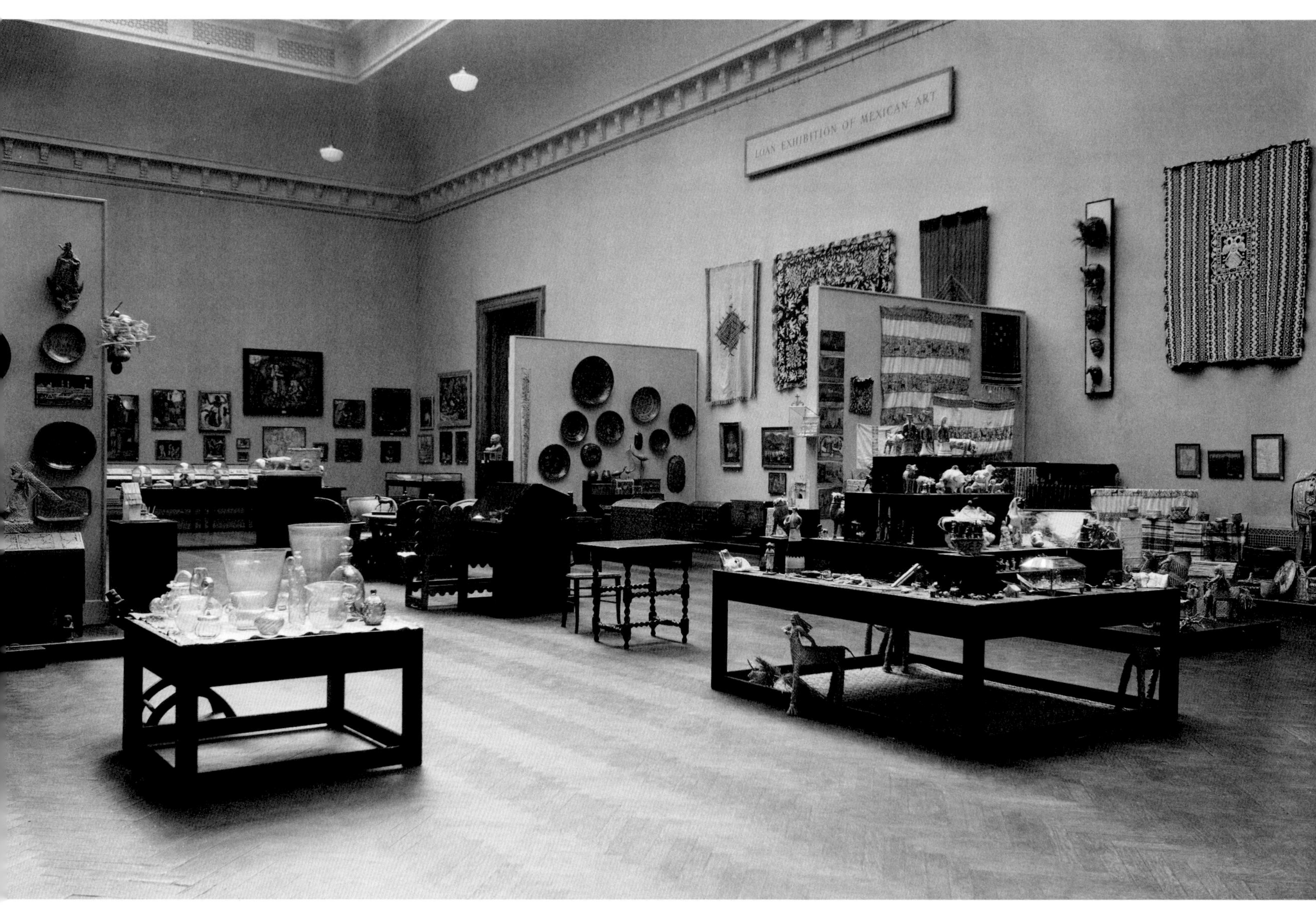

LOAN EXHIBITION OF MEXICAN ART

Indian Art of the United States

MoMA Exhibition #123; January 22–April 27, 1941

CURATOR: Assembled and installed under the direction of René d'Harnoncourt, in collaboration with Frederic H. Douglas, curator of Indian Art of the Denver Art Museum, and Henry Klumb, architect
NUMBER OF WORKS: Approximately 1,000
LOCATION: First-, second-, and third-floor galleries
CIRCULATING VENUES:
Gallup Art Center, Gallup, New Mexico:
    August 12–September 15, 1941
Worcester Museum of Art, Worcester, Massachusetts:
    October 22–November 23, 1941
Lyman-Allyn Museum, New London, Connecticut:
    December 1–December 29, 1941
Cleveland Art Museum, Cleveland, Ohio: January 9–February 8, 1942
Society of Liberal Arts, Joslyn Memorial, Omaha, Nebraska:
    February 19–March 22, 1942
The City Art Museum of St. Louis, St. Louis, Missouri:
    April 1–May 11, 1942
The Los Angeles County Museum of History, Science and Arts,
    Los Angeles, California: May 25–June 30, 1942
PUBLICATION: Frederic H. Douglas and René d'Harnoncourt, *Indian Art of the United States* (New York: The Museum of Modern Art, 1941)

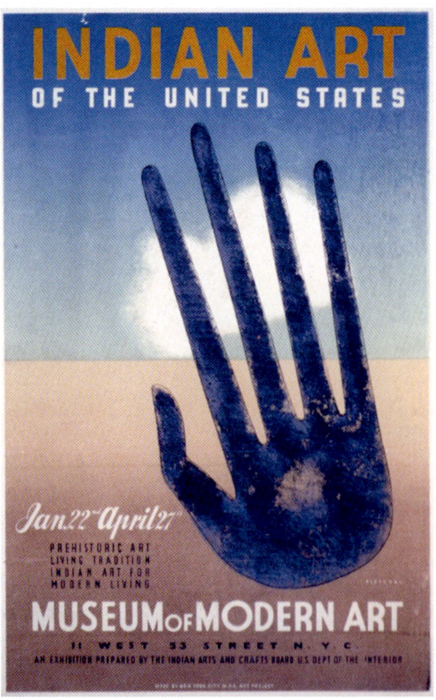

Poster for the exhibition *Indian Art of the United States*, 1941

Indian Art of the United States took place at MoMA two years after d'Harnoncourt's first foray into the subject at the Golden Gate International Exposition in San Francisco. D'Harnoncourt had hoped to obtain gallery space on one floor, but in an extraordinary coup, the entire Museum was turned over to him. MoMA clearly considered the installation of the exhibition newsworthy: the press release declared, in all capital letters, "MUSEUM OF MODERN ART REBUILDS THREE ENTIRE FLOORS TO INSTALL INDIAN EXHIBITION WITH UNDERGROUND CEREMONIAL CHAMBERS, TOTEM POLES, SIXTY-FOOT MURAL AND OTHER UNUSUAL FEATURES."[3] Novel "ultra-modern" installation techniques and display methods, including dramatic lighting effects and brilliantly colored backgrounds, were employed in the service of exhibiting more than one thousand items from the past 1,500 years.

The show progressed chronologically. Reversing the usual traffic pattern, it opened on the top floor with the prehistoric section (Indian art before the discovery of the tribes by Europeans); followed on the second floor by "Living Traditions," or historic and contemporary native art; and ended with "Indian Art for Modern Living," a selection of contemporary objects recontextualized as art for the home or the body in the modern world, on the ground floor. D'Harnoncourt then devised three different installation techniques or styles, one for each of the floors.

The works in the prehistoric section were divided into five general categories according to geography and the method used by their creators: Carvers of the Far West, Carvers of the Northwest Coast, Engravers of the Arctic, Sculptors of the East, and Painters of the Southwest. Within each grouping, d'Harnoncourt decontextualized the objects to amplify their aesthetic effect and presented them "with classic simplicity in rather severe white-walled rooms."[4] In two notable instances, he abandoned this austere presentation to evoke instead the original viewing conditions of the artifacts. He commissioned reproductions of prehistoric Pueblo mural paintings from the early sixteenth century, executed on plaster panels by modern Hopi painters. The original murals were found on the walls of a kiva, or underground ceremonial room, which was small and low, lit only from a hole in the middle of the ceiling. Thus, d'Harnoncourt installed the reproductions in a series of darkened, top-lit galleries. Then he presented pictographs of animals and figures on a canvas mural, twelve feet high and sixty feet wide, curved around the corner of the only daylit gallery on the floor. With this immersive experience, the mural simulated the effect of viewing the pictographs on the face of the sandstone walls of the Barrier Canyon in Utah. A participatory event space was set aside in this gallery, where members of the Navajo nation created sand paintings during Museum hours, while visitors watched.

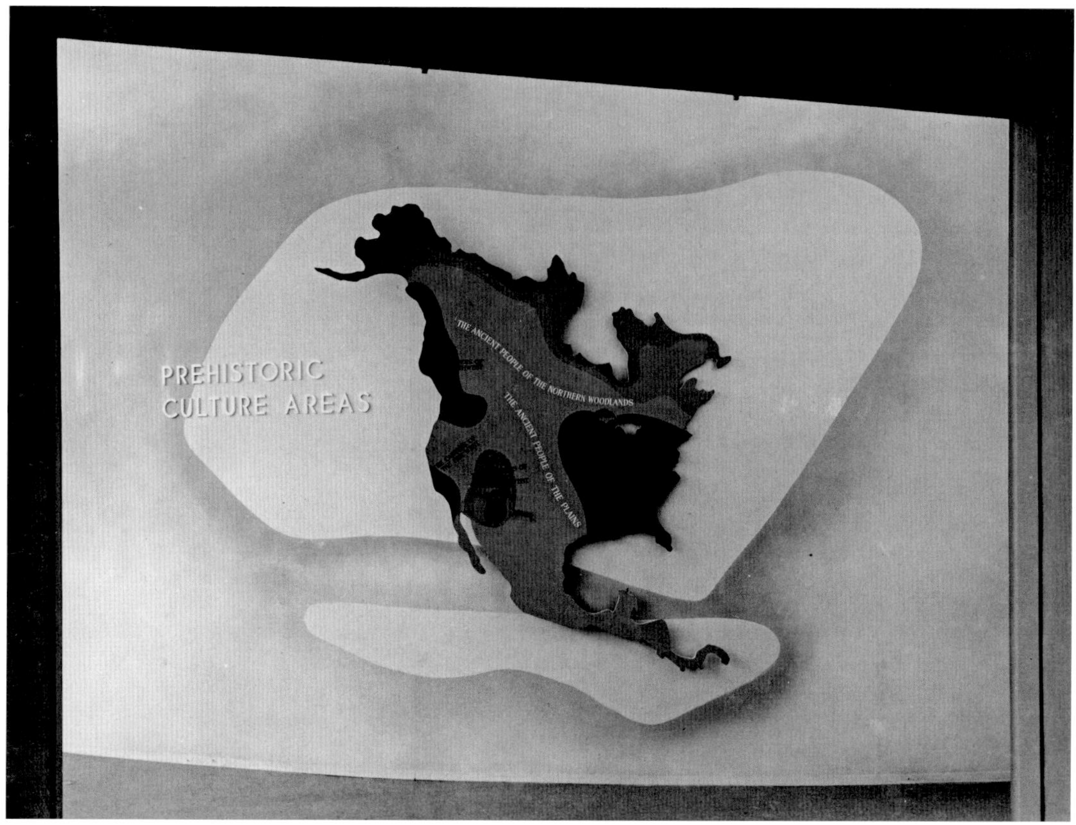

Map created by the New York City Works Progress Administration, introducing the prehistoric section of the exhibition on the third floor

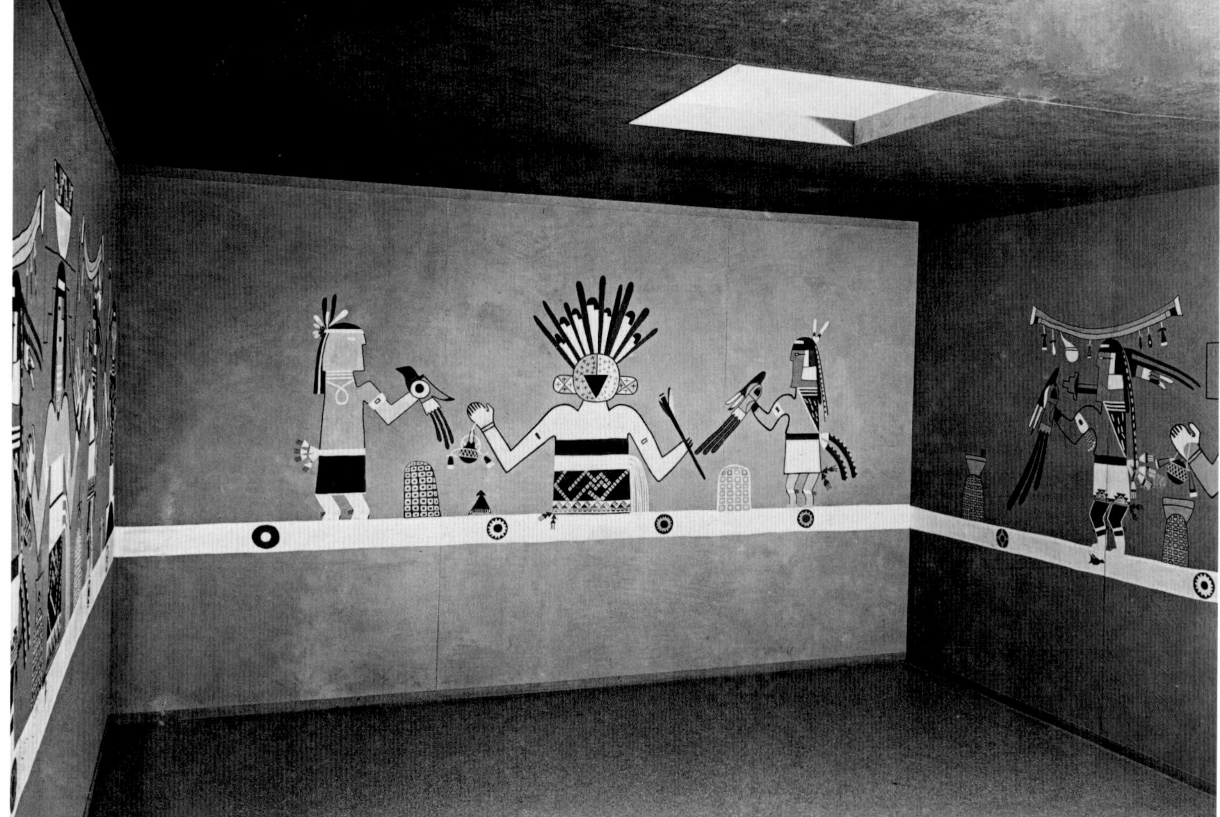

View of the gallery presenting reproductions of prehistoric Pueblo mural paintings, installed as if in a kiva, or small underground room lit from above

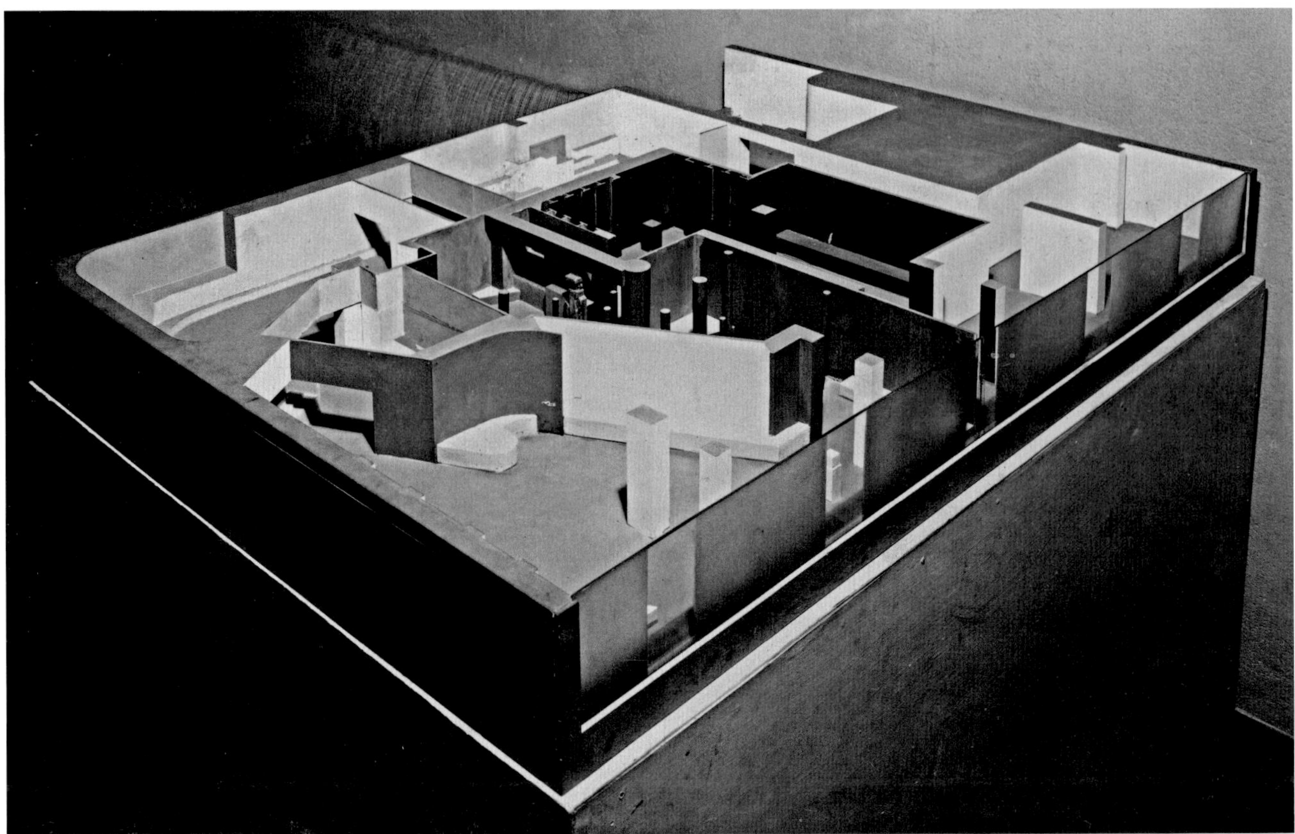

On the second floor, historic and contemporary native art was contextualized by region or tribe of origin: each room corresponded to one of the nine Indian culture areas identified by d'Harnoncourt (Pueblo Cornplanters, Navajo Shepherds, Apache Mountain People, Desert Dwellers of the Southwest, Seed Gatherers of the Far West, Hunters of the Plains, Woodsmen of the East, Fishermen of the Northwest Coast, and Eskimo Hunters of the Arctic). Here, d'Harnoncourt again subtly evoked the atmosphere of each culture and the physical surroundings of the objects in their original contexts. For example, in the Northwest Coast sculpture gallery, a darkened wall (its hue found in some of the works themselves) and dramatic lighting emphasized the physicality and monumentality of the sculpting, suggested the supernatural forces that imbued the figures, and evoked the dark forest.

On these two floors, d'Harnoncourt made use of introductory galleries placed at the entries, one with a model of the exhibition spaces and both with maps executed by the New York City Works Progress Administration Art Project. This technique of separating the didactic materials from the spaces occupied by the art would become a preferred approach for him. He also provided an element of the unexpected by changing the circulation path to the opposite direction on the second floor.

This scale model of the second-floor galleries was presented near the entrance to the exhibition to explain to visitors the structure and organization of the show.

Navajo sand painters at the exhibition,
March 26, 1941

View of the twelve-by-sixty-foot curved
wall presenting a canvas mural
depicting pictographs from Barrier
Canyon, Utah

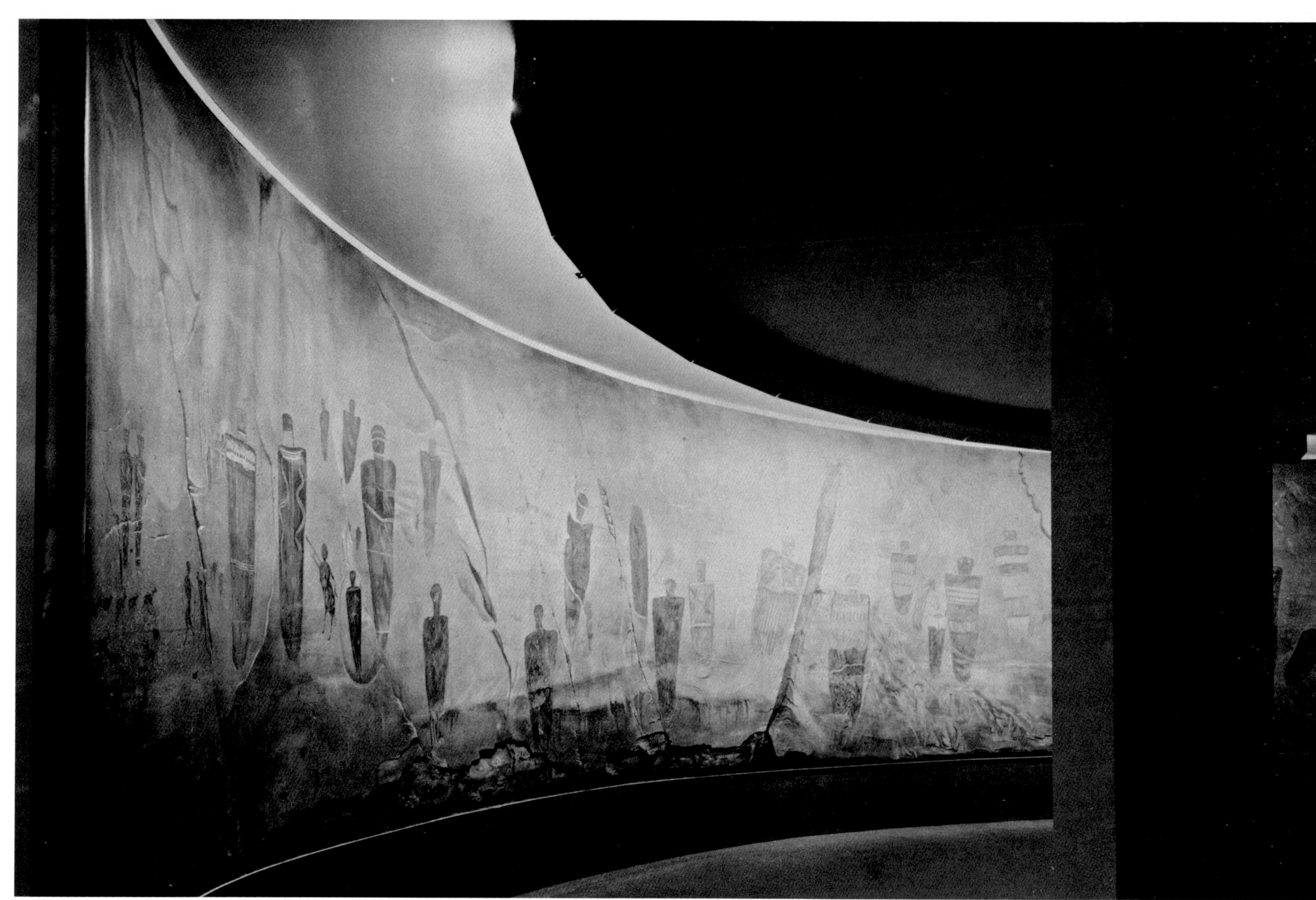

Finally, the ground floor, titled "Indian Art for Modern Living," presented a smaller group of contemporary objects particularly suited for the twentieth century. The objective here was to convey that Indian objects could be converted for use in modern society outside of their original context of creation. This contemporary section had three divisions: painting and sculpture; a study gallery to explain the role of art in the social life of a community, as well as its materiality, technique, and form; and a showcase of its role in modern decorative arts.

Despite the vast quantity of objects, the installation was spacious and uncluttered, with each display unit treated individually: *Newsweek* acknowledged that "such an all-inclusive exhibit could easily have been overwhelming, but . . . the show has been installed and lit with such superb taste and showmanship by René d'Harnoncourt . . . that it is a continuous delight to the ordinary spectator as well as to the art-minded connoisseur."[5] In each room, one object dominated, embodying a central thesis. Each transition from one cultural area to another was demarcated in "dramatic visual form," and methods were employed to relate "esthetic forms and choice of raw material and production methods to the basic elements that condition the particular culture."[6] Barr later reflected on the exhibition, noting it was "an installation possible only with long, deep, and original study. [D'Harnoncourt] avoided both the purely aesthetic isolation and the waxworks of the habitat group. . . . The varied galleries seemed informal at first glance but were calculated in size, perspective, sequence, color, light, level, sometimes dramatic but never theatrical, and functional rather than decorative."[7] In the *New York Times*, Edward Allen Jewell concurred, saying that the show represented "a high watermark in museum technique. It is a technique that, however bold and forthright, appears at all times subservient to the just pre-eminence of the art it so deftly sets off, correlates, differentiates and enhances."[8]

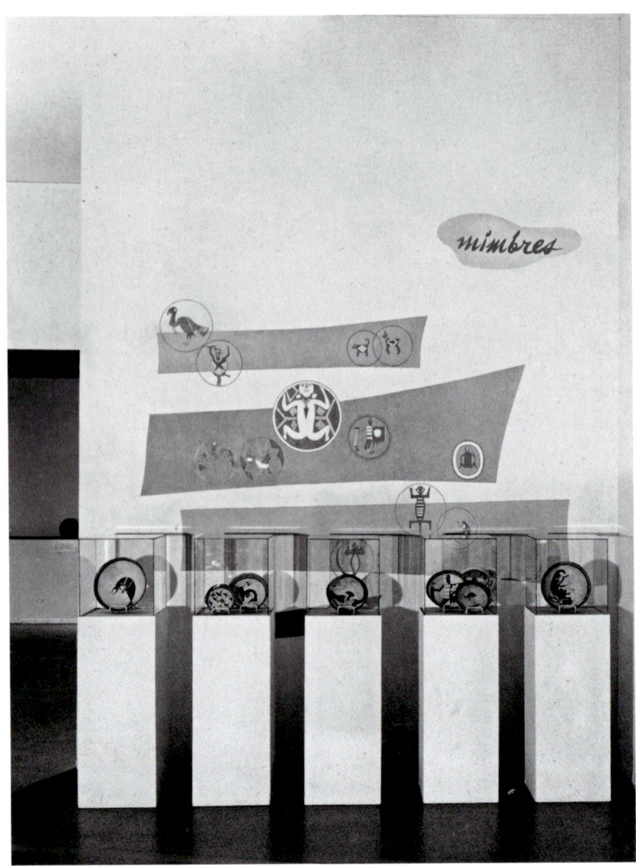

The elegant presentation of Mimbres pottery was surmounted by a graphic, to render more legible the original Mimbres designs.

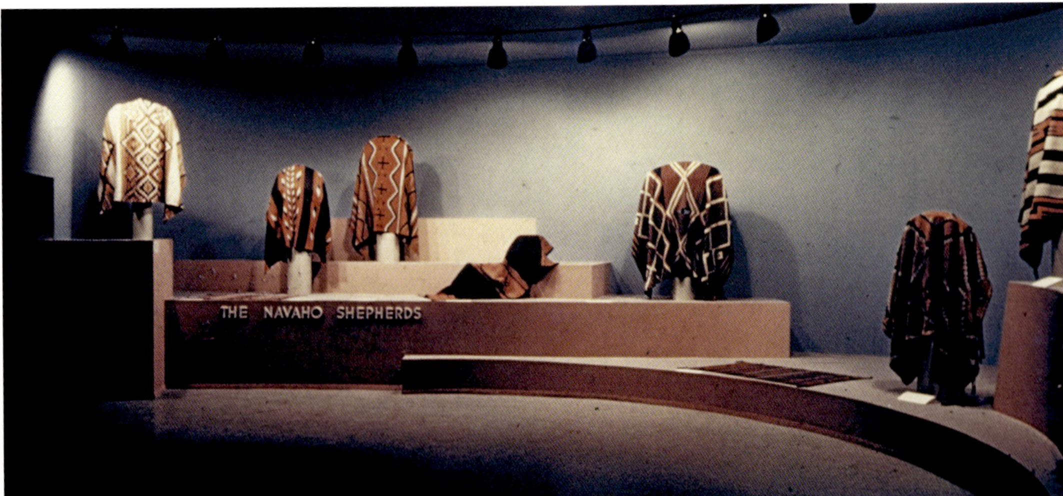

The presentation of Navajo ponchos evoked human proportions, as if they were being worn by individuals out in the fields; yet the arrangement was an abstracted and aestheticized one.

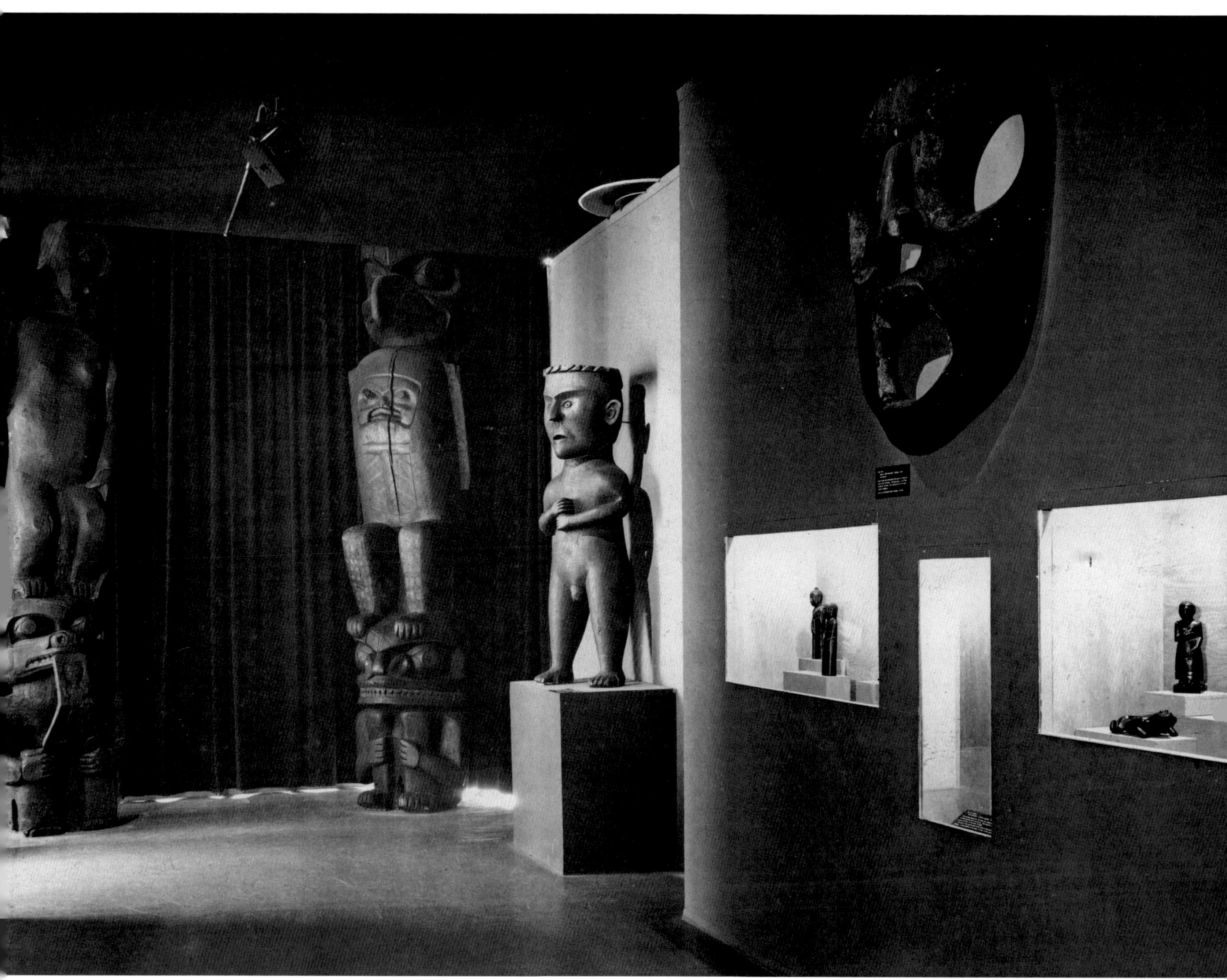

Installation view of the exhibition *Indian Art of the United States*, 1941

Arts of the South Seas

MoMA Exhibition #306; January 29–May 19, 1946

CURATOR: René d'Harnoncourt in collaboration with Dr. Ralph Linton, professor of Anthropology at Columbia University, and Dr. Paul S. Wingert, instructor in the Department of History of Art at Columbia University, with contributions from Miguel Covarrubias and the ethnologist Charles P. Mountford
NUMBER OF WORKS: 400
LOCATION: Second floor
PUBLICATION: Ralph Linton, Paul S. Wingert, and René d'Harnoncourt (with color illustrations by Miguel Covarrubias), *Arts of the South Seas* (New York: The Museum of Modern Art, 1946)
CIRCULATING VENUES:
Worcester Museum of Art, Worcester, Massachusetts:
    October 3—November 17, 1946

The first exhibition d'Harnoncourt organized as a Museum staff member, *Arts of the South Seas* was a presentation of some "400 strange and fantastic objects" that d'Harnoncourt prepared over the course of eighteen months.[9] As was his rule, he began by drawing each object selected for inclusion in the show. D'Harnoncourt then mapped a network of related cultures in the South Seas (or Oceania). He identified four major regions—Australia, Melanesia, Micronesia, and Polynesia—and within those, twenty distinct cultural areas.

D'Harnoncourt wanted to impress upon the viewer that the geographies of the various areas, their climates, and their available natural resources impacted the work produced. He suggested the atmosphere and environment within which each of the works had been made by imbuing the display with geographic and climatic cues. D'Harnoncourt sought to represent these variations through color, light, and spaciousness: red for Australia's deserts and steppes; green for New Guinea's tropical jungle and New Zealand's pine forests; the brilliant white light of Micronesia's small windswept coral

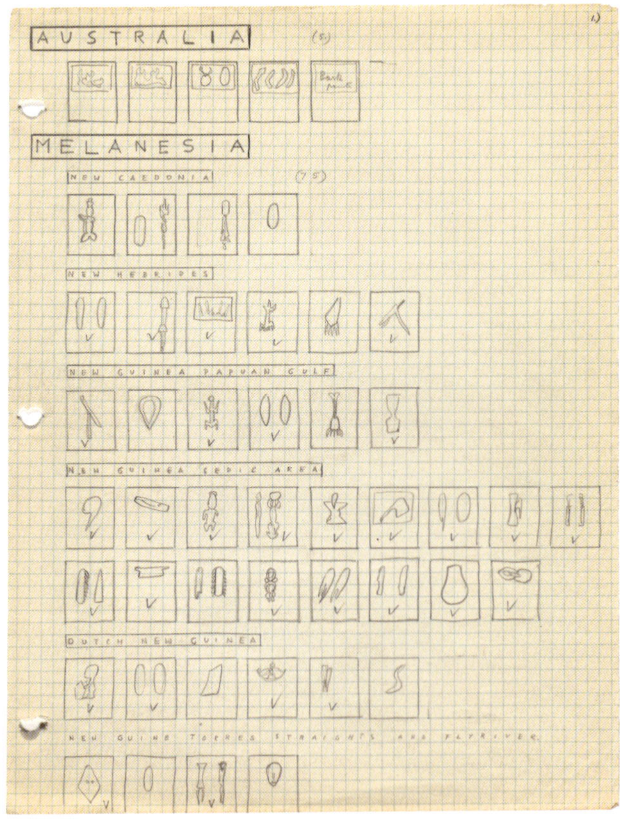

Checklist with hand-drawn illustrations of objects for the exhibition *Arts of the South Seas* grouped by region of provenance, 1946

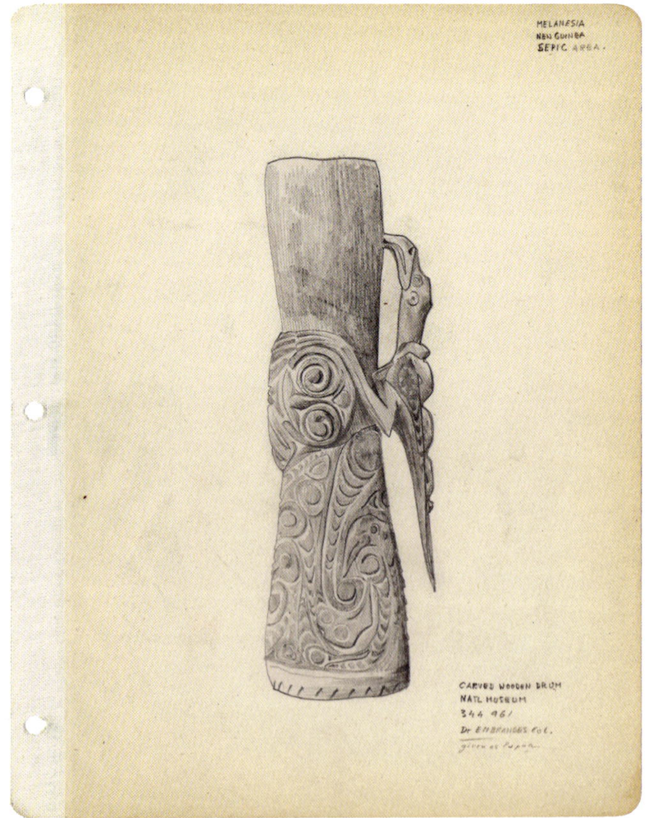

Study of an object included in the exhibition *Arts of the South Seas*, 1946

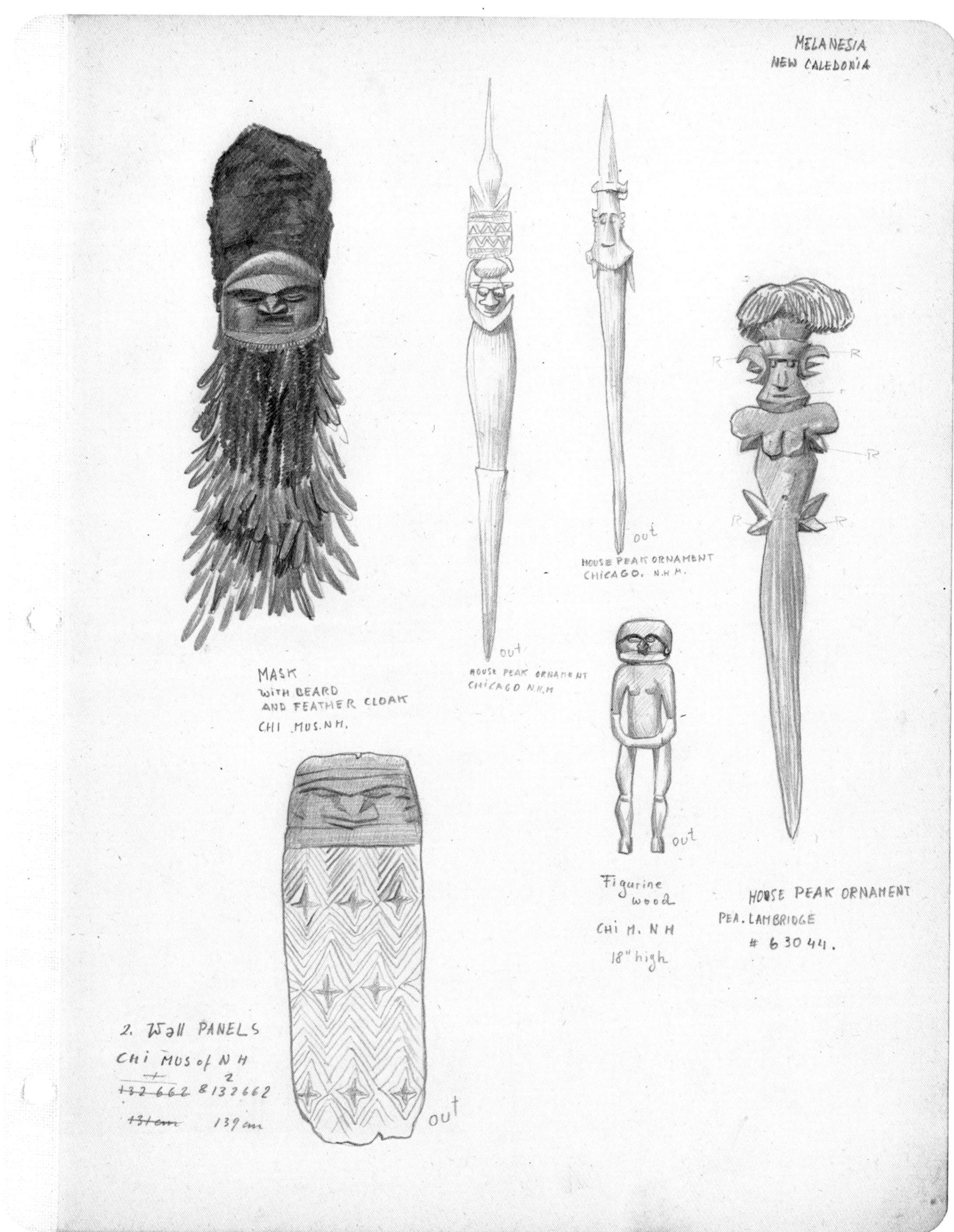

Scale drawings of objects included in the exhibition *Arts of the South Seas*, 1946

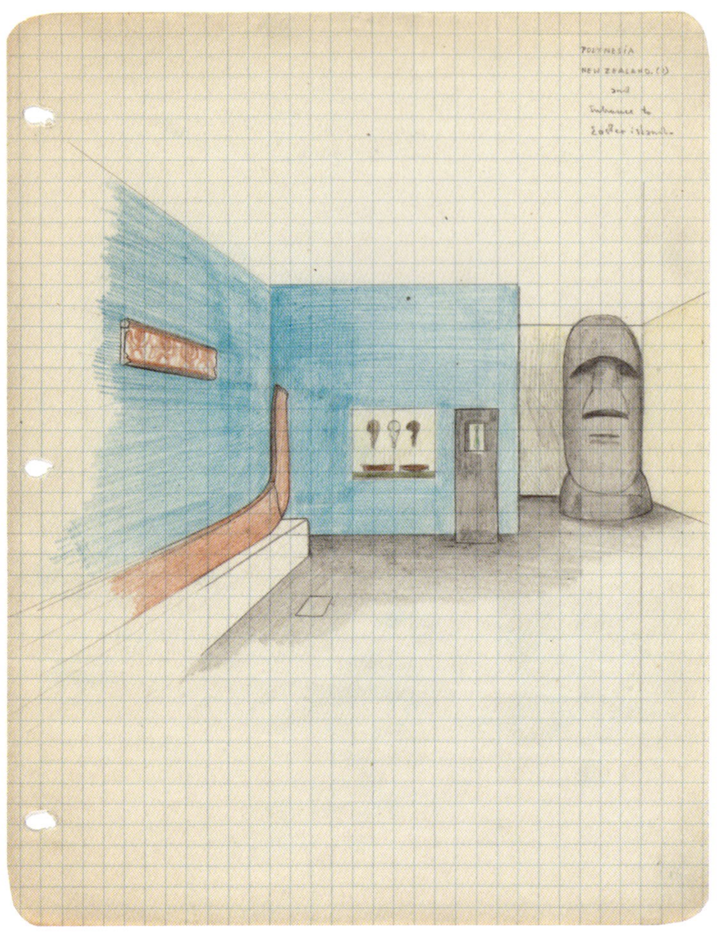

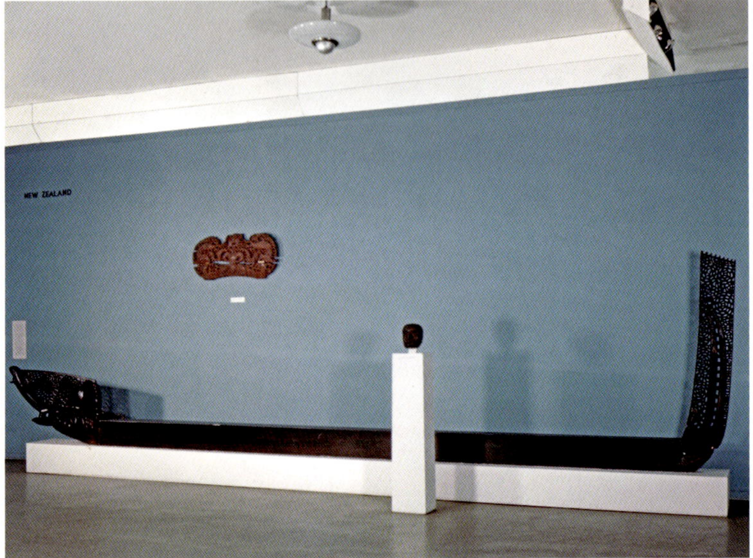

Preparatory vistas paired with installation views of the same sections of the exhibition, indicating the adjustments made by d'Harnoncourt in situ to the planned installation

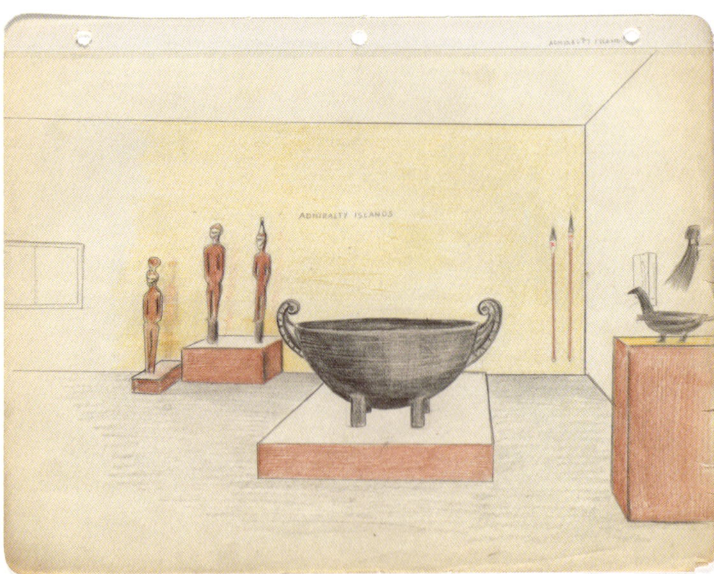

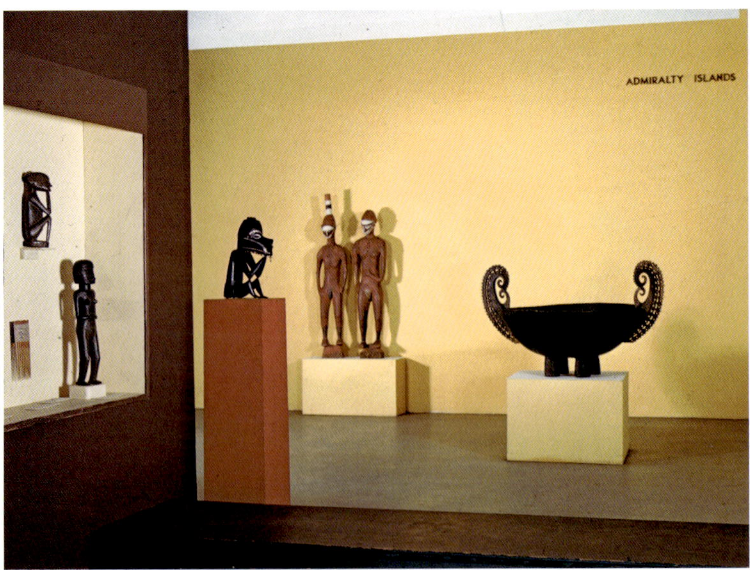

atolls; blue accents for Polynesia's temperate climate; and yellow for Fiji's barren coral formations. Throughout, d'Harnoncourt was sensitive to the color balance of the exhibition (see color wheel, page 60). He employed a total of eleven contrasting colors as visual aids, on ceilings, walls, and installation devices. A complete rarity for this time, the MoMA Archives include some color images of the installation, which brilliantly evoke the lushness of the palette employed. The images were found in a collection of glass lantern slides in d'Harnoncourt's papers, indicating that he himself likely used these images when delivering lectures.

D'Harnoncourt further identified three dominant stylistic trends: an extreme economy of means, or simplicity of sculpture and objects, largely found in Micronesia; geometric order, reflecting complex, highly structured social and religious concepts from Polynesia; and a dramatic emotional quality, resulting from distortion, exaggeration, and strong color, as found in Melanesia. While each region had a dominant tendency or style in the representation of form, these trends were also found to some extent in all the regions. D'Harnoncourt wanted to highlight these cross-pollinations and shared traits among the geographically distinctive areas with subtlety. It was while working on *South Seas* that he first reflected on ways to create vistas and open vistas, designing new display devices and vitrines that allowed viewing from multiple perspectives.

The anthropologist and social scientist Gregory Bateson penned an extraordinary review of the exhibition, which he viewed as a work of art in and of itself. He speculated that the exhibition depicted a sexual journey, representing the human reproductive cycle and ending in "a final statement of grotesque birth," an analysis that he noted was in line with modern anthropological thought. In a generous gesture, the author allowed d'Harnoncourt to publicly respond to the review; d'Harnoncourt diplomatically stated that the

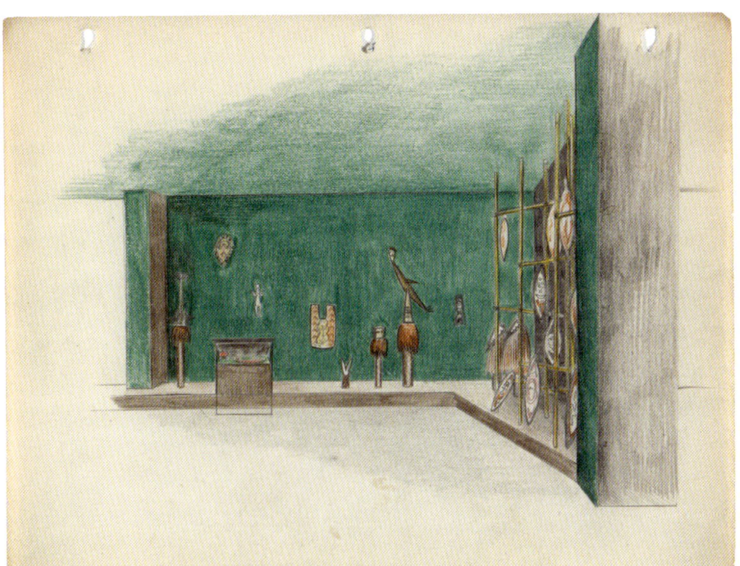
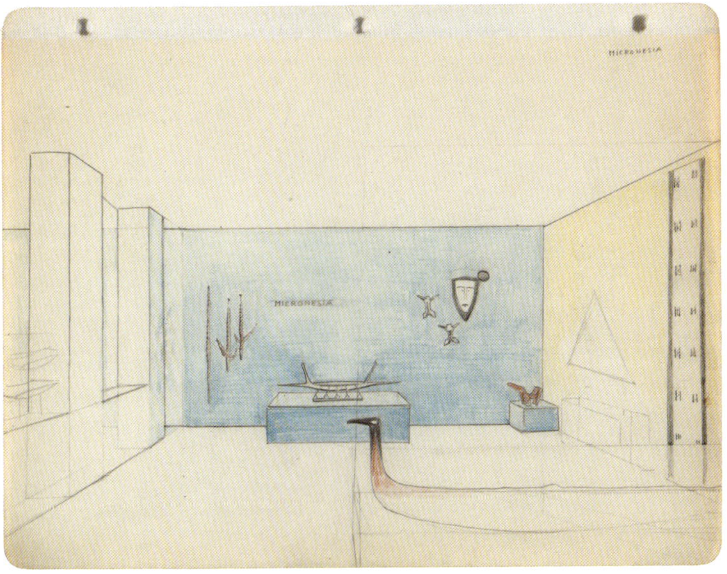

Preparatory vistas of the exhibition, showing sections dedicated to the Papuan Gulf and Micronesia, 1946

reproductive sequence was "perhaps not as important as you make it out," and that he would have stated it "in less concrete terms," if at all.[10]

Unlike *Indian Art*, which received nearly universally favorable reviews, there were some detractors to *Arts of the South Seas*. Robert M. Coates was a *New Yorker* writer who routinely criticized the Museum for straying from its domain of exclusively modern art. Coates decried that MoMA had gone "careening off after folk art and anthropology, as if determined to beat the Museum of Natural History on its own ground. After that there was a 'good neighbor' era, when the emphasis was on South American art . . . Now, however, with its present exhibition, called 'Arts of the South Seas,' it has veered off again, and your guess about its next tack is as good as mine." While concluding, "in brief, that [he] would like to see the Modern Museum stick to modern art," Coates was nonetheless compelled to acknowledge that this was "a singularly successful exhibition."[11]

Opposite, top: Installation views of the sections dedicated to the Sepik River and Australia, 1946

Opposite, bottom: Vista of the New Britain section of the exhibition, 1946

Below: Preparatory vista of the section dedicated to Central Polynesia, 1946

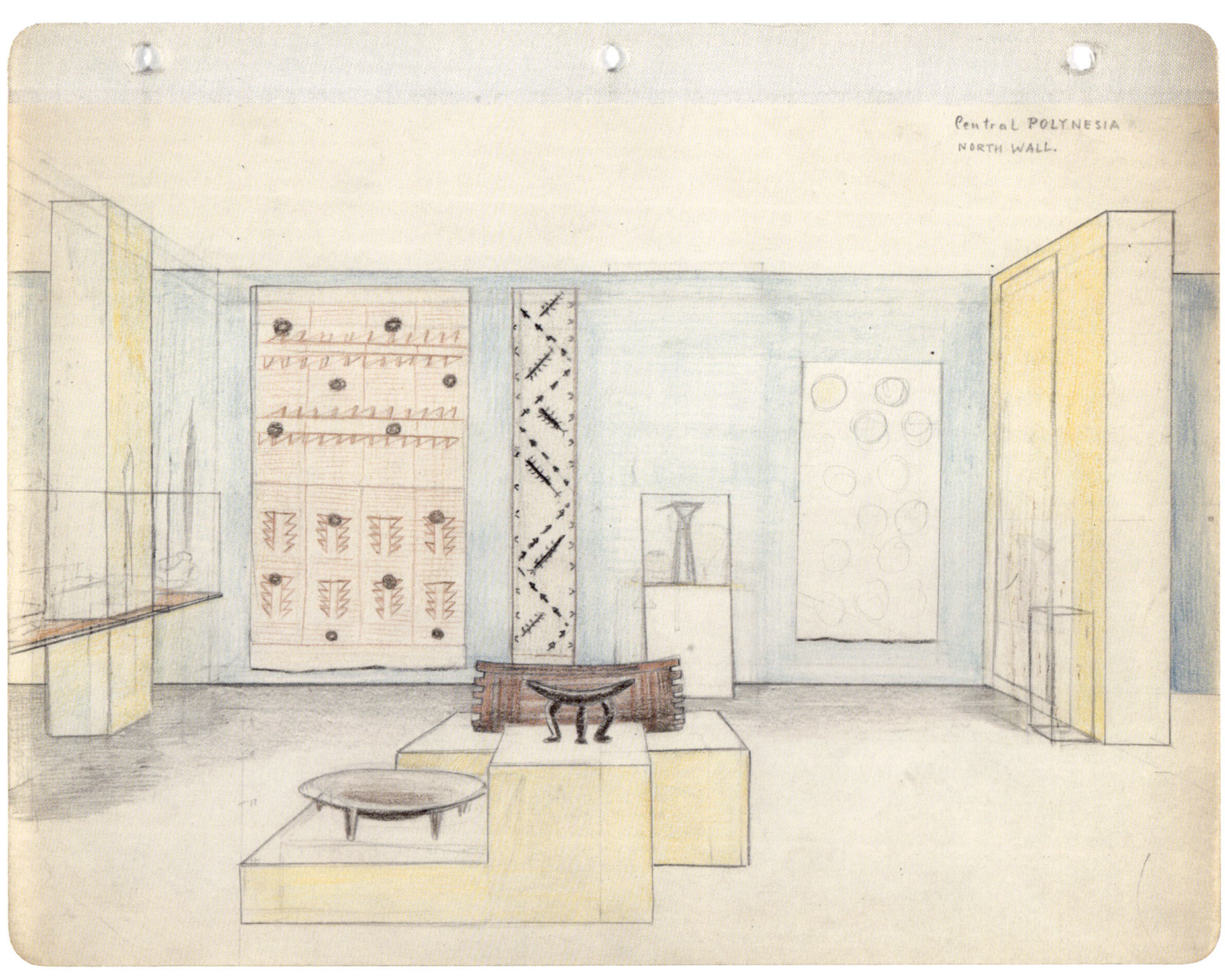

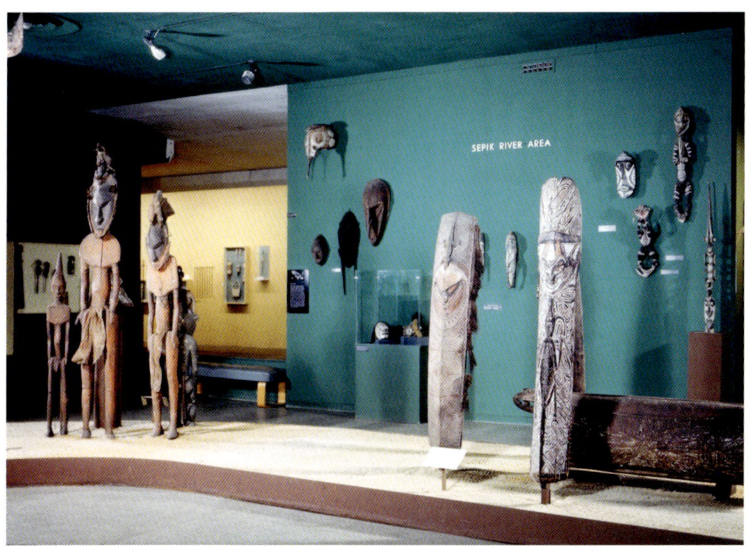

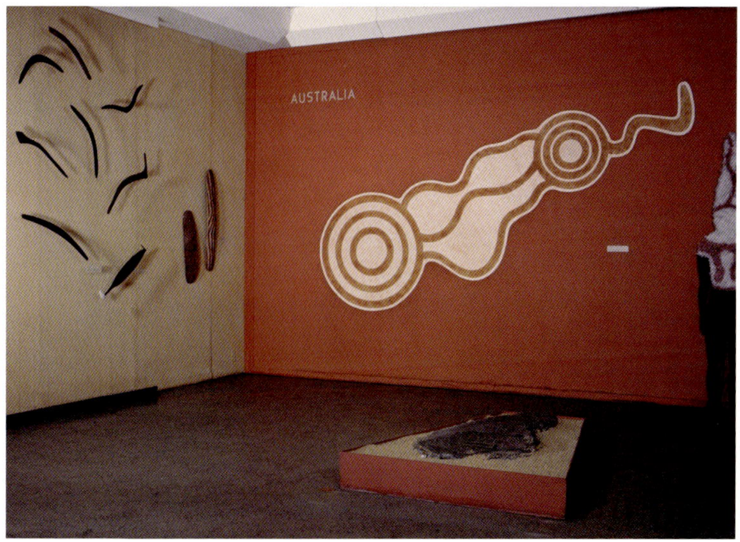
AUSTRALIA

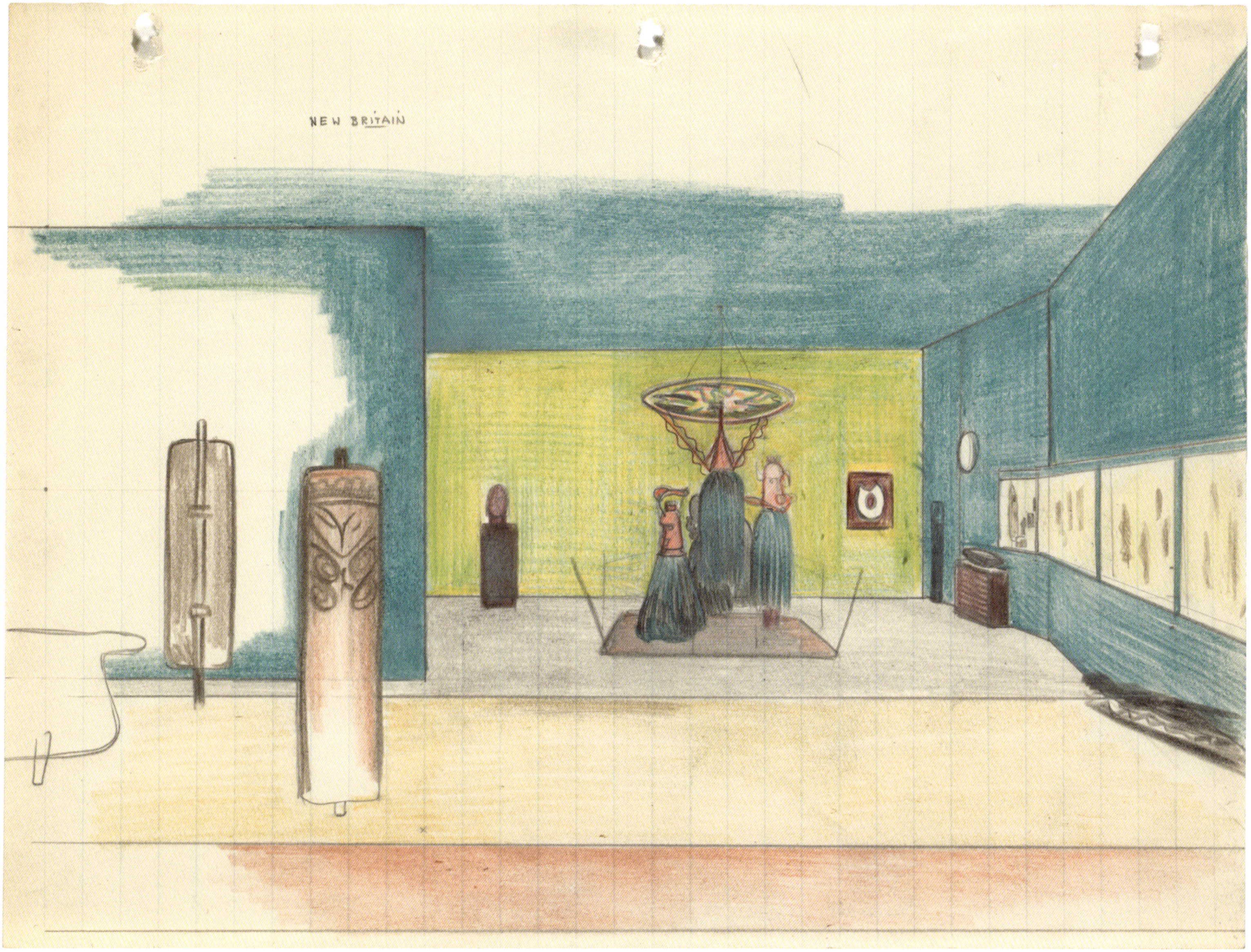

NEW BRITAIN

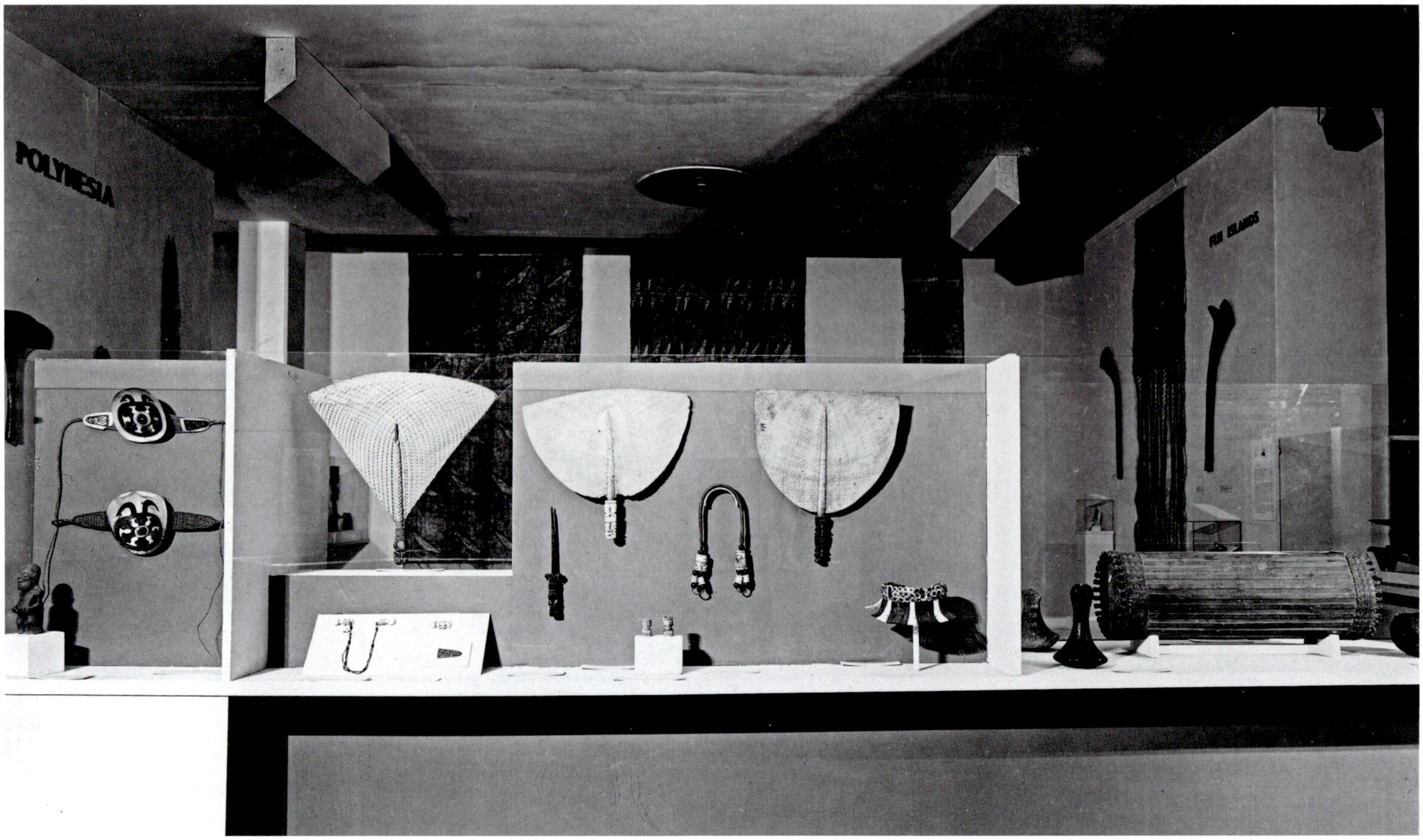

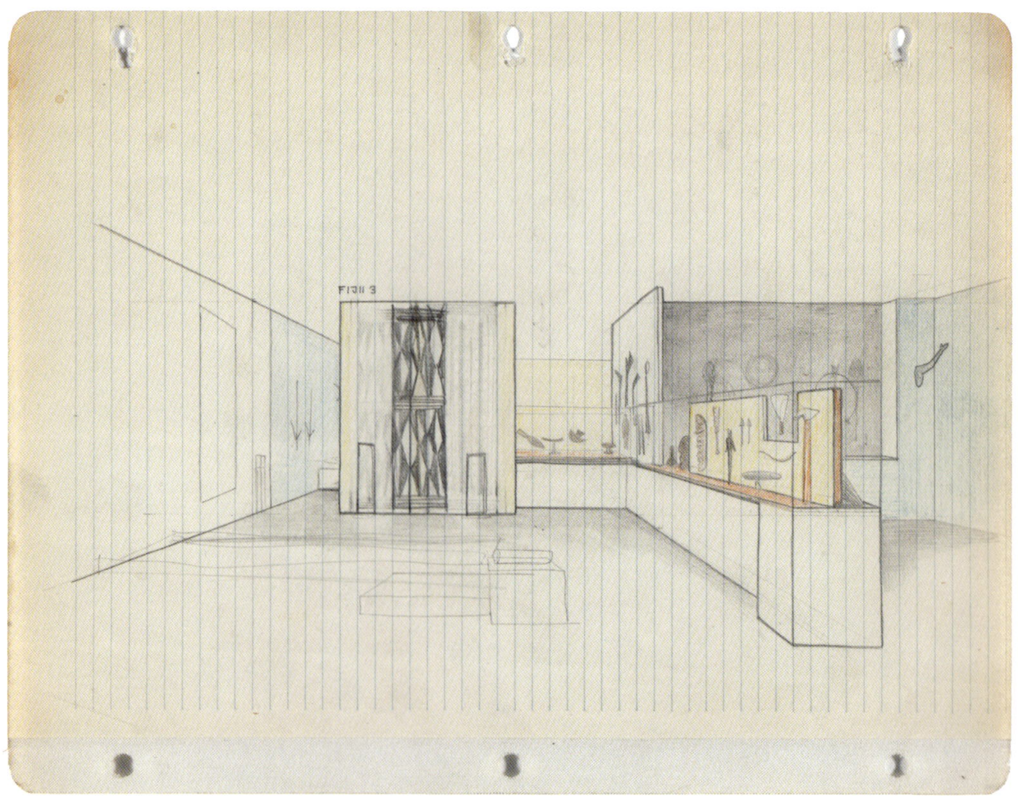

Above, left, and opposite: Vista and installation views of the Micronesia, Polynesia, and
New Zealand sections of the exhibition,
showing the interplay of affinities and transfer
between cultures, with the fan acting as a
formal connecting device, 1946

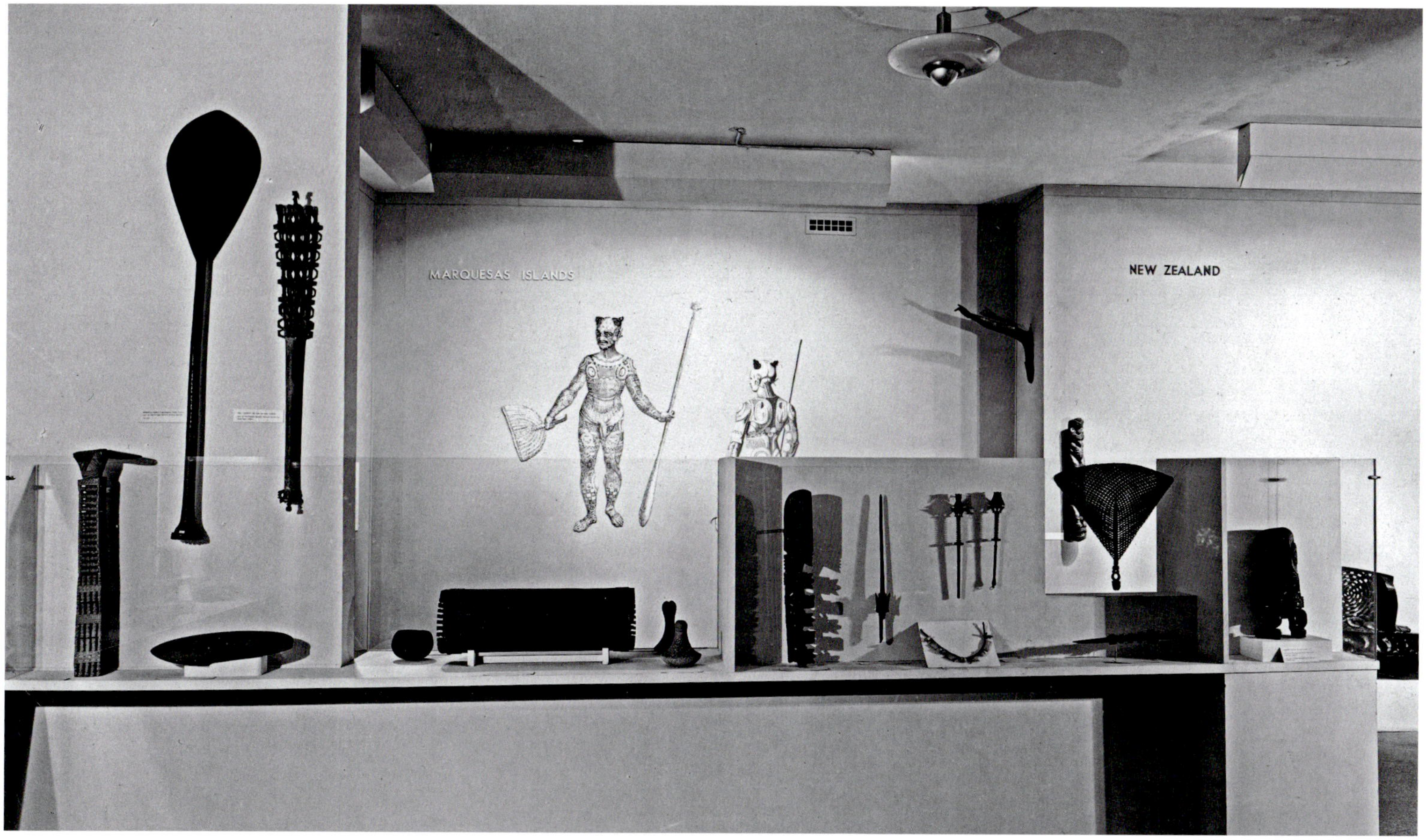

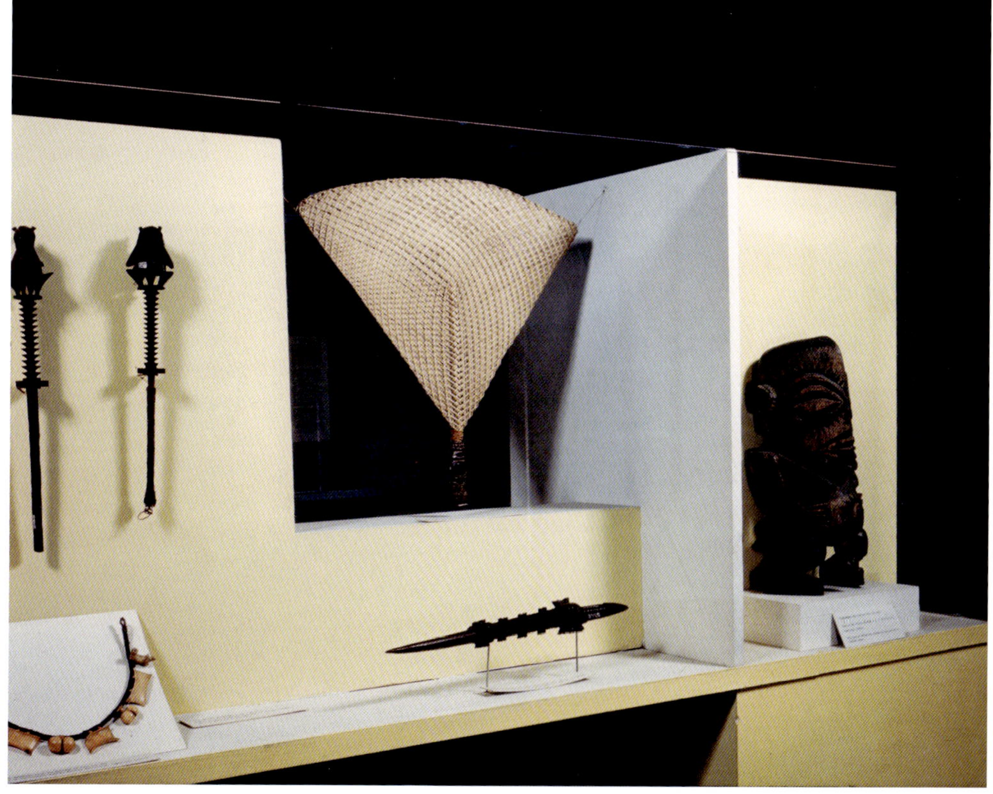

Naum Gabo and Antoine Pevsner

MoMA Exhibition #369; February 10–April 25, 1948

CURATOR: René d'Harnoncourt
NUMBER OF WORKS: Approximately 80, including
a few paintings and drawings
LOCATION: Third floor
PUBLICATION: Ruth Olson and Abraham Chanin, *Naum Gabo,
Antoine Pevsner* (New York: The Museum of Modern Art, 1948)

In 1948, the Museum presented its (surprisingly belated) first exhibition solely devoted to work by artists of the Russian avant-garde. *Naum Gabo and Antoine Pevsner*, two simultaneous and intertwined solo exhibitions of the two Constructivist sculptors and brothers, took place a few months before d'Harnoncourt assumed the role of director of the Museum. Interestingly, for his first foray into a modern artist's oeuvre, d'Harnoncourt chose work that seemed worlds away from his beloved primitive art and seemingly in opposition to his interest in manual industry: the exhibition included abstract sculptures constructed from industrial materials, such as translucent plastic for Gabo and sheets of oxidized tin and brass or colored plastics for Pevsner, rather than traditional materials of sculpture such as stone and bronze.

D'Harnoncourt provided an installation that mirrored the works' elegant simplicity. He offset the two shows, as the two brothers were oppositional in their approach to form and materials, providing a contrast while at the same time evoking the complementarity of their oeuvres. The first section contained Gabo's delicate plastic works and was separated from Pevsner's darker and more somber work of oxidized tin and brass by loosely hung fish-net curtains. Gabo's translucent sculptures were placed before a dark grey wall on a large pedestal, with multiple spot lighting, while Pevsner's metal sculptures were placed in white, brightly lit galleries.

Gabo thought d'Harnoncourt's solution was very satisfactory. In a letter to the Museum's director of exhibitions, Monroe Wheeler, he expressed his satisfaction with the exhibition, applauding d'Harnoncourt's success in creating different atmospheres: "In all the thirty odd years of our artistic career, with many exhibitions in diverse countries on the continent, I have never seen a more comprehensive understanding of the way our work should be presented to the general public in order to give them the opportunity to grasp the essence of each of our works."[12] Careful attention to detail continued to the stanchions used to protect the works. D'Harnoncourt selected a design made of wire for a light effect and to echo the elegant delicacy of the plastic constructions.[13]

Critics were sensitive to d'Harnoncourt's creation of vistas. Eleanor Bittermann of *Architectural Forum* wrote, "The exhibition is handsomely presented, continuing René d'Harnoncourt's tradition of open-vista grouping."[14] In the *Herald Tribune*, Carlyle Burrows agreed: "This show has been finely arranged by René d'Harnoncourt, the expert on display-planning, with a spaciousness which provides for intriguing vistas."[15]

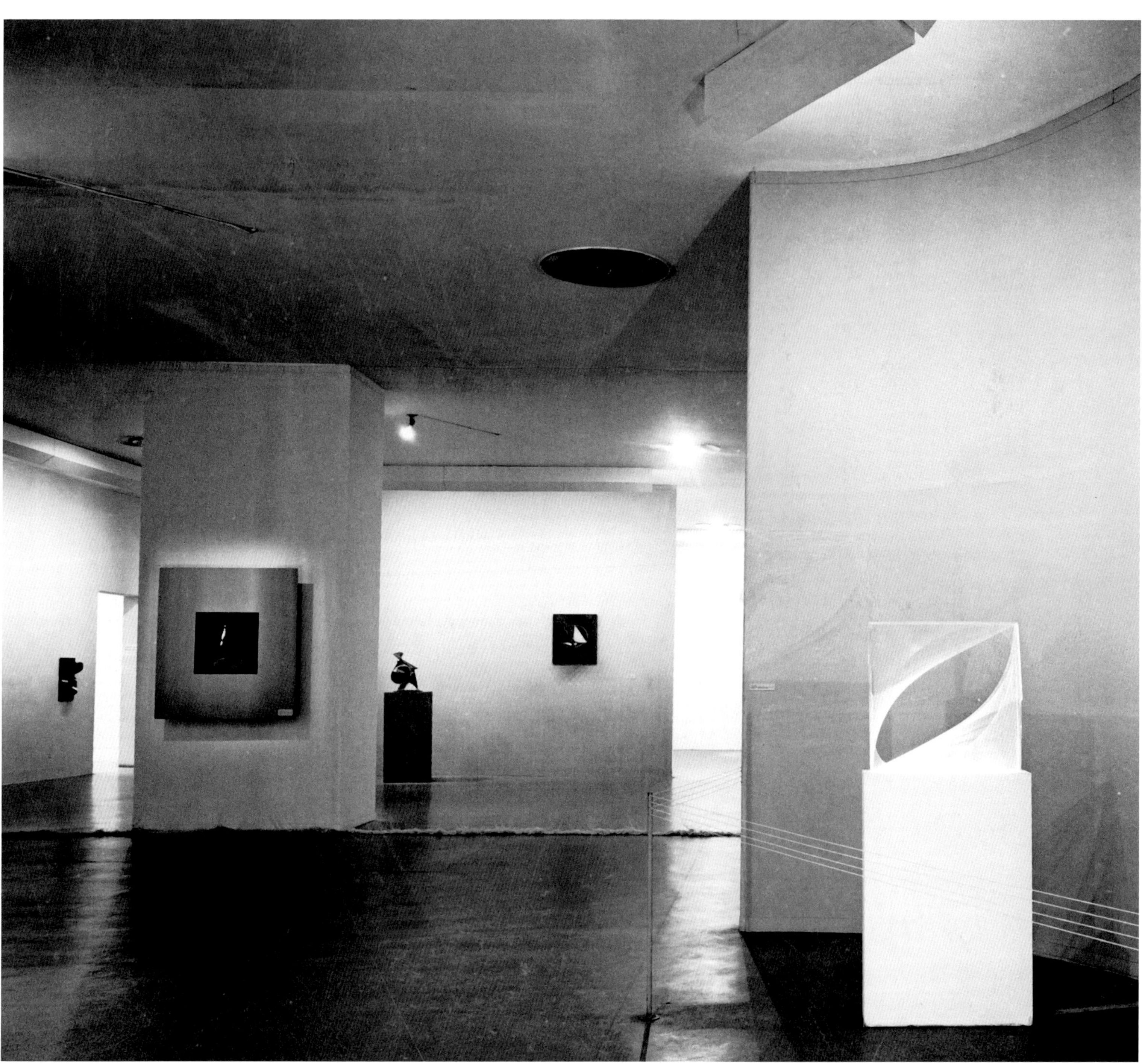

Installation view of the exhibition *Naum Gabo and Antoine Pevsner*, showing the fish-net curtains separating the two artists' respective galleries, 1948

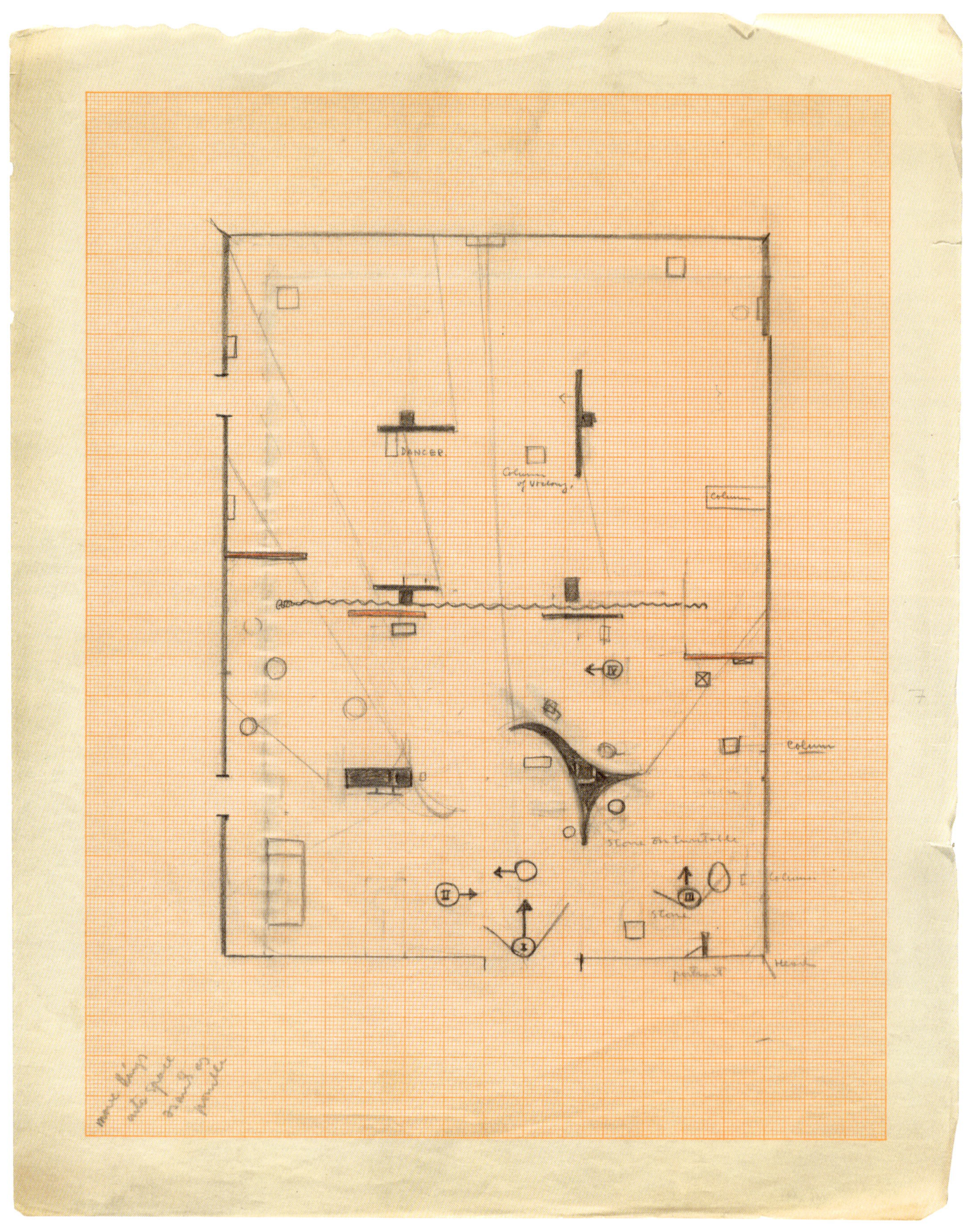

Floor plan of the exhibition, 1948

Scale sketches of works by Antoine Pevsner, 1948

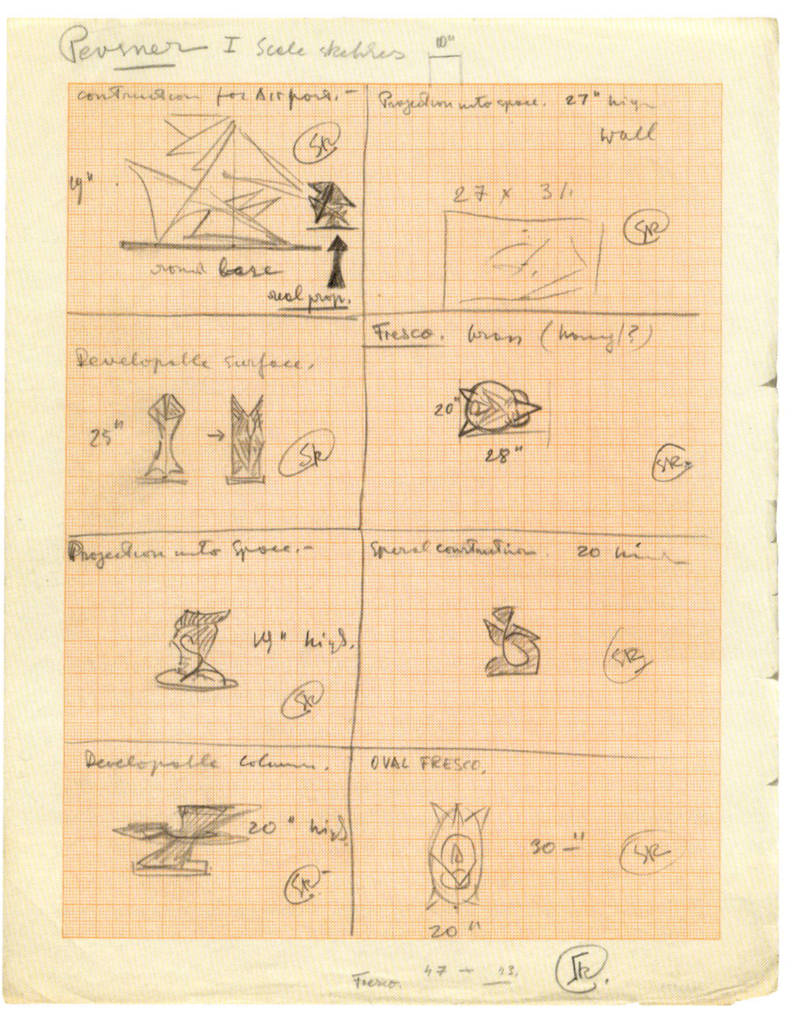

Vista of the exhibition *Naum Gabo and Antoine Pevsner*, 1948

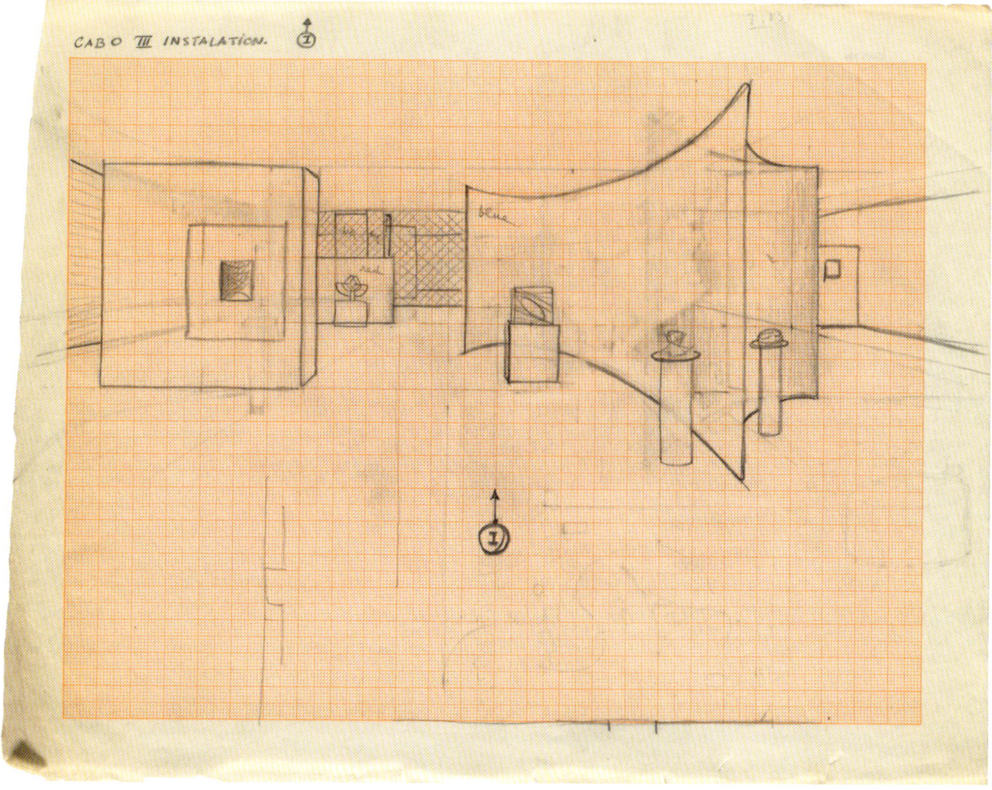

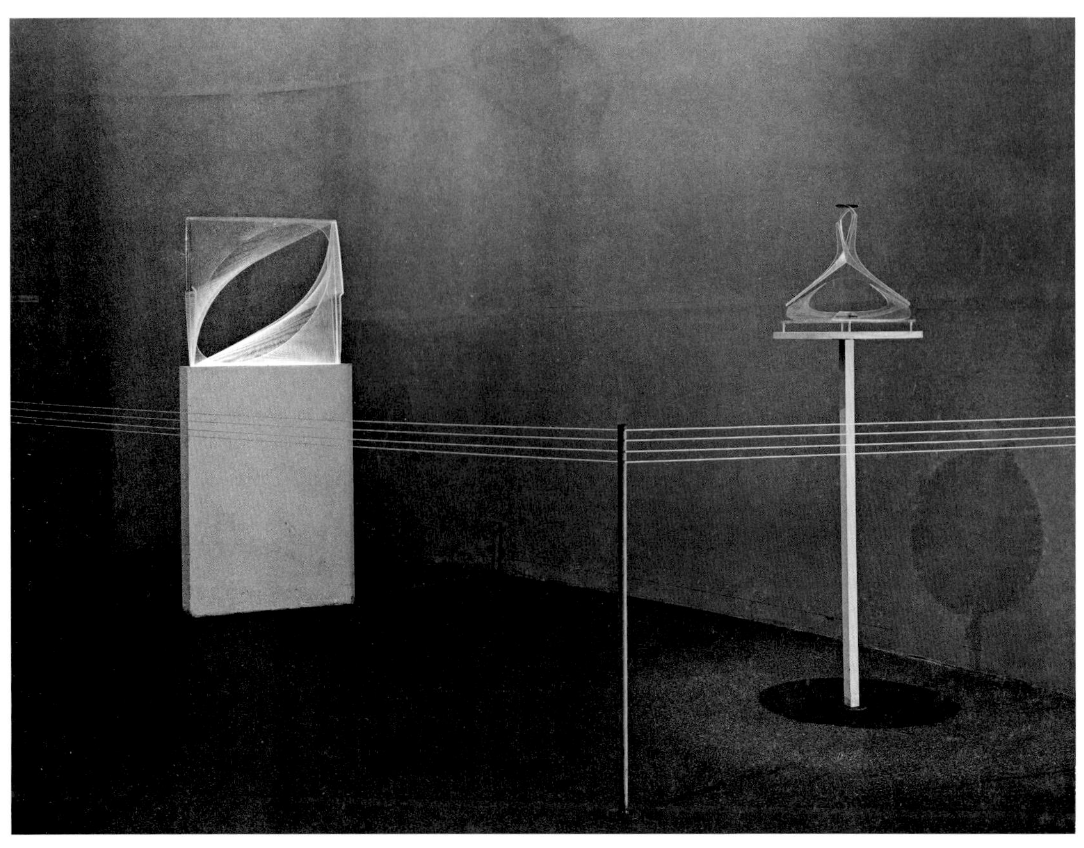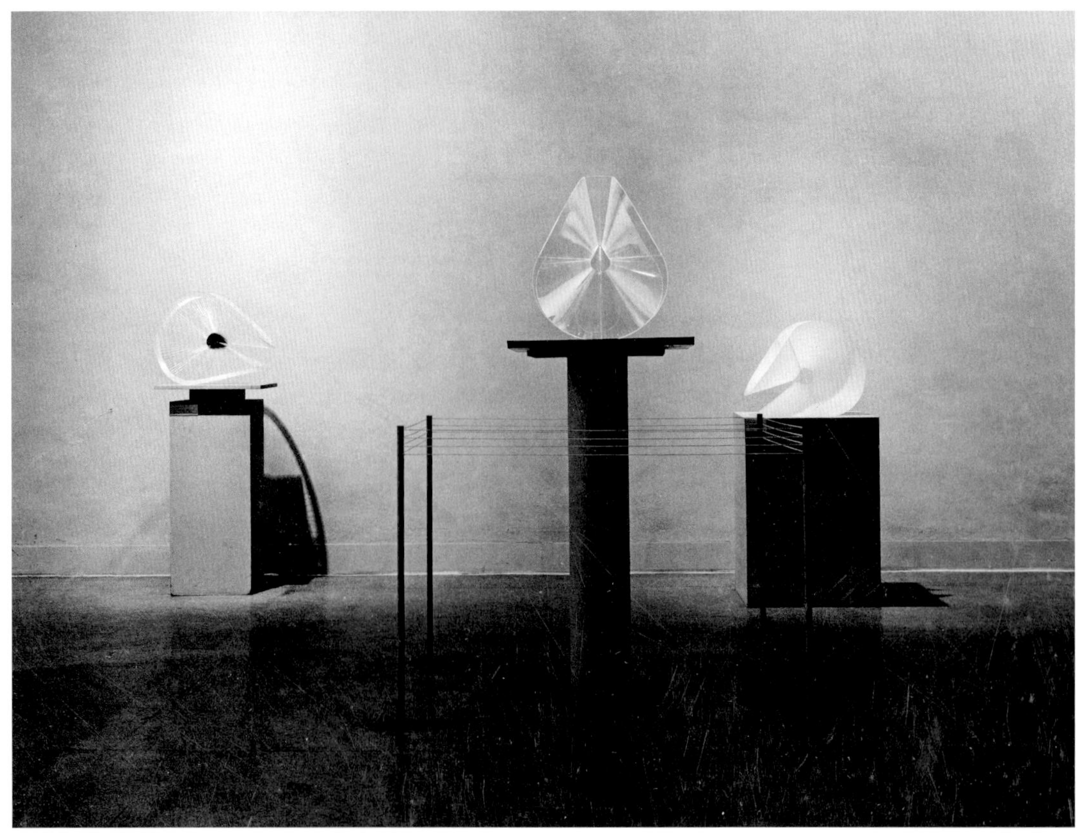

Installation views of works by
Naum Gabo, 1948

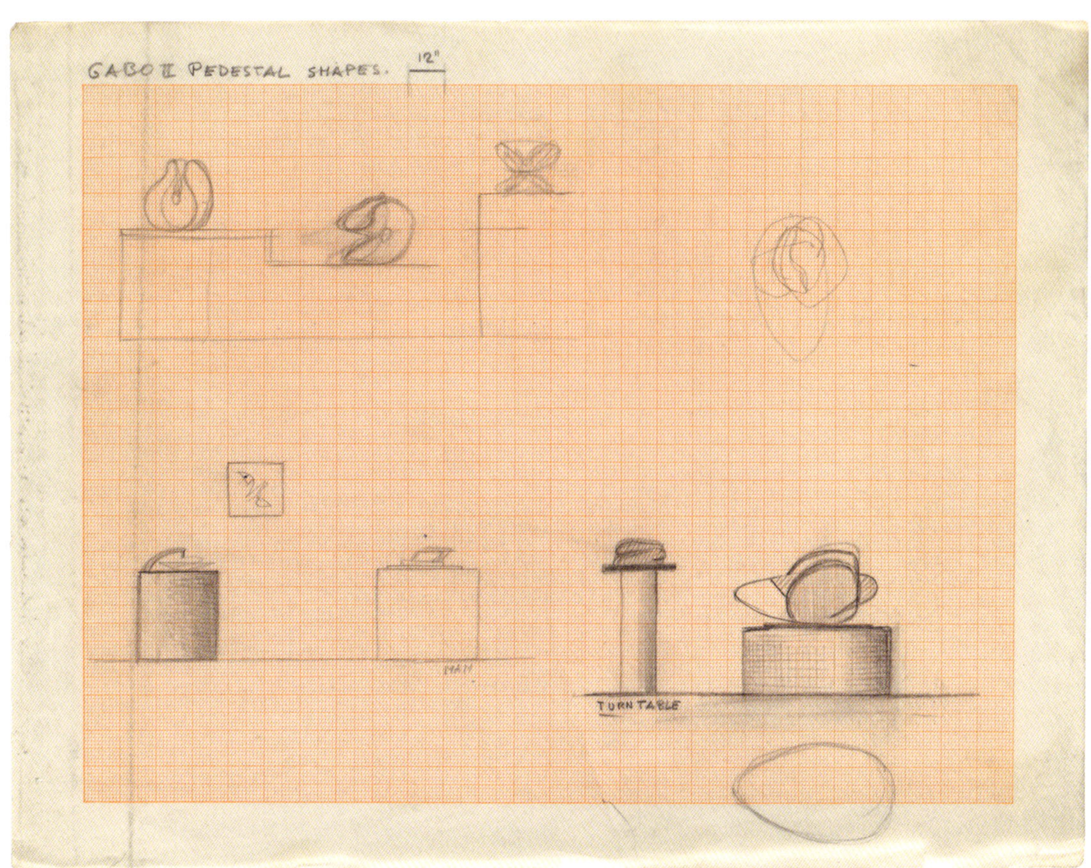

Sketch of pedestal shapes
for the exhibition, 1948

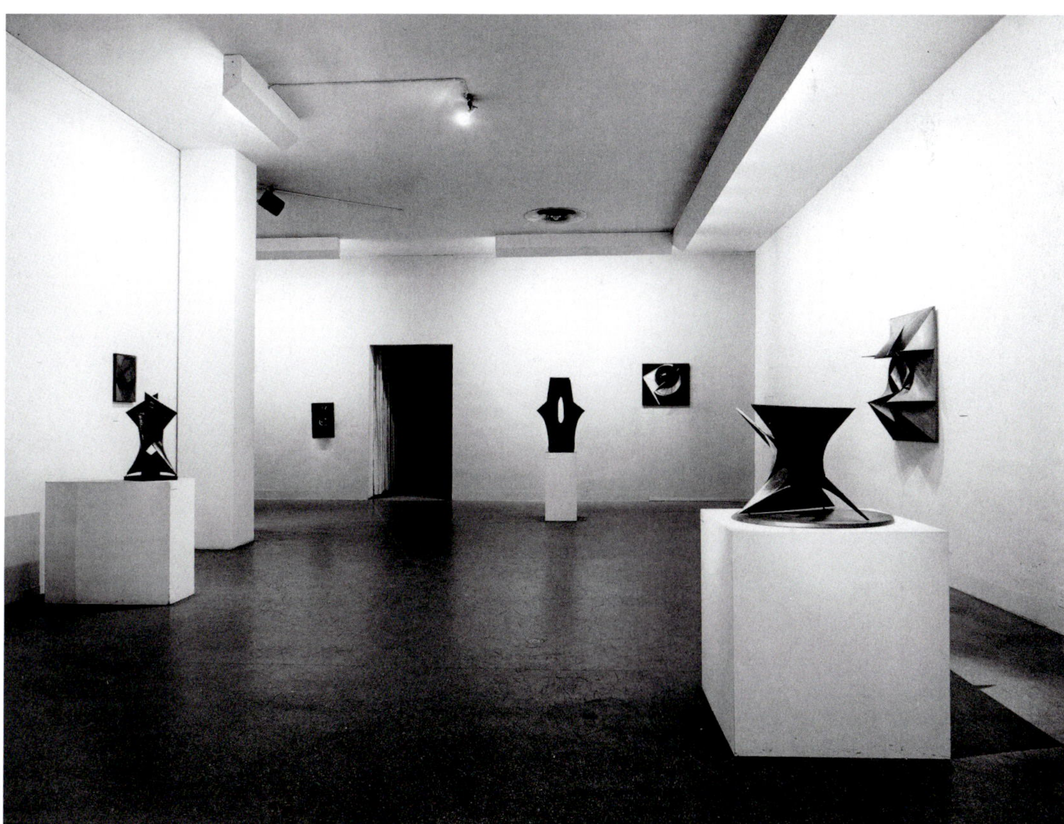

Installation view of works by
Antoine Pevsner, 1948

Elie Nadelman

MoMA Exhibition #388; October 5–November 28, 1948

CURATOR: Lincoln Kirstein
NUMBER OF WORKS: 43 sculptures in all media,
30 small plaster figures, and 6 drawings
LOCATION: Third floor
PUBLICATION: Lincoln Kirstein, *The Sculpture of Elie Nadelman*
(New York: The Museum of Modern Art, 1948)
CIRCULATING VENUES:
Baltimore Museum of Art, Baltimore, Maryland:
    December 19, 1948–February 15, 1949
Boston Institute of Contemporary Art, Boston, Massachusetts:
    March 1–April 15, 1949

Held two years after the death of the artist, the Elie Nadelman retrospective (d'Harnoncourt's second monographic exhibition devoted to sculpture) was assembled by Lincoln Kirstein, a longtime associate of the Museum and former member of its Advisory Committee. An expert on the work of Nadelman, Kirstein authored a monograph on the artist, the most definitive to date, which also served as the exhibition's catalogue. He selected some forty-five objects from the one thousand works, some in disrepair, found in the artist's home after his death.

D'Harnoncourt's installation evoked a refined elegance. A magnificent arrangement was presented at the entry to the show: a grouping of five classical figurines stood perched on three separate plinths in a niche, with behind them a floor-to-ceiling wall faux-finished to look like large panels of travertine and emblazoned with the artist's signature, a curlicue rendering of his initials. Later in the exhibition, a group of three seated figures perched atop a sheet-covered pedestal, in front of a curtained-off alcove, creating the impression of a very human and animate figure group.

The circulation path reflected the sinuousness of the human form as depicted by Nadelman. The pathway through the exhibition was roughly U-shaped, with the works arranged chronologically into groupings by style or theme, such as Neoclassic, the Circus, or Heroic, each of which d'Harnoncourt also identified on his drawings along with its influence, such as Tanagra Hellenistic Folk Art, Jugendstil, or Mannerism.

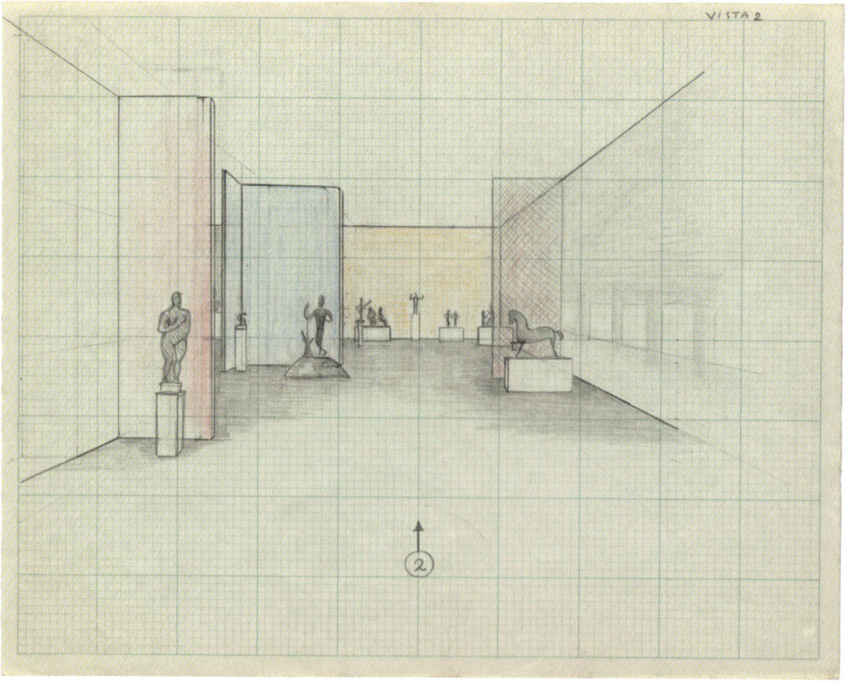

Exhibition vista, 1948

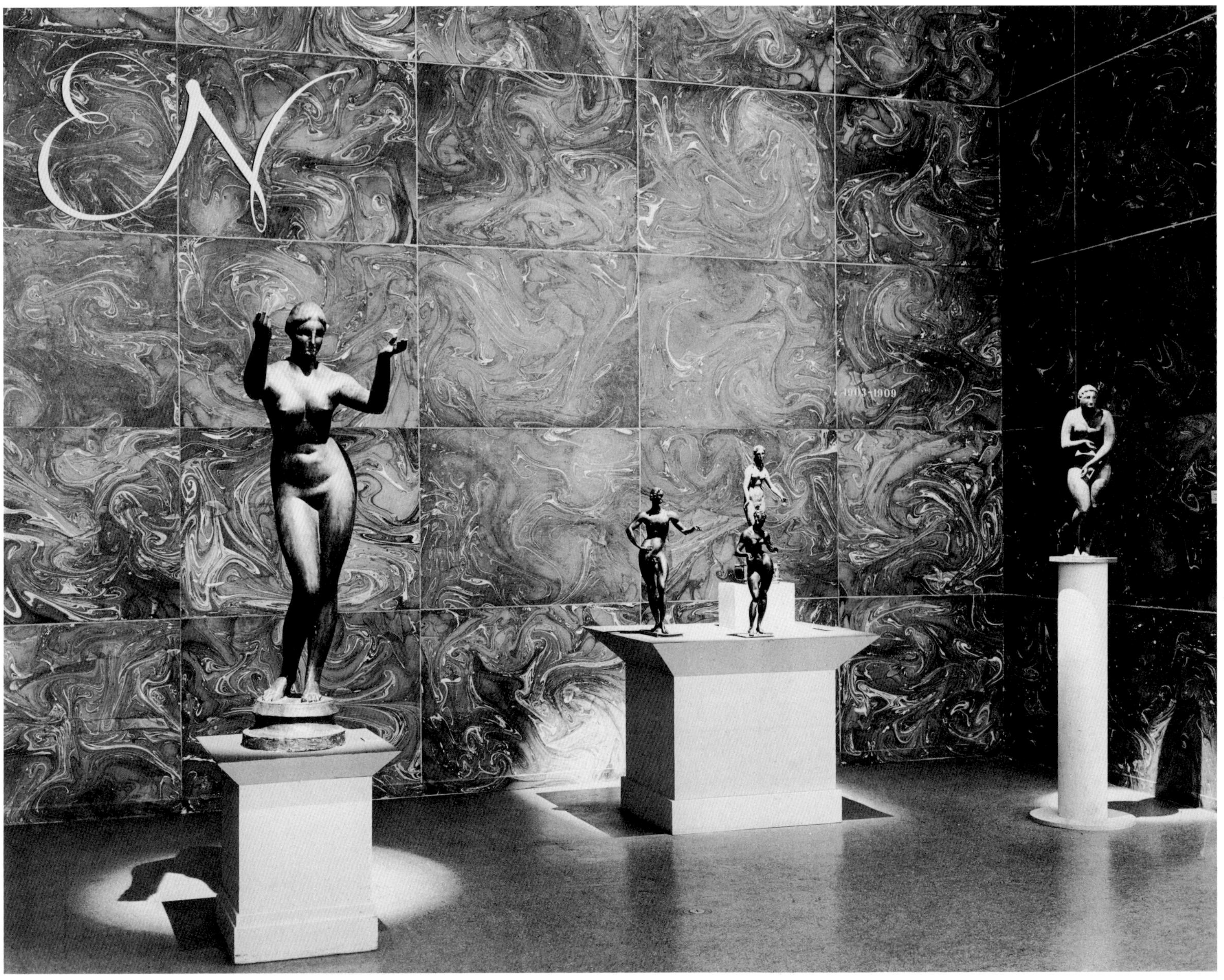

Entrance to the exhibition *Elie Nadelman*, 1948

These techniques did not go unnoticed. Critic Henry McBride wrote in the *New York Sun*: "The installation of the Nadelman show in the Museum is in itself a masterpiece; to be credited, I believe, to René d'Harnoncourt and Lincoln Kirstein. It has been dramatized to perfection, winning the visitor's respect at the outset with elegant bronzes and lovely marbles and then leading him without sense of shock to the astonishing satires of modern society which otherwise might have been difficult."[16] Kirstein credited his collaborator with the success of the exhibition, writing, "René had a strong visual sense, and his energy was adapted to the balance and arrangement of works which he exalted by their connection, combination, balance and surprise."[17]

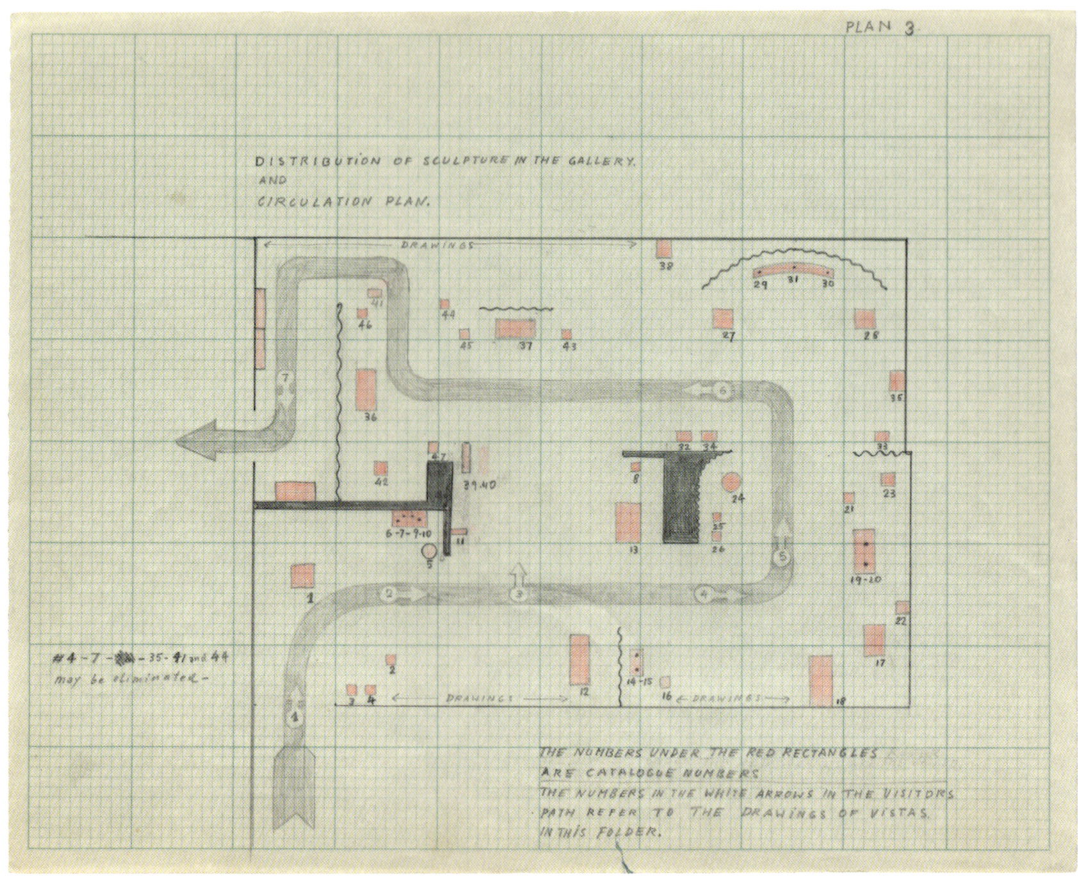

Floor plan illustrating the distribution of sculptures and the visitors' circulation path, 1948

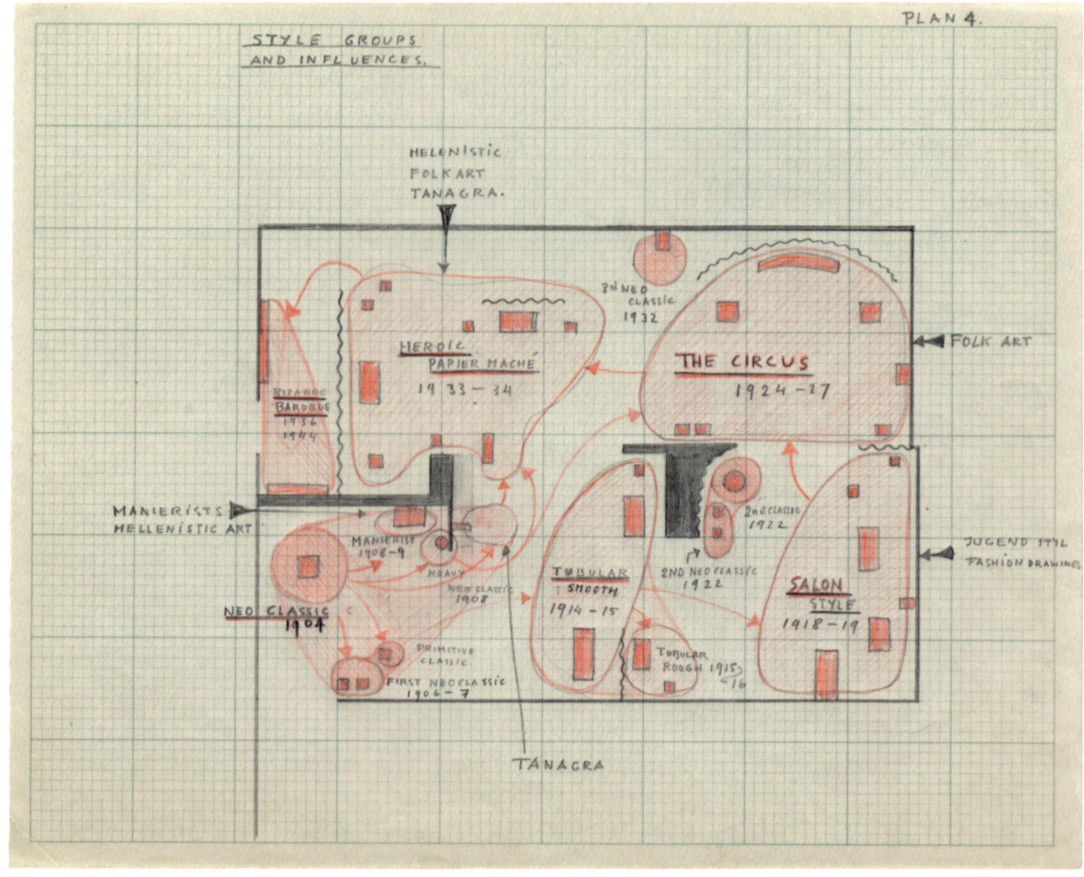

Floor plan showing style groups and influences in Nadelman's work, 1948

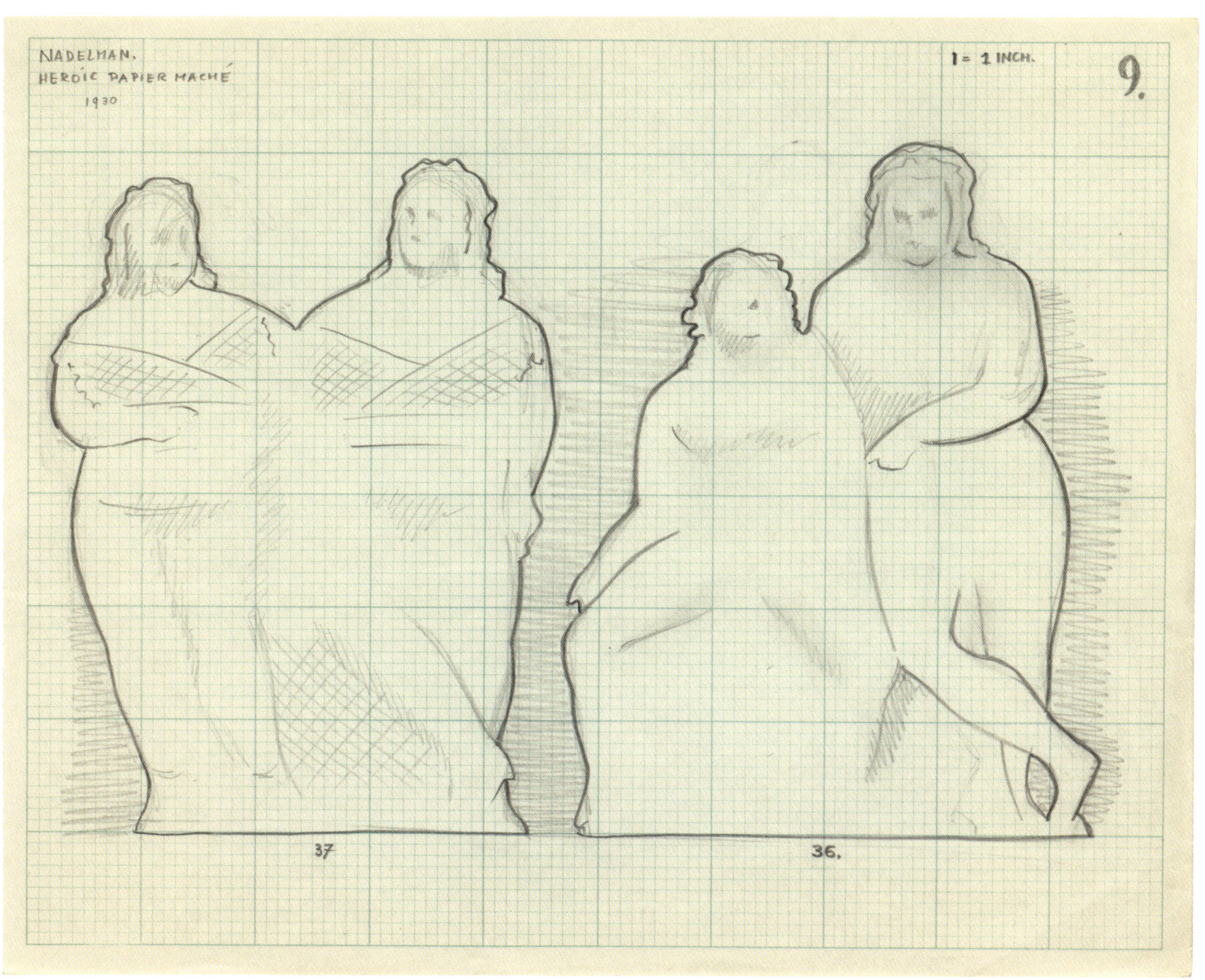

Sketch of Nadelman's "heroic papier maché" sculptures, 1948

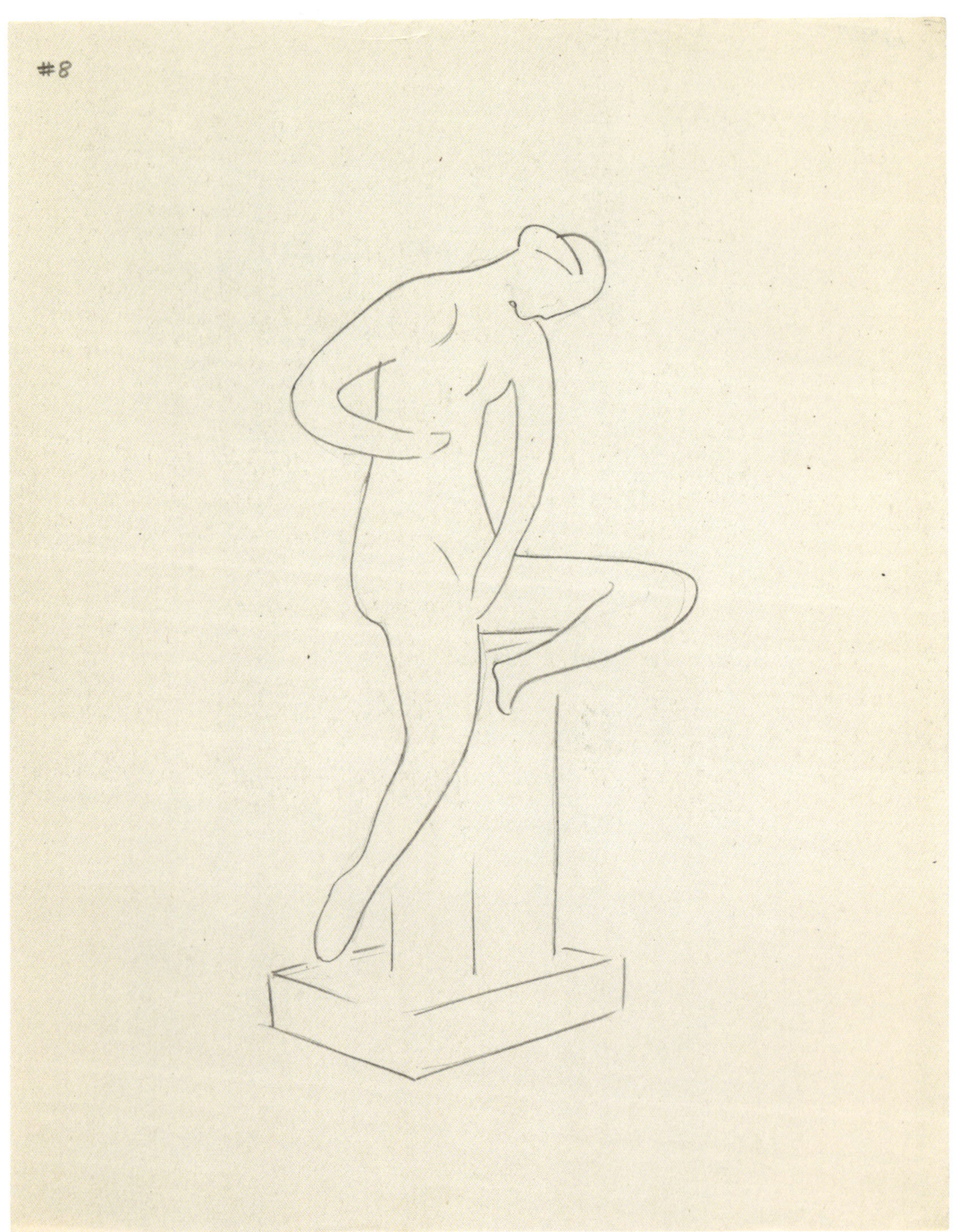

Sketch of a female nude, 1948

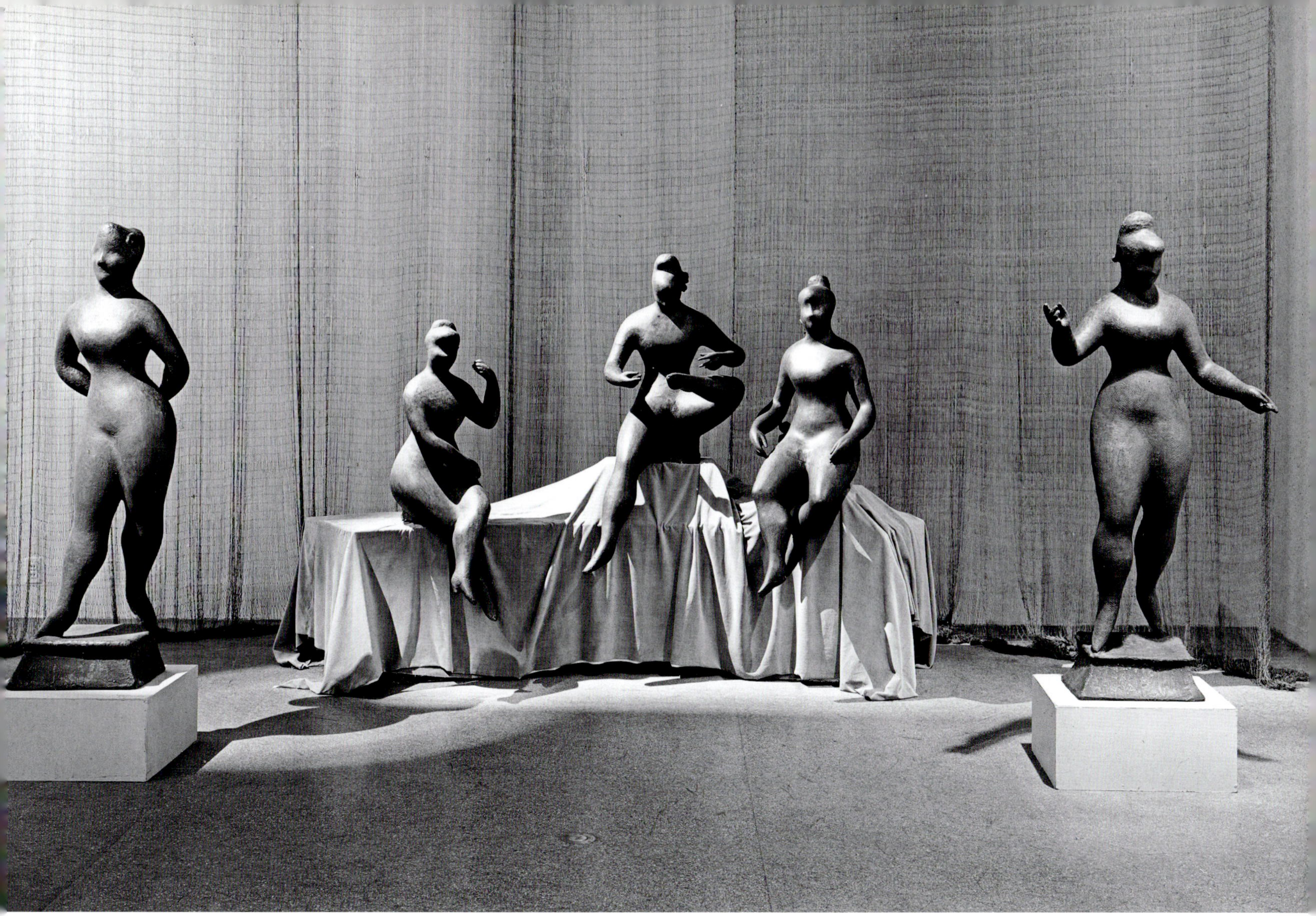

Installation view of sculptures installed on
multi-level pedestals, with curtain behind, and
corresponding exhibition vista, 1948

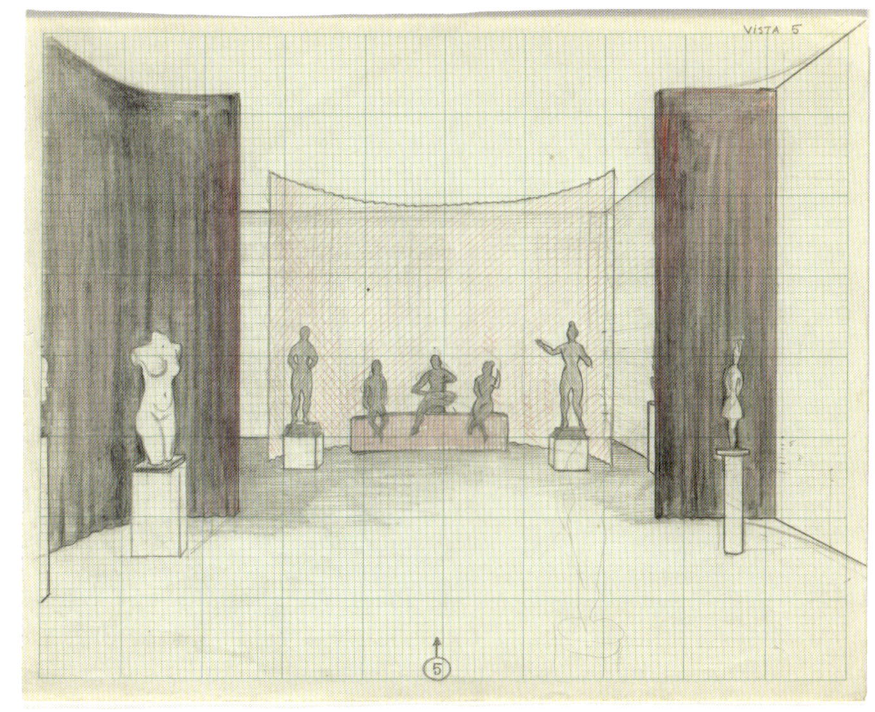

Timeless Aspects of Modern Art

MoMA Exhibition #393; November 16, 1948–January 23, 1949

CURATOR: René d'Harnoncourt
NUMBER OF WORKS: 56
LOCATION: Ground floor

Timeless Aspects of Modern Art brought together works of modern art, largely from the museum's permanent collection and some borrowed from other institutions, with works from other eras and cultures. They were grouped by affinity—Structure and Abstraction; Stylization and Emotional Content; Volume and Form; Fantastic and Mysterious—to illustrate that certain characteristics are, as the title of the show indicated, "timeless" and recurrent across eras and areas.

This premise required d'Harnoncourt to emphasize affinities among the works. In the section on stylization and emotional content, he paired a Romanesque crucifix with a painting of Christ by Georges Rouault; in the part devoted to volume and form, d'Harnoncourt made an elegant juxtaposition of Constantin Brancusi's *Bird in Space* with an ancient fertility symbol in the foreground, while behind them, in the Fantastic and Mysterious section, native Alaskan masks were installed next to an abstraction by Joan Miró, offering a similarity in spirit and technique.

In addition to the didactic devices and groupings by affinity, d'Harnoncourt also used dramatic lighting techniques. The Spanish Gothic cross was lit from below to heighten its emotional impact. Its lender Gordon B. Washburn, director of the Rhode Island School of Design Museum of Art, wrote that the lighting of the work was superb, better than in their past presentation, and that he hoped one day to imitate the technique. D'Harnoncourt replied that it was "on the dramatic side which I thought was permissible since we specifically wanted to show its content of religious fervor. I imagine that in its original setting [it] was lit up in a somewhat similar way, namely by candles from below."[18]

With this exhibition, d'Harnoncourt chose once again to separate the works from the exhibition didactics. Visitors were handed a brochure that not only included the floor plan of the exhibition with miniature reproductions of the works, but also situated them on both a timeline and a map of the world. In this way, it served to fully demonstrate his thesis while giving visitors the opportunity to focus on experiencing the works themselves and their juxtapositions, without the distracting presence of complex wall text.

The exhibition received very mixed reviews. One writer compared d'Harnoncourt's notion of affinity to Carl Jung's theory of the Collective Unconscious.[19] The critic for the *New York Times* empathized with d'Harnoncourt's intentions, though he was not entirely convinced by the result:

> This may well prove to be one of the most controversial in all [of MoMA's] exhibitions. As an exploration in depth of the affinities of the art of all ages, the exhibition is certainly not conclusive. As a thought-provoking and stimulating assemblage of material full of suggestion, and as an attempt to present certain ideas to aid the visiting public in grasping the fact that modern art is not a matter of spontaneous combustion without forbears, it is an arresting exhibition. With many of the details one might quarrel, but with the educational intent one must sympathize.[20]

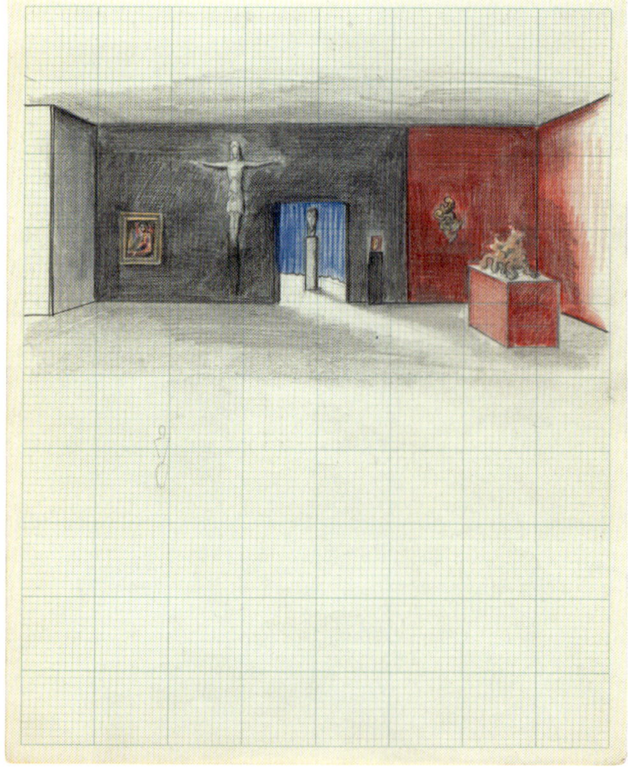

Vista of the exhibition showing Georges Rouault's *Christ Mocked by Soldiers* (1932), paired with a Romanesque *Christ on a Cross* (c. 1300 AD), 1948

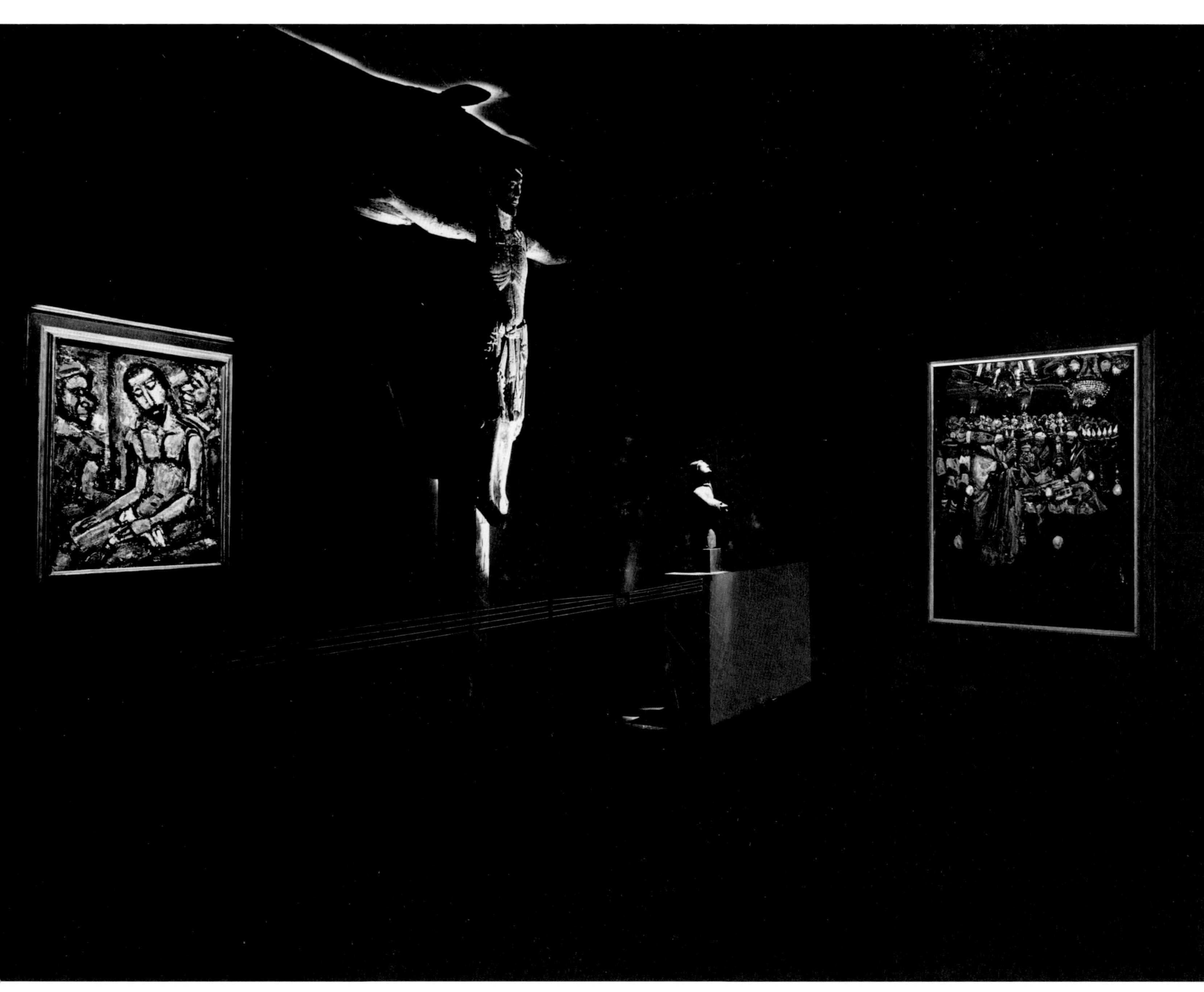

Installation view of the exhibition, showing d'Harnoncourt's
dramatic use of spot lighting, 1948

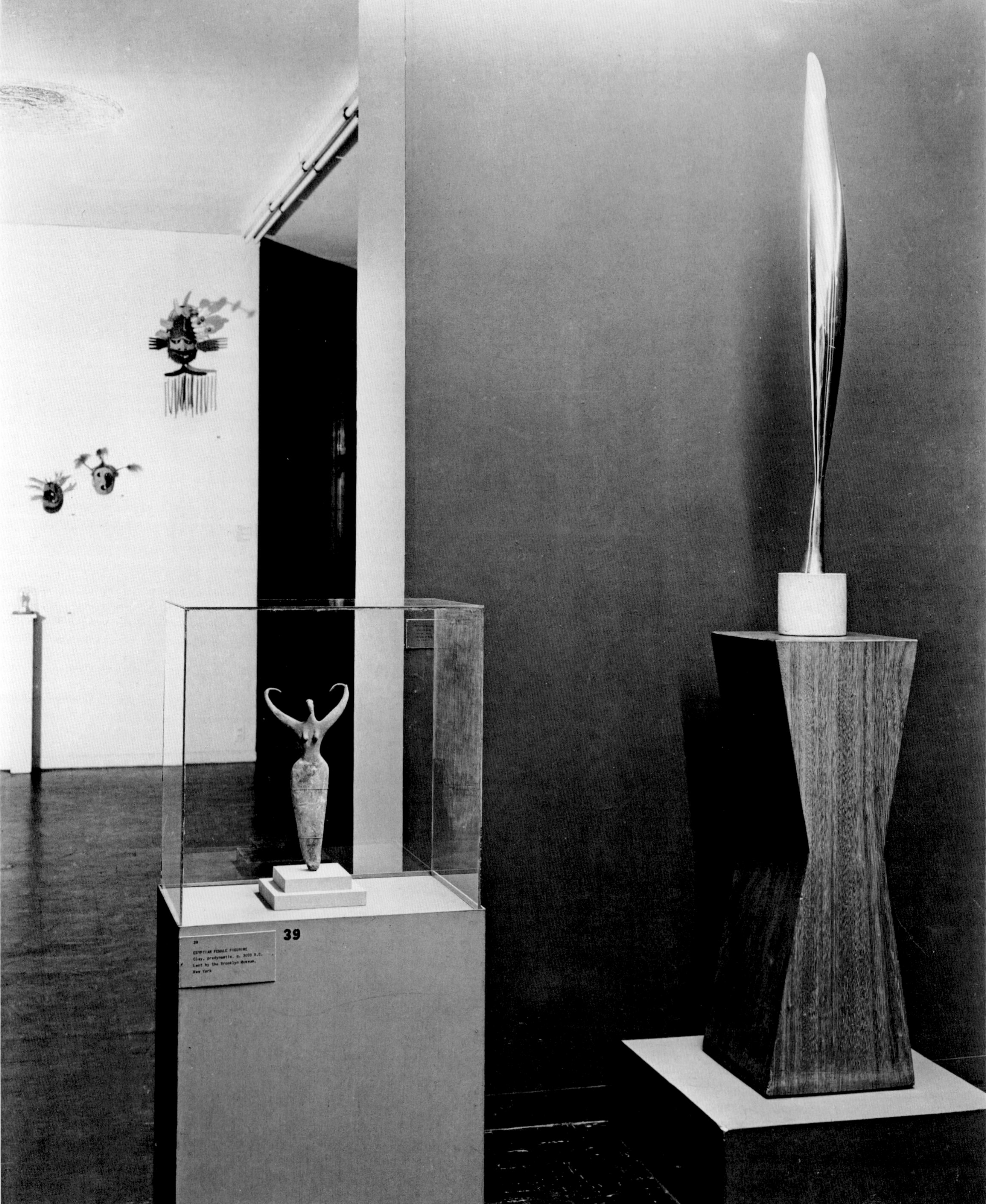
39
EGYPTIAN FEMALE FIGURINE
Clay, predynastic, c. 3000 B.C.
Lent by the Brooklyn Museum,
New York
39

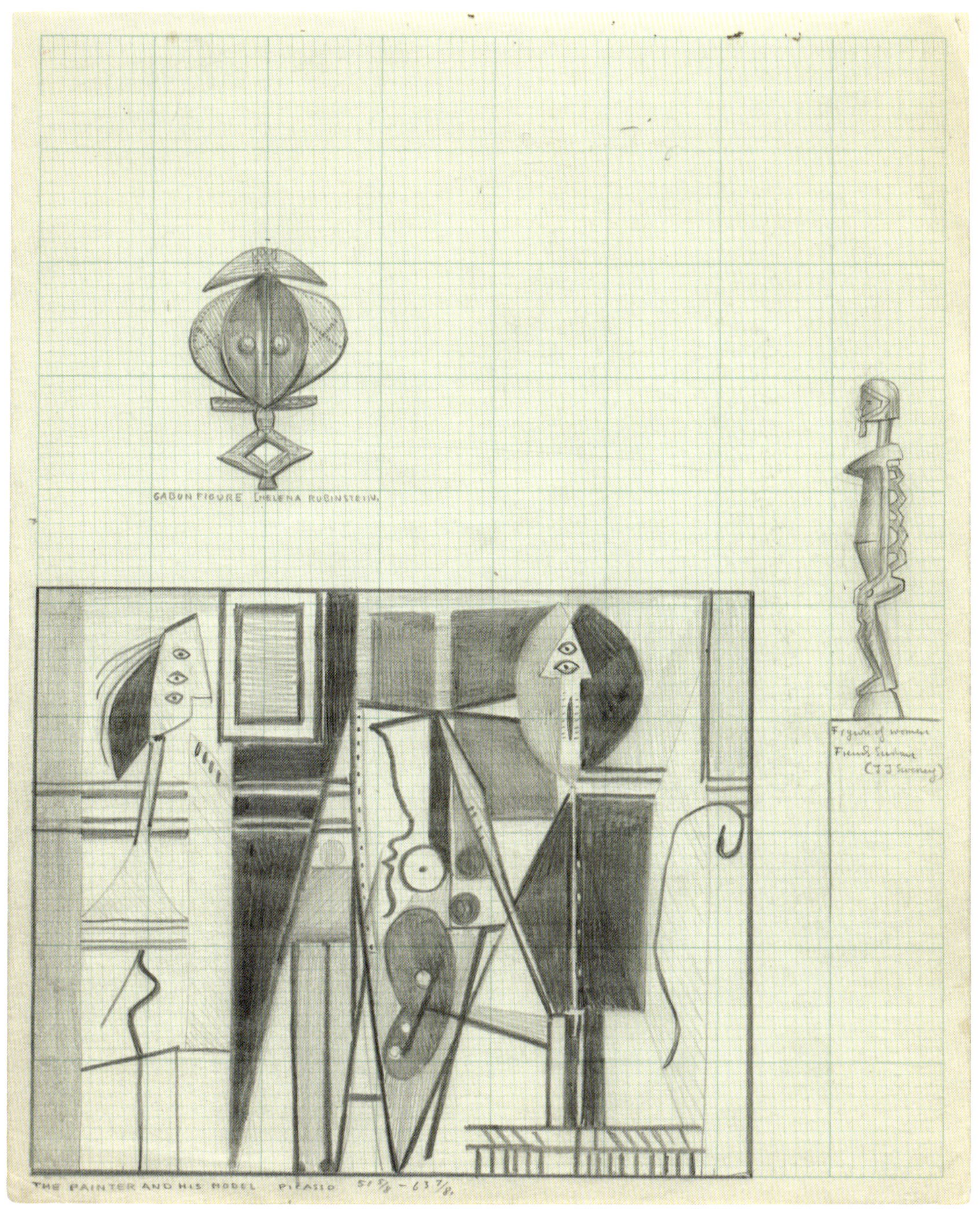

Opposite: Installation view of the exhibition showing Constantin Brancusi's bronze *Bird in Space* (1919) and an Egyptian female figurine (c. 3600 BCE) with native Alaskan masks in the background, 1948

Above: Scale drawing, grouping Pablo Picasso's *The Painter and his Model* (1928) with nineteenth-century wooden figures from Gabon and Sudan, 1948

But Emily Genauer, a long-time, vociferous critic of the Museum, praised the effort, calling it its most constructive exhibit. She applauded the fact that "the Museum of Modern Art, which in the past has made only the most mincing and reluctant of half-steps in the direction of the skeptical lay-public, now is prepared to go the whole way." She echoed d'Harnoncourt's intentions for her readers: "The point and plan of the show . . . demonstrate what René d'Harnoncourt, its director, describes as 'affinities and analogies' between modern art and that of other eras and cultures, and thereby 'to act as a reminder that such "modern" means of expression as exaggeration, distortion and abstraction have been used by artists since the very beginning of civilization to express their ideas and emotions.'"[21] She went on to say that the exhibition was "brilliantly installed," and requested that in a reduced form it should become a permanent component of the museum—a suggestion voiced by several other admirers.

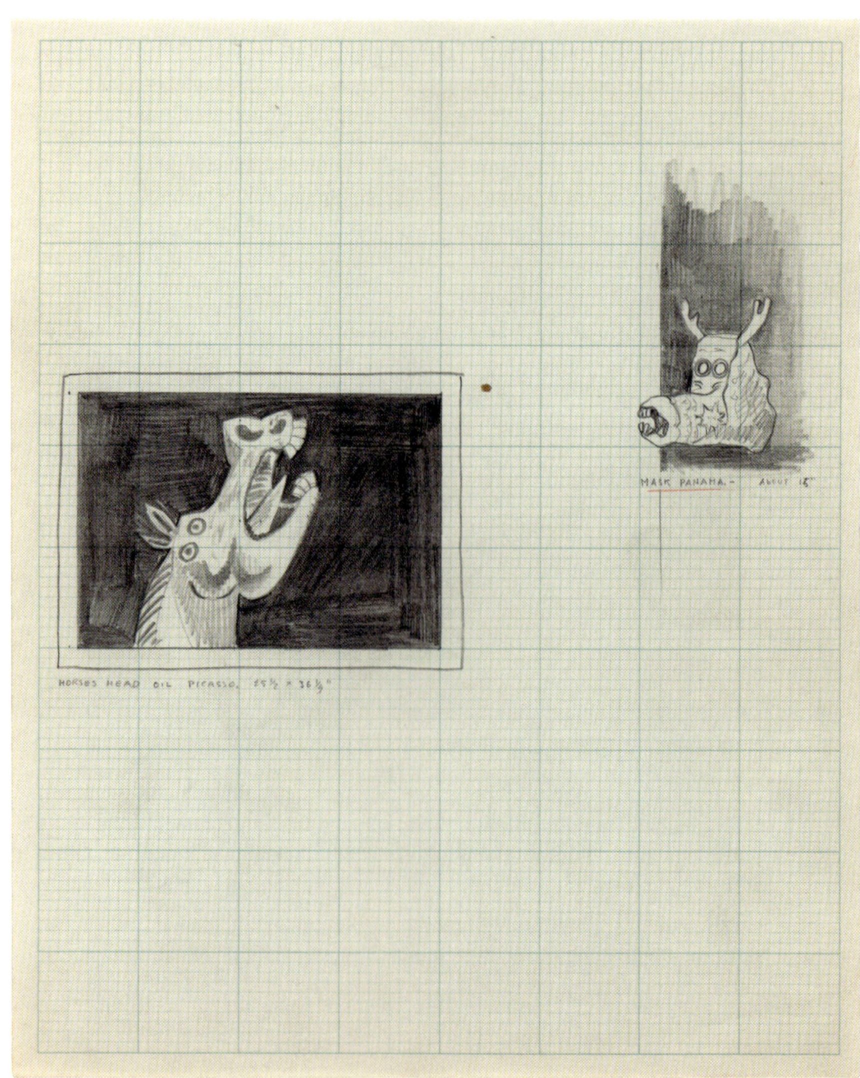

Left: Scale drawing, pairing Pablo Picasso's *Horse (Study for Guernica)* (1937) with a nineteenth-century bark cloth mask from Panama representing a deer, 1948

Opposite: Scale drawing, pairing Giorgio de Chirico's *Delight of the Poet* (c. 1913) with a group of marble Cycladic figurines from the third millennium BCE, 1948

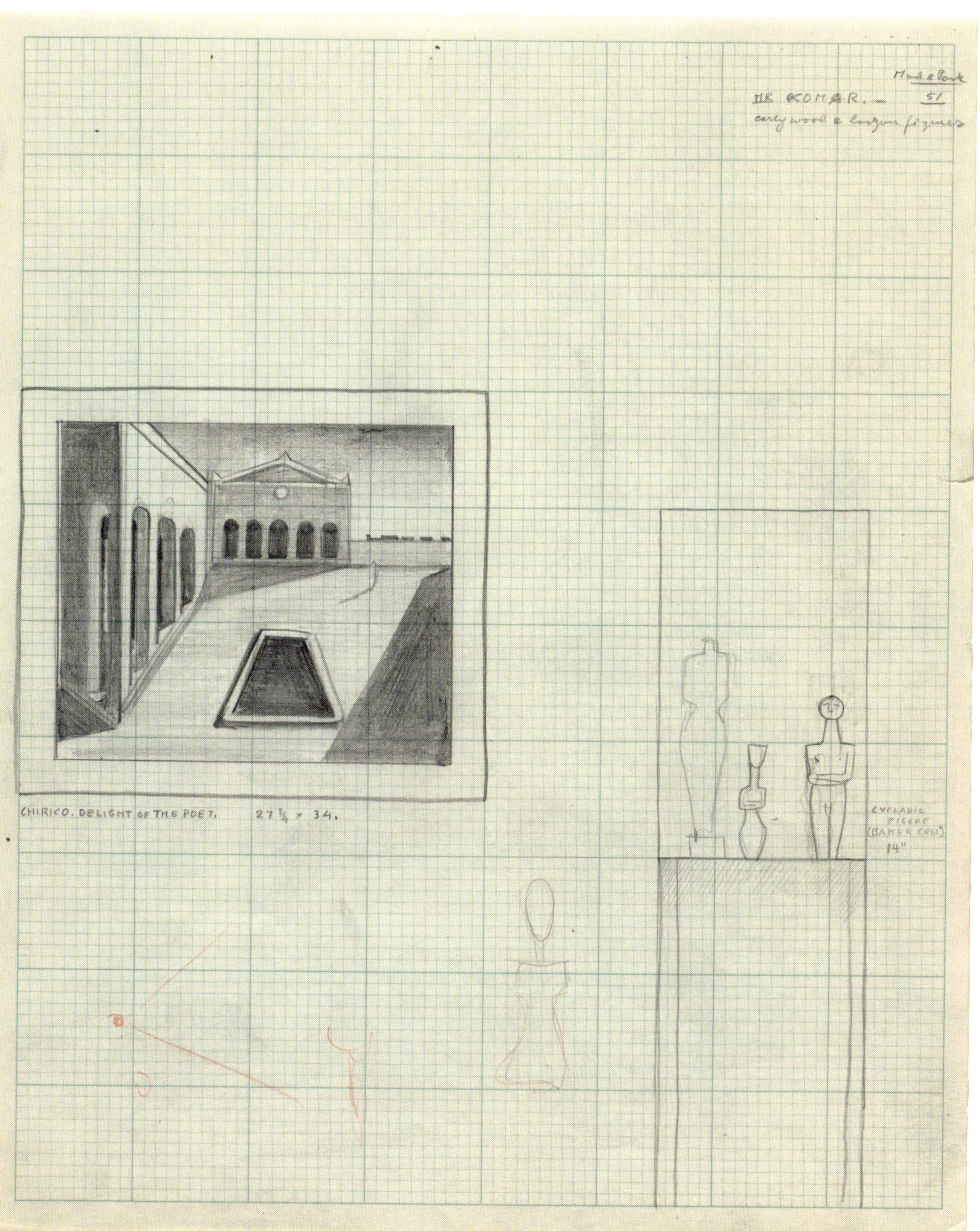

Mod & Cont
IIR KOMAR. —   51
early wood & bronze figures
CHIRICO. DELIGHT OF THE POET.   27 ¾ × 34.
CYCLADIC
FIGURE
(BAKER COLL)
14"

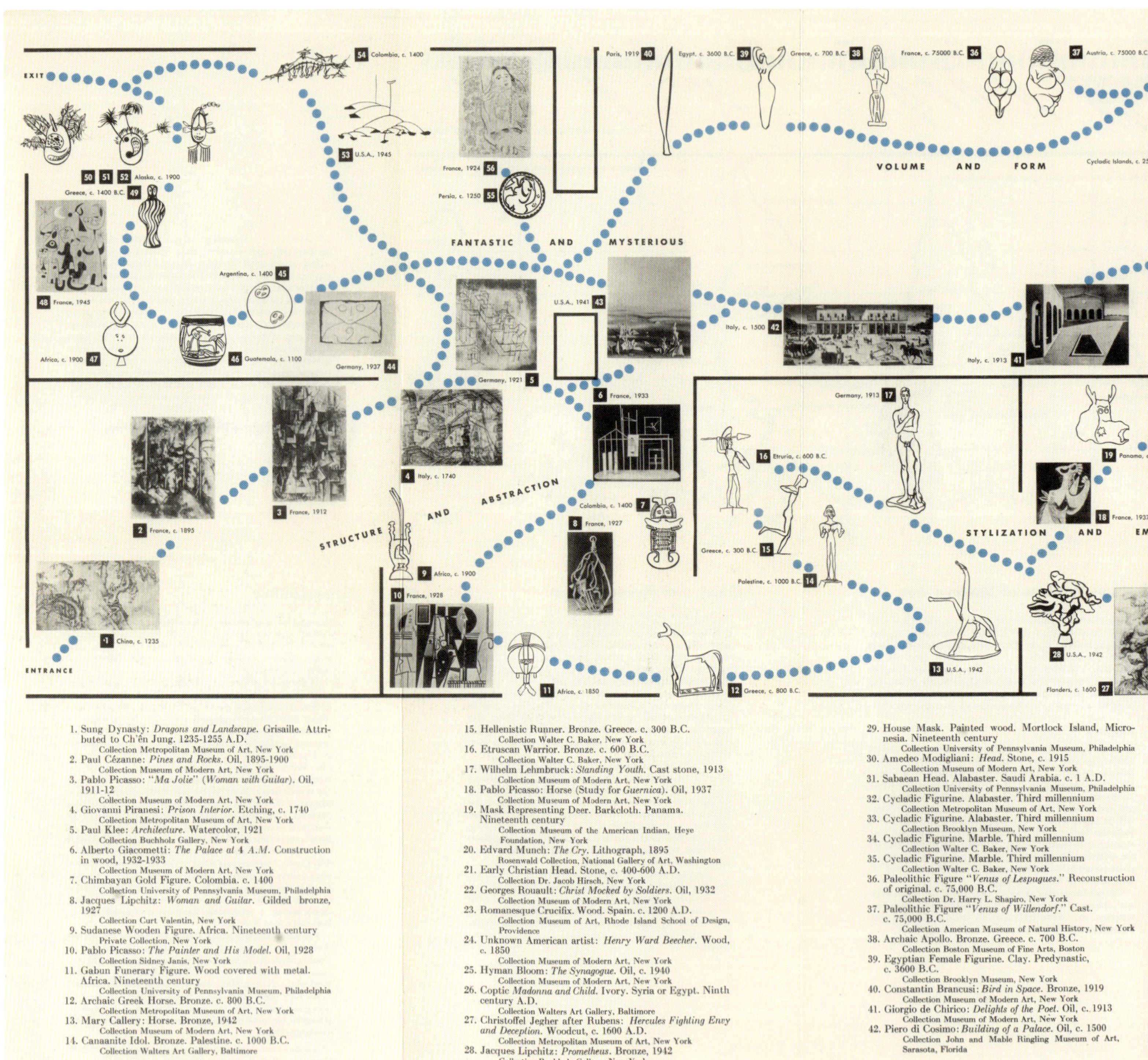

Brochure with a map of the exhibition, 1948

1. Sung Dynasty: *Dragons and Landscape.* Grisaille. Attributed to Ch'ên Jung. 1235-1255 A.D.
   Collection Metropolitan Museum of Art, New York
2. Paul Cézanne: *Pines and Rocks.* Oil, 1895-1900
   Collection Museum of Modern Art, New York
3. Pablo Picasso: *"Ma Jolie"* (*Woman with Guitar*). Oil, 1911-12
   Collection Museum of Modern Art, New York
4. Giovanni Piranesi: *Prison Interior.* Etching, c. 1740
   Collection Metropolitan Museum of Art, New York
5. Paul Klee: *Architecture.* Watercolor, 1921
   Collection Buchholz Gallery, New York
6. Alberto Giacometti: *The Palace at 4 A.M.* Construction in wood, 1932-1933
   Collection Museum of Modern Art, New York
7. Chimbayan Gold Figure. Colombia. c. 1400
   Collection University of Pennsylvania Museum, Philadelphia
8. Jacques Lipchitz: *Woman and Guitar.* Gilded bronze, 1927
   Collection Curt Valentin, New York
9. Sudanese Wooden Figure. Africa. Nineteenth century
   Private Collection, New York
10. Pablo Picasso: *The Painter and His Model.* Oil, 1928
    Collection Sidney Janis, New York
11. Gabun Funerary Figure. Wood covered with metal. Africa. Nineteenth century
    Collection University of Pennsylvania Museum, Philadelphia
12. Archaic Greek Horse. Bronze. c. 800 B.C.
    Collection Metropolitan Museum of Art, New York
13. Mary Callery: *Horse.* Bronze, 1942
    Collection Museum of Modern Art, New York
14. Canaanite Idol. Bronze. Palestine. c. 1000 B.C.
    Collection Walters Art Gallery, Baltimore

15. Hellenistic Runner. Bronze. Greece. c. 300 B.C.
    Collection Walter C. Baker, New York
16. Etruscan Warrior. Bronze. c. 600 B.C.
    Collection Walter C. Baker, New York
17. Wilhelm Lehmbruck: *Standing Youth.* Cast stone, 1913
    Collection Museum of Modern Art, New York
18. Pablo Picasso: Horse (Study for *Guernica*). Oil, 1937
    Collection Museum of Modern Art, New York
19. Mask Representing Deer. Barkcloth. Panama. Nineteenth century
    Collection Museum of the American Indian, Heye Foundation, New York
20. Edvard Munch: *The Cry.* Lithograph, 1895
    Rosenwald Collection, National Gallery of Art, Washington
21. Early Christian Head. Stone, c. 400-600 A.D.
    Collection Dr. Jacob Hirsch, New York
22. Georges Rouault: *Christ Mocked by Soldiers.* Oil, 1932
    Collection Museum of Modern Art, New York
23. Romanesque Crucifix. Wood. Spain. c. 1200 A.D.
    Collection Museum of Art, Rhode Island School of Design, Providence
24. Unknown American artist: *Henry Ward Beecher.* Wood, c. 1850
    Collection Museum of Modern Art, New York
25. Hyman Bloom: *The Synagogue.* Oil, c. 1940
    Collection Museum of Modern Art, New York
26. Coptic *Madonna and Child.* Ivory. Syria or Egypt. Ninth century A.D.
    Collection Walters Art Gallery, Baltimore
27. Christoffel Jegher after Rubens: *Hercules Fighting Envy and Deception.* Woodcut, c. 1600 A.D.
    Collection Metropolitan Museum of Art, New York
28. Jacques Lipchitz: *Prometheus.* Bronze, 1942
    Collection Buchholz Gallery, New York

29. House Mask. Painted wood. Mortlock Island, Micronesia. Nineteenth century
    Collection University of Pennsylvania Museum, Philadelphia
30. Amedeo Modigliani: *Head.* Stone, c. 1915
    Collection Museum of Modern Art, New York
31. Sabaean Head. Alabaster. Saudi Arabia. c. 1 A.D.
    Collection University of Pennsylvania Museum, Philadelphia
32. Cycladic Figurine. Alabaster. Third millennium
    Collection Metropolitan Museum of Art, New York
33. Cycladic Figurine. Alabaster. Third millennium
    Collection Brooklyn Museum, New York
34. Cycladic Figurine. Marble. Third millennium
    Collection Walter C. Baker, New York
35. Cycladic Figurine. Marble. Third millennium
    Collection Walter C. Baker, New York
36. Paleolithic Figure *"Venus of Lespugues."* Reconstruction of original. c. 75,000 B.C.
    Collection Dr. Harry L. Shapiro, New York
37. Paleolithic Figure *"Venus of Willendorf."* Cast. c. 75,000 B.C.
    Collection American Museum of Natural History, New York
38. Archaic Apollo. Bronze. Greece. c. 700 B.C.
    Collection Boston Museum of Fine Arts, Boston
39. Egyptian Female Figurine. Clay. Predynastic, c. 3600 B.C.
    Collection Brooklyn Museum, New York
40. Constantin Brancusi: *Bird in Space.* Bronze, 1919
    Collection Museum of Modern Art, New York
41. Giorgio de Chirico: *Delights of the Poet.* Oil, c. 1913
    Collection Museum of Modern Art, New York
42. Piero di Cosimo: *Building of a Palace.* Oil, c. 1500
    Collection John and Mable Ringling Museum of Art, Sarasota, Florida

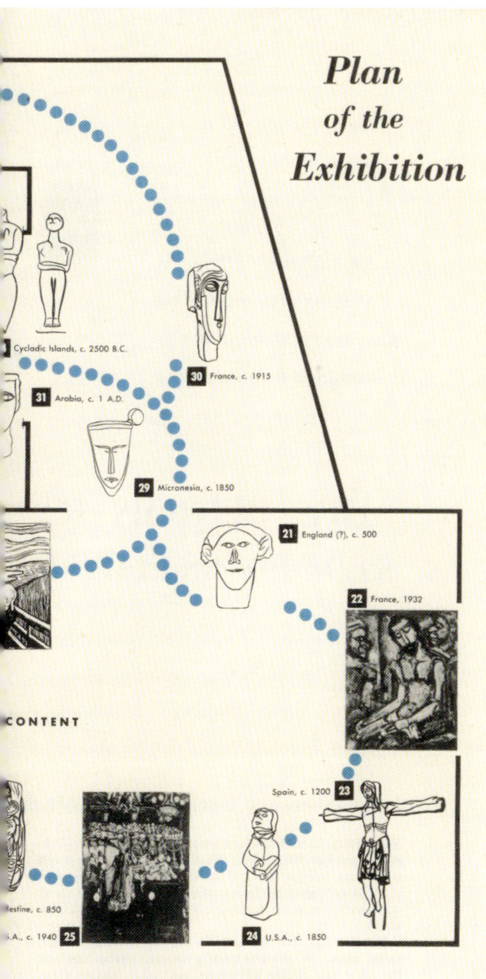

43. Yves Tanguy: *The Five Strangers*. Oil, 1941
    Collection Wadsworth Atheneum, Hartford
44. Paul Klee: *Letter Ghost*. Gouache, 1937
    Collection Museum of Modern Art, New York
45. Disk with Two Faces. Copper. Northern Argentina. Before 1500 A.D.
    Collection Museum of the American Indian, Heye Foundation, New York
46. Maya Painted Bowl. Ceramic. Guatemala. Eleventh or twelfth century A.D.
    Collection University of Pennsylvania Museum, Philadelphia
47. African Mask. Wood. Ivory Coast. Nineteenth century
    Collection Brooklyn Museum, New York
48. Joan Miro: *Woman in the Night*. Gouache on canvas. 1945
    Collection Mrs. Pierre Matisse, New York
49. Mycenaean *Figurine*. Clay. c. 1400 B.C.
    Collection Metropolitan Museum of Art, New York
50. Eskimo Mask. Wood. Nineteenth century
    Collection University of Pennsylvania Museum, Philadelphia
51. Eskimo Mask. Wood. Nineteenth century
    Collection American Museum of Natural History, New York
52. Eskimo Mask. Wood. Nineteenth century
    Collection Museum of the American Indian, Heye Foundation, New York
53. Alexander Calder: *Petals and Yellow Half-Moon*. Mobile. 1945
    Private Collection, New York
54. Chibcha Gold Ornaments. Colombia. c. 1400 A.D.
    Collection University of Pennsylvania Museum, Philadelphia
55. Persian Deep Plate. Rayy Ware. c. 1250 A.D.
    Collection Walters Art Gallery, Baltimore
56. Henri Matisse: *Arabesque I*. Transfer lithograph, 1924
    Collection Museum of Modern Art, New York

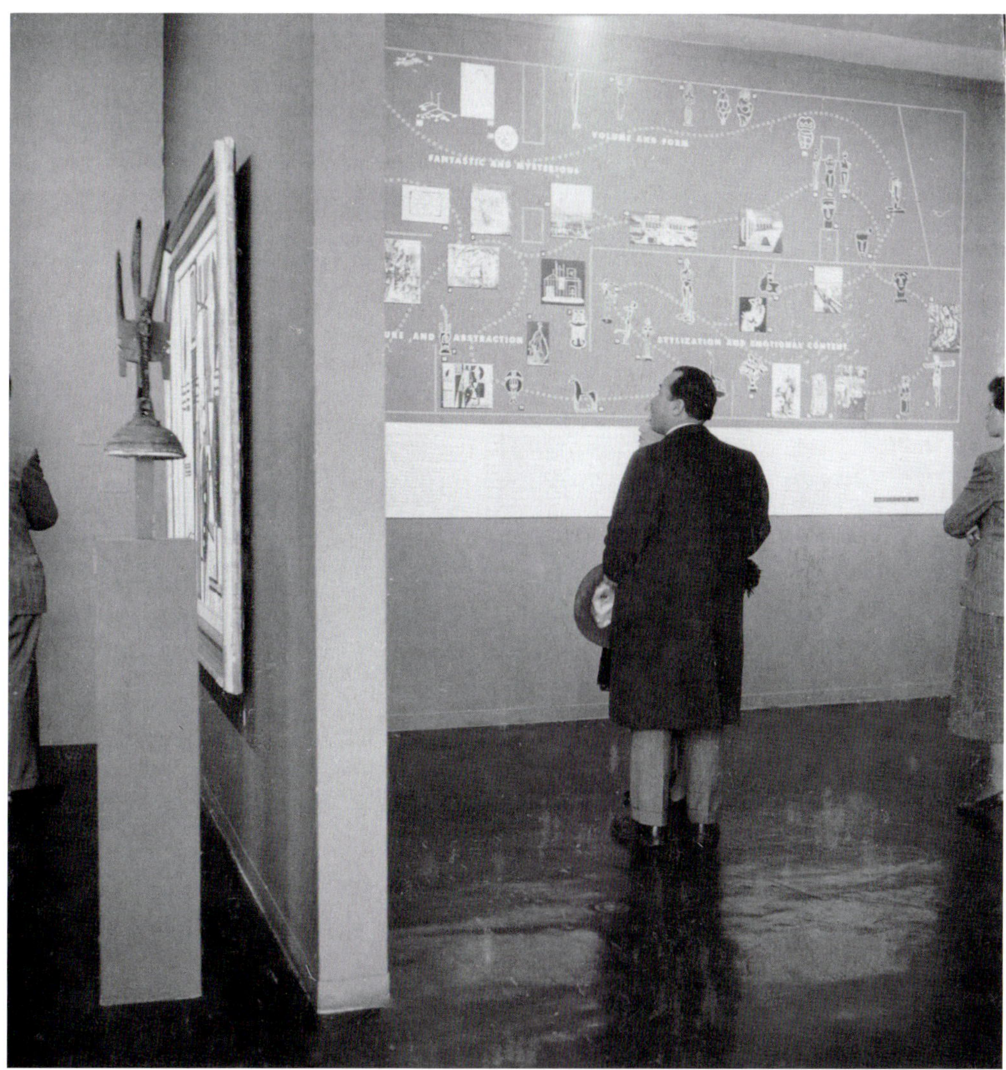

D'Harnoncourt presented the map of the exhibition at the entrance to the galleries, at a remove from the artworks themselves, so that visitors could know what to expect while being able to focus on the artworks on display.

Modern Art in Your Life

MoMA Exhibition #423; October 5–December 4, 1949

CURATOR: René d'Harnoncourt and Robert Goldwater
NUMBER OF WORKS: 202
LOCATION: Third floor
PUBLICATION: Robert Goldwater and René d'Harnoncourt, *Modern Art in Your Life* (New York: The Museum of Modern Art, 1949)

The educational objective of *Modern Art in Your Life* was to associate fine art and the applied arts, in an effort to make modern art more accessible: the basic tenet was to impress upon the (sometimes doubting) American public the importance of modern art by illustrating how it had informed the design of everyday items. The exhibition was assembled in collaboration with Robert Goldwater (at the time associate professor of Art History at Queens College and editor of the *Magazine of Art*), who wrote the accompanying catalogue. In it, Goldwater explained that the goal of the exhibition was to show how "the appearance and shape of countless objects of everyday environment are related to, or derived from, modern painting and sculpture."[22] Or, simply stated, how twentieth-century painters and sculptors impacted industrial design, advertising, typography, etc.

The exhibition layout began with a long tunnel with a low drop ceiling, lined by semitransparent curtains, then spilled out onto a large central gallery, an open, high-ceilinged, and bright room anchored by a large midnight-blue wall. This gallery housed paintings and sculptures representing five main trends in modern art—Geometric Abstraction, Geometric Stylization, Organic Abstraction, Organic Stylization, and Surrealism—which were paired with examples of architecture, industrial design, graphics, advertising, and window display that share a similar essence or formal logic. For example, geometric abstract art, represented by works by Piet Mondrian and Theo van Doesburg, was complemented by a display of International Style architecture and design objects; geometric stylizations were paired with posters and advertisements, while organic abstraction was paired with anthropomorphic chair designs. In perhaps the most striking example, Surrealist paintings led to a dramatically darkened gallery containing spotlit three-dimensional tableaux, which were examples of contemporary department-store window design.

Another (and perhaps earlier) proposal stated the goal was, "to help the public find in modern art those elements that reflect the characteristics of our specific phase of civilization and make modern art as a whole an expression of our time." It was to address how modern art relates "to other aspects of our civilization in the twentieth century, to our knowledge of psychology, of political science, of economics and war."[23] The fields to be covered were to include science, literary devices to expose the influence of psychoanalysis and new developments in philosophy, and social problems that have produced entire movements, such as the School of Mexico. These earlier efforts carried the working title of "Modern Art in the Modern World." The final realized scenario, of the parallels and affinities between contemporary art and design, represented a significant narrowing of focus. While Thomas Hess noted in *ARTnews*

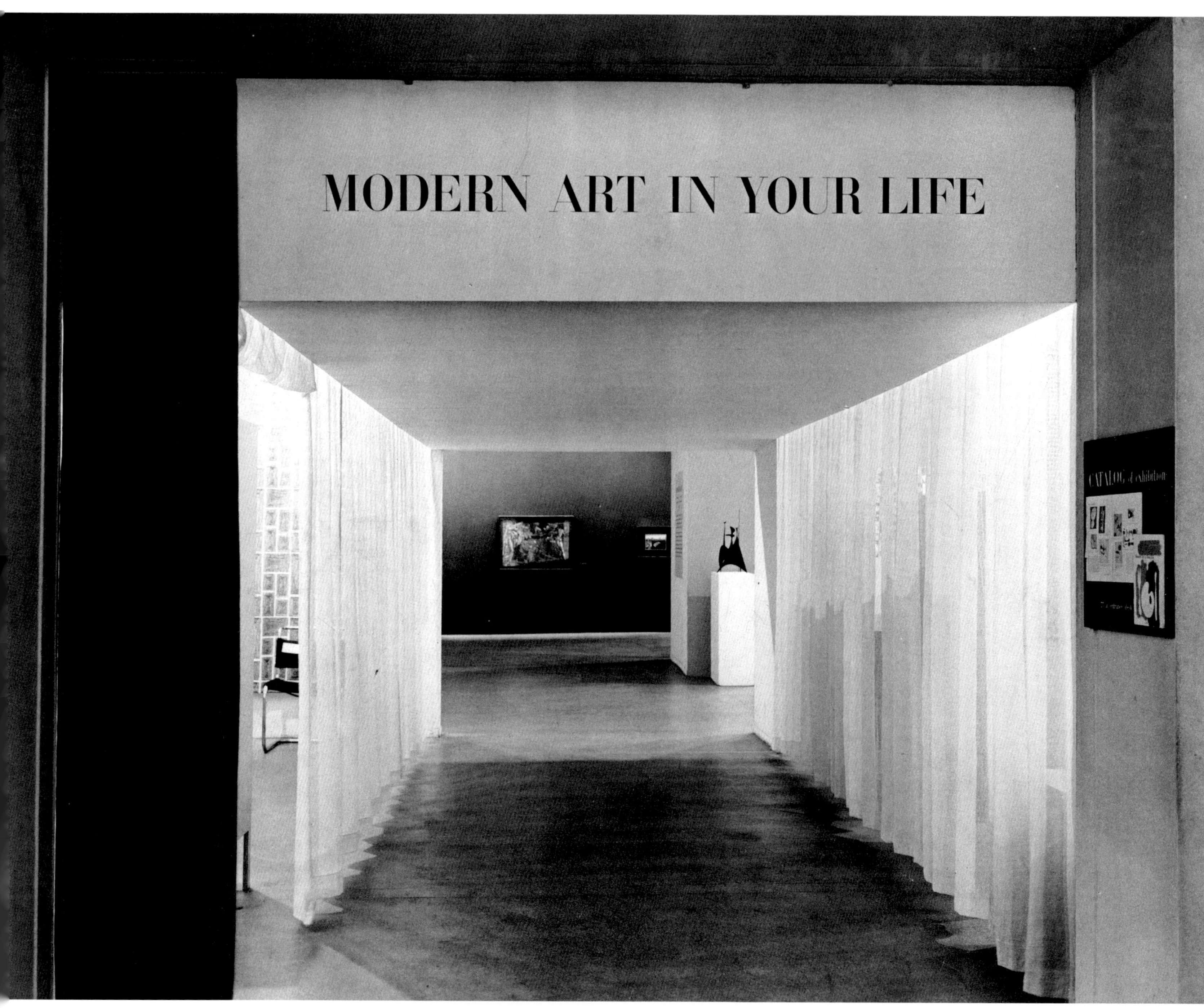

Entrance to the exhibition, 1949

that d'Harnoncourt was "supplying one of his most spectacular installations,"[24] others were less praiseful. The critic from the *New Yorker*, Robert M. Coates, noted the exhibition was intended to illustrate "how the theories of modern painting and sculpture have affected contemporary living. Such a showing, it seems to me, was overdue, and if this one doesn't entirely succeed in its effort, it should be given credit for a fairly good try."[25]

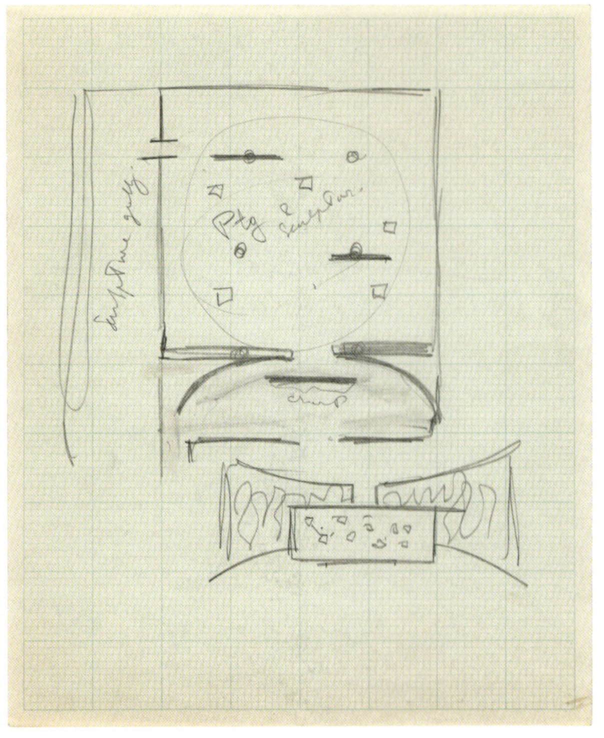

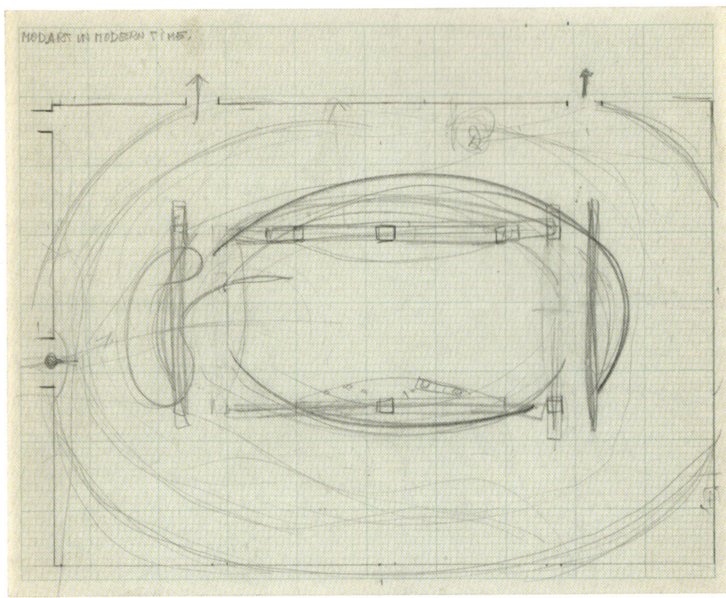

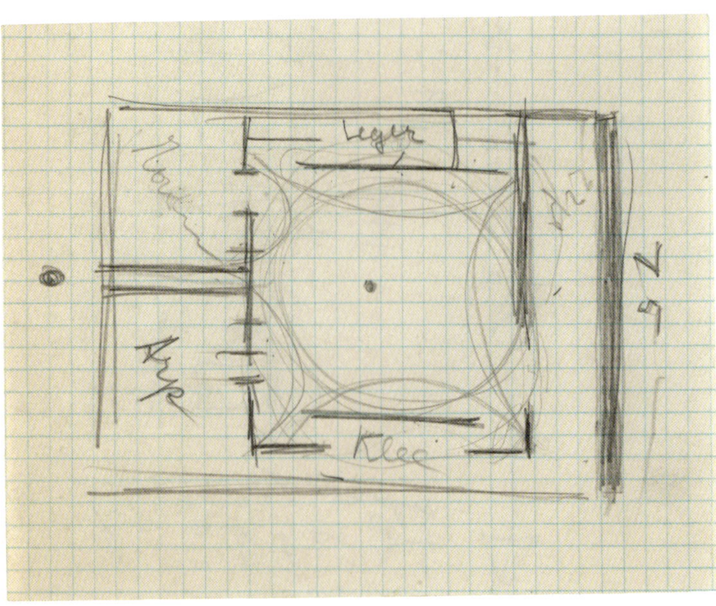

Above and left: Draft proposals for the floor plan layout, indicating the evolution of d'Harnoncourt's thinking about the exhibition, 1949

Opposite: Final floor plan of the exhibition, 1949

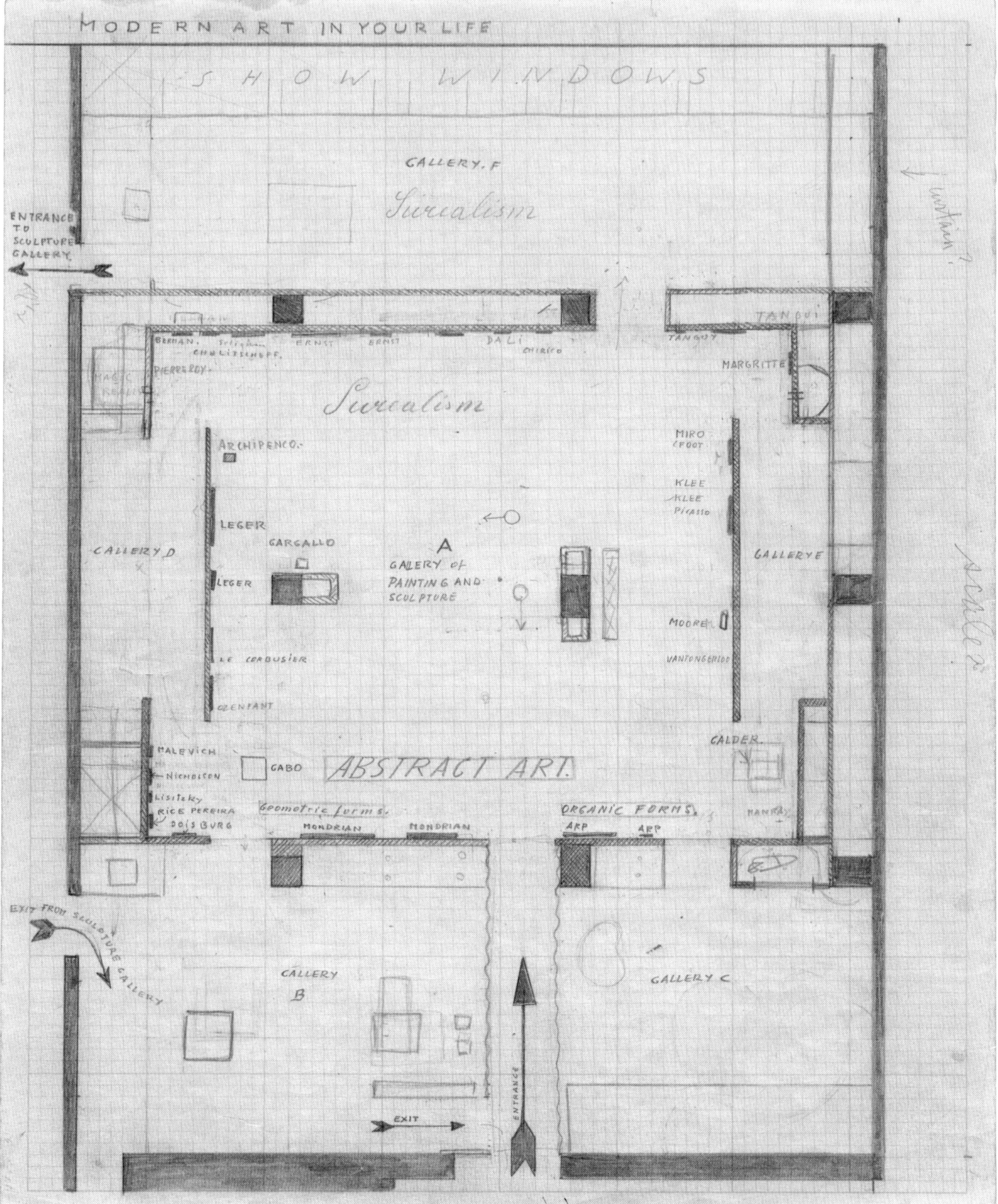

MODERN ART IN YOUR LIFE
SHOW WINDOWS
GALLERY. F
Surrealism
ENTRANCE TO SCULPTURE GALLERY
BERMAN
SELIGMAN
TCHELITSCHEFF
PIERRE ROY
MAGIC REALISM
ERNST
ERNST
DALI
CHIRICO
TANGUY
TANGUY
MARGRITTE
Surrealism
ARCHIPENCO.
MIRO
GALLERY D
LEGER
GARGALLO
KLEE
KLEE
PICASSO
A
GALLERY OF PAINTING AND SCULPTURE
LEGER
GALLERY E
LE CORBUSIER
MOORE
VANTONGERLOO
OZENFANT
MALEVICH
NICHOLSON
LISITZKY
RICE PEREIRA
DOISBURG
GABO
ABSTRACT ART.
CALDER
Geometric forms.
MONDRIAN
MONDRIAN
ORGANIC FORMS
ARP
ARP
MANRAY
EXIT FROM SCULPTURE GALLERY
GALLERY B
GALLERY C
EXIT
ENTRANCE

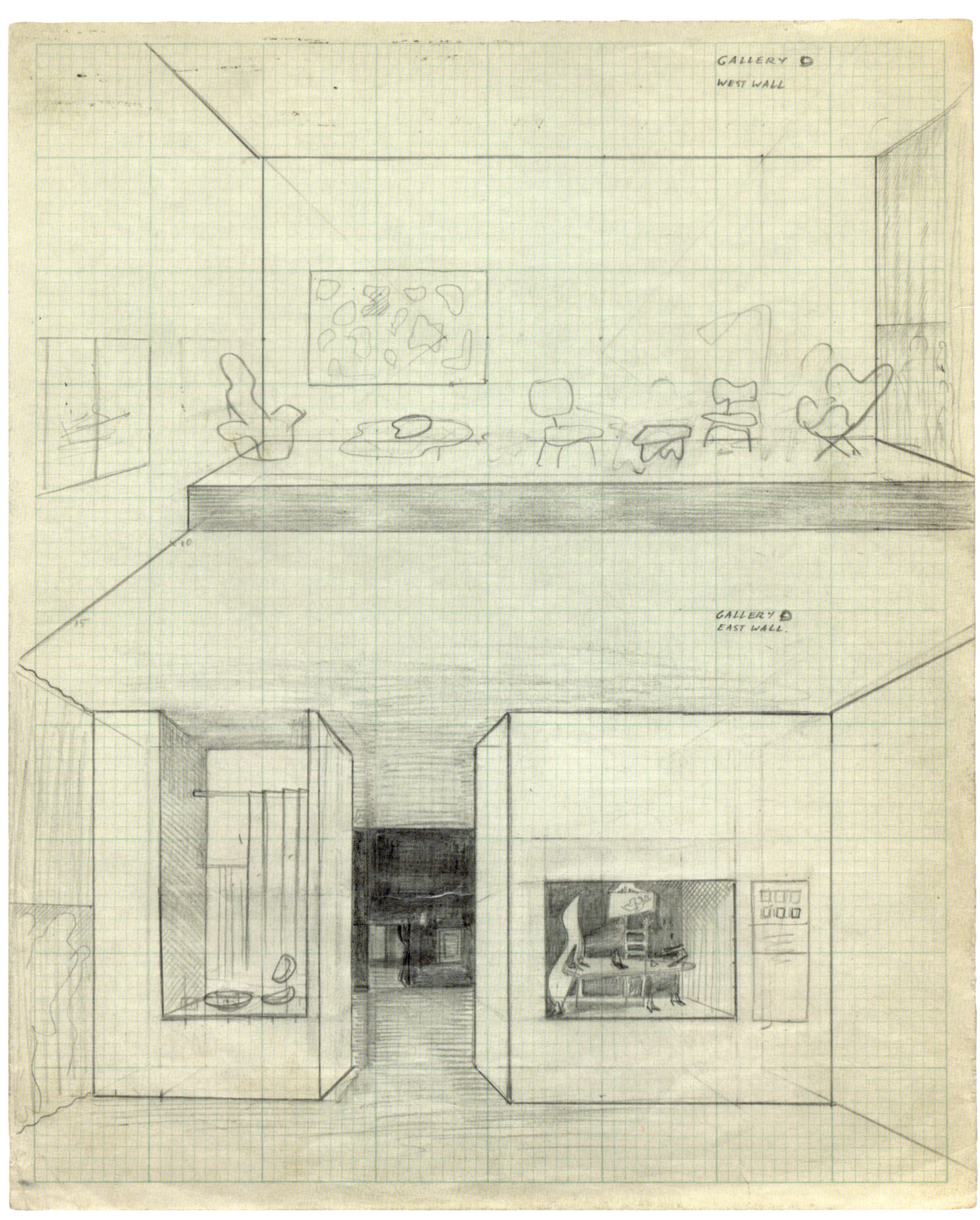

GALLERY C
WEST WALL
GALLERY D
EAST WALL.

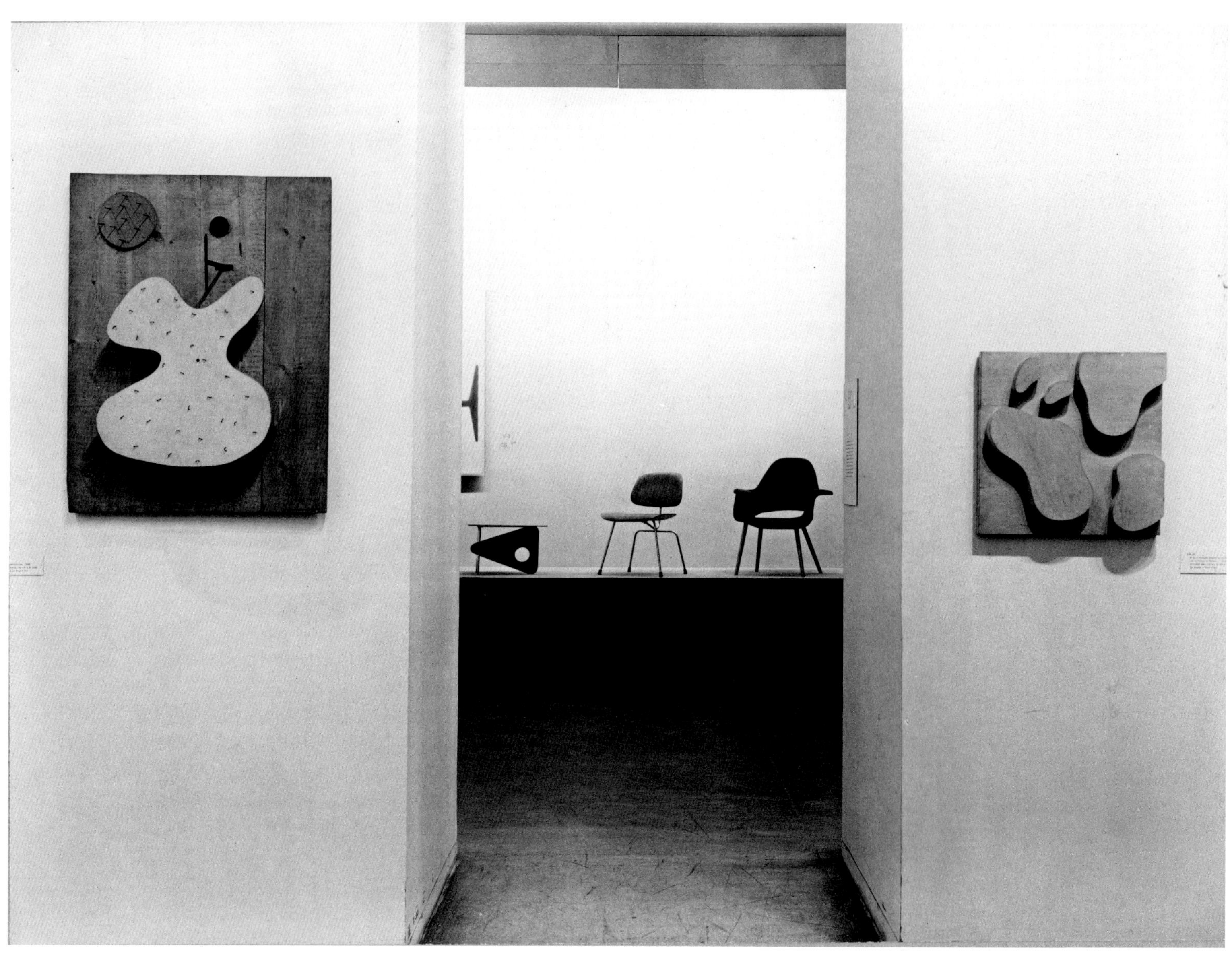

Opposite: Drawing of an installation of modern industrial design furniture, 1949

Above: View of the Abstract Organic Form installation, bringing together modern
industrial design furniture with works by Jean Arp, 1949

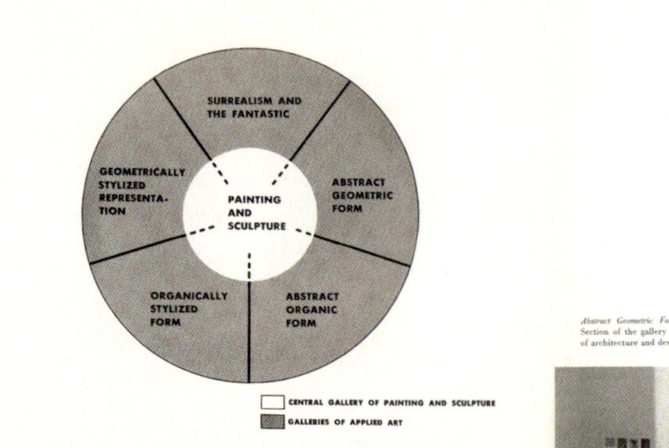

The chart shown above is a schematic ground plan of the exhibition on which this publication is based. It also serves as a graphic presentation of the problems dealt with on the preceding pages.

The center circle corresponds to the gallery of painting and sculpture that occupied the center of the exhibition. The works of art shown in this gallery were arranged in five groups, each representing a major style of modern art. Five doors, each in the center of one of these style groups, led to the five outer galleries devoted to the display of corresponding styles in architecture, industrial design and graphic design.

Thus the exhibition and this chart invite comparison not only between various branches of art within the same style but also between the various art styles within the same branch.

The photographs on the following pages were taken at the time of the showing of the exhibition *Modern Art In Your Life* held at the Museum of Modern Art in 1949. They are reproduced here to enable the reader to make his comparisons on the basis of impressions received from seeing entire groups of objects rather than particular pieces. For the purposes of this study it is dangerous to judge affinities between painting and sculpture and the applied arts of any given period from isolated examples. The resemblance between two individual works of art is often superficial and irrelevant and should always be checked by comparison of entire groups.

44

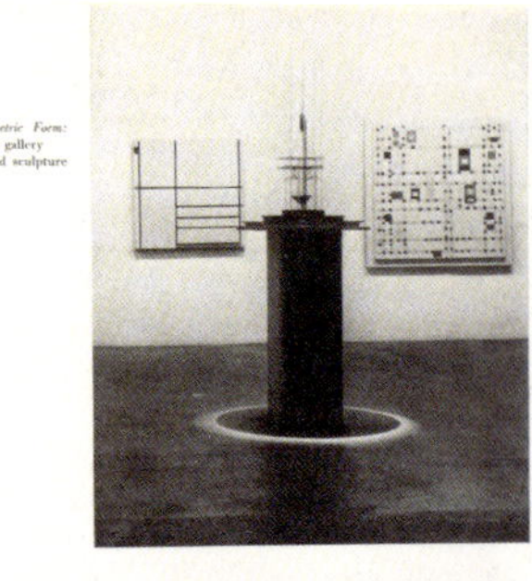
Abstract Geometric Form: Section of the gallery of painting and sculpture

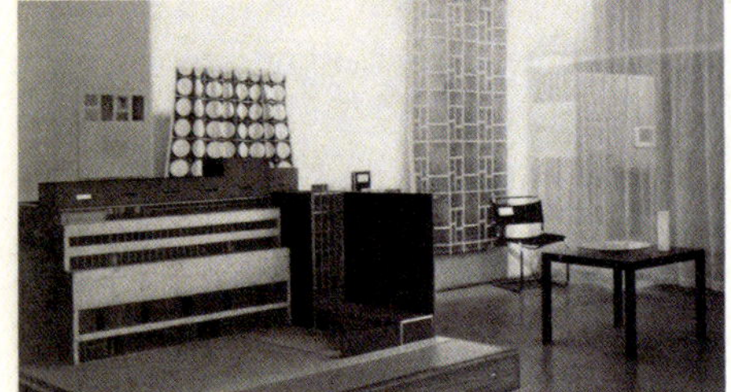
Abstract Geometric Form: Section of the gallery of architecture and design

45

Left: This schema of the exhibition, included in its catalogue, illustrates how works of modern art were arranged in five groups, each representing a major style, and each connecting to outer galleries devoted to corresponding styles in architecture, industrial design, and graphic design.

Below: Vista of an installation of architectural models and posters in the Abstract Geometric Form section of the exhibition, 1949

Opposite, top: View of the Surrealism and the Fantastic installation, with works by Salvador Dalí and Yves Tanguy on either side of the entrance to a gallery presenting modern retail window displays, 1949

Opposite, bottom: Vista of the Magic Realism and Surrealism section of the exhibition, 1949

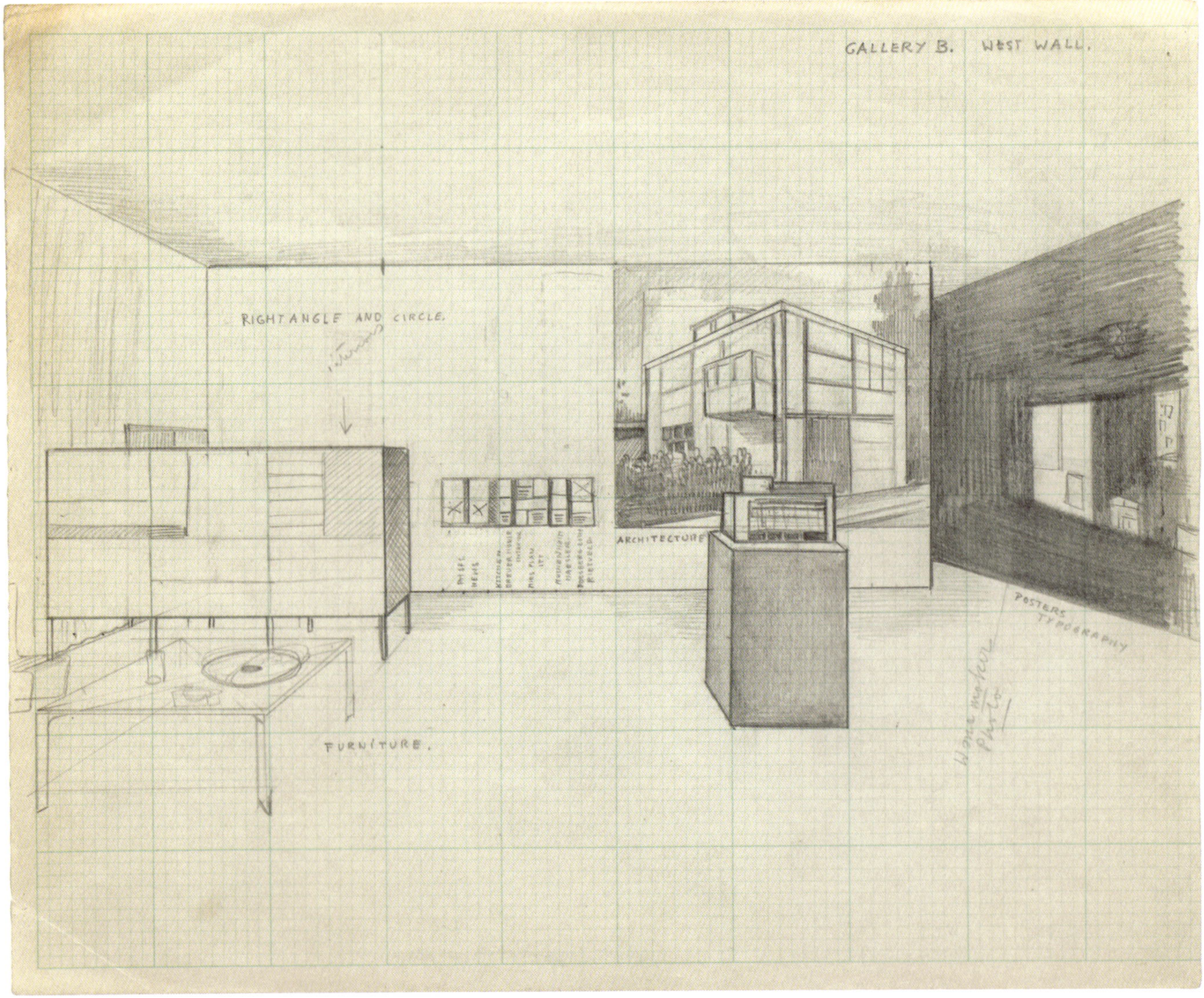

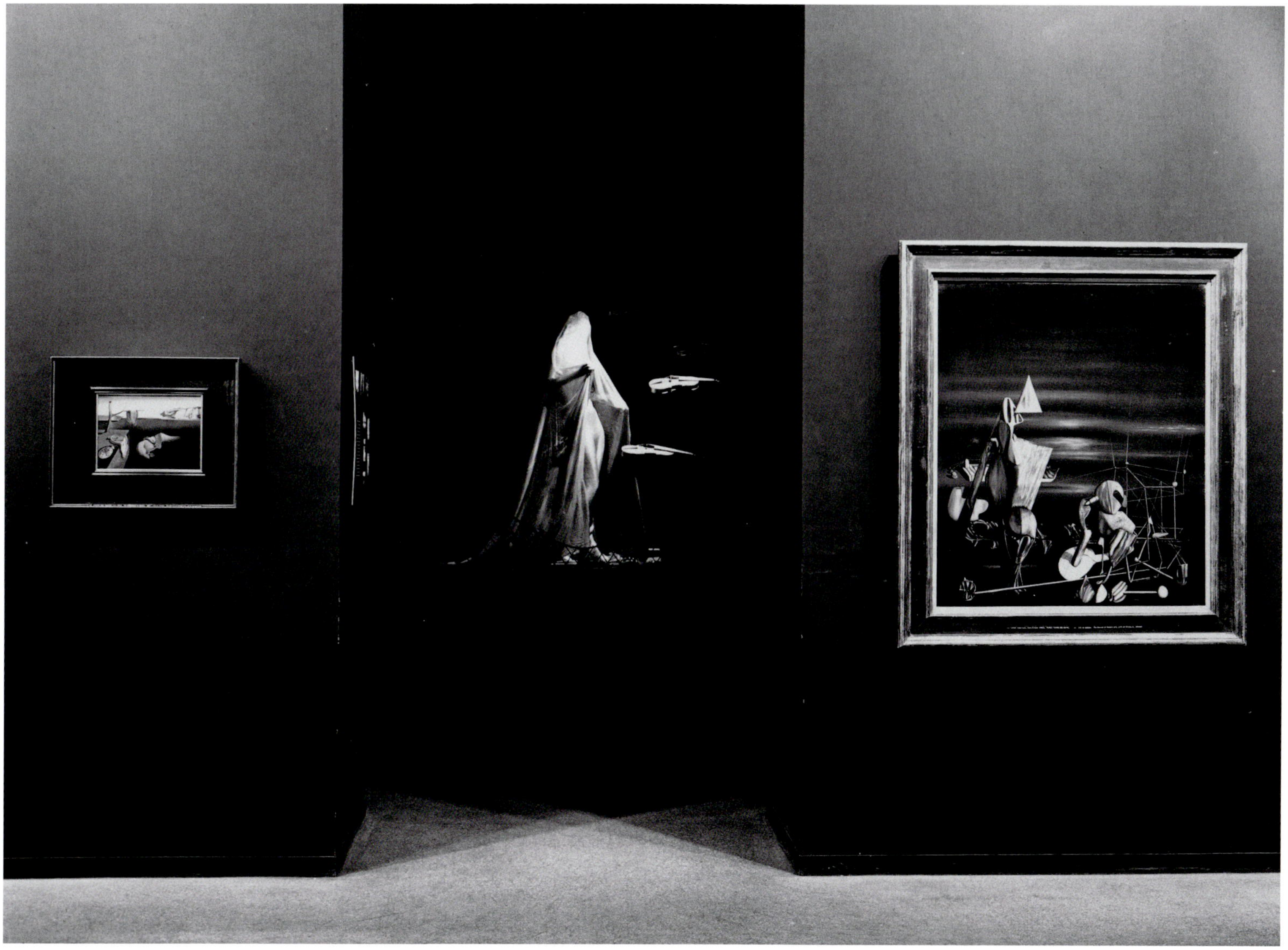

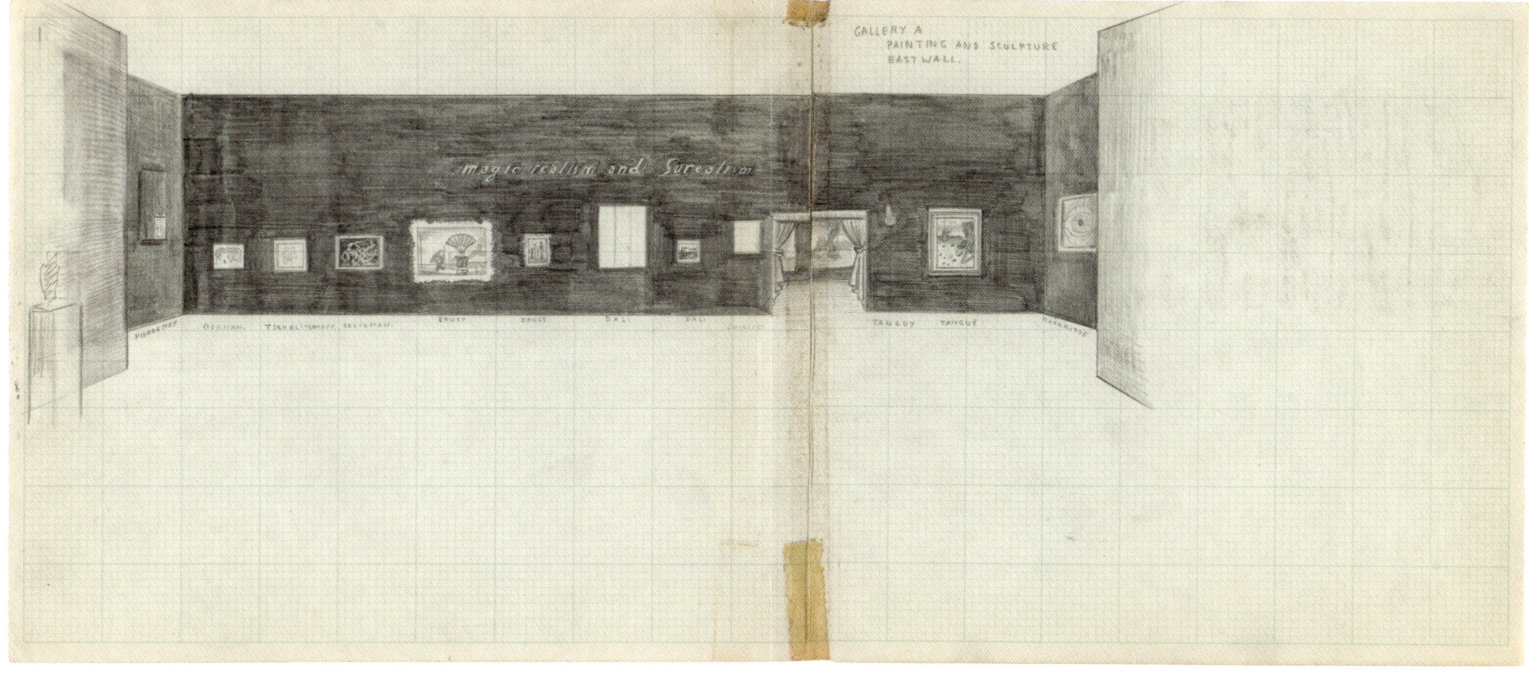
GALLERY A
PAINTING AND SCULPTURE
EAST WALL.
magic realism and Surealism
ERNST
DALI
TANGUY
TANGUY

Ancient Arts of the Andes

MoMA Exhibition #550; January 25–March 21, 1954

CURATOR: René d'Harnoncourt, assisted by Mildred Constantine
NUMBER OF WORKS: More than 400
LOCATION: Third floor
PUBLICATIONS: Wendell C. Bennett (introduction by René d'Harnoncourt), *Ancient Arts of the Andes* (New York: The Museum of Modern Art, 1954). Supplement: *32 Masterworks of Andean Art from the Exhibition Ancient Arts of the Andes*, with a preface by René d'Harnoncourt (New York: The Museum of Modern Art, 1955)
CIRCULATING VENUES:
The Minneapolis Institute of Arts, Minneapolis, Minnesota:
    April 20–June 13, 1954
California Palace of the Legion of Honor, San Francisco, California:
    July 19–September 19, 1954

In his original proposal, d'Harnoncourt stated his belief that this exhibition, at the time titled "The Empire of the Andes," would be the first attempt to show the finest works of art from all the major South American countries together.[26] D'Harnoncourt gathered more than four hundred objects, including gold and silver pieces, ceramics, stone and wood sculptures, and tapestries dating from roughly 1200 BC to the time of the Spanish conquest in the sixteenth century. The Andes are one of the few great prehistoric civilizations from which items made of perishable materials, such as fabrics and feathers, are extant; yet its art was relatively unknown, even as compared to the arts of Africa, Oceania, and pre-Columbian Mexico.[27] Many of the archeological findings were recent, and several of the countries had placed bans on exporting their ancient cultural artifacts.

The process of assembling the artworks to be included was a particularly adventurous and colorful one. One lender, the eminent collector and scholar in the field of ancient art Don Rafael Larco Hoyle, who had a private museum near Lima, Peru, stipulated that d'Harnoncourt carry the cache of Peruvian goldwork (valued at $130,000) in a suitcase from Lima to the Museum. Not surprisingly, there was an escalated concern about security and insurance due to the gold pieces, which led to deploying special security systems, including custom-made burglar alarms; when the works traveled to Minneapolis and San Francisco, they were transported in a sealed and guarded train. Knowing that the expenses for the undertaking would be considerable, the Museum sought institutions to co-sponsor the exhibition, and in the end the Minneapolis Institute of Arts and the California Legion of Honor in San Francisco signed on.[28] With the supplemental funding, d'Harnoncourt was able to travel twice to Brazil, Ecuador, Chile, and Peru to make arrangements for the objects, many of which had never been publically exhibited before. Other lenders were as far away as Japan and as close as the American Museum of Natural History.

D'Harnoncourt compared this exhibition to *Indian Art of the United States* and *Arts of the South Seas* in that "it will stress the artistic quality of the work shown, but at the same time attempt to give a portrait of the great Indian civilization of South America."[29] The structure of the show was geographical. The exhibition was organized into three sections, in two galleries: one devoted to the Central Andes (Peru and Bolivia) and the Southern Andes (Chile and northwest Argentina); the other to the Northern Andes (Ecuador, Colombia, and Venezuela), plus Panama, Costa Rica, and the Amazon region of Brazil.

D'Harnoncourt used some of the more dramatic effects he had developed in his previous exhibitions of primitive arts. One highlight was a cast of El Lanzon (1200 to 400 BC), a 13-foot-tall sculpture depicting the head of a snake with feline features, carved from black rock; thought to be the oldest prehistoric sculpture, it was borrowed from the National Museum of Anthropology and Archaeology in Peru. The original would have been placed at the intersection of two subterranean corridors in a temple complex, lit from below by a fire; so

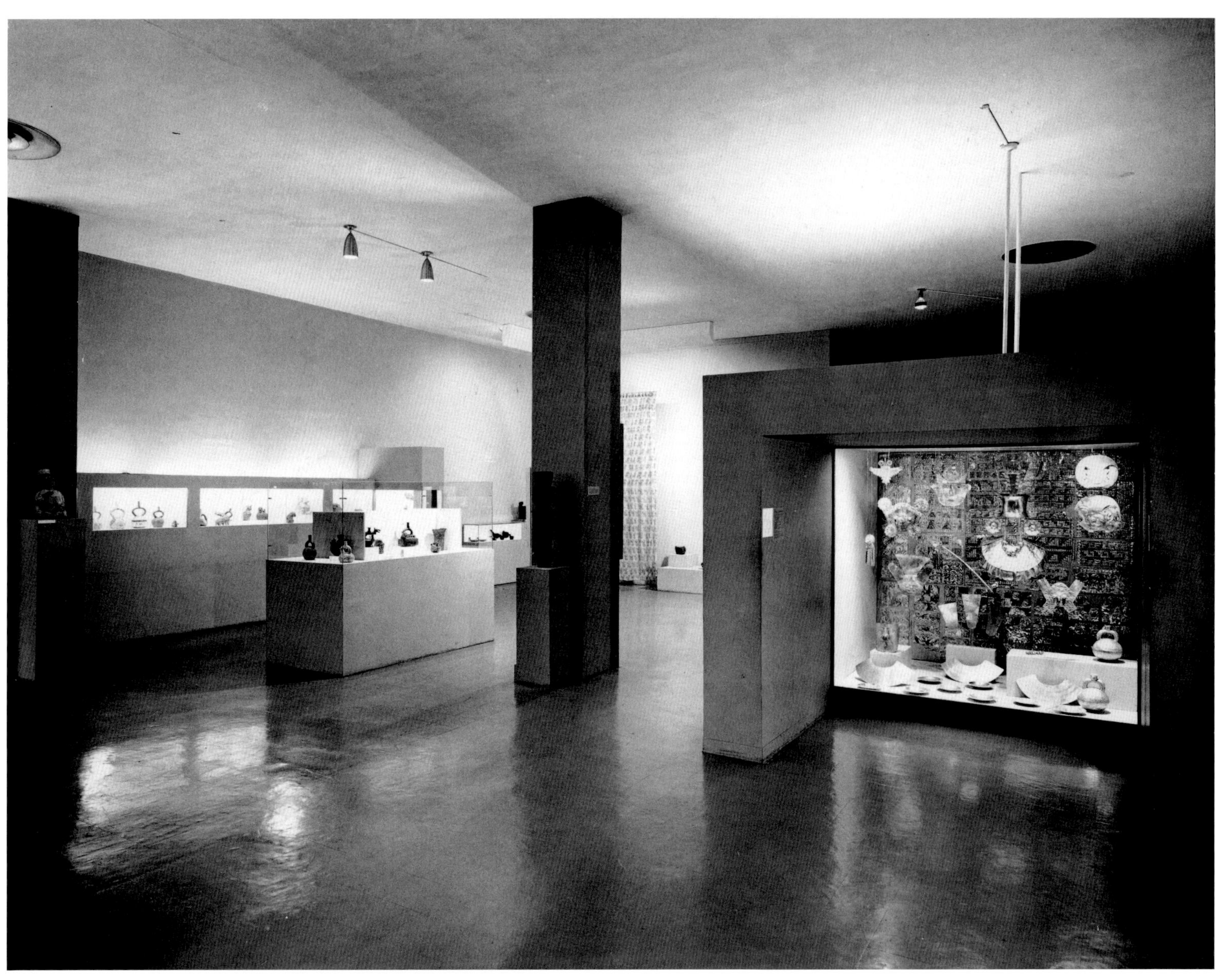

Installation view of the large main gallery, including, on the right,
a vitrine filled with gold objects and referred to as "the bunker"

d'Harnoncourt tried to replicate those conditions. The main gallery, a large, brightly lit room suggesting desert surroundings, was broken into a series of alcoves displaying textiles, ceramics, and gold objects. Behind this was a long, darkened gallery devoted to the Northern Andes (painted green to evoke the jungle), which included sculpture, ceramics, and nearly one hundred beautiful and precious gold objects. To show more concretely the environment in which these were produced, d'Harnoncourt included a gallery of photographs of Inca highland architecture, such as Machu Picchu.

The large gallery notably included a gold-paneled room (affectionately titled "the bunker" by Museum staff) containing forty-seven repoussé gold plaques from Peru's National Museum of Anthropology and Archaeology. As explained in the catalogue, gold was used decoratively in Peru, similarly to how velvet was used to cover the surfaces of large objects, even walls, during the Renaissance, resulting in less precious objects than in, for instance, the Northern Andes. The experience of visiting this show was conveyed on a contemporary radio show on WQXR, "Nights in Latin America," sponsored by Pan American-Grace Airways (also a corporate sponsor of the exhibition). Host Pru Devon recounted: "When I emerged from the darkened corridors which dramatized the pre-historic Andean art at the Modern Museum, I took a deep breath and almost shouted, 'GOLD!' For I came upon an exhibition of Peruvian gold that shone like the sun! The Peruvians had gold galore and were certainly lavish with it."[30]

The accompanying publication by collaborator Wendell C. Bennett was notable not just for its groundbreaking scholarship, but because it included four color-plate photographic reproductions, evidently a source of pride for the Museum, which emphasized this aspect of the book in its promotional materials. This was no small endeavor at the time: each of those four plates cost $1,000. The Museum solicited donations to cover the expense, and Museum trustee (and primitive art collector) Gertrud A. Mellon underwrote one. In addition, the Museum issued *32 Masterpieces of Andean Art*, a supplemental publication, as the works from South America arrived too late to be photographed for inclusion in the catalogue.

The exhibition was incredibly well received, with the *New York Times* hailing it as "one of the most spectacular shows and installations that the museum has yet housed. By careful selection and installation revealing the contrasts within the successive cultures Mr. d'Harnoncourt has presented a dramatic display with stress always on the art rather than the primarily archaeological aspects of the material."[31] Emily Genauer, in the *New York Herald Tribune*, called it "one of the handsomest exhibitions in a quarter-century career" and commended d'Harnoncourt's "pure esthetic approach."[32] The exhibition was equally well received in California as it was in New York. The director of the California Palace of the Legion of Honor, Thomas C. Howe, Jr., wrote to d'Harnoncourt: "The Andean show is very beautiful and impressive and I am happy to report that the public response is gratifying in the extreme. The unqualified success of your exhibition should indeed be a great satisfaction to you." He also noted that the demand for the catalogue was so great they had to triple their order, especially surprising due to its high price point.[33]

Letter from Max Weber to René d'Harnoncourt, complimenting him on his exhibition *Ancient Arts of the Andes*, February 24, 1954 (incorrectly dated 1953 by Weber)

Opposite: Vitrine (nicknamed "the bunker") lined with forty-seven repoussé gold bricks, with eighteen gold objects resting on its base and another dozen suspended from above

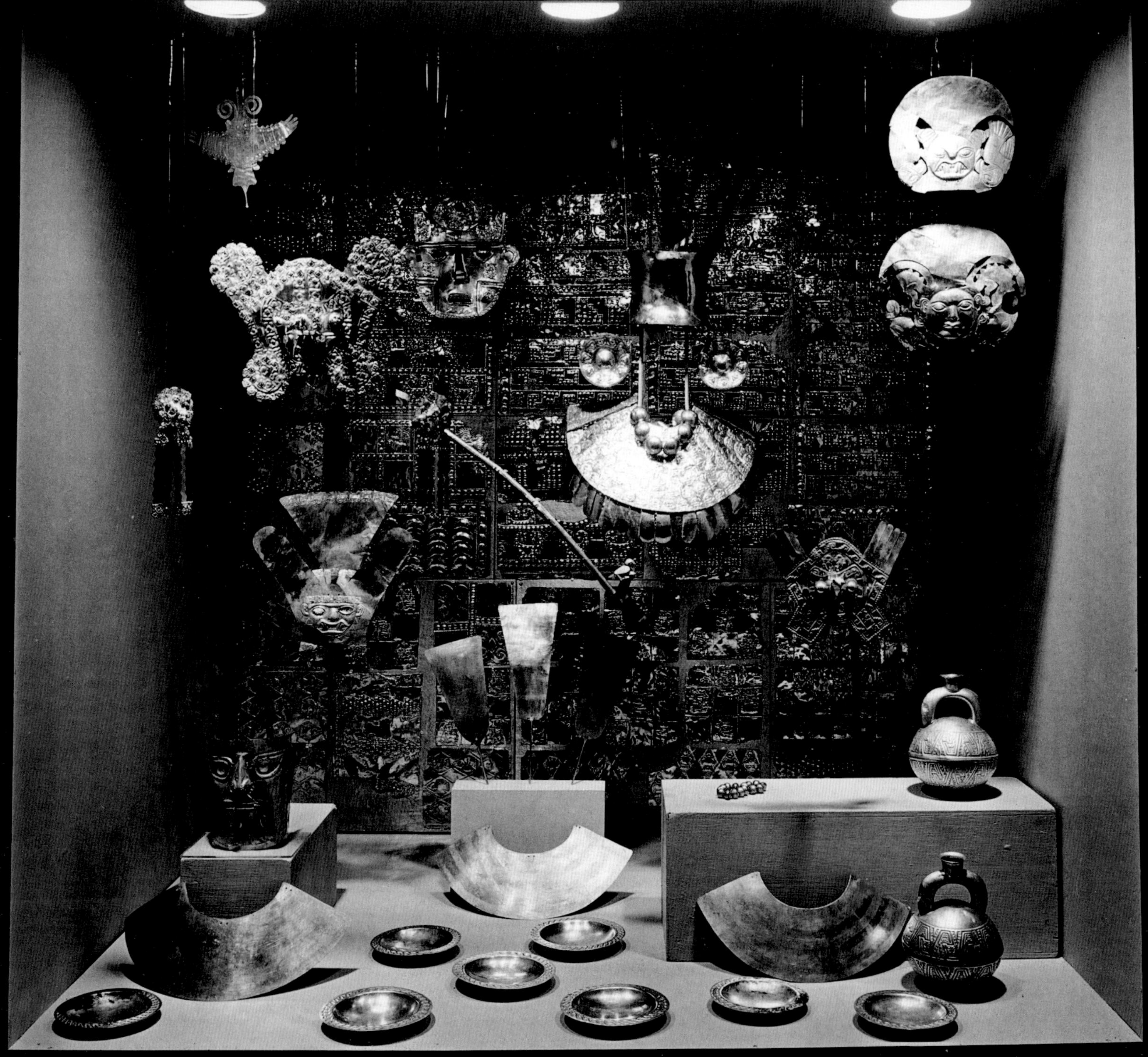

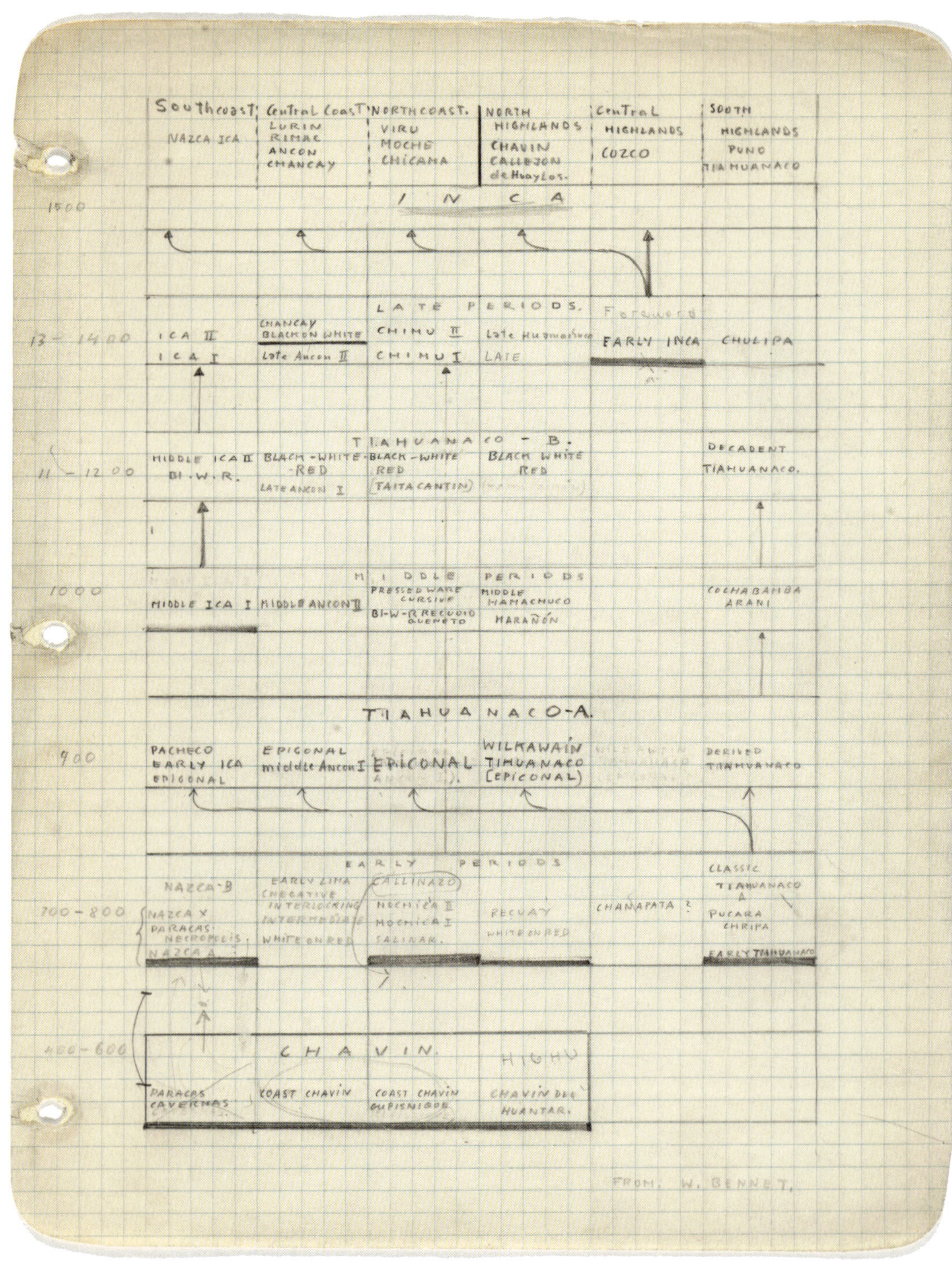

Above: Style chart of Andean art organized by period and region, 1953

Opposite: Drawings of objects, grouped according to provenance, 1953

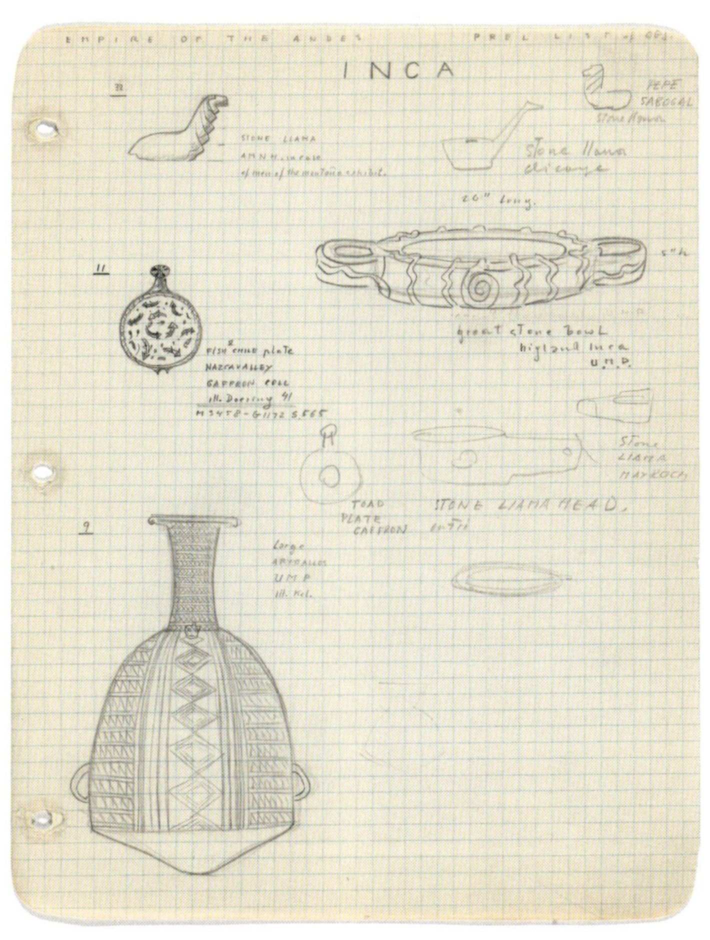

EMPIRE OF THE ANDES   PREL LIST OF OBJECTS
INCA
PEPE SABOGAL
STONE LLAMA
STONE LLAMA
AMNH in case
STONE LLAMA HEAD.
GREAT STONE BOWL
highland Inca
U.M.P.
TOAD PLATE CAJAMARCA
Large AMPHORAS U.M.P.

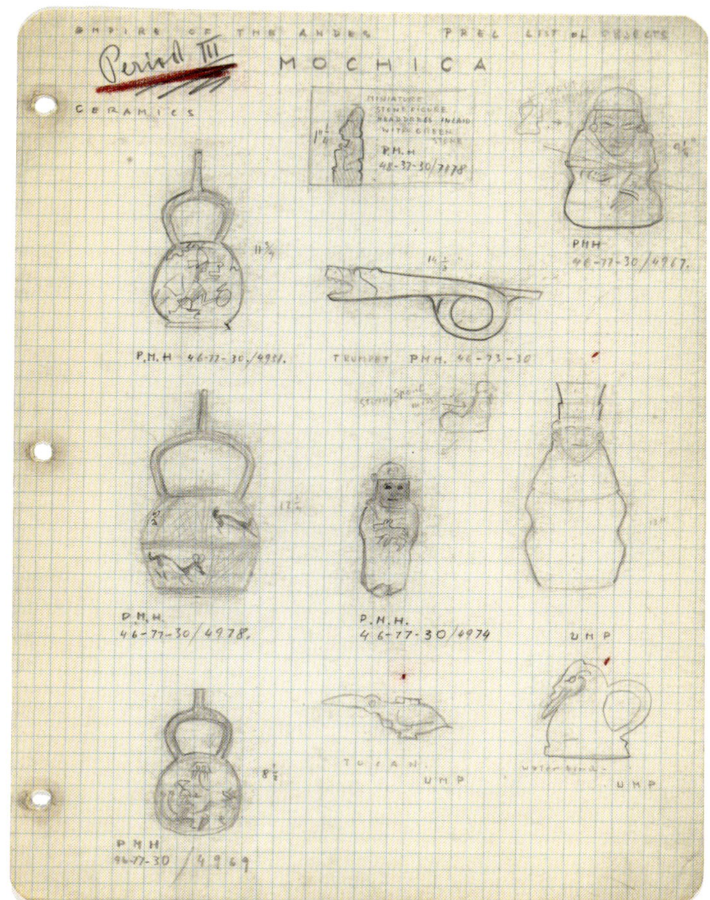

EMPIRE OF THE ANDES   PREL LIST OF OBJECTS
Period III   MOCHICA
CERAMICS
P.H.H 46-77-30/4951.
TRUMPET P.M.H. 46-73-30
P.M.H. 46-77-30/4978.
P.N.H. 46-77-30/4974
U.M.P
P.M.H 46-77-30/4969
P.H.H 46-77-30/4967.
U.M.P
U.M.P

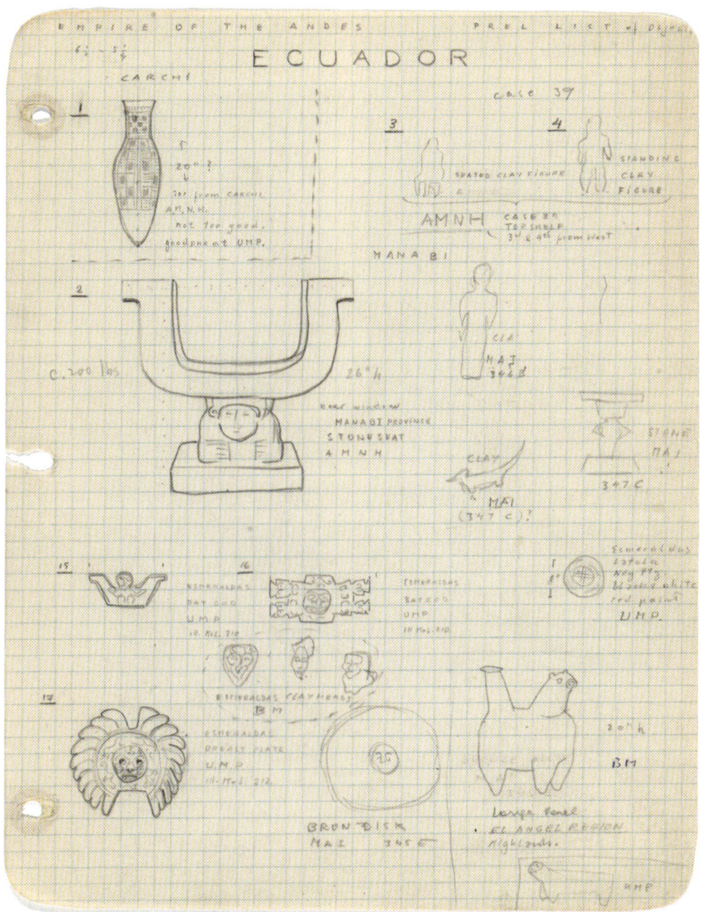

EMPIRE OF THE ANDES   PREL LIST OF OBJECTS
ECUADOR
CARCHI
CASE 39
AMNH
MANABI
STONE SEAT AMNH
BRONZE DISK
BM

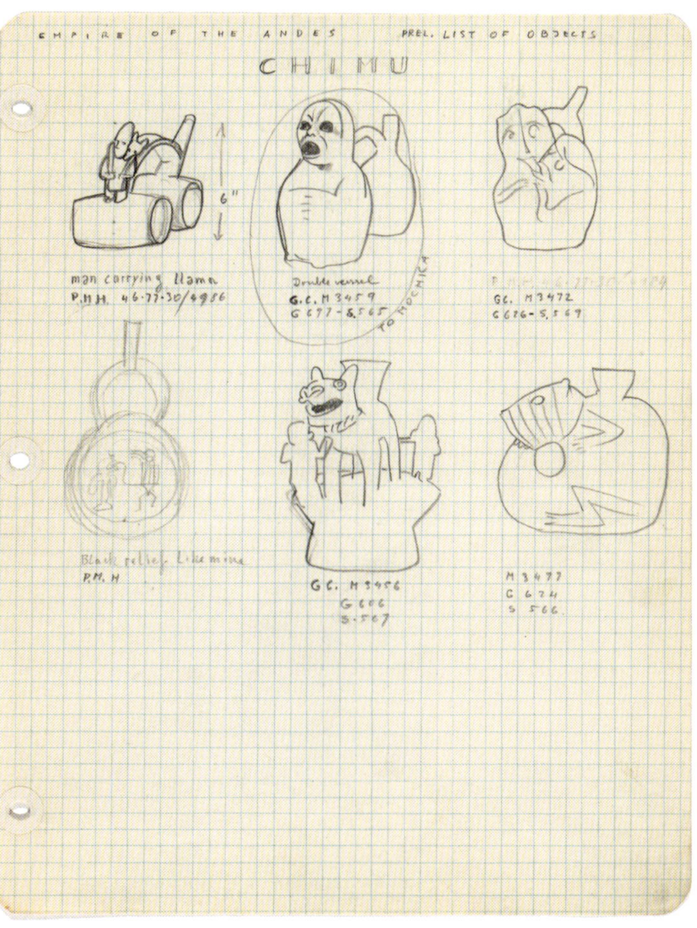

EMPIRE OF THE ANDES   PREL. LIST OF OBJECTS
CHIMU
man carrying llama
P.H.H. 46-77-30/4956
Double vessel
G.C. M3459
G.C. M3472
Black relief like mine
P.M.H
G.C. M3456
M3477

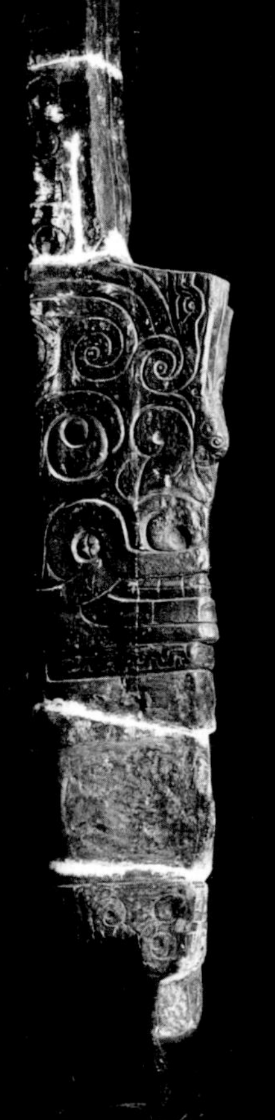
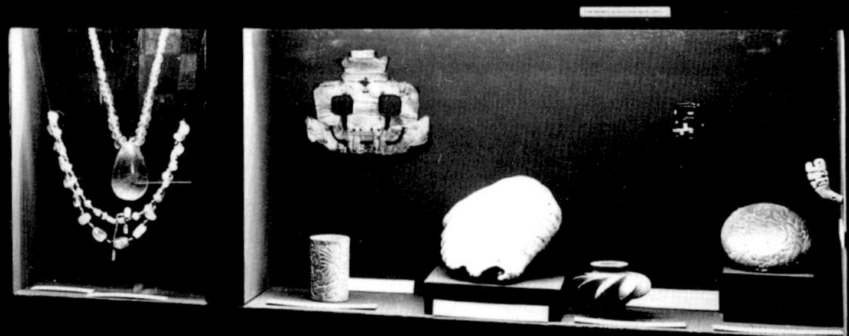

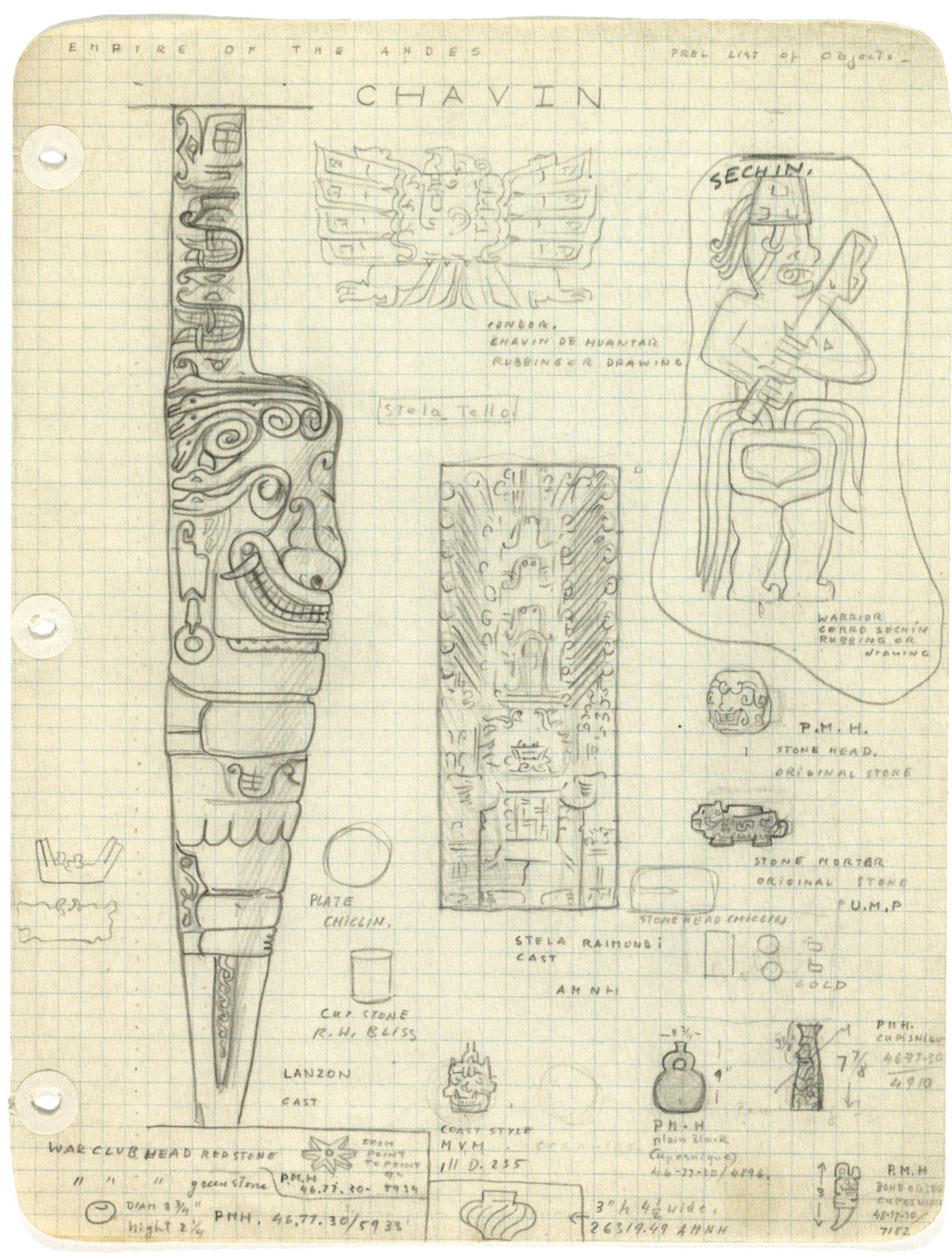

Opposite: Installation view of the darkened entry passageway gallery, featuring the cast of "El Lanzon," a highlight of the exhibition, 1953

Above: Drawings of Chavin objects, including "El Lanzon," 1953

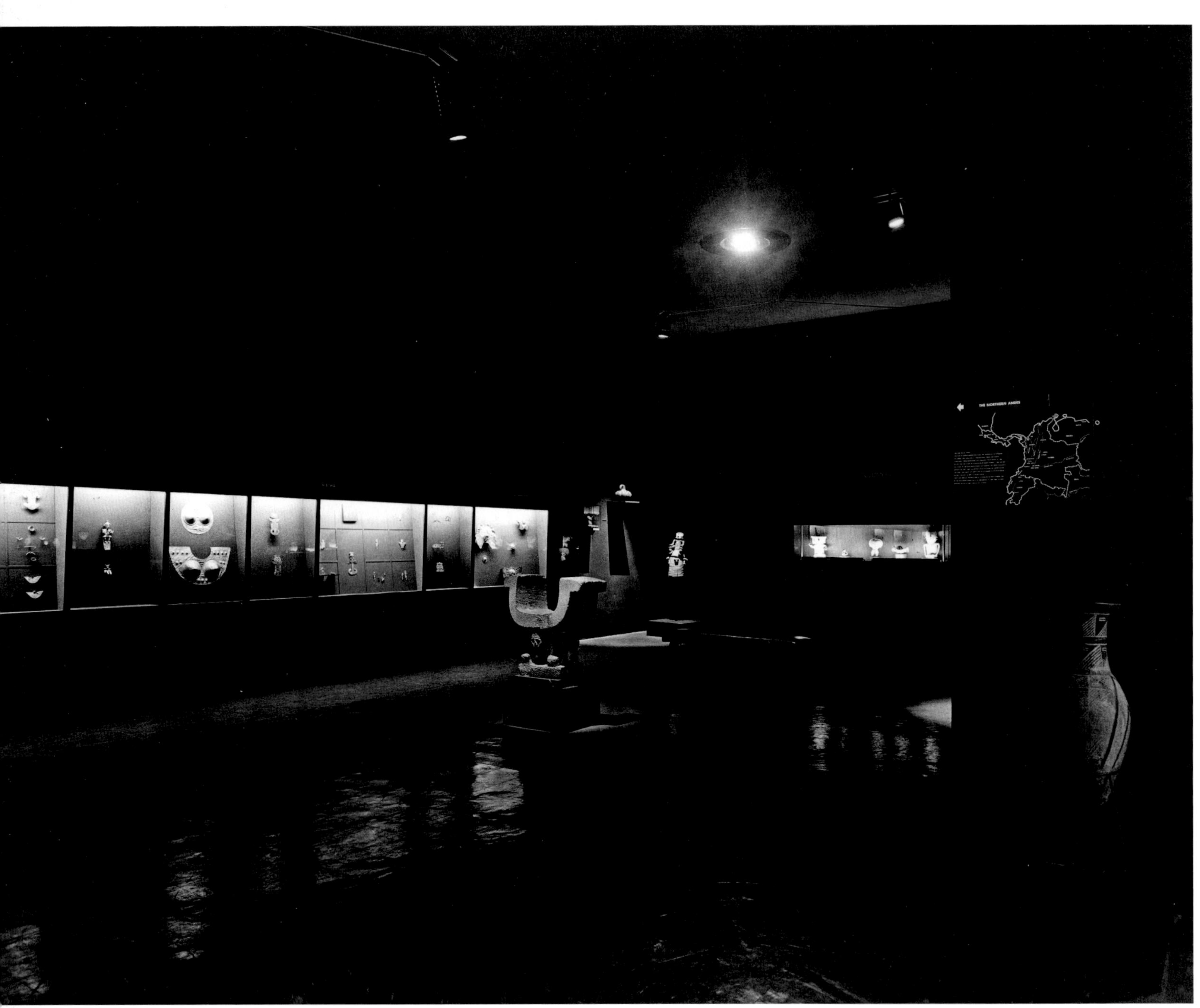

Installation view of the dark gallery dedicated to the Northern Andes. D'Harnoncourt strategically placed the didactic map and text around the corner from the main gallery so that viewers could focus on the objects in the vitrines.

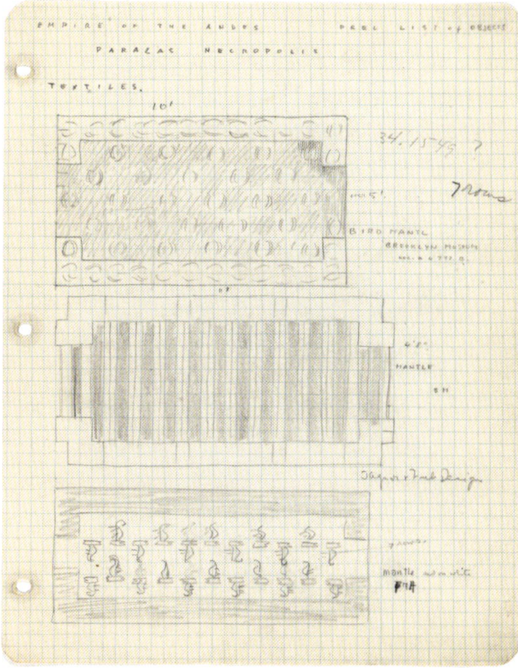

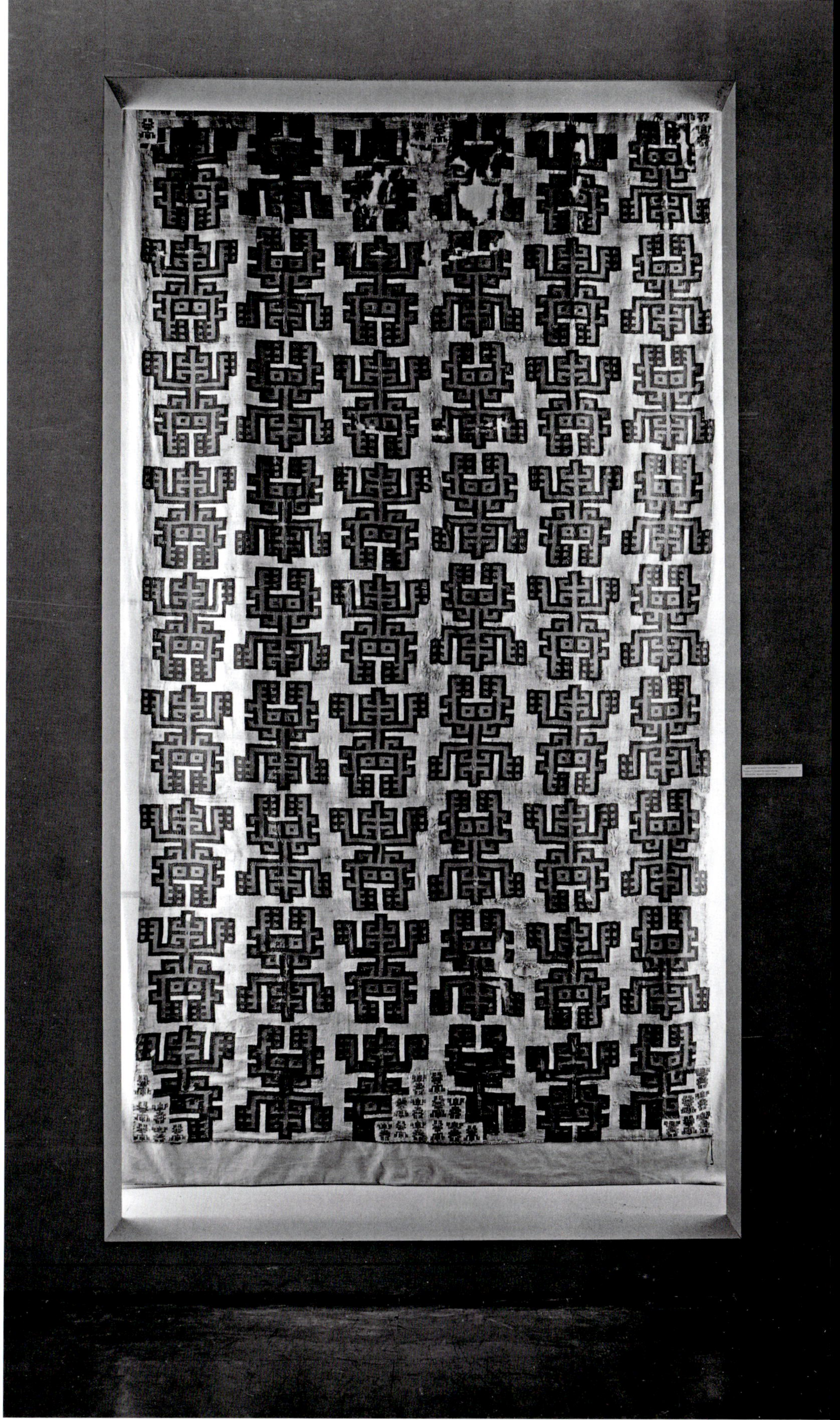

Above: Drawings of textiles, 1953

Right: Installation view of a textile work, 1953

Seurat Paintings and Drawings

MoMA Exhibition #629; March 24–April 15, 1958;
May 1–May 11, 1958

CURATOR: William S. Lieberman
NUMBER OF WORKS: 175
LOCATION: Third-floor galleries, rebuilt specifically for the exhibition
(original installation, before the fire); ground floor (following the fire)
PUBLICATION: Daniel Catton Rich, ed., *Seurat Paintings and
Drawings* (Chicago: The Art Institute of Chicago, 1958)
CIRCULATING VENUES:
The Art Institute of Chicago, Chicago, Illinois:
    January 16–March 7, 1958

In 1958, the Museum mounted a major retrospective of the work of Georges Seurat, originally organized by Daniel Catton Rich for the Art Institute of Chicago. The exhibition included 175 works, perhaps none more significant than *A Sunday on La Grande Jatte— 1884* from the Art Institute's collection. It was the first and last time the great painting ever left that museum: its donor stipulated that it could never be moved from the Institute, but on his deathbed he conceded it could travel once—to MoMA. A grand affair, the painting (estimated to be worth $1 million at the time) was sent by special railroad car to Hoboken, then transported to the Museum, with a police escort, in an insulated truck. The canvas formed a focal point of the exhibition, along with three other large works.

D'Harnoncourt ably arranged the large number of pictures included in the exhibition. The largest paintings were each assigned an entire wall within a large gallery, while the medium-sized works were organized into groups of three or four in room-sized galleries. The remaining 138 smaller works on paper were grouped and distributed among galleries and hallways. These groups were sometimes staggered along a long wall, or in one case, recessed in a "false" wall similar to a jewelry showcase.

D'Harnoncourt's organization of the exhibition into sections revealed a sensitivity to color employed for the best effect. To create a contrast with the black and white of the drawings on paper, he placed them in galleries painted red and green, which also mitigated the visual static of differing mats and frames. The painting galleries, by contrast, were painted white and dark grey. D'Harnoncourt was particularly concerned that the lighting be strong enough to clarify the subtle colors, and a unique solution was devised: lightbulbs were shielded behind baffles and pointed obliquely at the pictures, so their beams wouldn't reflect on the glass. Further, the use of alternating white- and blue-hued lightbulbs produced the effect of natural light. For *La Grand Jatte*, a second set of lights was placed on the floor, and the room was painted grey with the great painting hung on a white accent wall. This exhibition provided what was perhaps one of d'Harnoncourt's most radical installation gestures: in the last gallery there was a freestanding, massive, dark table with recesses cut into the surface. It operated like a giant light table: in these niches, some half-dozen drawings were displayed, illuminated from below.

On April 15, 1958, just three weeks after the exhibition opened, a fire broke out on the second floor of the Museum, damaging six works from the Museum collection and killing one employee. D'Harnoncourt had to deliver

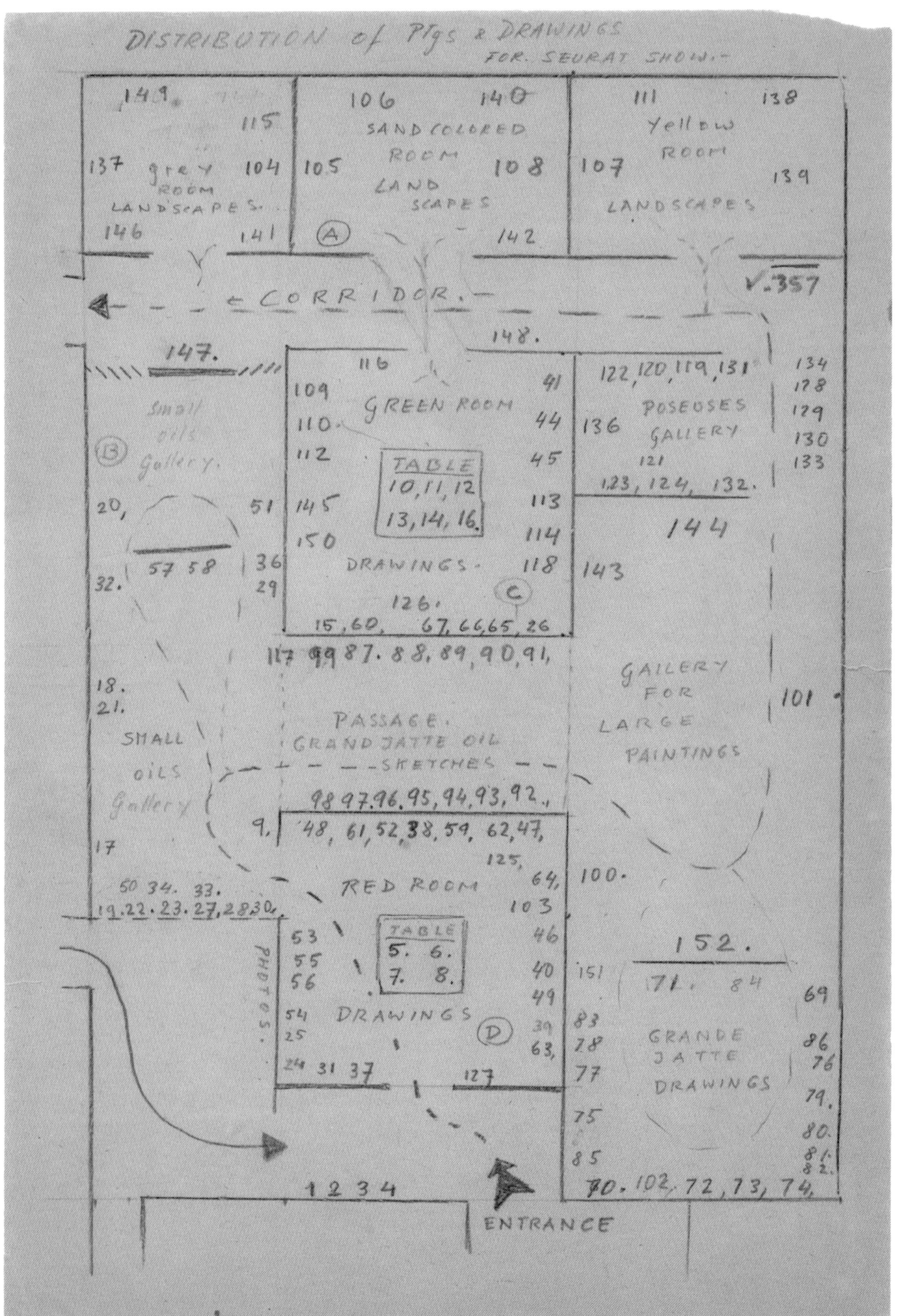

Floor plan for the exhibition, c. 1958

the regrettable news to the director of the Chicago Art Institute; none of the works in the Institute's collection had been damaged. The Museum quickly redesigned its ground-floor galleries, creating partitions with cinder-block walls so as to be fireproof. Once the plaster on the new partitions was dry, the exhibition reopened, but d'Harnonourt's installation was not reprised, and regrettably, the official installation photographs that exist for the exhibition document the presentation after the fire.[34]

The exhibition was warmly received, as attested by the review in the *New York Times*, which declared it "one of the most interesting and best installed shows devoted to the work of a single artist that the Museum has ever put on."[35] John Maxon, director of the Museum of Art of the Rhode Island School of Design, wrote to d'Harnoncourt: "This is but a note to tell you that the installation of the Seurat Show is quite the handsomest in my memory of the many elegant ones in the history of your Museum. As it must have been a particularly hard task, I was especially impressed. At any rate, it is a superb presentation and I congratulate you."[36]

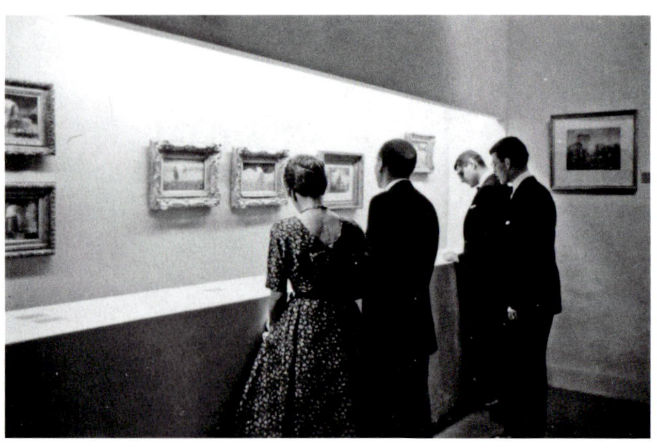

Installation of drawings recessed into a "false" wall, 1958

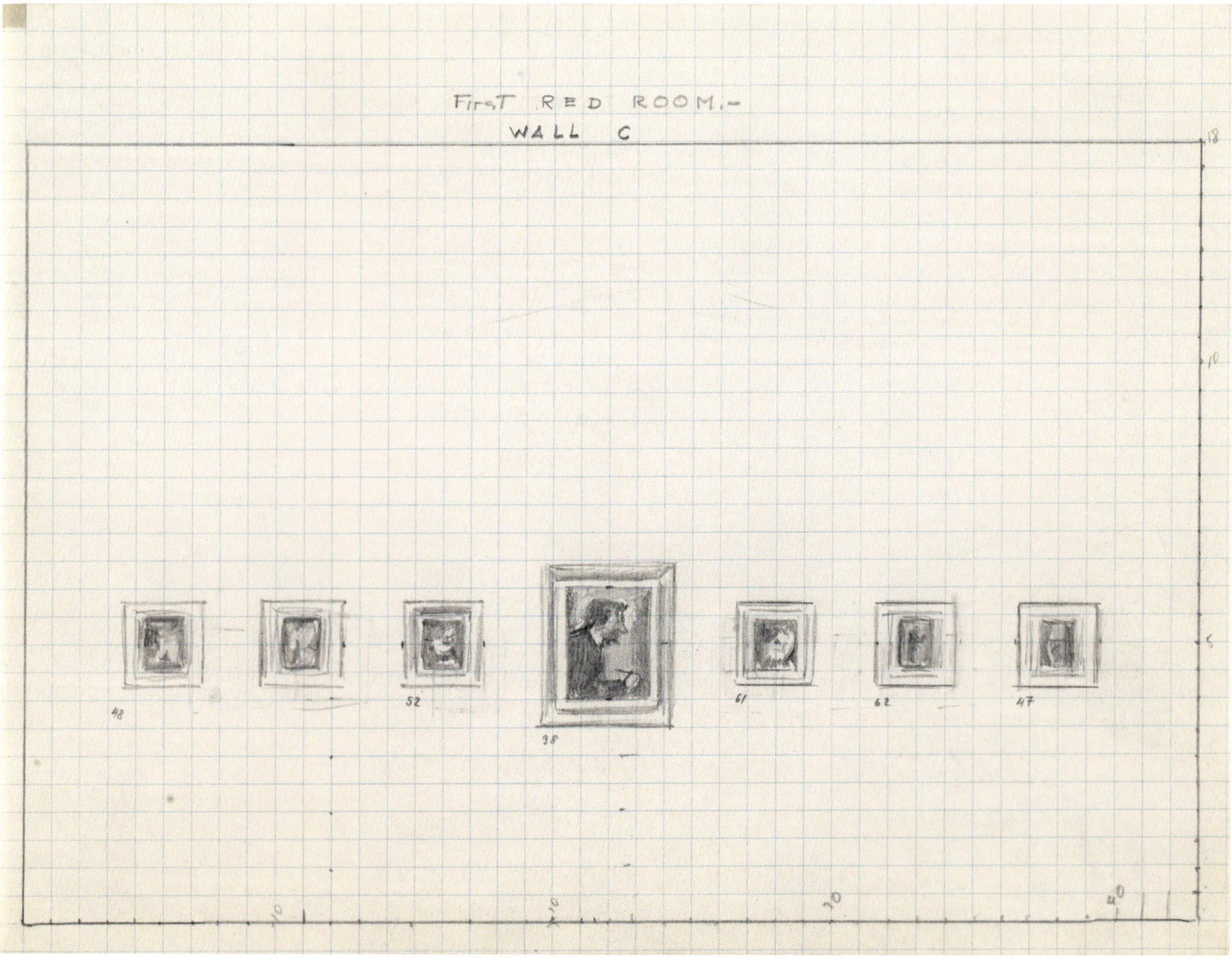

Vista of conté crayon drawings, to be hung on a red wall, c. 1958

D'Harnoncourt and guest at the opening of the exhibition, standing in the passage leading to *La Grande Jatte* lined with oil preparatory sketches for that painting. The addition of vertical elements on the wall, creating a series of niches, established a rhythm. In the ceiling, baffles made it possible to hide and control the lighting.

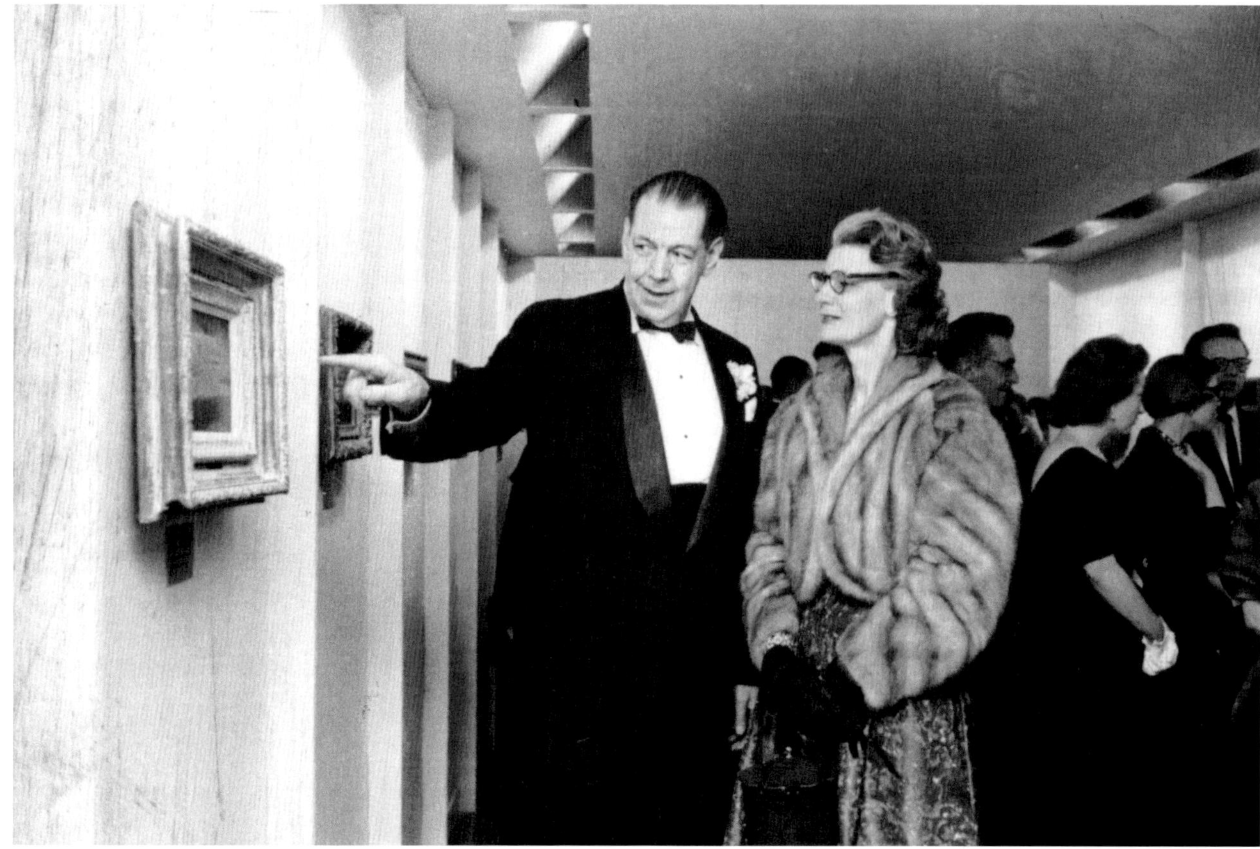

D'Harnoncourt and guest at the opening, leaning over the "light table" designed by d'Harnoncourt to display unframed drawings in the recesses, lit from below.

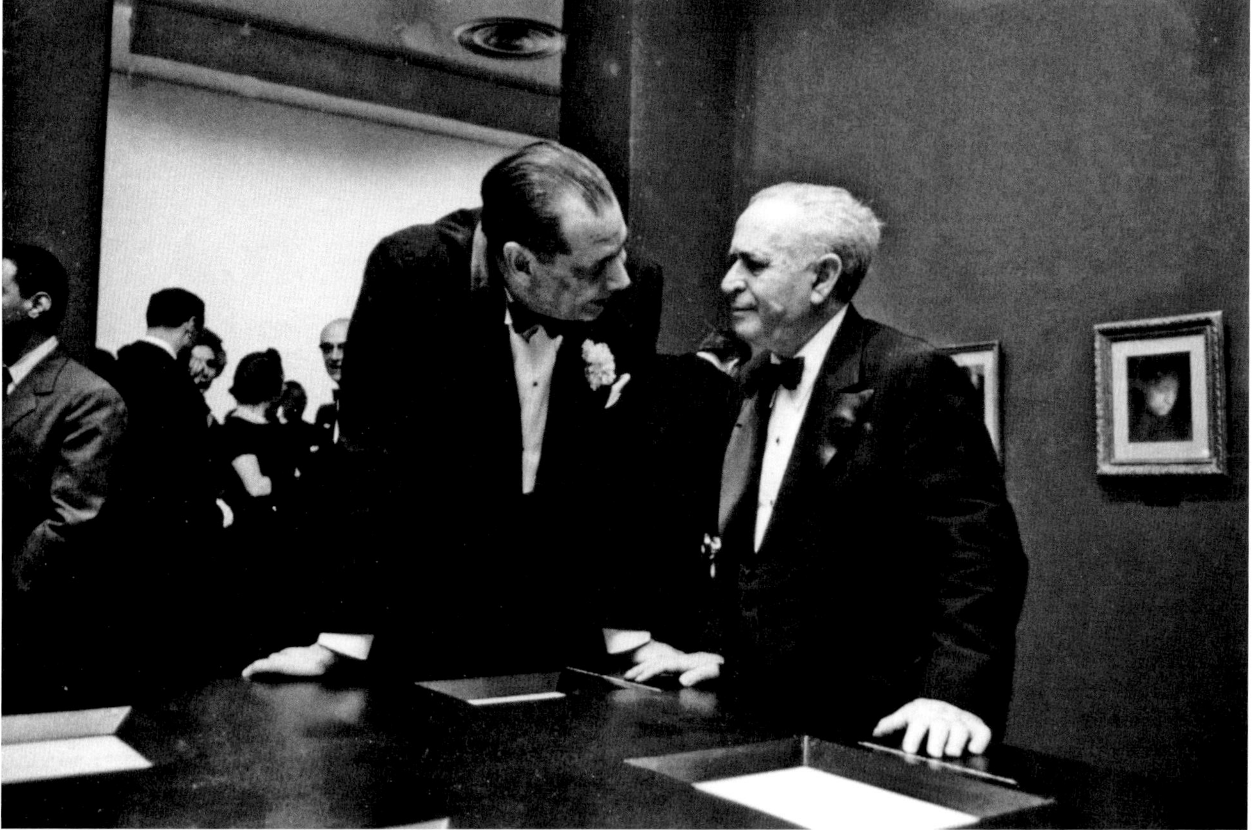

Jean Arp: A Retrospective

MoMA Exhibition #631; October 8–November 30, 1958

CURATOR: James Thrall Soby
NUMBER OF WORKS: 113 collages, string pictures, wood reliefs, and stone sculptures
LOCATION: Third floor
PUBLICATION: James Thrall Soby, ed., *Arp* (New York: The Museum of Modern Art, 1958)

D'Harnoncourt's next monographic exhibition (and one of four exhibitions marking the reopening of the Museum after the fire of 1958), *Jean Arp: A Retrospective* was curated by James Thrall Soby. It presented d'Harnoncourt with a number of new challenges. It was a full career retrospective; yet Arp's work displayed little stylistic evolution, as the artist established his style in 1926 and thereafter kept investigating and reexamining it in various media. The exhibition included an abundance of small works—another challenge in installation. In d'Harnoncourt's care, the exhibition was nonetheless realized with great panache. He found a way to allow the visitor ample space to circum-navigate the works, while providing a background screen to remove the distraction of seeing too many works together by segmenting the main hall with piers and four wing-like canvas structures. He also arranged the works to progress from small to large, so that in the end *Ptolemy I*, which was only forty inches tall, had the effect of a monumental sculpture.

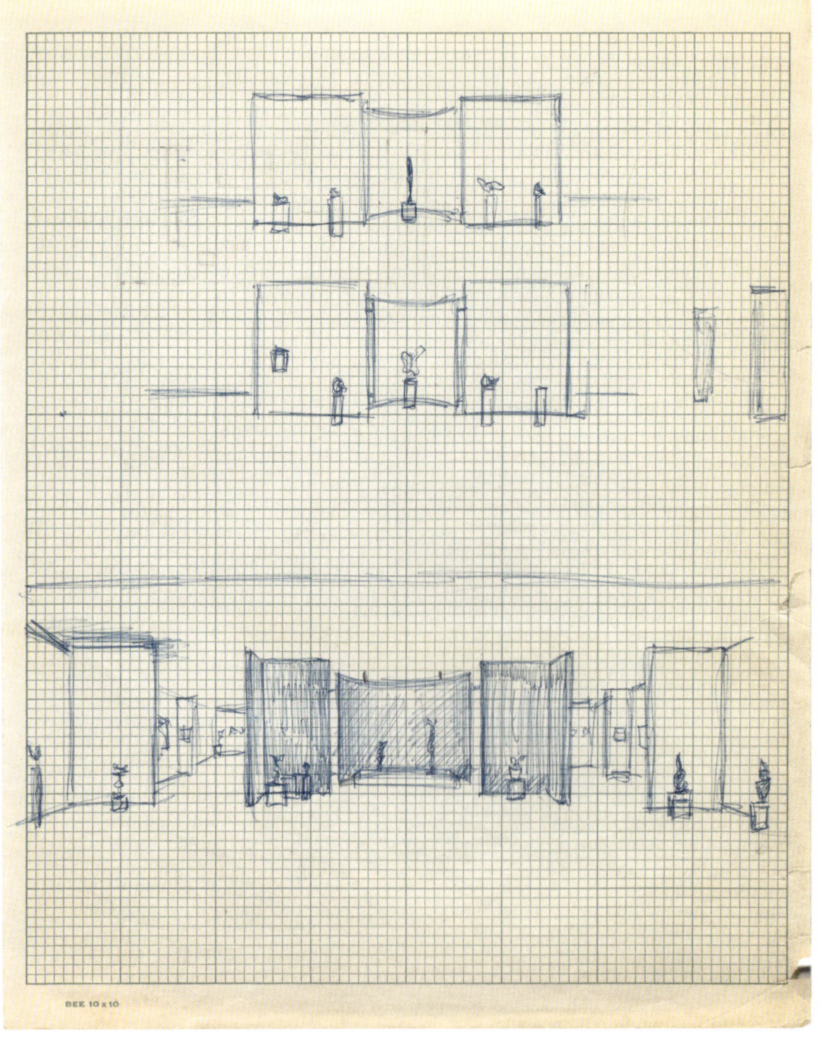

Vista of the exhibition, 1958, showing the contrast of the dark and light walls

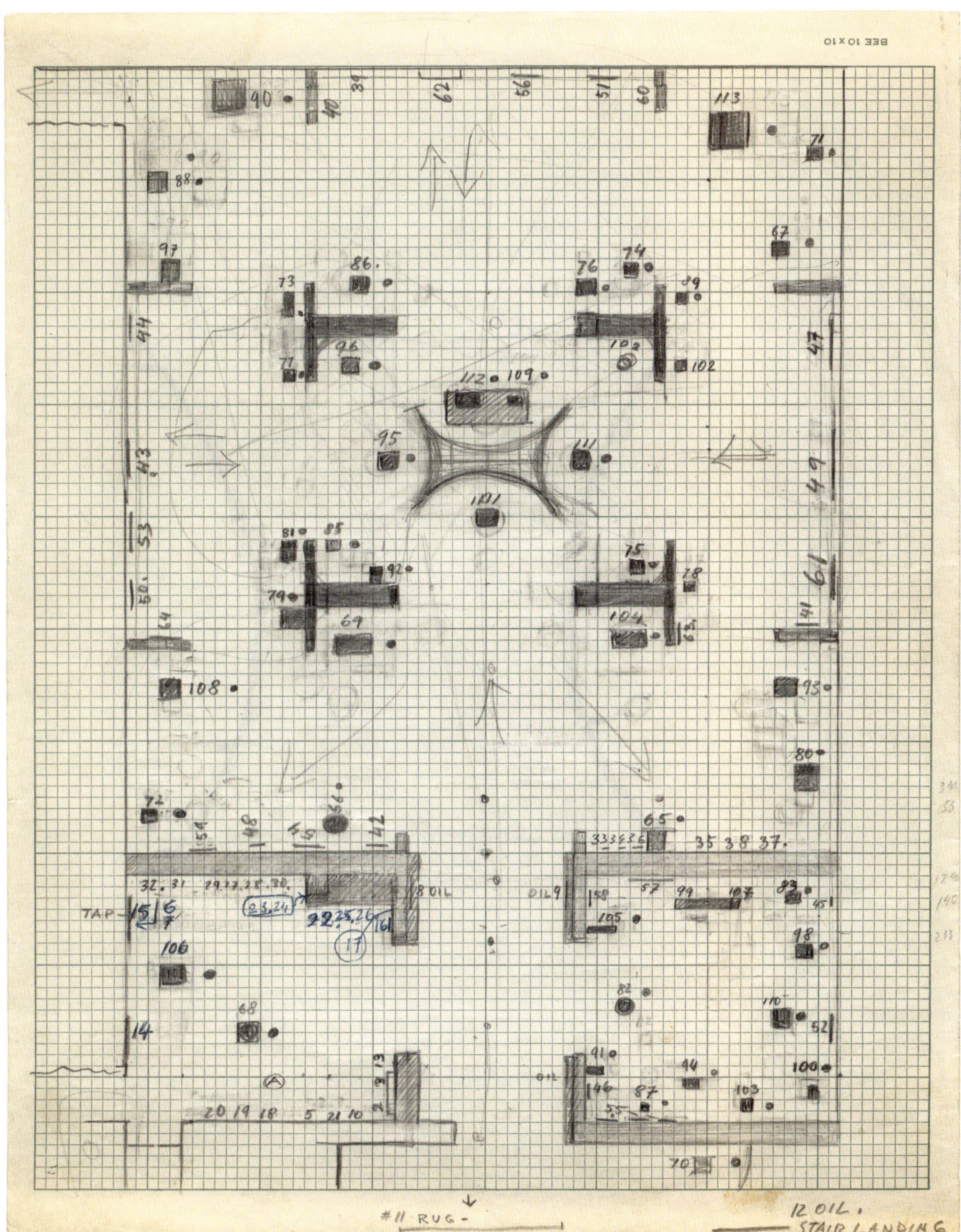

Floor plan for the exhibition, 1958

D'Harnoncourt effectively employed a suite of neutral tones. He placed the white marble works against white walls; black walls were provided behind composite stone objects; grey walls appeared behind bronze sculpture; and canvas framed the dark granite works. He paired this with the use of soft-effect lighting.

These details did not go unnoticed. Reviewer Dorothy Adlow described how the viewer was gradually able to perceive the affinities among the works:

> At first glance, these highly simplified shapes seem elementary and possibly without meaning. But with long viewing, they come alive and there seems to be a likely logic in the arrangements, such logic as we take for granted in a pile of leaves swept on the ground, or in a handful of pebbles dropped on the beach.[37]

William Rubin, who in 1967 joined the Museum where he would establish his prodigious career, reviewed the exhibition for *Arts Magazine*, showing an acute sensitivity to the problem of display. He wrote:

> In Arp's case, installation constituted a greater challenge than selection, and Mr. d'Harnoncourt responded with a beautifully conceived exhibition. . . . The novel arrangement of the main hall . . . creates a continuous flow of space. . . . With newly installed lights providing a softer effect, the over-all appearance of the main hall is superb.[38]

Arp attended the opening of the exhibition, and according to Soby, "He was delighted with René d'Harnoncourt's installation and to see so many of his works again after a number of years."[39] Carola Giedion-Welcker, whose book on Arp was sold concurrently with the Museum's exhibition catalogue, wrote Soby that Arp was very pleased with the show and its generosity of spirit. She continued: "[Arp] showed me photos of René d'Harnoncourt's installation— superb! I thought that <u>never</u> have Arp's works been shown in such an orchestration and correspondence."[40] A year after d'Harnoncourt's death, trustee James Thrall Soby wrote: "It goes without saying that René was *the* master in this field. Indeed, I will never forget Arp's rather wistful, sad comment when he and I were walking through his show just before it closed. 'I know,' he said quietly, 'that my work will never again look this well.'"[41]

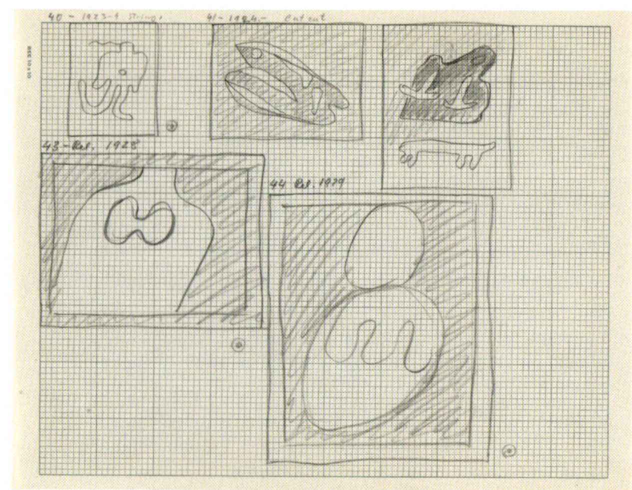

Scale drawings of sculptures, 1958

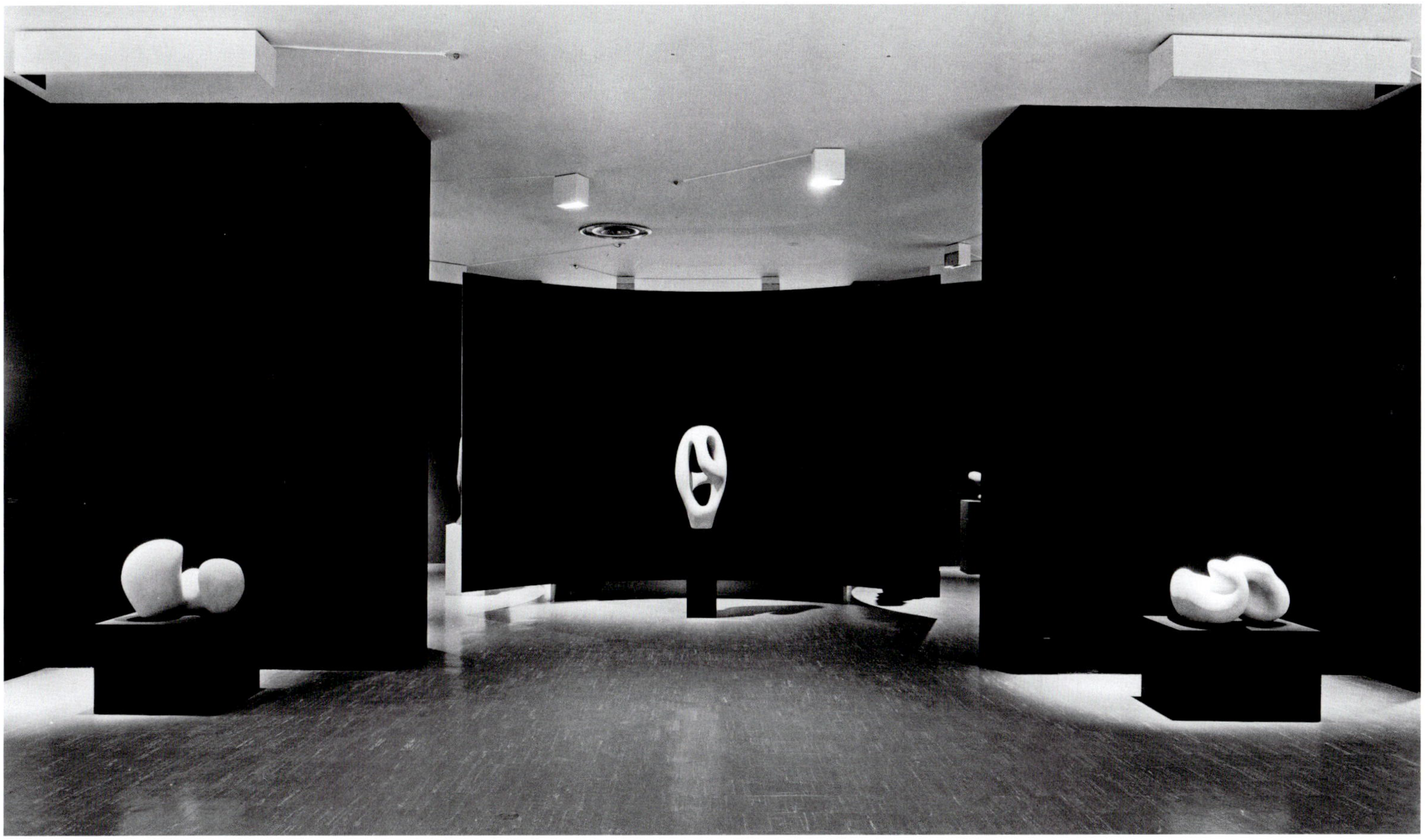

Above: Installation view of three sculptures, including *Ptolemy I* (1953), 1958. Arp's organic white forms looked particularly striking against a black wall and mounted on black pedestals.

Right: Scale drawings of sculptures, 1958

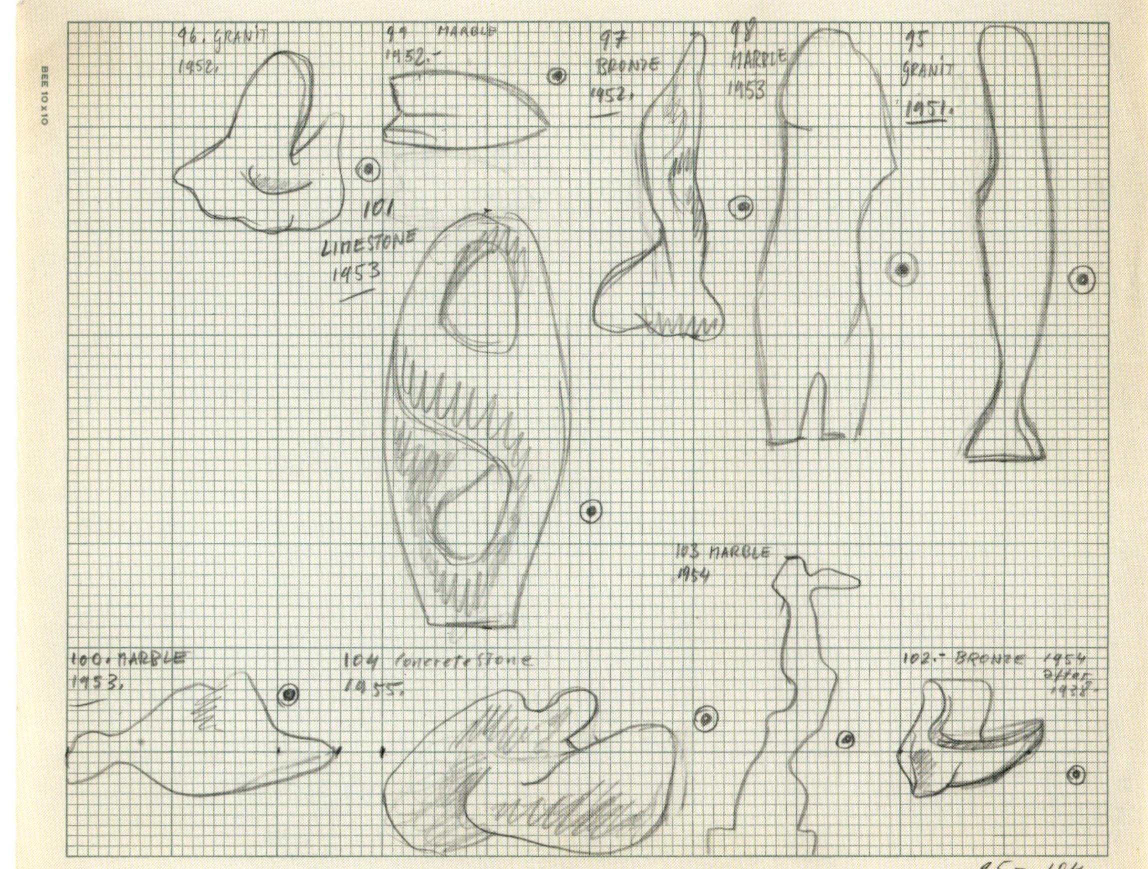

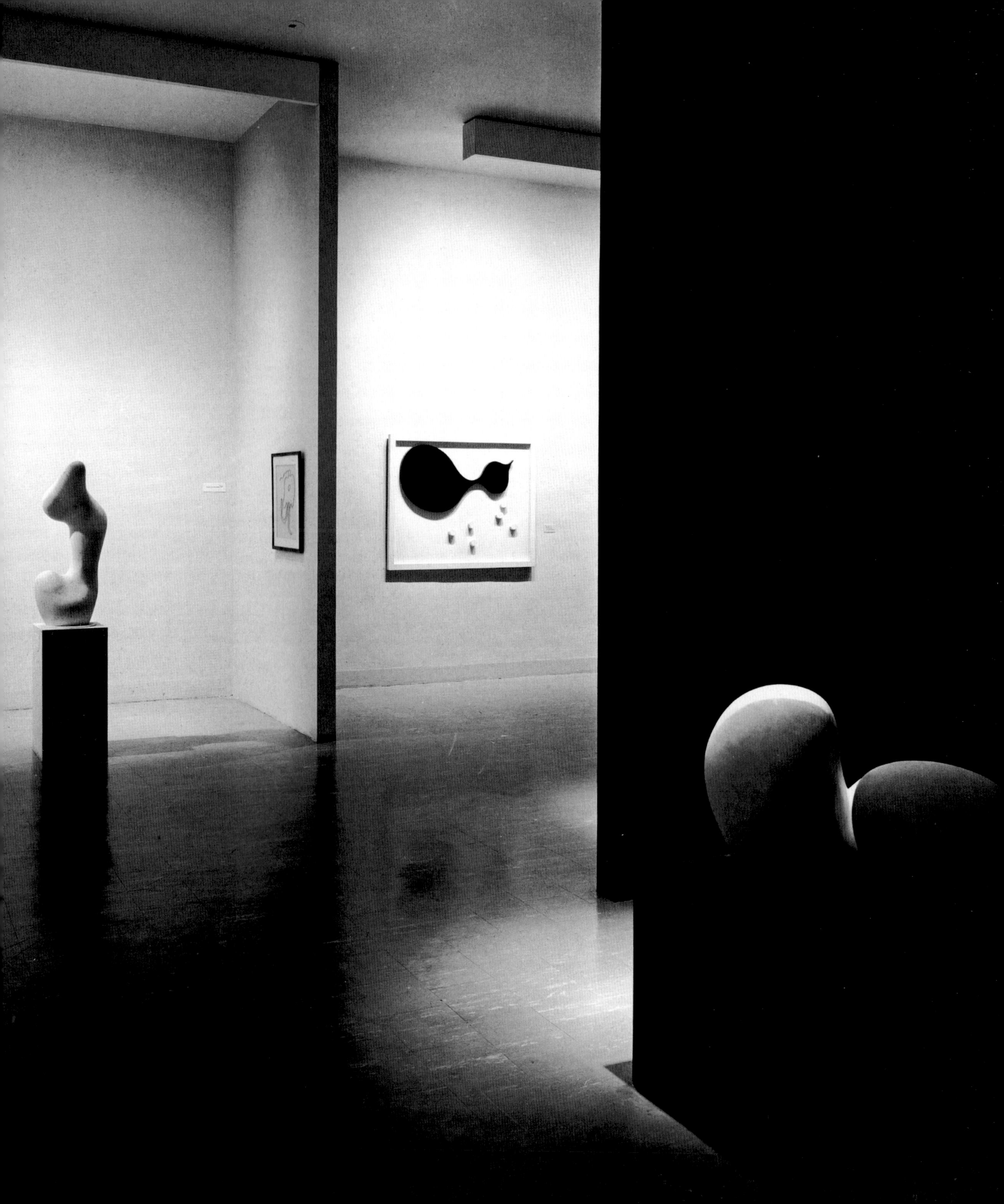

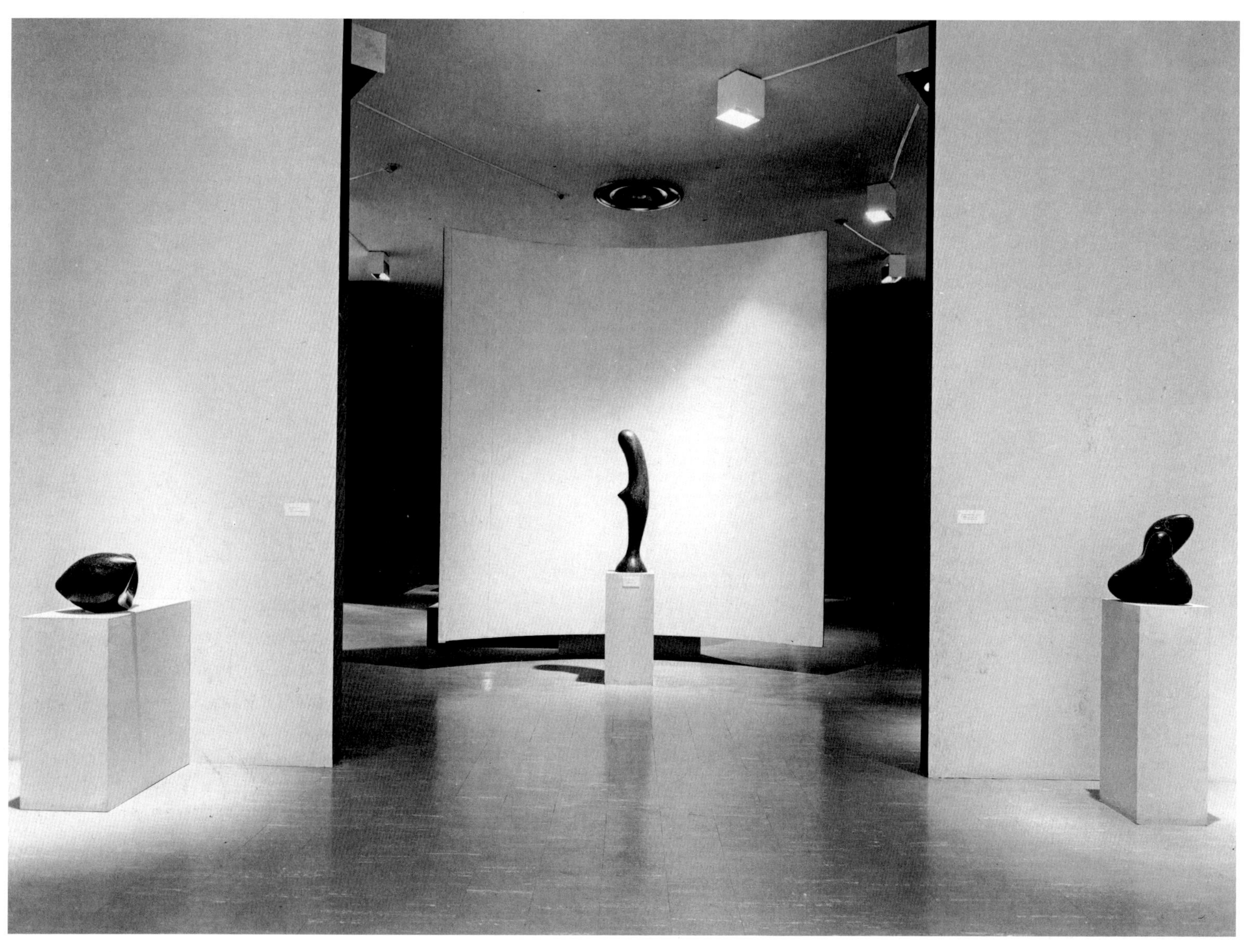

Installation views of the exhibition, 1958

Art of the Asmat - The Collection of Michael C. Rockefeller

MoMA Exhibition #709a; September 11–November 6, 1962

CURATOR: Collected by Michael C. Rockefeller
NUMBER OF WORKS: 135
LOCATION: 16 West 54th Street (Sculpture Garden)
PUBLICATION: *The Art of the Asmat, New Guinea: Collected by Michael C. Rockefeller*, notes by A. A. Gerbrands (New York: The Museum of Primitive Art, 1962)

The *Art of the Asmat* exhibition was devoted to the artistic production, in the southwest region of New Guinea, of a native population that called itself the Asmat, meaning "the people." The works on view formed part of the collection gathered during two trips to the region by Michael C. Rockefeller, a trustee of the Museum of Primitive Art and son of Nelson Rockefeller, co-founder of the Museum of Primitive Art.[42] The exhibition served as a tribute to Michael, who disappeared during his second research expedition. The show was officially organized by the Museum of Primitive Art, with MoMA acting as a cosponsor. It was on view in a pavilion in MoMA's Abby Aldrich Rockefeller Sculpture garden at 16 West 54th Street and continued in a gallery at the Museum of Primitive Art across the street.

This purpose-built, one-story pavilion was designed by MoMA's chief curator of Architecture and Design Arthur Drexler with the architect Guster Henschell. Its layout was developed by d'Harnoncourt with Douglas Newton, curator of the Museum of Primitive Art. The pavilion had a simple, light metal frame with a roof and wall panels, and a big gallery with canvas walls to let light filter in; it was meant to be evocative of Asmat houses.

The Asmat had a strong spiritual tradition, which was embodied in their sculptural production. For them, life, art, and magic were one; their creation myth held that a lonely magician placed carved figurines in a clearing and that they came to life when he played his drum. Among the hallmarks of their artistic output are *bisj* poles, created to honor recently slain Asmat warriors. Examples of these were featured in the show, presented outdoors in the open central courtyard, as they would have been in the Asmat village; they were "certainly the dramatic climax of the Exhibition," acknowledged d'Harnoncourt.[43] The interior spaces included shields, spears, masks, ancestral figures, and animal sculptures, all intensely illuminated, many suspended or hanging from poles, to evoke an Asmat ceremonial house. The exhibition, in its dramatic installation, sought to convey "the expressive force of Asmat art, its bold design, its ritual function and its symbolic content."[44]

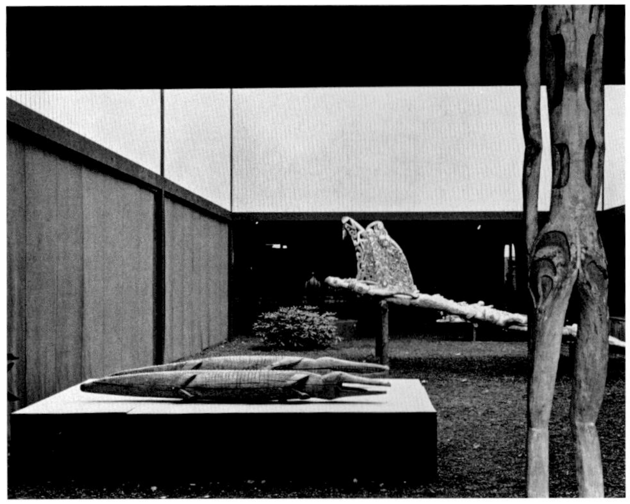

Installation view of wooden sculptures, 1962

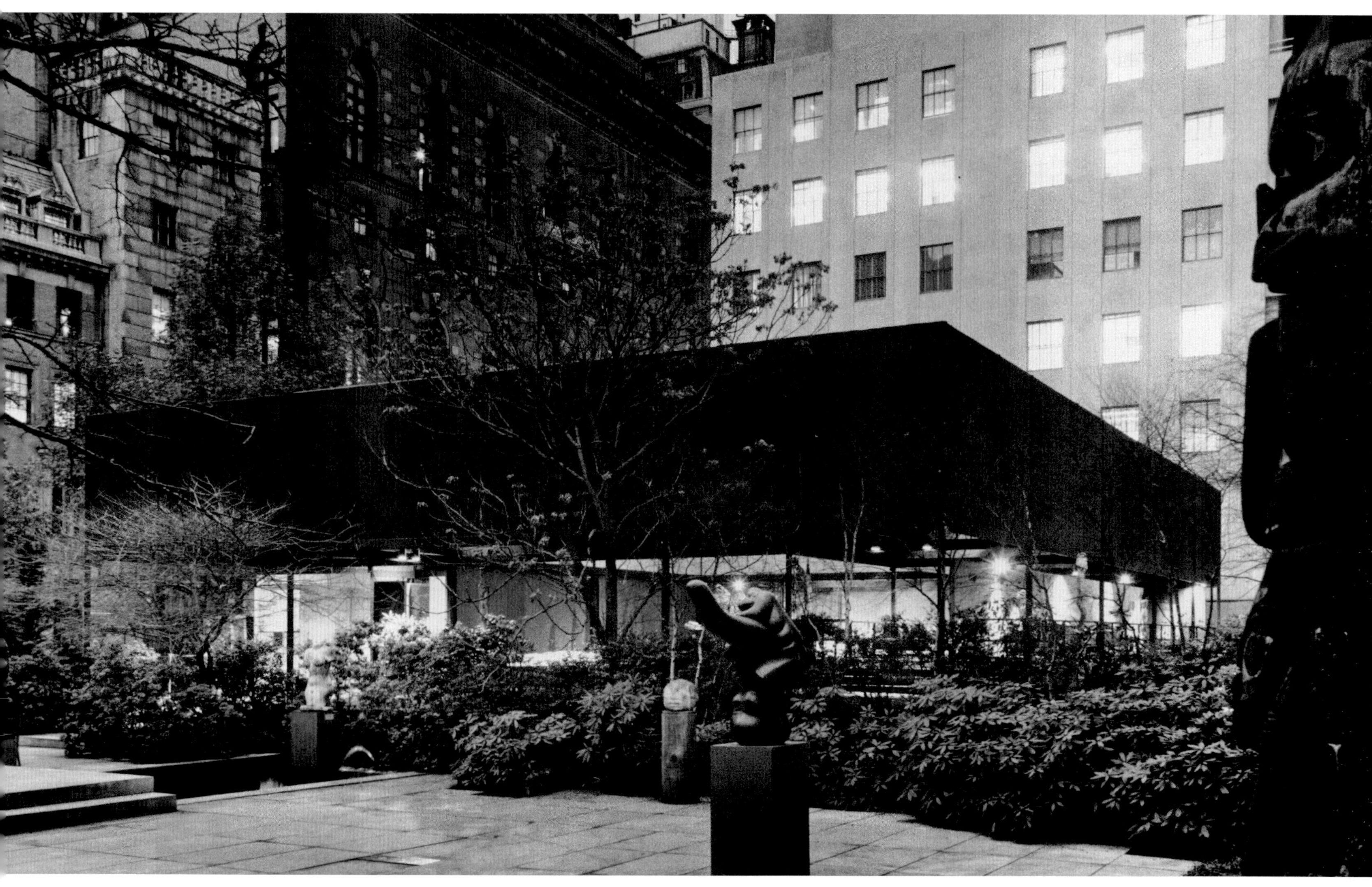

Pavilion built for the exhibition in the Museum's garden, 1962

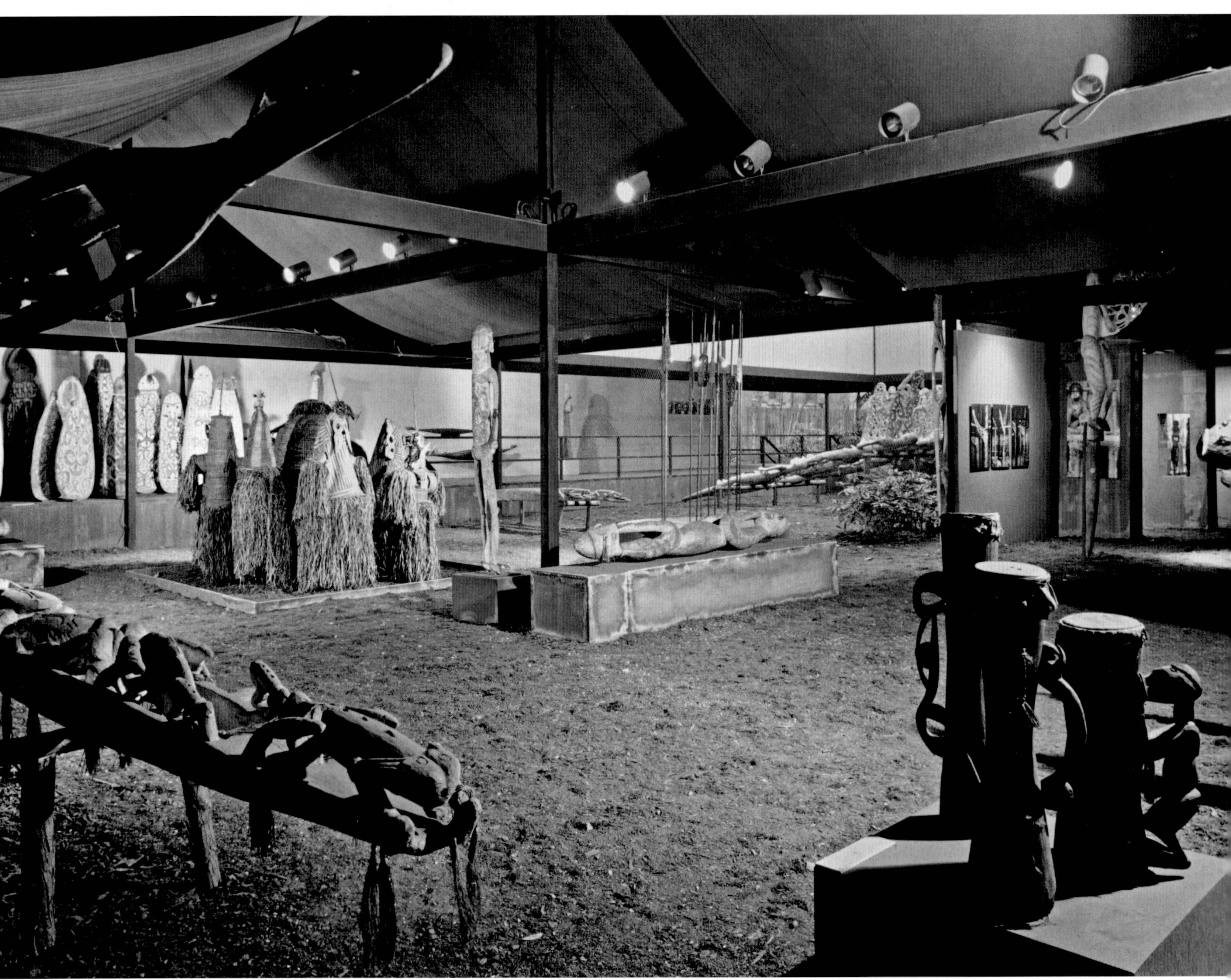

Above and opposite: Installation views of the exhibition, 1962, including *bisj* poles

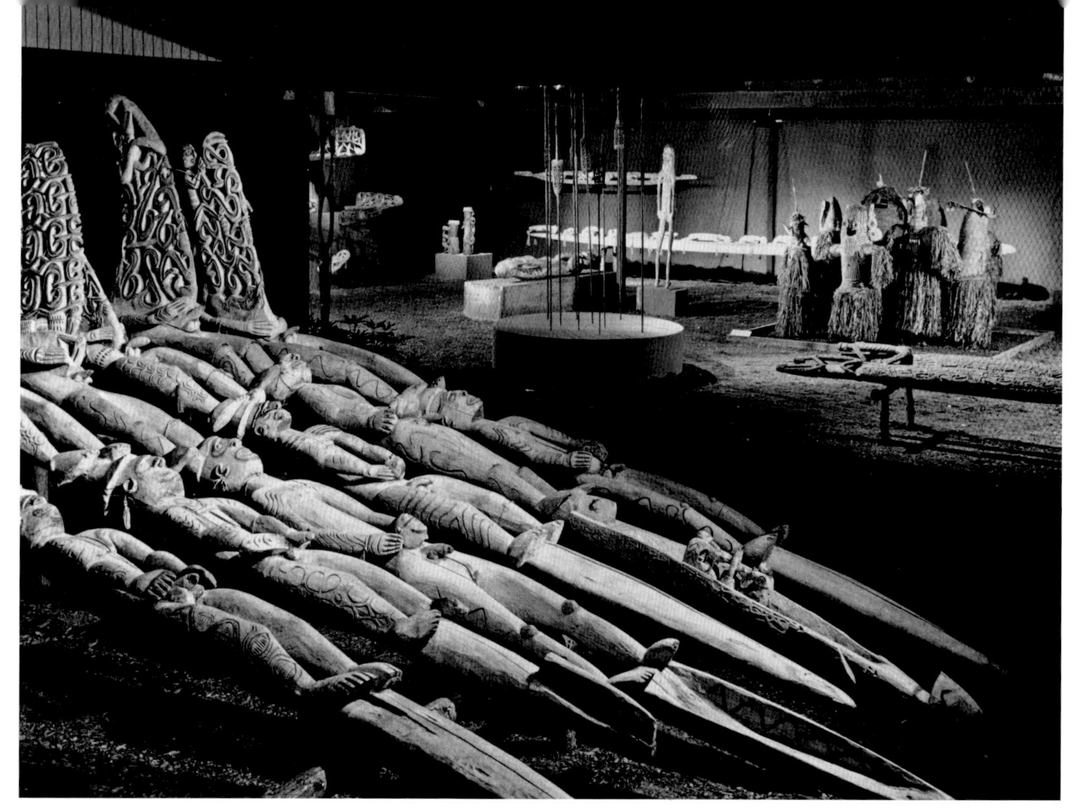

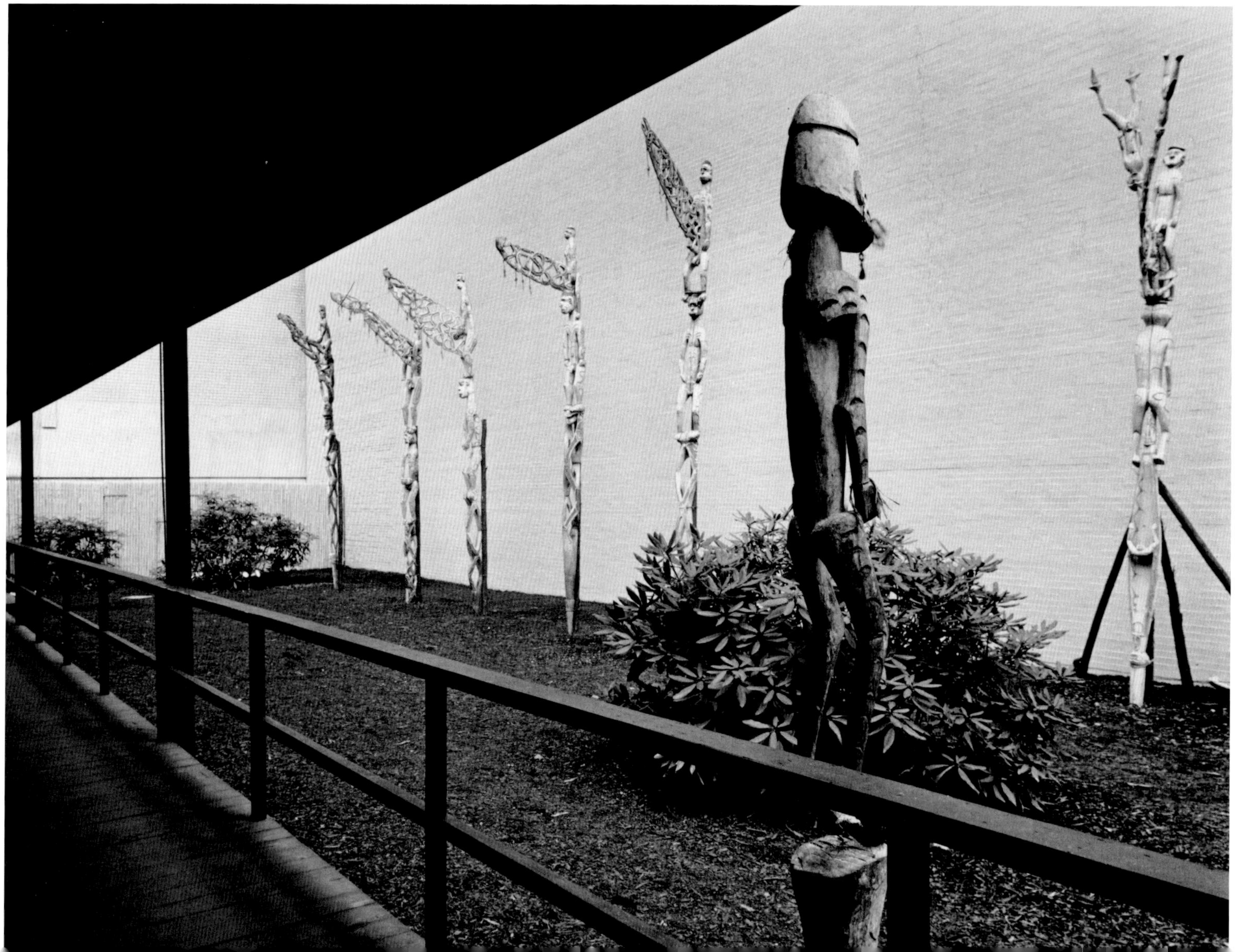

Rodin

MoMA Exhibition #721; May 1–September 8, 1963

CURATOR: Peter Selz
NUMBER OF WORKS: 100 sculptures in bronze, marble, terra cotta, and plaster; 45 drawings, watercolors, and prints
LOCATION: First floor and Sculpture Garden
PUBLICATION: Albert E. Elsen, *Rodin* (New York: The Museum of Modern Art, 1963)
CIRCULATING VENUES:
The Works of Auguste Rodin (1840–1970), California Palace of the Legion of Honor, San Francisco, California: October 19–December 8, 1963

The 1963 *Rodin* exhibition comprised one hundred sculptures and forty-five works on paper by the well-known and beloved artist, selected by Peter Selz, curator of the Department of Paintings and Sculpture since 1958 (year of his celebrated exhibition *New Images of Man*). Prints were presented on the second floor, while d'Harnoncourt's installation of Rodin's sculptures took over the entire first floor and garden. Reviewing the show for the *New York Times,* John Canaday almost seemed bored with praising the museum over and over with each new show: "Everyone knows Rodin by now and everyone knows that the museum always does a fine job of installation, so there you are." He appreciated the rearrangement of the Museum's garden to accommodate certain large pieces, centering on *The Burghers of Calais* and dominated by a series of versions of *St. John the Baptist.* "The only way to see sculpture better than in a well illuminated interior disposition is in the open air with greenery, water and architecture as complements," he noted. "The museum has come up with a beautiful show, indoors and out."[45]

The exhibition was resoundingly well received. According to *Time* magazine, it "was near perfection—the superb work of a giant superbly installed. The critics were all superlatives."[46] The eminent Rodin scholar Albert Elsen, author of the exhibition catalogue, commented, "D'Harnoncourt, who installed the exhibition, made no attempt at an art historical or didactic arrangement. On the basis of deep feeling for each piece and its visual rightness in combination with others, as well as a desire to let each work receive full attention, he created a superb installation that avoided the temptations of distracting dramatic effects."[47]

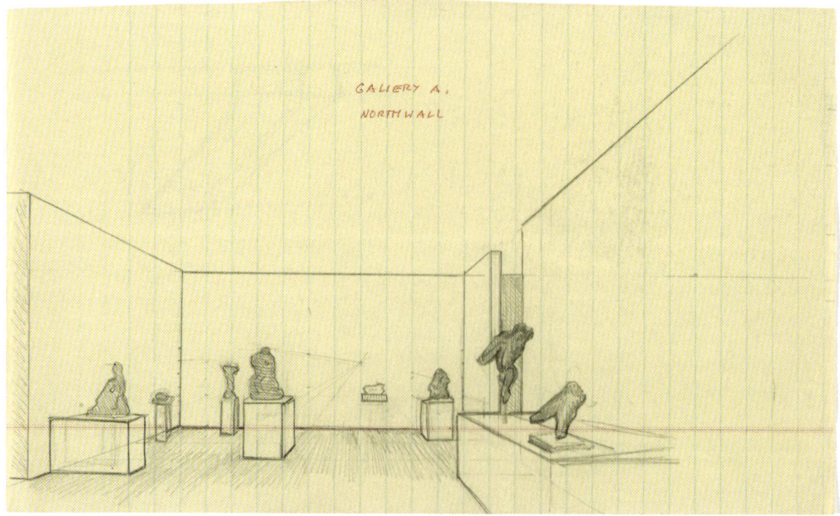

Vista of Gallery A, North Wall, 1963

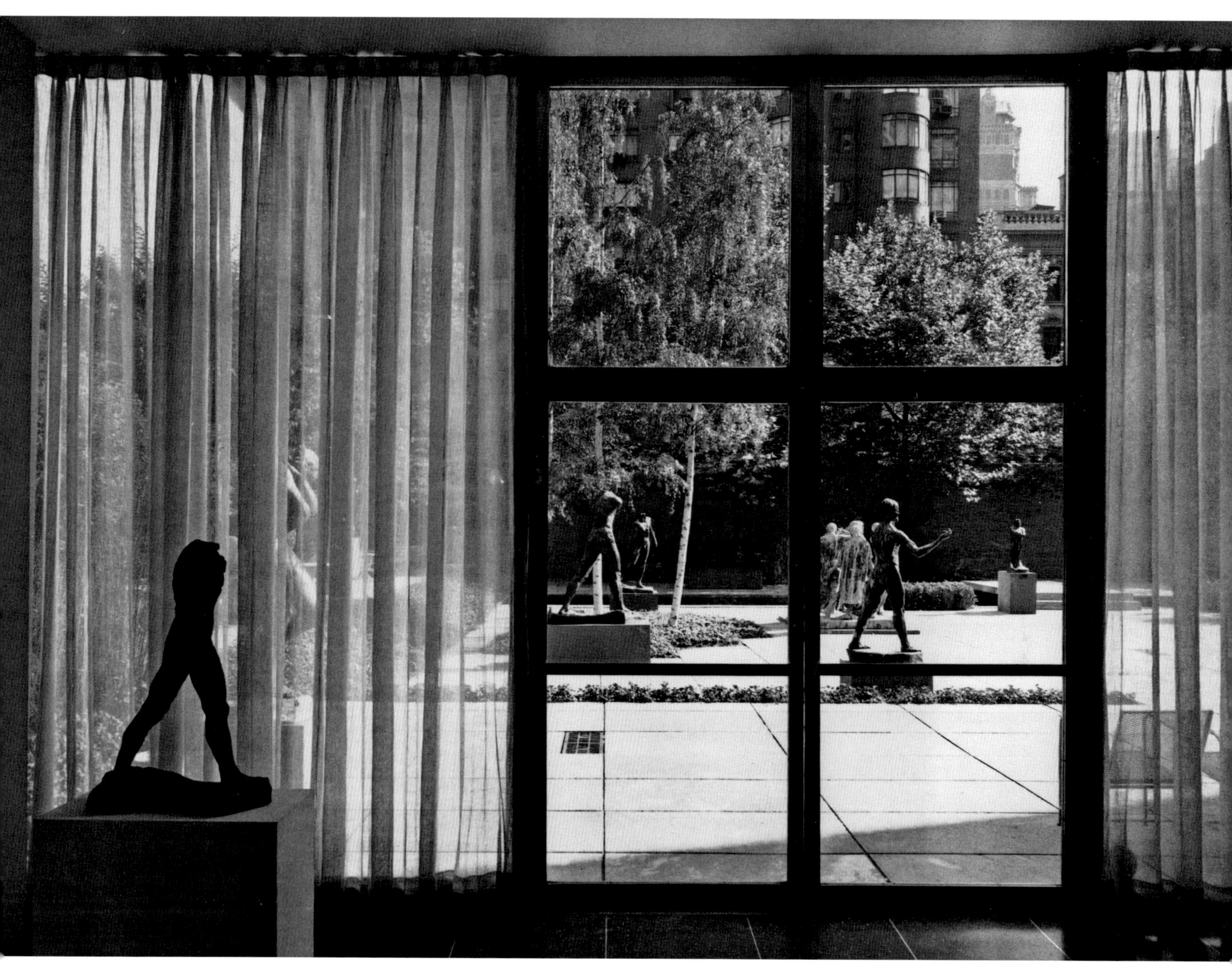

Installation view of the exhibition looking out into the Sculpture
Garden, where sculptures by Rodin were installed in plein air, 1963

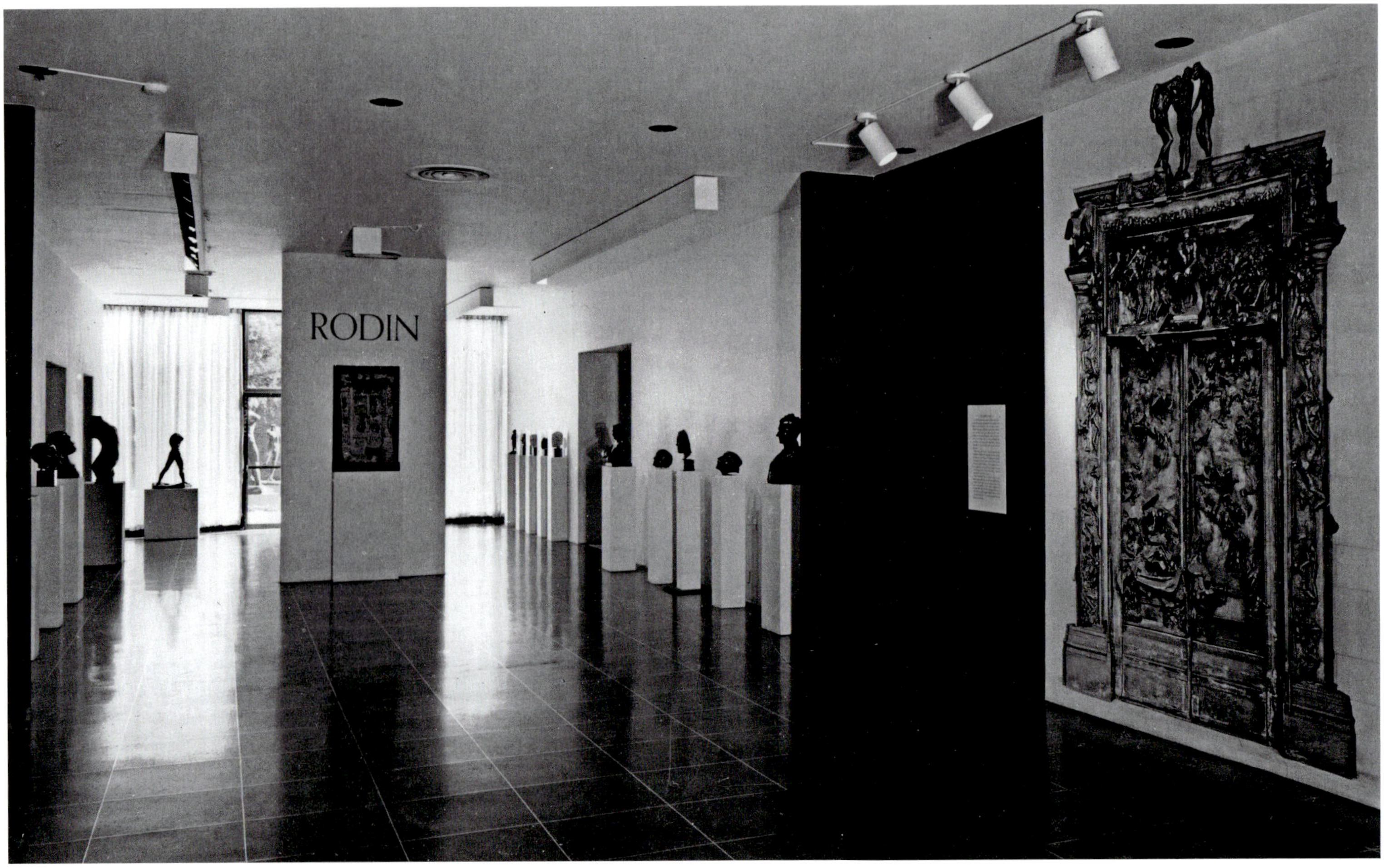

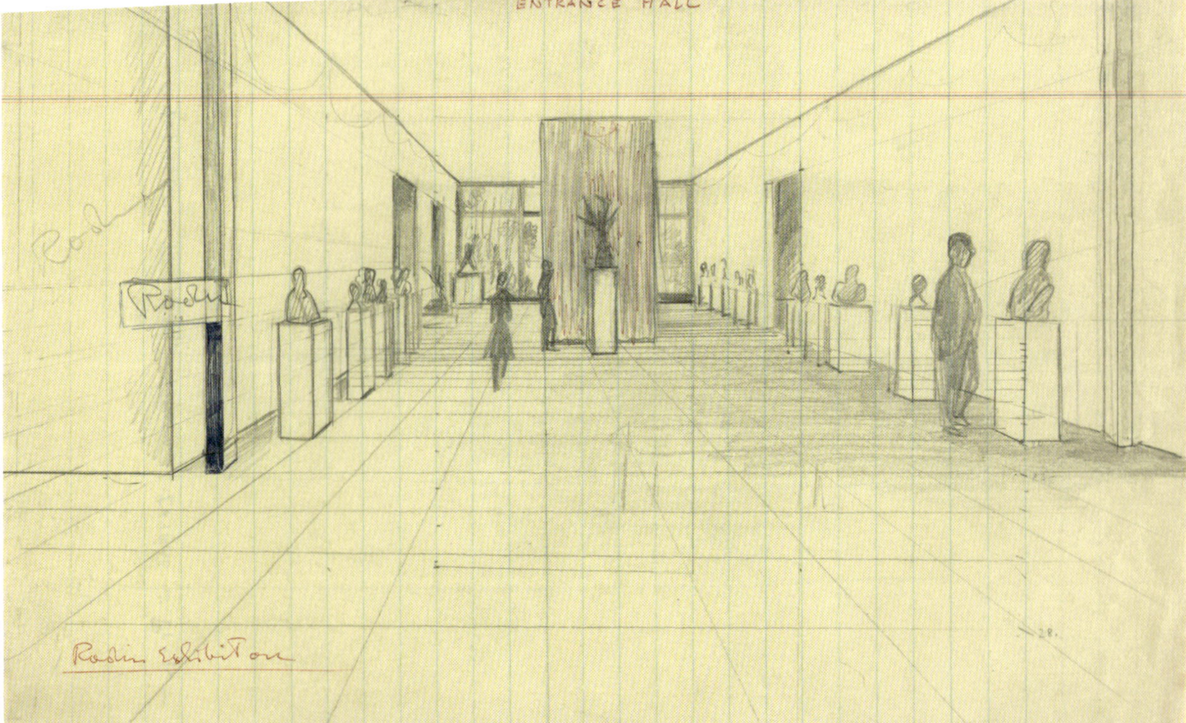

Above: Installation view of the entrance hall, 1963

Left: Vista of the entrance hall, including Museum visitors for scale, 1963

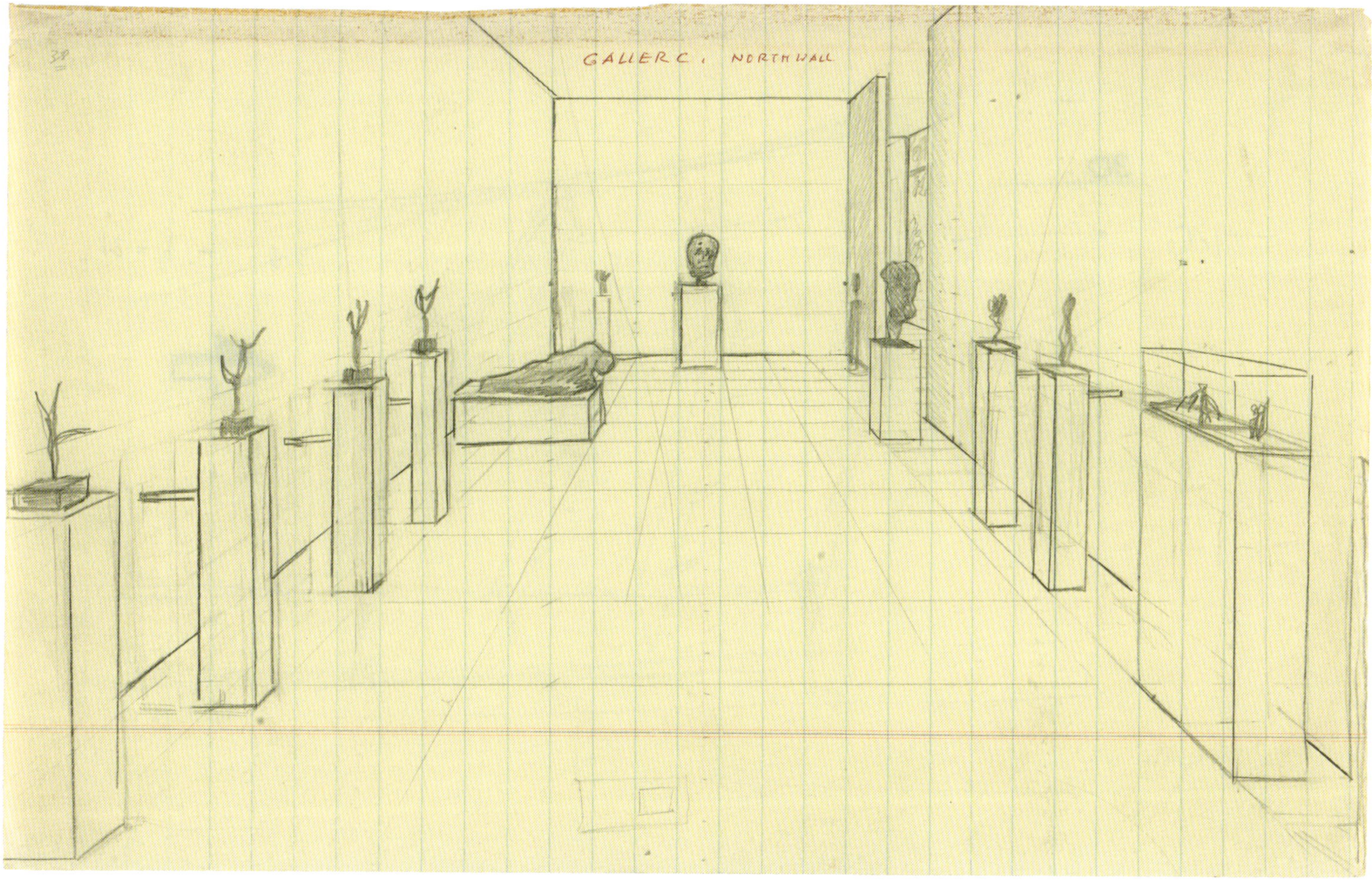

Vista of Gallery C, North Wall, 1963

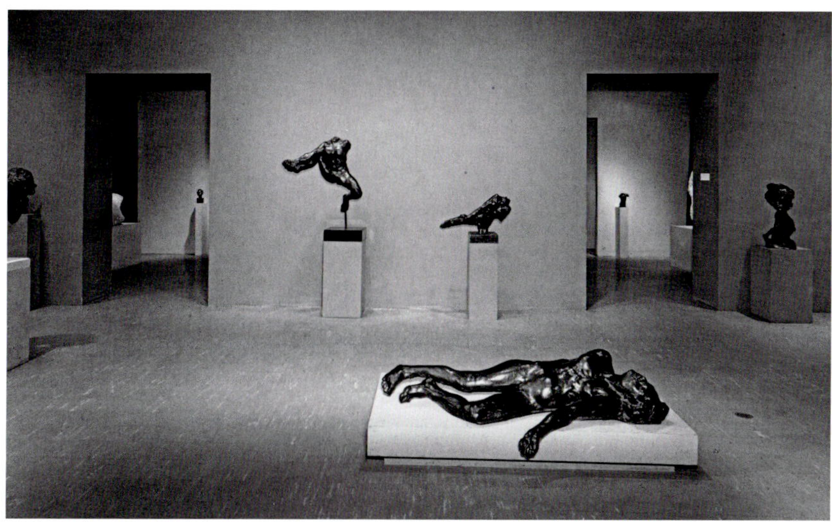

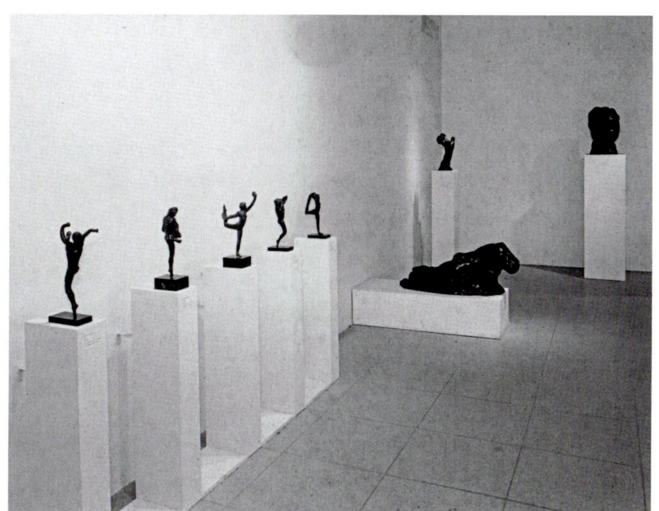

Installation views of figurines on pedestals of various heights, 1963

The Sculpture of Picasso

MoMA Exhibition #841; October 11, 1967–January 1, 1968

CURATOR: Roland Penrose
NUMBER OF WORKS: More than 200 bronze, paper, wood, and sheet-metal sculptures
LOCATION: First floor
PUBLICATION: Roland Penrose, *The Sculpture of Picasso* (New York: The Museum of Modern Art, 1967)
CIRCULATING EXHIBITIONS:
Hommage à Pablo Picasso (Dessins, Sculptures, Céramiques), Petit and Grand Palais, Paris, France: November 18, 1966–February 12, 1967
Picasso: Sculpture, Ceramics, Graphic Work, Tate Gallery, London, United Kingdom: June 9–August 13, 1967

The culminating masterwork of d'Harnoncourt's distinguished career of exhibition installation was the 1967 *The Sculpture of Picasso*, the first major retrospective of Picasso's sculpture to be shown in the United States. A vast majority of the works were on loan from the artist himself. The exhibition was originally organized by Professor Jean Leymarie in Paris at the Petit Palais, then traveled to the Tate Gallery in London, under the direction of Sir Roland Penrose, chairman of the Institute of Contemporary Art, a writer, painter, and collector who was also Picasso's friend and biographer.

D'Harnoncourt viewed the Paris version of the exhibition and made sketches onsite, then bought the catalogue and sketched the sculptures anew from the published images, referring to his original drawings; finally, to really acquaint himself with the work, he saw the show again in its London iteration. Both European venues presented the work chronologically. D'Harnoncourt took an altogether different approach for the installation in New York, choosing instead—as was his custom—to show the sculptures in complementary groupings, emphasizing aggregations by affinity of form and content.

"Except for the American Indian show we had in 1941, this show presented the greatest number of problems," d'Harnoncourt noted. "The variety of style and raw materials, the variety of content and form, all those are greater than almost any show I had done."[48] He juxtaposed objects similar in their use of Surrealist vocabulary; those sharing themes and forms; and those that worked together emotionally, that had, in d'Harnoncourt's words, the same "visual weight." He explained: "In one room, for example, there are two big figures facing each other. They're both constructions, but in one work each piece was shaped by the artist and the other is made up of found objects. They're the same height and the same visual weight but of different periods."[49]

D'Harnoncourt's approach was bolstered by the artist's own words, which appeared on a wall label in the exhibition: "The several manners I have used in my art must not be considered as an evolution, or as steps toward an unknown ideal. . . . All I have ever made was made for the present and with the hope that it will always remain in the present."[50] D'Harnoncourt had deployed a very similar quote by Picasso—"To me there is no past or future in art"—as the organizing rationale for the *Timeless Aspects of Modern Art* exhibition some two decades earlier. This aligns with d'Harnoncourt's philosophy on art, encapsulating his lifelong engagement with the arts of both yesterday and today, from near and far. He explained in an interview concurrent with the show: "Well, works of art are funny things. They speak different languages to different people at different times and I think, by and large, that it's a wonderful thing to see the same work of art occasionally under different circumstances."[51]

The exhibition opened with a beautiful, classical symmetry of entrance halls, followed by the formal space of the main hall, which dazzled with the

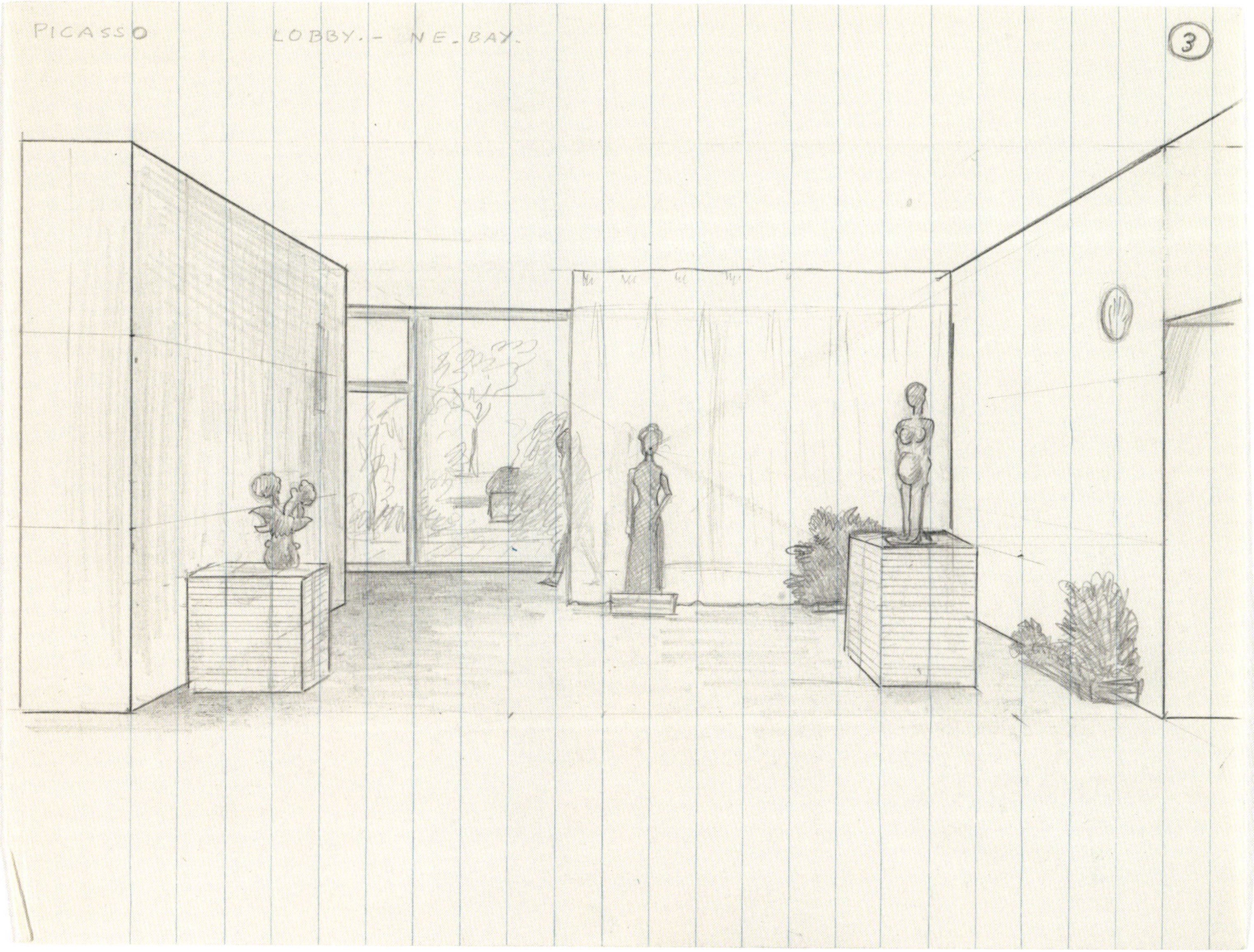

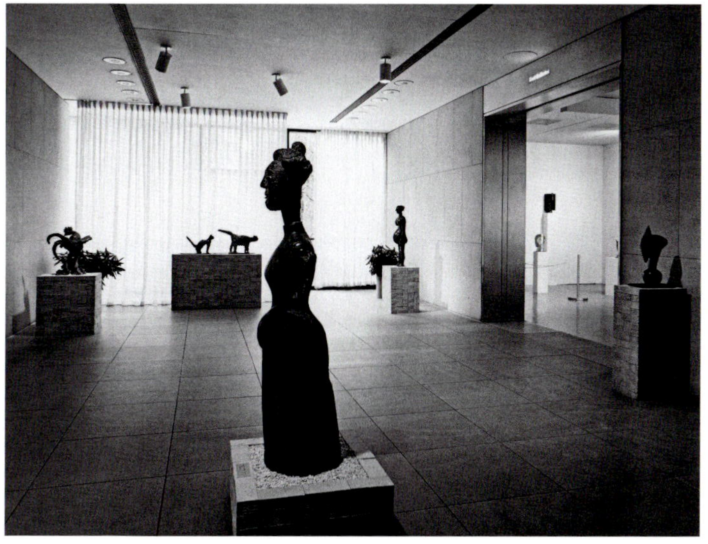

Above: Vista of the lobby of the exhibition, 1967

Right: Installation view of the exhibition, 1967. Here the pebbles that d'Harnoncourt used to cover the top of his brick pedestals are clearly visible.

inclusion of three of Picasso's world-famous, life-size bronzes: *Man with Sheep* (1944), *She-Goat* (1950), and *Pregnant Woman* (1950). Further into the show, a major sculptural group could not be included: *The Bathers* (1956)*,* owned by Nelson Rockefeller, which had been previously committed to another show. Instead, d'Harnoncourt installed a large photomural of the *Bathers*, flanked by two groups of similar works—four bronze figures and five flat-wood assemblages—endowing the entire grouping with a sense of completeness.

For his final installation, d'Harnoncourt employed a variety of novel techniques. First, he commissioned specially built pedestals constructed of buff-colored brick, topped with pebbles, for the main gallery. He thought the brick pedestals would be much more beautiful than painted wood, providing a contrast with the granite background and cast-bronze sculptures. He also had the ceilings in the main entrance gallery covered with unobtrusive plain white panels to create a clean and seamless backdrop to the space, and installed new lighting. In the gallery for Cubist experiments and constructions, he deployed a mirror-lined vitrine within a column that spanned the full height of the space. The presentation of monumental heads was carefully studied:

> I had this group of drawings of enormous heads, but they were enormous only in scale, not in size. Only when you are close can you see how big they really are. A nose may be 20 times as big as a real nose. I wanted a place where you wouldn't see them from far away. I also felt that because of their size they should not be cramped. That's why I used the round room. In a square room, the corners tell you the size. Here the effect is one of infinite space.[52]

He achieved this effect by deploying a large, curved wall to create a rounded gallery.

The Museum had initially wanted to take just a selection of the work from the European venues, but the artist insisted that all the works be exhibited. In his characteristic, mischievously self-effacing manner, d'Harnoncourt replied, "I can only say that if one is willing to have a dialogue with each individual sculpture by Picasso one finds out soon that it is the sculpture itself that demands its specific setting—All one has to do is to coordinate the demands of 220 sculptures."[53]

Barr, an expert on Picasso (in 1946, he had published the definitive reference work on the artist, *Picasso: Fifty Years of His* Art) in writing to Henry Kahnweiler, Picasso's dealer, noted that "d'Harnoncourt presented the show superbly after months of study. The whole ground floor of the Museum has been rebuilt; all the walls and lighting have been changed with much thought and great sensibility."[54] Praise for the show also came from other Museum employees. Grace Mayer, curator of Photography, wrote to d'Harnoncourt: "I know that you have been told many times, and in many ways, but I feel impelled to tell you again that your genius matches that of Picasso!"[55]

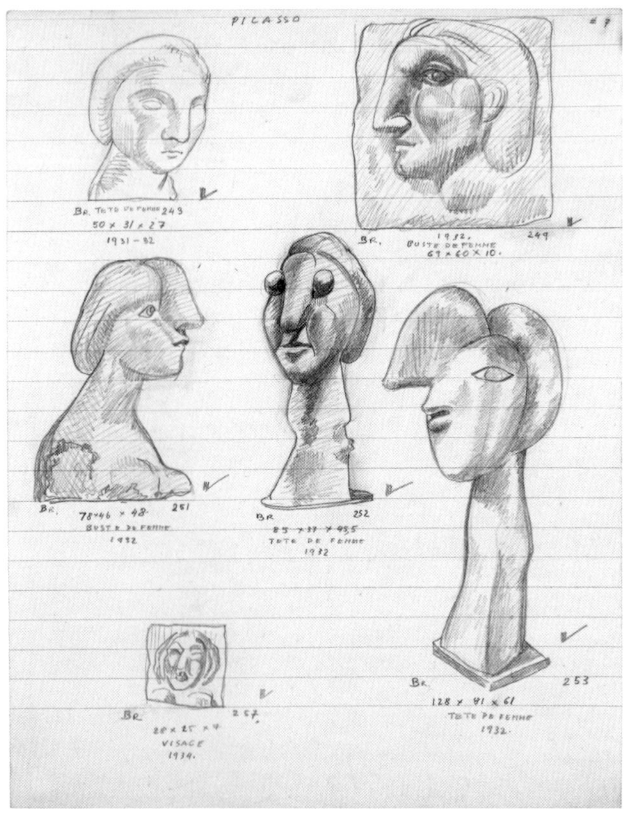

Group scale drawings for the exhibition *The Sculpture of Picasso*, 1967

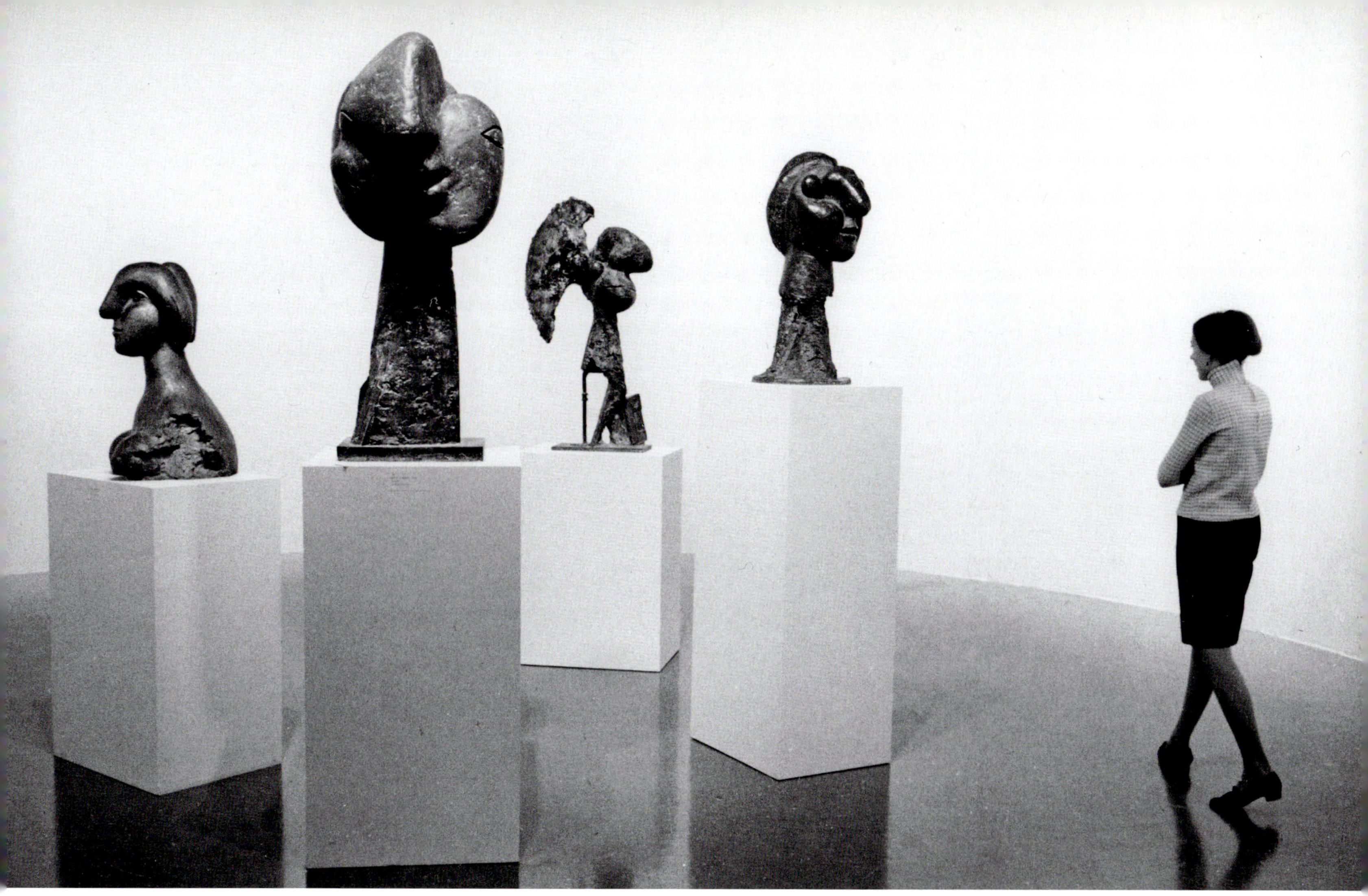

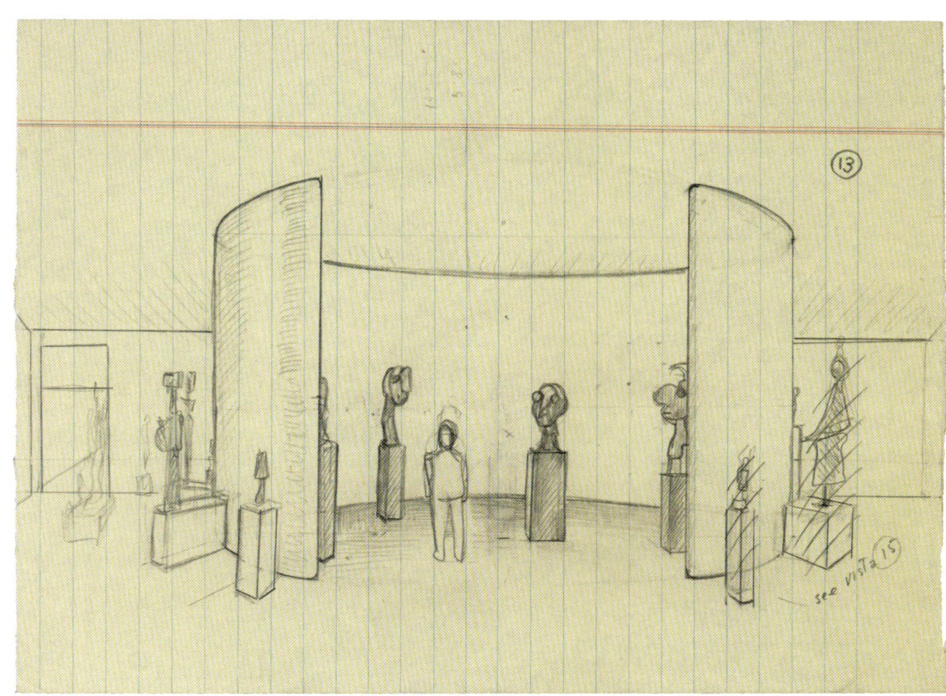

Installation view and corresponding vista of
the exhibition showing the gallery with the
curved wall, 1967

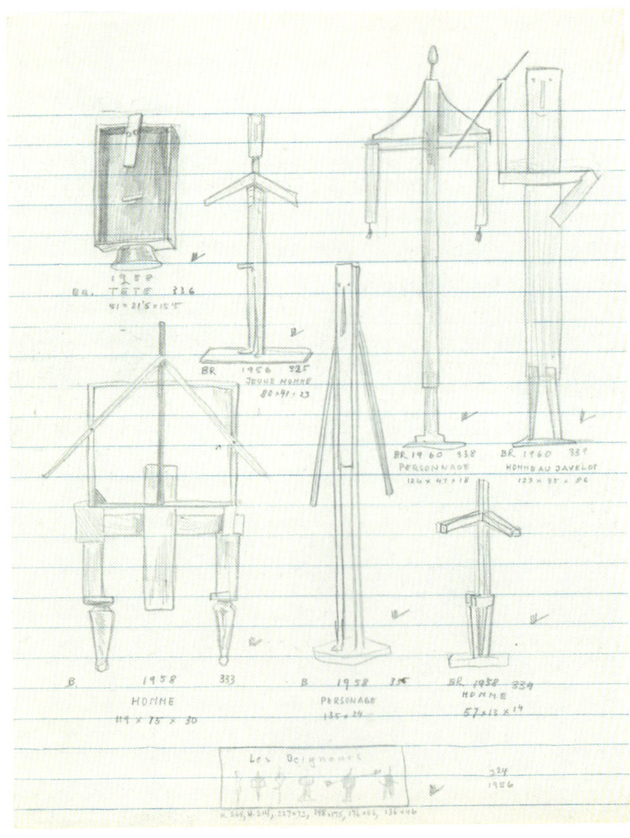

Group scale drawings for the exhibition
The Sculpture of Picasso, 1967

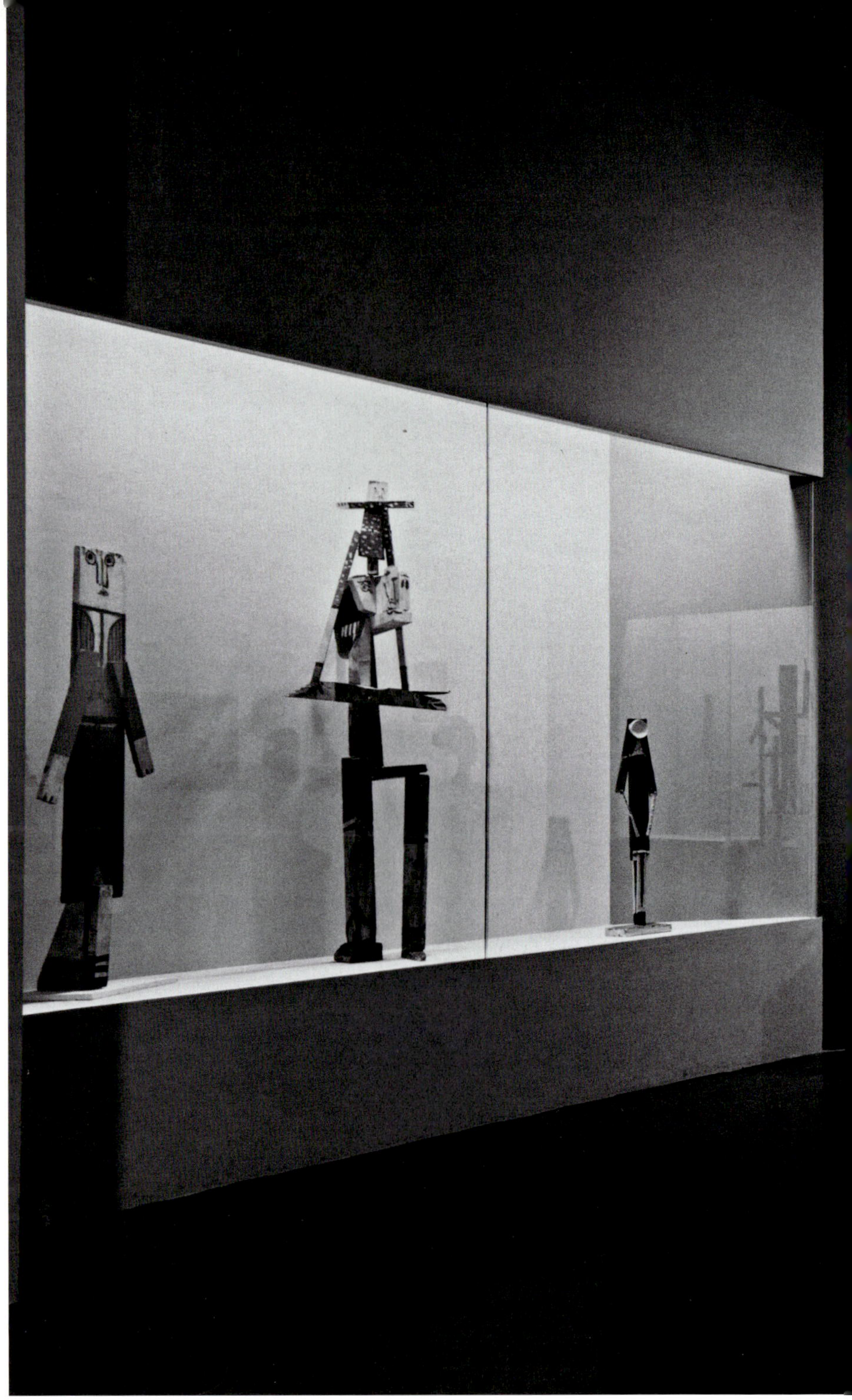

Installation view of the exhibition with at center the photomural of
The Bathers

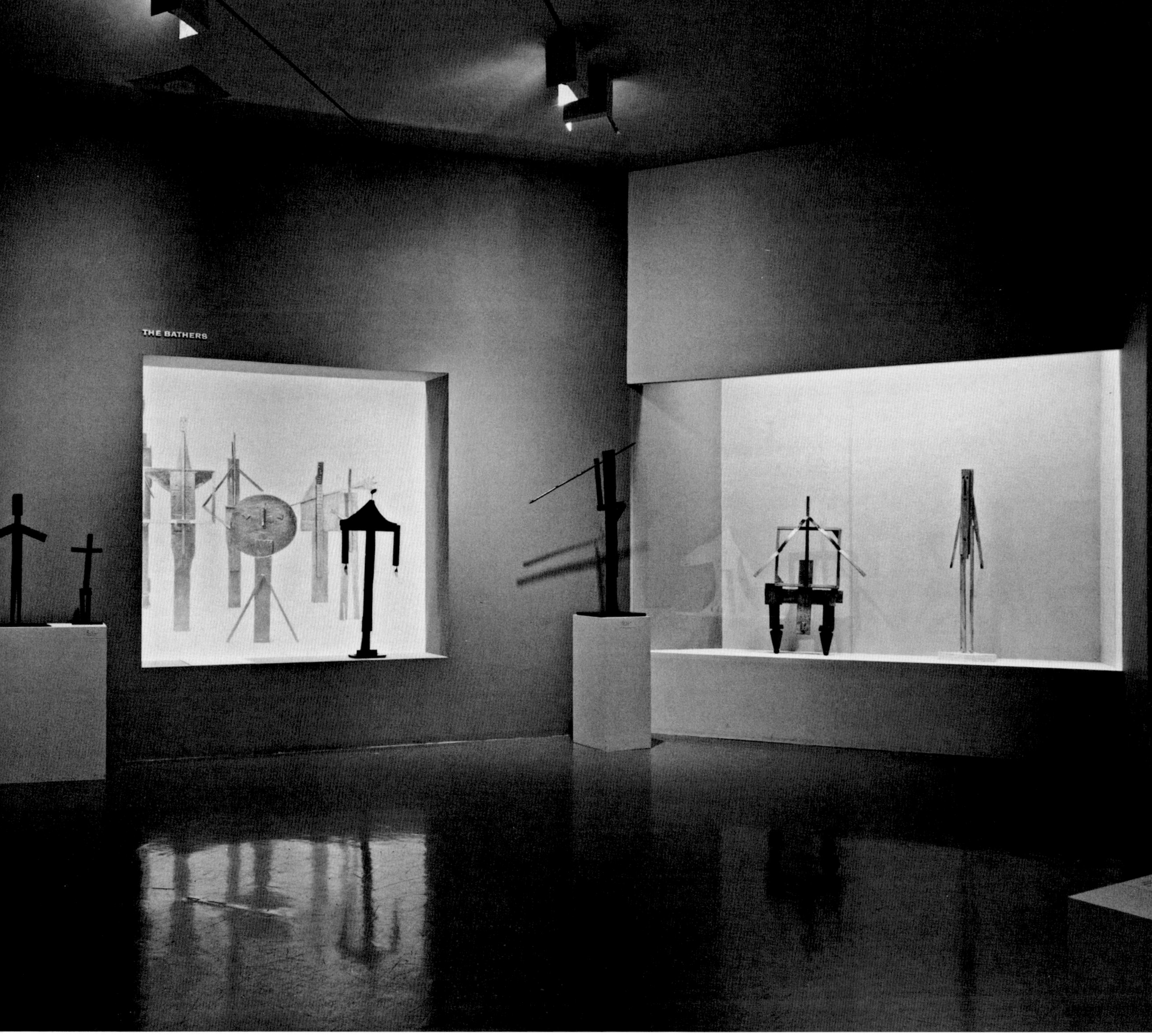

THE BATHERS

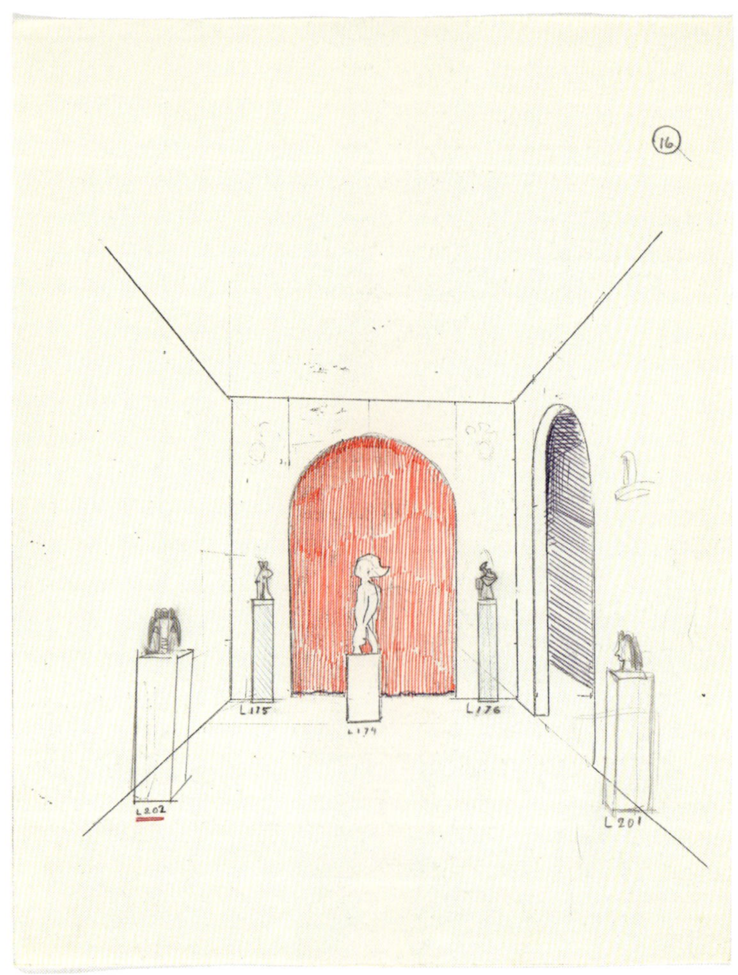

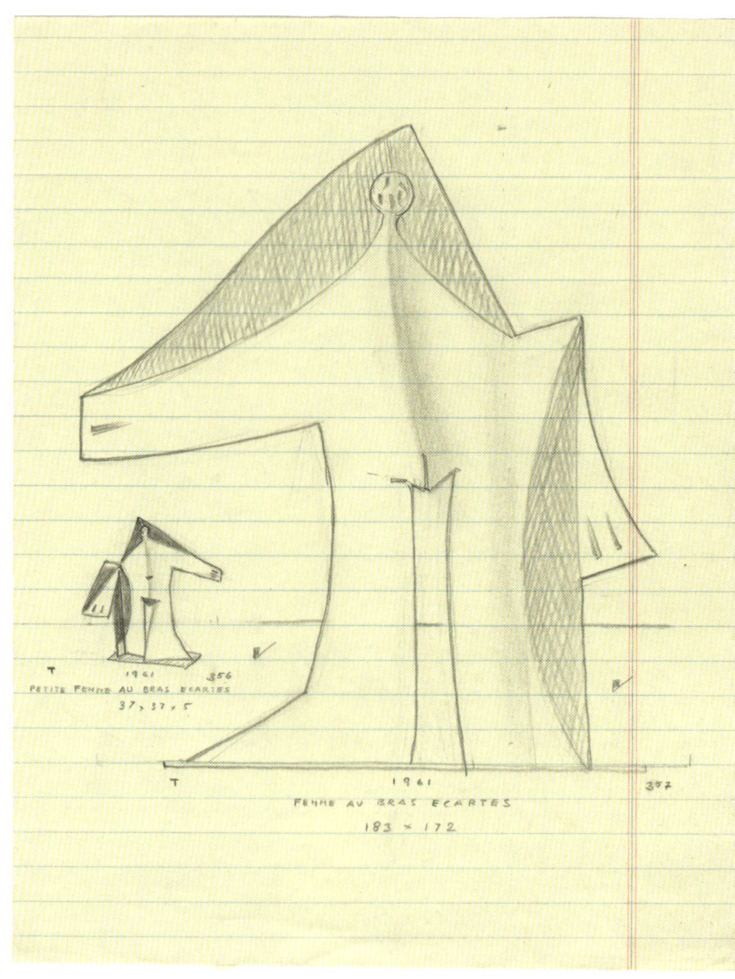

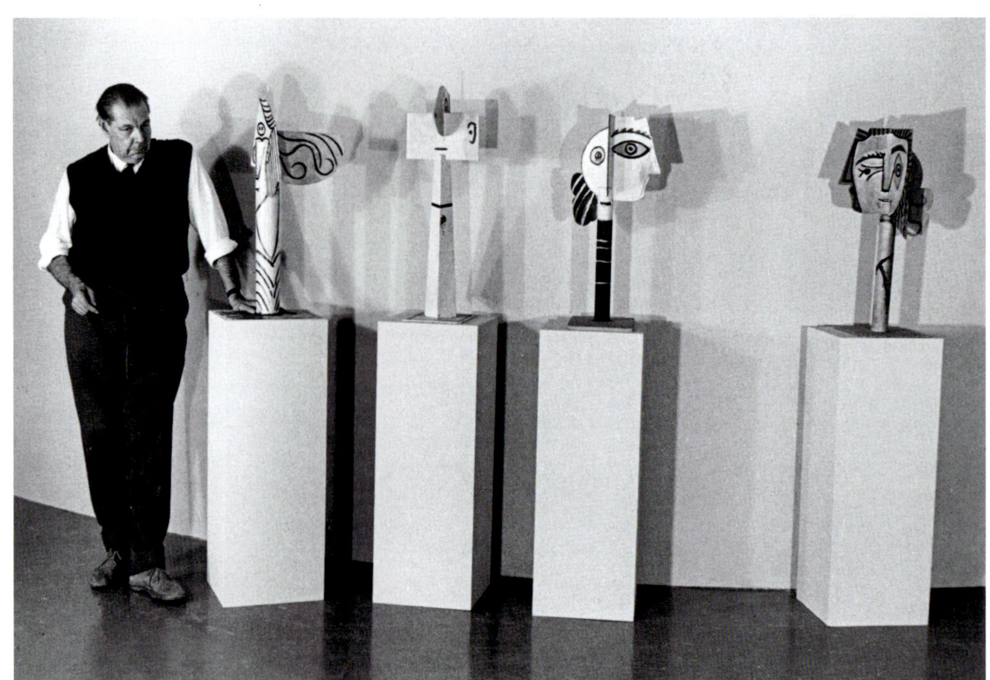

Above, left: Color study for a curtain to hang behind a sculpture (see page 59 for related fabric samples), 1967

Above, right: Sketch of Picasso's *Woman with Outstreched Arms* (1961), 1967

Left: René d'Harnoncourt installing the exhibition, October 1967

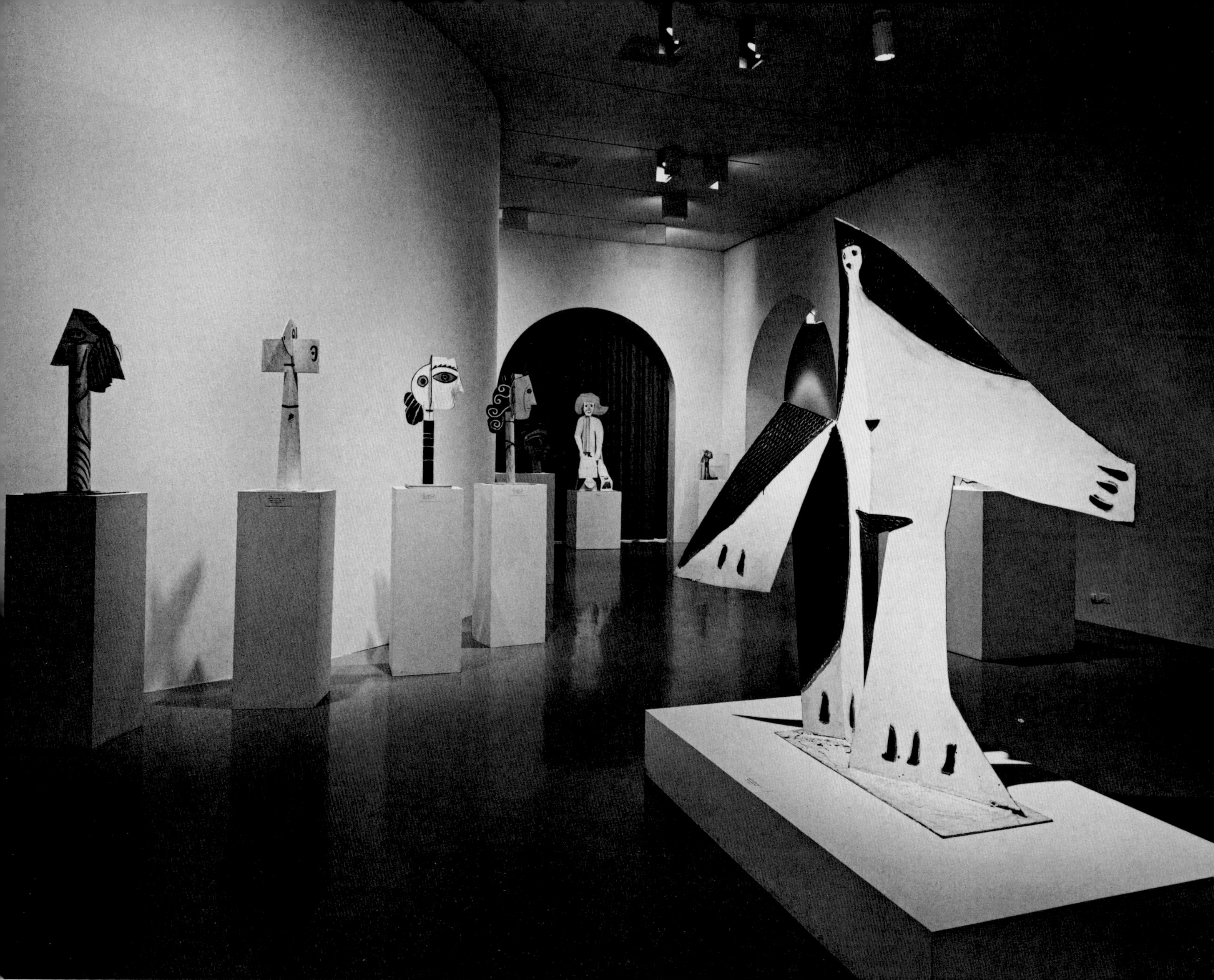

Above: Installation view, including *Woman with Outstretched Arms* (1961), 1967

Following spread: Installation view of the main lobby gallery, seen from the Museum's entrance, 1967

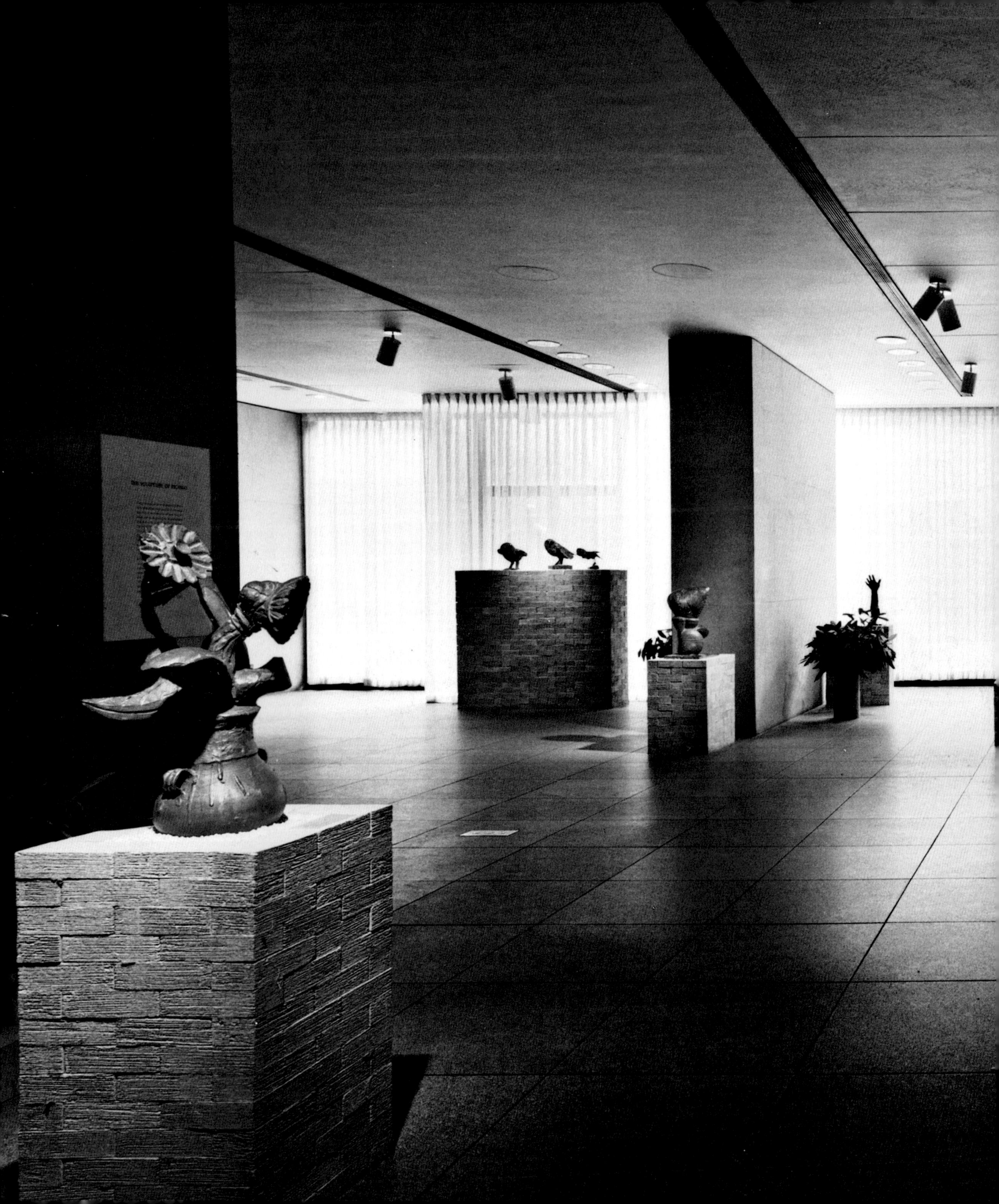

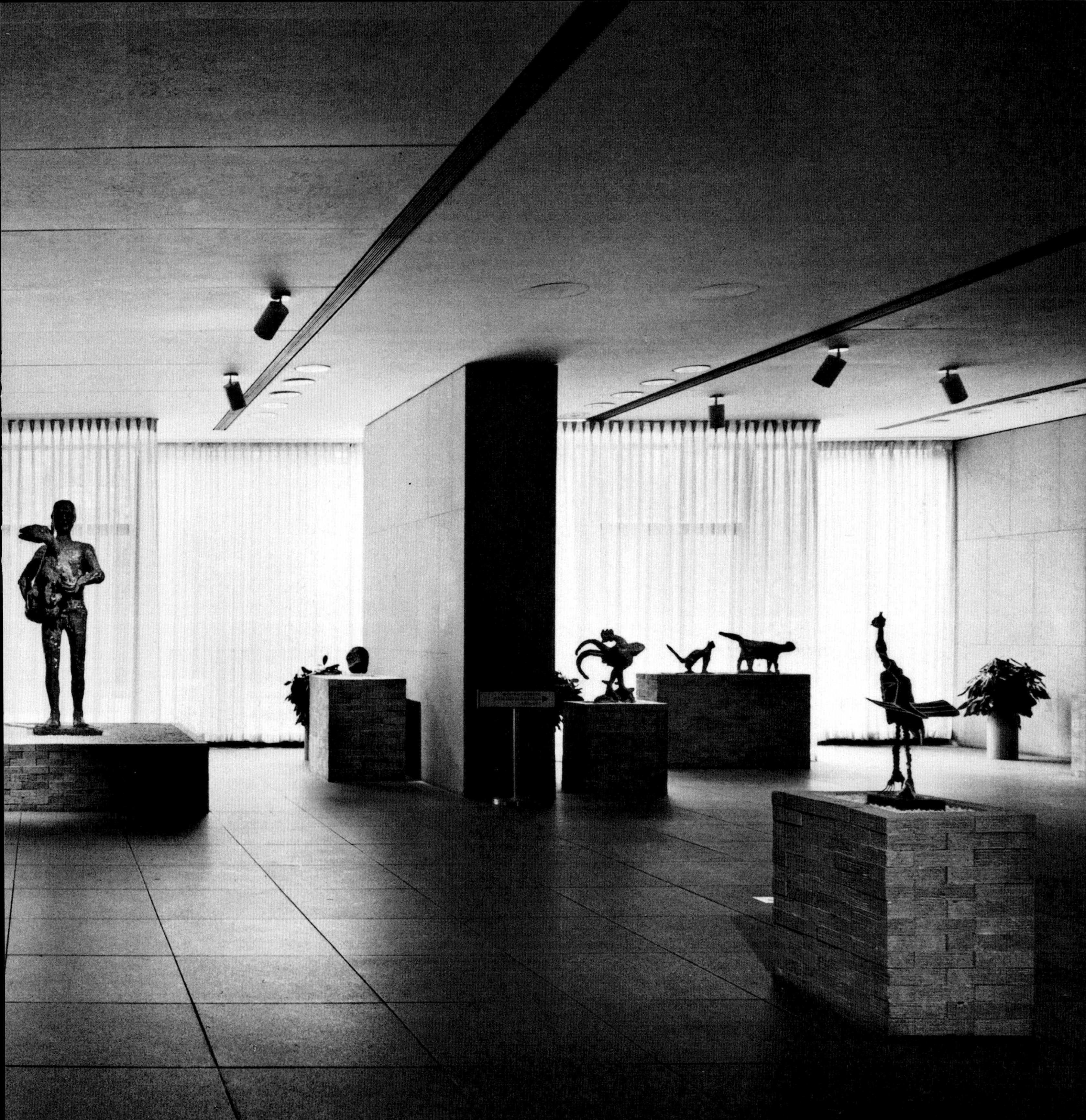

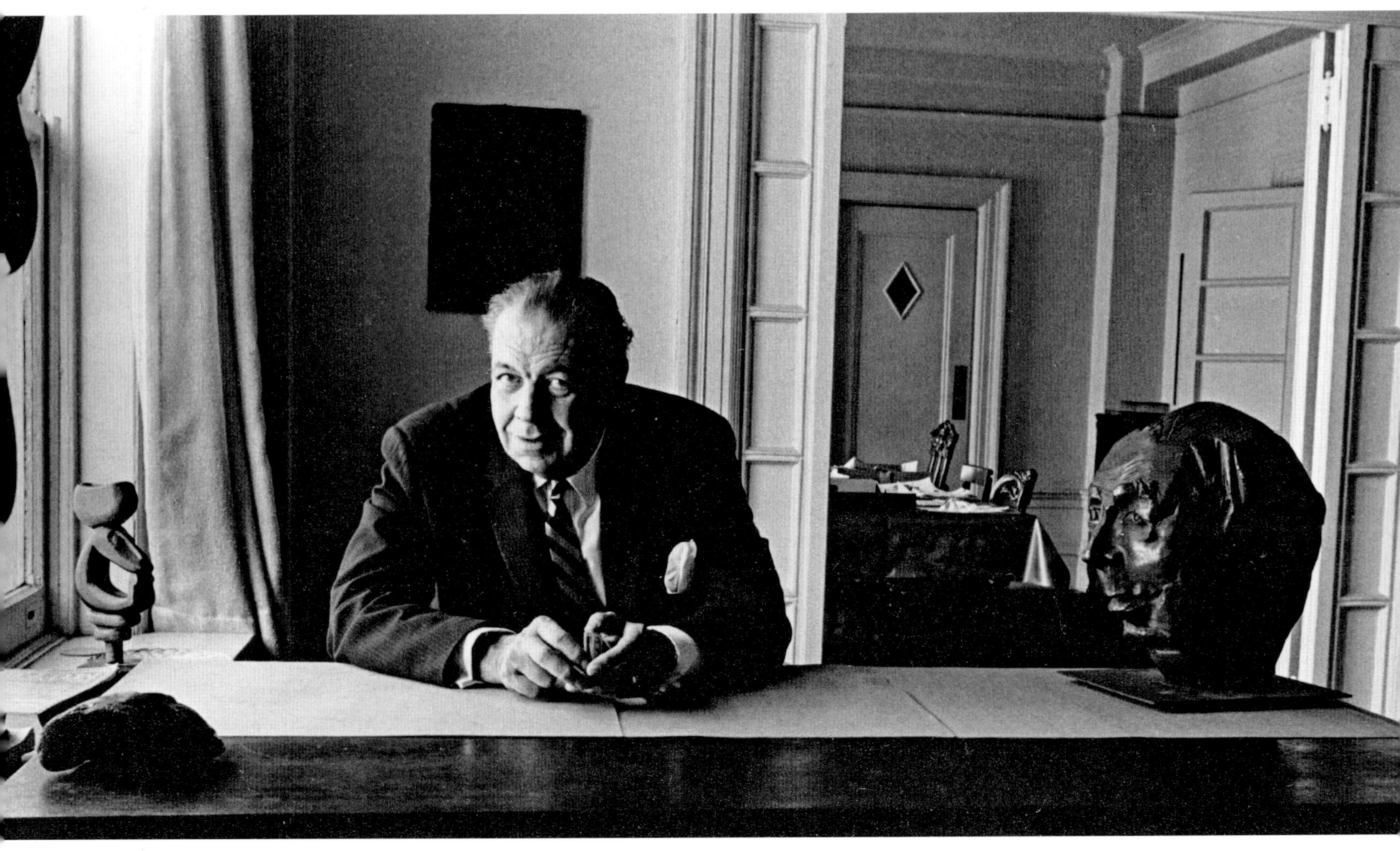

René d'Harnoncourt, n.d.

René d'Harnoncourt: A Life

For René d'Harnoncourt

The heart pervaded by the calmness that belongs to things—pure waiting—opens up, free from contingencies and guilt, in spite of fate—lo, like a garden that succeeds, surrendering, in its attempt to give.

—Rainer Maria Rilke (translated by Walter Kaufman)[1]

1901

Count René Wladimir Hubert Maria de la Fontaine und d'Harnoncourt-Unverzagt is born to Hubert d'Harnoncourt and Julie Mittrowsky in Vienna on May 17. For centuries, according to d'Harnoncourt's later recollections, the aristocratic Austrian family of French descent owned vast lands near the Belgian border, including three castles, two of which had two hundred rooms apiece, owned by his mother's family.[2] His siblings are Hubert (1891–1924), Johann Eberhard (1896–1970), and Renata (1906–1983).

1904

The family moves to Baden bei Wien.

1909

The family moves to Graz. René enjoys a comfortable childhood, tended to by a governess and servants.

1911

D'Harnoncourt begins studies at Realgymnasium, Graz.

1918–22

D'Harnoncourt studies at the Realschule of Graz then the University of Graz, following courses in chemistry and philosophy. He collects engravings by Dürer and other German Old Masters, and his hobbies include drawing, painting, and writing poetry and plays, including *Das Licht* (a philosophical drama) and *Pierrot, Pierrette und der Riese* (a short play). With three friends, he creates Freiland, a literary group and organization for modern art. They organize and mount exhibitions, including the first in Graz of prints by Matisse and Picasso, as well as balls, with decorations by members of the Stadt Theater. The club enlists contributions from poets Stefan George and Rainer Maria Rilke (with whom d'Harnoncourt exchanges letters when he is only nineteen years old).

1922–24

D'Harnoncourt enrolls at Technische Hochschule in Vienna, studying chemical engineering. His thesis, "The Creosote Contents of Certain Soft Coals of Southern Yugoslavia," is published in the German technical journal *Brennstoff-Chemie.* He continues to collect paintings and engravings.

1924

D'Harnoncourt finds himself suddenly impoverished: following the dissolution of the Austro-Hungarian empire, the family estate he was to inherit is expropriated by Czechoslovakia. D'Harnoncourt elects to immigrate to Mexico, leaving university without graduating, and partially finances his trip by selling some valuable fifteenth- and sixteenth-century drawings and prints, including works by Dürer and Holbein and a manuscript poem by Rilke.

1925–26

D'Harnoncourt travels to Mexico, via Paris, on board the ship *Lafayette* from Saint-Nazaire, arriving in Veracruz on January 6, 1926. Unable to secure employment as a scientist, d'Harnoncourt turns to a variety of odd jobs as a commercial artist to support himself. His fortunes improve when he meets affluent American collectors of colonial antiquities and folk and native art and begins buying works for their collections. D'Harnoncourt begins to make trips across Mexico to the interior, visiting all twenty-eight Mexican states.

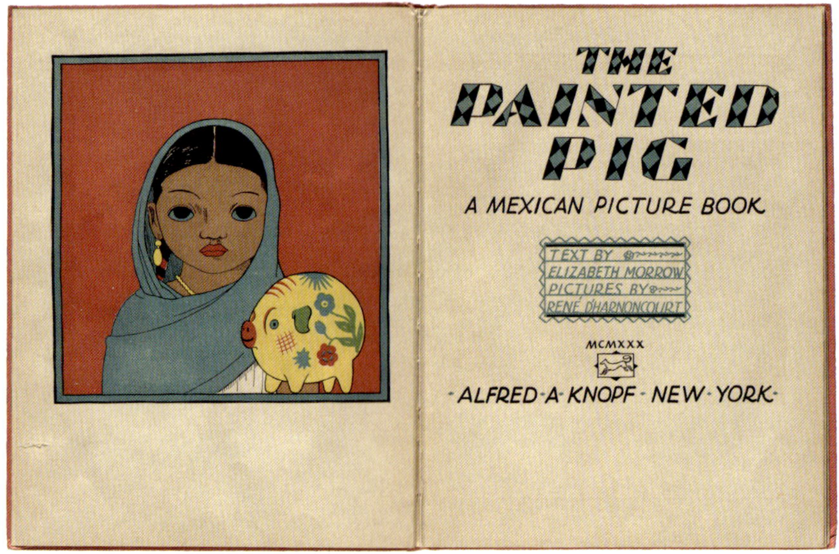

Frontispiece and title page of *The Painted Pig: A Mexican Picture Book*, a children's book written by Elizabeth Morrow and illustrated by René d'Harnoncourt (New York: Alfred A. Knopf, Inc., 1930)

1927–28

D'Harnoncourt travels extensively across Mexico to acquire indigenous artifacts, both antique and contemporary, to sell at Frederick Davis's Sonora News Company store in Mexico City. He organizes the first commercial exhibitions in Mexico of work by the so-called Modern Mexican Muralists, Diego Rivera, José Clemente Orozco, and Rufino Tamayo.

Domingos Mexicanos (*Mexican Sundays*), a collection of reproductions of watercolor tableaux by René d'Harnoncourt, is published by Davis in an edition of three hundred copies.

D'Harnoncourt publishes the article "Pancho the Toy Maker" in *Mexican Folkways* 4, no. 2 (April–June 1928).

1929–30

D'Harnoncourt is invited by the Mexican Ministry of Education to assemble a collection of folk art on behalf of the government and to lecture on the subject as a member of the faculty of the Seminar for Cultural Relations with Latin America. *Mexican Folk Art* comprises forty-eight collections of Mexican folk art, one for each state, to be sent to schools in the United States.

D'Harnoncourt illustrates the children's book *The Painted Pig* by Elizabeth Morrow, published by Alfred A. Knopf. In Mexico, he meets Carl Zigrosser of Weyhe Gallery, New York, who agrees to represent him.

He publishes the article "Mexican Popular Arts" in *Mexican Folkways* 6, no. 2 (1930).

1930–32

D'Harnoncourt organizes the *Mexican Arts* exhibition for the American Federation of Arts and Carnegie Foundation (see portfolio). A preview of the painting section is shown in the fall of 1930 in Mexico City at the Ministry of Education, prior to being sent to the United States. D'Harnoncourt accompanies the exhibition of one thousand two hundred objects as it travels to fourteen cities.

1931

D'Harnoncourt writes and illustrates *The Hole in the Wall*, a children's book, and *Mexicana: A Book of Pictures,* both published by Alfred A. Knopf. He places thirty-six

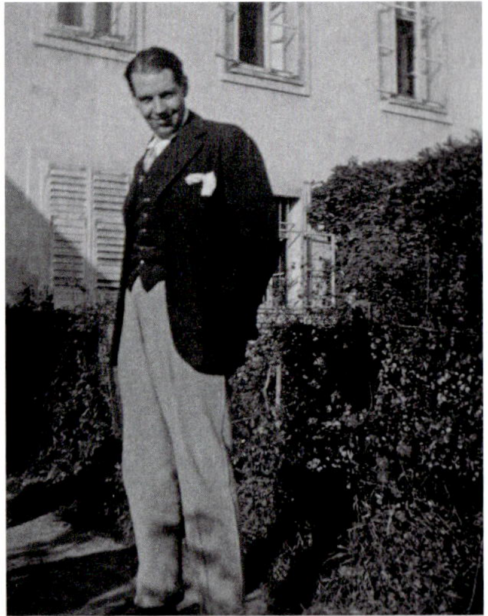

René d'Harnoncourt in 1932, photographed by a family member during his visit to Austria to obtain his US immigration documents

works on consignment at Weyhe Gallery, with prices
    ranging from $25 to $150 (or $400 to $2,400,
    adjusted for inflation).

1932

D'Harnoncourt returns to Austria to receive an immigra-
    tion visa and remains there for six months. Some four
    dozen of his drawings are included in his solo exhibi-
    tion *Drawings by René d'Harnoncourt* at Weyhe
    Gallery (May 16–30).

1933

D'Harnoncourt reenters the US as an immigrant. On
    May 29, he marries Sarah Carr of Chicago, an adver-
    tising copy editor for Marshall Field and Company's
    in-house magazine, *Fashions of the Hour*, and the
    daughter of a wealthy cracker manufacturer.
    The couple settles in New York.
In New York, he directs a two-year project for the *Art in
    America* radio program, organized by the American
    Federation of Arts with a grant from the Carnegie
    Corporation and sponsored by the General Federation
    of Women's Clubs. The first series, organized by the
    Metropolitan Museum of Art, covers American art
    before 1900; the second focuses on art after 1900
    and is organized by MoMA. On this occasion, d'Har-
    noncourt meets Alfred Barr, who provides the scripts,
    for the first time.[3] It is the first nationally broadcast
    radio program on the subject, airing on thirty-six radio
    stations of the NBC network.
In the summer, d'Harnoncourt is on the faculty of the
    Seminar for Cultural Relations with Latin America,
    Mexico City.
Contemporary Work by Cartoonists and Caricaturists
    (January 13–February 12) at the Cleveland Museum
    of Art includes four works by d'Harnoncourt.
    D'Harnoncourt illustrates the children's book *Beast,
    Bird, Fish*, by Elizabeth C. Morrow, published by
    Alfred A. Knopf.

1934

D'Harnoncourt holds a two-year faculty position at Sarah
    Lawrence College, Bronxville, New York. In the sum-
    mer, he returns to Mexico City for the Seminar for
    Cultural Relations with Latin America.

1936

D'Harnoncourt is a faculty member of the New School for
    Social Research, New York; in the summer he is once
    again in Mexico City.

He is appointed assistant to the general manager of the
    newly created Indian Arts and Crafts Board, part of the
    Department of the Interior's Bureau of Indian Affairs.

1937

D'Harnoncourt is promoted to full-time general manager
    of the Indian Arts and Crafts Board, a position he
    holds until 1944.

1939–40

D'Harnoncourt becomes a naturalized US citizen.
He organizes and installs the exhibition *Indian Art in
    the United States and Alaska* at the Golden Gate
    International Exposition in San Francisco.
He is named vice-president, Laboratory of Anthropology,
    Santa Fe, New Mexico.

1941

D'Harnoncourt organizes and installs his first MoMA
    exhibition *Indian Art of the United States* (January 22–
    April 27; see portfolio) in collaboration with
    Frederic H. Douglas of the Denver Art Museum.
He is a member of the Advisory Committee on Art,
    Department of State, until 1943.
He writes the preface to *Mexican Costume* (Chicago:
    Pocahontas Press, 1941) by Carlos Merida.

1942

D'Harnoncourt is named chairman, Committee on Manual
    Industries, Inter-American Development Committee,
    Washington, DC.

1943

D'Harnoncourt is named by Nelson A. Rockefeller to
    acting secretary, Section of Art, Office of Inter-
    American Affairs, Washington, DC.
With Frederic H. Douglas, he co-authors *El Arte del Indio
    en Los Estados Unidos*, published by the Indian
    Institute, Department of the Interior.
Daughter Anne Julie is born.

1944

D'Harnoncourt becomes chairman, Indian Arts and Crafts
    Board, US Department of the Interior. He is charged
    with visiting reservations throughout the country to
    encourage the growth of indigenous arts and
    handicrafts.

He officially joins the MoMA staff with a dual title: vice-president in charge of Foreign Activities, and director of the newly formed Department of Manual Industry. As vice-president in charge of Foreign Activities, he embarks in December on a three-month trip, initiating a membership campaign for the Museum, in Mexico City, Mexico; Lima, Peru; Santiago, Chile; Buenos Aires, Mar del Plata, Rosario, Argentina; Rio de Janeiro, São Paulo, Brazil; and Port-au-Prince, Haiti.

He is responsible for installing the temporary exhibit of post-Columbian arts and crafts for the reopening of the Mexican and Central American Hall of the American Museum of Natural History, New York, on February 25. The display includes works borrowed from the collections of Elizabeth Morrow and d'Harnoncourt.[4]

1945

With Miguel Covarrubias, d'Harnoncourt co-curates the exhibition *El Arte Indigena de Norteamerica*, March 20–April 20, National Museum of Anthropology, Mexico City.

1946

He organizes and installs the MoMA exhibition *Arts of the South Seas* (January 29–May 19, 1946; see porfolio) in collaboration with Dr. Ralph Linton and Dr. Paul S. Wingert; and assists the artist Henry Moore in installing his exhibition at the Museum (December 17, 1946–March 16, 1947).

On November 14, 1946, he is elected a trustee of the Museum, for a term to expire on June 30, 1949.

During the summer, while on leave from MoMA, d'Harnoncourt is named senior counsellor of visual arts, UNESCO.

1947

D'Harnoncourt is named director of Curatorial Departments and chairman, Coordination Committee, MoMA.

He becomes an advisor to the US Delegation to the Second Session of the General Conference on UNESCO in Mexico City.

1948

D'Harnoncourt is appointed chairman, Committee of Museums and Industry, International Council of Museums (ICOM).

At MoMA, he curates and installs the exhibition *Naum Gabo and Antoine Pevnser* (February 10–April 25;

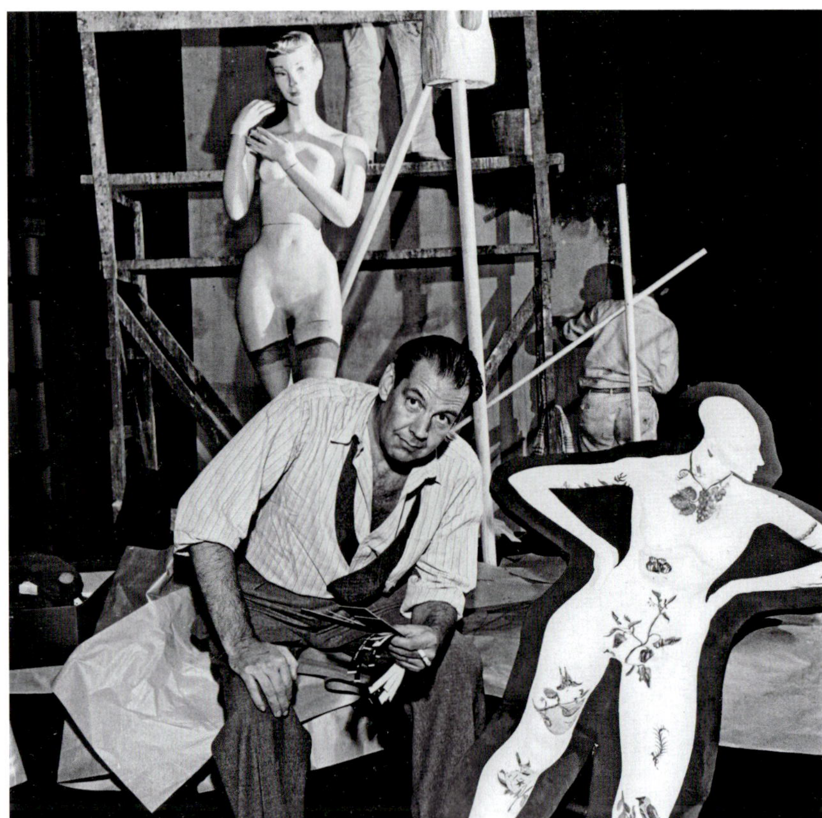

René d'Harnoncourt during the installation of the exhibition *Modern Art in Your Life,* 1949

see portfolio) and *Timeless Aspects of Modern Art* (November 16, 1948–January 23, 1949; see portfolio). He installs the exhibition *Elie Nadelman,* curated by Lincoln Kirstein (October 5–November 28; see portfolio).

In May, d'Harnoncourt delivers a speech at the annual meeting of the American Federation of Arts; an expanded version is published under the title "Challenge and Promise: Modern Art and Society" in the November issue of *Magazine of Art*.

1949

On October 14, d'Harnoncourt is appointed director of The Museum of Modern Art.

In collaboration with Robert Goldwater, he curates and installs *Modern Art in Your Life* (October 5–December 4; see portfolio).

1950

D'Harnoncourt publishes *Teaching Portfolio No. 3, Modern Art Old and New* (New York: The Museum of Modern Art, 1950).

1951

He installs the US Exhibition (a selection of works in
MoMA's collection) at the first São Paulo Bienal, Brazil.

1952

D'Harnoncourt is instrumental to the creation and launch
of the International Program and International
Council at MoMA.

1953

He installs the MoMA exhibition *12 Modern American
Painters and Sculptors* at the Musée National d'Art
Moderne, Paris, and *Primitive Sculpture from the
Collection of Nelson A. Rockefeller* at the Century
Association, New York.

1954

D'Harnoncourt is named commissioner of the US Pavilion
at the Venice Biennale.

He organizes and installs the MoMA exhibition *Ancient
Arts of the Andes* (January 25–March 21; see
portfolio).

He is named Chevalier of the Légion d'Honneur by the
French government.

1955

D'Harnoncourt directs the large MoMA exhibition in Paris,
American Art of the Twentieth Century. With more
than 200 works of art by 114 artists, it is part of a
festival of cultural events presented by the American
Embassy at the invitation of the French government.

He installs the MoMA exhibition *Fifteen Paintings by French
Masters of the Nineteenth Century from the Louvre
and the Museums of Albi and Lyon* (February 25–
April 24); *50 ans d'art aux États-Unis* at the Musée
National d'Art Moderne, Paris; and *El Arte Moderno
Estados-Unidos* at the Palacio de la Virreina and
Museo de Arte Moderno, Barcelona.

He is awarded an Honorary Doctor of Humane Letters,
Dartmouth College, Hanover, New Hampshire.[5]

1956

D'Harnoncourt is named vice-president of Nelson
Rockefeller's newly created Museum of Primitive
Art (MPA).

He pens a defense of "Modern Art and Freedom" for *Facts
Forum News*, June 1956. It is a rebuttal against Esther
Julia Pels's article "Art for Whose Sake?" (published in

American Legion magazine in February 1956) linking
modern art to communism.

1957

D'Harnoncourt installs the opening exhibition of the MPA,
Selected Works from the Collection.

1958

At MoMA, d'Harnoncourt installs the exhibitions *Seurat
Paintings and Drawings* (March 24–May 11; see
portfolio) and *Jean Arp: A Retrospective* (October 8–
November 30; see portfolio).

D'Harnoncourt installs *Art of Ancient Peru (Selected
Works from the Collection)* at the MPA and *New
American Painting* at the Museo Nacional de Arte
Contemporaneo, Madrid.

He is awarded an Honorary Doctor of Humane Letters,
Columbia University, New York, and the Officer's
Cross of the Order of Merit of the Federal Republic
of Germany.

1959

D'Harnoncourt installs the MoMA exhibitions *Recent
Sculpture U.S.A* (May 13–August 16) and *New Images
of Man* (September 30–November 29).

1961

D'Harnoncourt installs the MoMA exhibition *Steichen the
Photographer* (March 28–May 30).

The exhibition *Two Private Collections: Gertrud A. Mellon
and René d'Harnoncourt* at the MPA (November 29,
1961–February 11, 1962) includes some seventy
objects owned by d'Harnoncourt, and hailing from
Arizona to Peru, Ghana, and New Guinea.

D'Harnoncourt is appointed commissioner of the Indian
Arts and Crafts Board, US Department of the Interior,
a position he holds until 1965.

1962

D'Harnoncourt installs the MoMA exhibition at the United
States Pavilion of the Venice Biennale, Italy, and *Art of
the Asmat - The Collection of Michael C. Rockefeller*
at the MPA and in the MoMA Sculpture Garden
(September 11–November 6; see portfolio).

1963

D'Harnoncourt installs the MoMA exhibition *Rodin*
(May 1–September 8; see portfolio).

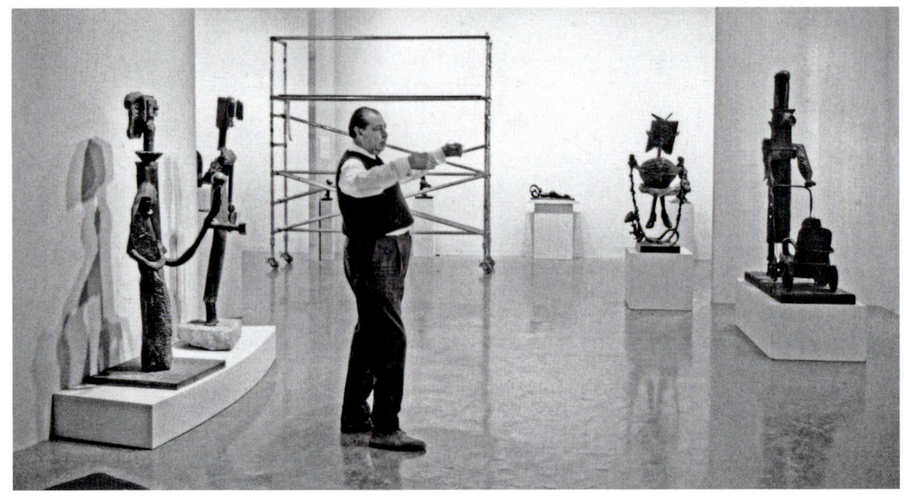

René d'Harnoncourt installing
The Sculpture of Picasso,
October 1967

1964

He installs the MoMA exhibition *The Edward Steichen Photography Center* (May 27–unknown closing date).

D'Harnoncourt writes "Foreword: The Museum of the Future, A Pictorial Chronicle," published in *Art in America* 1, no. 52.

1965

He installs an exhibition of masterworks from MoMA's collection, *États-Unis Sculptures du XXe siècle,* at the Musée Rodin, Paris.

1966

D'Harnoncourt is appointed to a subcommittee of the National Council on the Arts to develop the Visual Arts Program. He remains on the National Council until his death.

1967

D'Harnoncourt installs his final MoMA exhibition *The Sculpture of Picasso* (October 11, 1967–January 1, 1968; see portfolio).

1968

D'Harnoncourt retires from The Museum of Modern Art on June 30.

He begins planning for a major Native American exhibition for Paris, Frankfurt, and Zurich, to open in 1969.

On August 13, he dies when struck by an intoxicated driver while walking along a country road in Long Island, New York. A memorial service is held in the Museum Sculpture Garden on October 8. Speakers include William Paley, David Rockefeller, Robert Motherwell, and Arthur Drexler, and his nephew Nikolaus Harnoncourt conducts the Concentus Musicus ensemble from Vienna.

1969

The exhibition *Institute of International Education: Artists Abroad: An Exhibition in Memory of René d'Harnoncourt* is organized by the American Federation of Arts, in cooperation with the Institute of International Education. D'Harnoncourt had begun to assemble this exhibition of work by former Fulbright grantees prior to his death.

1970

The commemorative exhibition *René d'Harnoncourt: Exhibitions of Primitive Art* is mounted by the MPA (February 25–May 10). It is a survey of a dozen museum shows designed by d'Harnoncourt. Ludwig Glaeser, a curator in MoMA's Department of Architecture and Design, selects and installs the show, and Mordechai Omer researches and prepares texts.

1975

A gallery at MoMA is dedicated to d'Harnoncourt (on the former first floor, garden wing).

Opposite: René d'Harnoncourt, n.d.

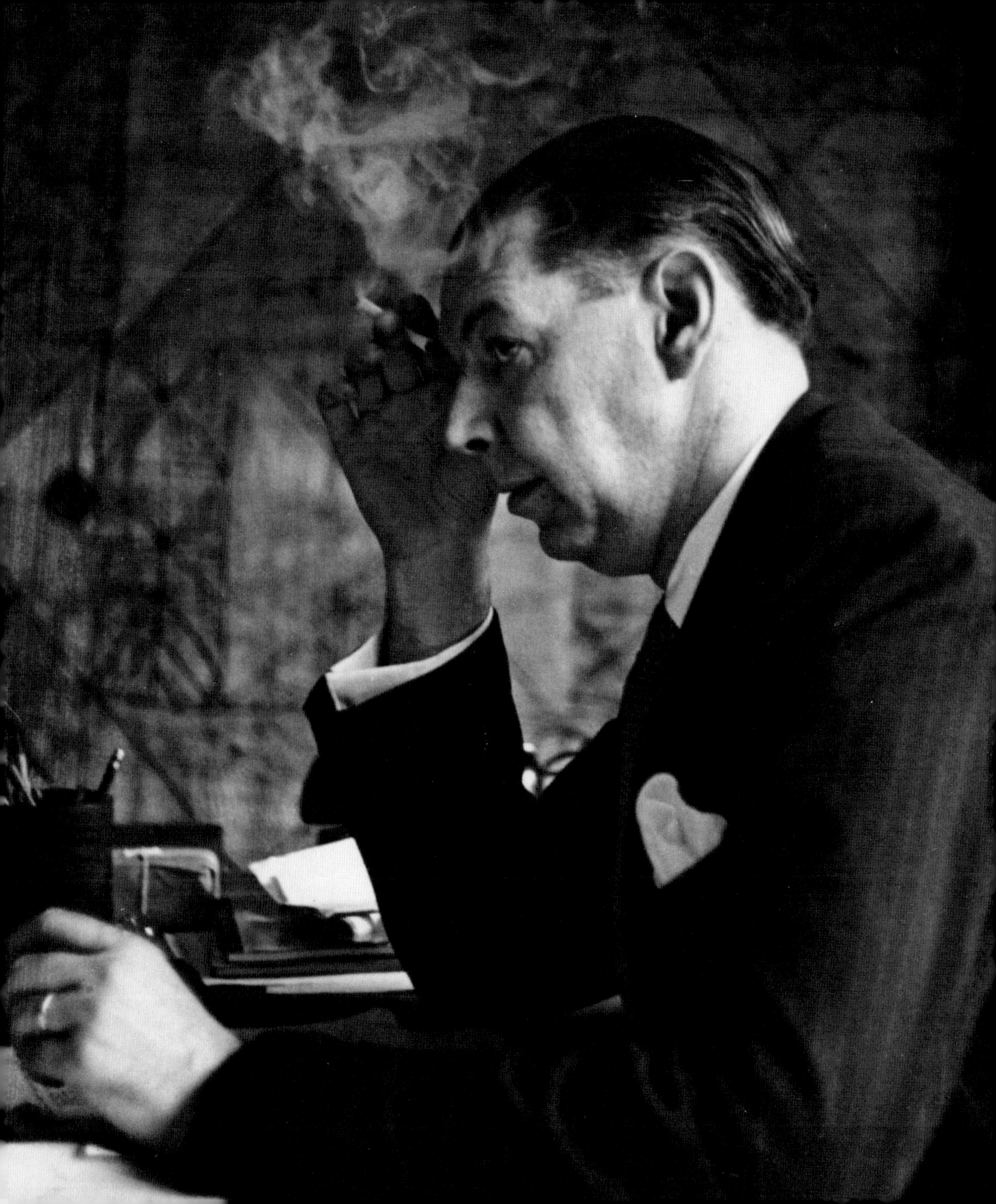

Notes

René d'Harnoncourt: *Installateur*

1. Geoffrey T. Hellman, "Profiles: Imperturbable Noble," *The New Yorker* 36, no. 12 (May 7, 1960): 104.

2. Robert Motherwell, "Robert Motherwell: Artist's Eulogy for René d'Harnoncourt," unpublished remarks, October 8, 1968. Department of Public Information Records [PI], II.C.85. The Museum of Modern Art Archives, New York.

3. Oral History Program [OHP], interview with Anne d'Harnoncourt, September 11, 2003, 18. MoMA Archives, NY.

4. Sarah d'Harnoncourt, loose notes regarding her husband, n.d. René d'Harnoncourt Papers [RDH], X.A.3. MoMA Archives, NY.

5. Nelson Rockefeller, in *René d'Harnoncourt, 1901–1968: A Tribute, October 8, 1968, Sculpture Garden, The Museum of Modern Art* (New York: The Museum of Modern Art, 1968), 5.

6. Obituary, "Art: The Best Qualities," *Newsweek* 72, no. 9 (August 26, 1968): 82.

7. OHP interview with Anne d'Harnoncourt, 27.

8. Sanka Knox, "'Head of Museum Recalls Career," *New York Times*, June 27, 1968.

9. Louis Carré, letter to d'Harnoncourt, April 4, 1958. RDH, VIII.61. MoMA Archives, NY.

10. Board of Trustee Meeting Minutes, June 13, 1968, 4. MoMA Archives, NY.

11. OHP interview with Anne d'Harnoncourt, 13, 27.

12. Many members of d'Harnoncourt's aristocratic circle owned such items and now needed money in the postwar years. My understanding of d'Harnoncourt's activities in his homeland was enhanced by a review of a memoir written by Nikolaus d'Harnoncourt, which was privately published posthumously. I am grateful to the family for sharing with me the chapter concerning René.

13. Hellman, "Imperturbable Noble": 72.

14. Press release, Museum of Primitive Art, November 29, 1961. The Metropolitan Museum of Art Archives [MMAA], AR.1991.1.43.

15. Hellman, "Imperturbable Noble": 79.

16. Sarah d'Harnoncourt on René in the René d'Harnoncourt papers, 1921–1983, [mf 3831;766]. Archives of American Art, Smithsonian Institution.

17. Edward Alden Jewell, "Art: Exhibition by d'Harnoncourt," *New York Times*, May 19, 1932.

18. Hellman, "Imperturbable Noble": 102.

19. Richard F. Shepard, "Placing Picassos Required Art, Too," *The New York Times*, October 19, 1967; *Nine Days to Picasso*, directed by Warren Forma and featuring René d'Harnoncourt (New York: The Museum of Modern Art and Forma Art Associates, Ltd., 1967).

20. René d'Harnoncourt, quoted in Mordechai Omer, "René d'Harnoncourt: His Art of Installation," unpublished manuscript, 19, 1968–74. RDH, IX.D.2. MoMA Archives, NY.

21. Mildred Constantine and Douglas Newton, "Letters: In Defense of René d'Harnoncourt," *Craft Horizons* 30, no. 5 (October 1970): 6.

22. Hellman, "Imperturbable Noble": 52–54.

23. Wheeler in *René d'Harnoncourt, 1901–1968*, 11.

24. The eccentric painter and writer Dr. Atl had originally been proposed as a co-director with d'Harnoncourt, but that did not come to pass.

25. René d'Harnoncourt, introduction, *Mexican Arts: Catalogue of an Exhibition Organized for and Circulated by the American Foundation of Arts, 1930–1931* (Washington, DC: American Federation of Arts, 1930), xi.

26. For further discussion of d'Harnoncourt's involvement in the arts of Mexico, see Anna Indych-López, *Muralism without Walls: Rivera, Orozco, and Siqueiros in the United States: 1927–1940* (Pittsburgh: University of Pittsburgh Press, 2009).

27. Hellman, "Imperturbable Noble": 84.

28. The program was funded by the Carnegie Corporation, and it was through d'Harnoncourt's relationship with Keppel that he obtained the position. Keppel also provided testament to d'Harnoncourt's employment so that he was able to immigrate to the United States.

29. The annual Seminar's objective was to share accurate information about Latin America. Participants from the United States traveled to Mexico for a few weeks in the summer to meet and exchange ideas. See Helen Delpar, *The Enormous Vogue of Things Mexican: Cultural Relations between the United States and Mexico, 1920–1935* (Tuscaloosa: University of Alabama Press, 1992), 73–74.

30. Indian Arts and Crafts Act of 1935, US Department of the Interior, accessed December 15, 2017, https://www.doi.gov/iacb/indian-arts-and-crafts-act-1935. For an in-depth study of the role of the IACB, see Robert Fay Schrader, *The Indian Arts and Crafts Board: An Aspect of New Deal Indian Policy* (Albuquerque: University of New Mexico Press, 1983).

31. For a full description of this nuanced story, see Rick A. López, *Crafting Mexico: Intellectuals, Artisans, and the State after the Revolution* (Durham, NC: Duke University Press, 2010).

32. See W. Jackson Rushing, "Marketing the Affinity of the Primitive and the Modern: René d'Harnoncourt and Indian Art of the United States,'" in *The Early Years of Native American Art History*, ed. Catherine Berlo (Seattle: University of Washington Press; Vancouver: University of British Columbia Press, 1992), 203–5.

33. Alfred Frankenstein, "Art on Treasure Island: The Critic Rushes Down an Indian Trail," *San Francisco Chronicle*, October 22, 1939. For a contemporary discussion of the show and its novel devices, see Carlos Emmons Cummings, *East Is East and West Is West: Some Observations on the World's Fairs of 1939 by One Whose Main Interest Is in Museums* (Buffalo: Buffalo Museum of Science, 1940).

34. For an overview of this subject, see Leonard S. Marcus, *The American Store Window* (New York: Whitney Library of Design, 1978).

35. René d'Harnoncourt, letter to Alfred H. Barr, Jr., November 8, 1939; quoted in Rushing, "Marketing the Affinity of the Primitive and the Modern," 208.

36. Milton Brown, "The Indians Discovered," *Parnassus* 13 (March 1941).

37. Eleanor Roosevelt, *My Day* column, January 27, 1941.

38. René d'Harnoncourt and Frederic H. Douglas, *Indian Art of the United States* (New York: The Museum of Modern Art, 1941), 11.

39. OHP interview with Anne d'Harnoncourt, 16–17.

40. Press release, PR 11131—4, 1944, The Museum of Modern Art, New York; Minutes of the Coordination Committee, December 22, 1943. Records of the Coordination Committee, 2. MoMA Archives, NY.

41. Readers interested in the evolution in the use of the terms "primitive art" and "primitivism" should refer to the anthology *Primitivism and Twentieth-Century Art: A Documentary History*, Jack Flam and Miriam Deutch, eds. (Berkeley: University of California Press, 2003), which brings together texts pertaining to the use of the term and its problematic history, from the "discovery" of that art by European artists and writers at the beginning of the twentieth century to today, when the term has been radically reappraised.

42. Robert J. Foster, "Art/Artefact/Commodity: Installation Design and the Exhibition of Oceanic Things at Two New York Museums in the 1940s," *Australian Journal of Anthropology* 23, no. 2 (August 2012): 130.

43. Rushing, "Marketing the Affinity of the Primitive and the Modern," 195.

44. Barr's papers include handwritten notes titled "Attitude Toward Primitive Art," n.d. In them he lists: "Curios and Relics; Appreciation of Japanese Prints; Appreciation of Romanesque and Byzantine; Appreciation of Egyptian and Mesopotamian; Appreciation of Indian, Persian and Musulman; Appreciation of Negro, Polynesian and American; Appreciation of the Art of Children; among others." Alfred H. Barr, Jr., Papers, VII.A.28. MoMA Archives, NY.

45. Alfred H. Barr, Jr., "Letters to the Editor," *College Art Journal* 10, no. 1 (Fall 1950): 57.

46. OHP interview with Anne d'Harnoncourt, 14.

47. This interest in art from other cultures and times existed at the institution throughout d'Harnoncourt's tenure at the institution, then waned after he retired. The topic was reprised most famously by the Museum in 1984 with curators William Rubin and Kirk Varnedoe's sprawling *"Primitivism" in Twentieth-Century Art: Affinity of the Tribal and the Modern*, which showcased 150 modern artworks together with 200 tribal objects. The exhibition was widely criticized for its approach, which decontextualized the primitive arts and positioned them as mere inspiration to the modern works. With the denial of cultural specificity and emphasis on pure form, the show was accused of advancing the role of appropriation and the point of view of the superiority of Western culture.

48. René d'Harnoncourt, undated typed manuscript with hand annotations, attached to a handwritten note from Sarah d'Harnoncourt to Mordechai Omer calling it "so characteristic" of René, n.d. PI, II.C.85. MoMA Archives, NY.

49. René d'Harnoncourt, Ralph Linton, and Paul S. Wingert, *Arts of the South Seas* (New York: The Museum of Modern Art, 1946), 8.

50. Wheeler in *René d'Harnoncourt, 1901–1968*, 13.

51. Shepard, "Placing Picassos Required Art, Too."

52. D'Harnoncourt, Linton, and Wingert, *Arts of the South Seas*, 7.

53. A.B.L, "'Modern' Art from the Andes," *The New York Times Magazine* (January 24, 1954): 22. PI [15;16]. MoMA Archives, New York.

54. Constantine and Newtown, "Letters: In Defense of René d'Harnoncourt": 6.

55. Robert Goldwater, *Primitivism in Modern Painting* (New York: Harper and Brothers Publishers, 1938), xvii.

56. René d'Harnoncourt, letter to Bruno Adriani, February 25, 1955. MMAA, AR.1999.14.11. D'Harnoncourt later served as Rockefeller's emissary in brokering an agreement with the Metropolitan Museum of Art to create a department encompassing the holdings of the MPA and Rockefeller's personal collection. When the Museum of Primitive Art closed in 1974, its library, its staff, and 3,500 works were transferred to the Michael C. Rockefeller Wing at the Metropolitan.

57. Handwritten notes, signed RdH, n.d. MMAA, AR.1999.14.11.

58. As recounted by Sarah d'Harnoncourt. René d'Harnoncourt Papers, 1921–1983, [mf 3831;766]. Archives of American Art, Smithsonian Institution.

59. The original has since been lost, but it was reproduced as a print by the Pacific House in 1940.

60. For a complete study of the introduction of primitive art into museums of art, see Flam and Deutch, *Primitivism and Twentieth-Century Art*.

61. For a detailed account of this exhibition, see Rushing, "Marketing the Affinity of the Primitive and the Modern," 191–236; Records of the Indian Arts and Crafts Board, National Archives Record Group 435, at the National Archives and Records Administration, College Park, Maryland; as well as Foster, "Art/Artefact/Commodity": 134.

62. Dorothy Adlow, "Arts of the Andes Assembled," *The Christian Science Monitor*, February 6, 1954. PI [15;20]. MoMA Archives, NY.

63. Barnett Newman, "Arts of the South Seas" [June 1946], published in *Studio International* 179, no. 919 (February 1970): 71.

64. Max Weber, letter to d'Harnoncourt, February 24, 1953 [*sic*]. RDH, VIII.45. MoMA Archives, NY.

65. René d'Harnoncourt, letter to David H. Stevens, Director for the Humanities, Rockefeller Foundation, December 7, 1945. RF, 1.1, 200R, box 250, folder 2981. Rockefeller Archive Center.

66. Press release no. 5, January 29, 1946. The Museum of Modern Art, New York. It is remarkable that such a detailed description of the arrangement was deemed important enough to mention in the *Arts of the South Seas* press release.

67. D'Harnoncourt to Stevens. The support of the Rockefeller Foundation was noted in the catalogue's acknowledgements ("The Rockefeller Foundation made possible the additional experimental and research work necessary to demonstrate through a new display method the complex relationships between the various Pacific cultures") as well as in the "Installation Notes," posted at the exhibition's entryway, which directly addressed the display technique employed. See d'Harnoncourt, Linton, and Wingert, *Arts of the South Seas*, 6, and The Museum of Modern Art Exhibition Records [MoMA Exhs.], 306.5. MoMA Archives, NY.

68. Press release, 491014-73, October 14, 1949. The Museum of Modern Art, New York.

69. Tentative proposal, n.d. MoMA Exhs., 393.2. MoMA Archives, NY.

70. Hellman, "Imperturbable Noble": 104.

71. Tentative proposal, n.d. MoMA Exhs., 393.2. MoMA Archives, NY.

72. Exhibition brochure, n.d. Department of Circulating Records, I.4.2.14. MoMA Archives, NY.

73. Ibid.

74. Howard Devree, "Modern Art Opens Exhibition Today," *New York Times*, October 5, 1949.

75. Speech given at the Annual Meeting of the American Federation of Arts; René D'Harnoncourt, "Challenge and Promise: Modern Art and Society," *Magazine of Art* (November 1948): 251–52.

76. Hellman, "Imperturbable Noble": 102.

77. Installation notes, n.d. MoMA Exhs., 306.5. MoMA Archives, NY; Lists, n.d. RDH, IX.A.34. MoMA Archives, NY.

78. René d'Harnoncourt, radio interview by Martha Deane, WOR, New York, October 16, 1967. Transcripts, 7. MoMA Archives, NY.

79. René d'Harnoncourt quoted in Eleanor Freed, "The Alchemy of Picasso," *The Houston Post*, September 24, 1967. PI, II.A.250. MoMA Archives, NY.

80. Tentative proposal, n.d. MoMA Exhs., 393.2. MoMA Archives, NY.

81. Alfred H. Barr, Jr., *What Is Modern Painting?* (New York: The Museum of Modern Art, 1943), 5.

82. Hellman, "Imperturbable Noble": 52.

83. Edward Alden Jewell, "The Redman's Culture," *New York Times*, January 26, 1941; Foster, "Art/Artefact/Commodity": 134.

84. Edward Alden Jewell, "Art from Oceania," *The New York Times*, February 3, 1946.

85. Peter Selz, interview with the author, August 17, 2017.

86. For further reading on installations at MoMA, see Charlotte Klonk, *Spaces of Experience: Art Gallery Interiors from 1800 to 2000* (New Haven: Yale University Press, 2009); Mary Anne Staniszewski, *The Power of Display: A History of Exhibition Installations at The Museum of Modern Art* (Cambridge, MA: The MIT Press, 1998).

87. In 1955, Kiesler wrote to d'Harnoncourt thanking him for a recommendation for a grant from the Chapelbrook Foundation: "You, who have so much dwelt in the realm of the work of early cultures, where the ritual is the very core and meaning of life, art and architecture, I'm sure will understand me better than anyone else . . . Remembering the many conversations we had in the past years and your, can I say sympathy you documented so often for me and my work. . . ." Frederick Kiesler, letter to d'Harnoncourt, March 22, 1955. RDH, III.42. MoMA Archives, NY.

88. Master checklist, n.d. MoMA Exhs., 682.1. MoMA Archives, NY.

89. Press release no. 31, March 28, 1961. The Museum of Modern Art, New York.

90. Freed, "The Alchemy of Picasso."

91. Perhaps the standard-bearer was Richard Lohse's *New Design in Exhibitions: 75 Examples of the New Form of Exhibitions* (published in German in 1953 and in English by Praeger in 1954, and acquired by the MoMA Library by March of that year). The book included a half-dozen MoMA exhibitions. Lohse sought to analyze an exhibition technique reliant on form and function, which he saw as distinctive of the era. After an introductory essay touching on various aspects of and historical moments in exhibition design, the book presented seventy-five case studies that included a summary of the subject, form, and construction of the show, accompanied by a fine selection of photographs and plans. Robert Gutmann and Alexander Koch published the profusely illustrated *Exhibition Stands* in 1954, in German, English, and French editions. The authors reviewed the manners of display for merchandise or a theme, and emphasized the importance of exhibitions and trade fairs in communicating ideas with a mass public. They enlisted seven noted experts (including George Nelson, Misha Black, and Gio Ponti) to gain an international perspective. The book only includes three examples from MoMA, one of which is *Arts of the South Seas*. Although the authors did not credit d'Harnoncourt by name, they noted that the secret of the exhibition's success was its use of skillful lighting techniques. Some volumes focus specifically on practical aspects of installation. Klaus Franck's volume *Exhibitions* (1961) included an introduction delineating various elements of exhibition design, including available space, display armatures, lighting, graphics and didactics, followed by well over 100 examples of exhibition and trade show installations. It included only a half-dozen from MoMA, none of which were by d'Harnoncourt. In 1962, James H. Carmel published *Exhibition Techniques: Traveling and Temporary*. This detailed manual considered every single component of exhibition-making, from installation to crating and shipping. Carmel cited several examples of d'Harnoncourt exhibitions; he criticized *Arts of South Seas* for its rigid, maze-like circulation plan. While he conceded such a layout allowed one to focus the

attention of the visitor on specific locations, he argued against the technique particularly for institutions like MoMA, which expected large numbers of visitors to crowd the galleries (H. Carmel, *Exhibition Techniques: Traveling and Temporary* [New York: Reinhold Publishing Corp., 1962], 30.).
92. Hellman, "Imperturbable Noble": 104.
93. Omer, a scholar who had come to the United States in 1966 to study museum installation, may have assisted d'Harnoncourt with *The Sculpture of Picasso*, though he was not credited with any official role in the press release or exhibition catalogue. After many months of work and a couple drafts of the manuscript, the project was abandoned, as the Museum found Omer's text to be inadequate, poorly written, and fraught with errors. Mordechai Omer, unpublished manuscript. RDH, X.D.4. MoMA Archives, NY.
94. Ibid.
95. Hellman, "Imperturbable Noble": 50.
96. René d'Harnoncourt, *Teaching Portfolio Number Three: Modern Art Old and New* (New York: The Museum of Modern Art, 1950).
97. René d'Harnoncourt, interview by Ruth Bowman, "Views on Art," WNYC, October 23, 1967. Transcripts, 8. MoMA Archives, NY.
98. René d'Harnoncourt, "Challenge and Promise": 252.
99. Robert Goldwater, in *René d'Harnoncourt, 1901–1968*, 31.

Exhibition Portfolios

1. Reminiscences of René d'Harnoncourt (1968), *Carnegie Corporation project*, 9. Columbia University Center for Oral History Archives, Rare Book & Manuscript Library, Columbia University in the City of New York.
2. Alfred Barr in *René d'Harnoncourt, 1901–1968: A Tribute, October 8, 1968, Sculpture Garden, The Museum of Modern Art* (New York: The Museum of Modern Art, 1968), 19.
3. Press release, January 20, 1941. The Museum of Modern Art, New York.
4. René d'Harnoncourt, "Living Arts of the Indians," *Magazine of Art* 34, no. 2 (February 19, 1941): 76.
5. "20,000 Years of Indian Art Assembled for New York Show," *Newsweek* (February 3, 1941): 57–58.
6. D'Harnoncourt, letter to Frederick Keppel, August 19, 1938; quoted in W. Jackson Rushing, "Marketing the Affinity of the Primitive and the Modern," in *The Early Years of Native American Art History*, ed. Catherine Berlo (Seattle: University of Washington Press; Vancouver: University of British Columbia Press, 1992), 201.
7. Barr in *René d'Harnoncourt, 1901–1968*, 19.
8. Edward Alden Jewell, "The Redman's Culture," *New York Times,* January 26, 1941.
9. Press release no. 5, January 29, 1946. The Museum of Modern Art, New York.
10. Gregory Bateson, "Arts of the South Seas," *Arts Bulletin* 28, no. 3 (June 1946): 121–23.
11. Robert M. Coates, "The Art Galleries: The Modern Museum and Other Problems," *The New Yorker* 21, no. 52 (February 9, 1946): 64–67.
12. Naum Gabo, letter to Monroe Wheeler, February 22, 1948. Naum Gabo Papers, Beinecke Rare Book and Manuscript Library, Yale University.
13. The resulting use of multiple strings was distracting and competed with the sculpture, making this, in the opinion of the author, perhaps one of the few design mishaps in d'Harnoncourt's long career.

14. Eleanor Bittermann, "Review: Exhibitions," *Architectural Forum* 88, no. 3 (March 1948): 146. She is referring to her previous review of *Arts of the South Seas*, published in *Architectural Forum,* May 1946.
15. Carlyle Burrows, "Art of the Week," *Herald Tribune*, February 15, 1948.
16. Henry McBride, "Lyrical Sculpture," *New York Sun*, October 15, 1958. Pl [11;575]. MoMA Archives, NY.
17. Lincoln Kirstein, letter to Mordechai Omer, November 29, 1970, cited in Omer, "René d'Harnoncourt: His Art of Installation," unpublished manuscript, 16, 1968–1974. RDH, IX.D.2. MoMA Archives, NY.
18. René d'Harnoncourt, letter to Gordon B. Washburn, January 27, 1949. MoMA Exhs., 393.3. MoMA Archives, NY.
19. Typescript, Amy Spingarn, "A Jungian's View of *Timeless Aspects of Modern Art*," December 1948. MoMA Exhs., 393.3. MoMA Archives, NY.
20. Howard Devree, "Place of Moderns in Art is Depicted," *The New York Times*, November 17, 1948.
21. Emily Genauer, "Museum Contrasts Paintings of All Ages," *New York World Telegram*, November 27, 1948.
22. Robert Goldwater and René d'Harnoncourt, *Modern Art in Your Life* (New York: The Museum of Modern Art, 1949), preface.
23. Tentative proposal, n.d. MoMA Exhs., 393.2. MoMA Archives, NY.
24. Thomas Hess, "Of Arts and the Man," *Art News* 48, no. 6 (October 6, 1949): 16.
25. Robert M. Coates, "The Art Galleries: Mondrian, Kleenex, and You," *The New Yorker* 25, no. 34 (October 15, 1949): 61–63.
26. Draft exhibition proposal, n.d. RDH, VIII.1. MoMA Archives, NY.
27. René d'Harnoncourt, talk on *Ancient Arts of the Andes*, February 24, 1954. Transcripts, 2. MoMA Archives, NY.
28. René d'Harnoncourt, letter to Richard S. Davis, May 7, 1953, asking the Minneapolis Institute of Arts to co-sponsor the exhibition. RDH, VIII.1. MoMA Archives, NY.

29. Draft exhibition proposal, n.d. RDH, VIII.1. MoMA Archives, NY.
30. "Pan-American-Grace Airways: Nights in Latin America," advertisement script, n.d. RDH, VIII.24. MoMA Archives, NY.
31. Howard Devree, "Andes Exhibition on Display Today," *The New York Times*, January 27, 1954.
32. Emily Genauer, "Art and Artists: Andean Exhibit at Modern Museum," *New York Herald Tribune*, January 31, 1954.
33. Thomas C. Howe, Jr., letter to René d'Harnoncourt, August 3, 1954. RDH VIII.13. MoMA Archives, NY.
34. The few traces of the original installation design can be gleaned from photographs from the opening party and in Cynthia Kellogg, "Seurat Art Gives Ideas for Walls," *The New York Times*, April 2, 1958.
35. Howard Devree, "Art: Seurat Exhibition," *The New York Times*, March 26, 1958.
36. John Maxon, letter to d'Harnoncourt, April 3, 1958. RDH, VII.61. MoMA Archives, NY.
37. Dorothy Adlow, untitled review, *The Christian Science Monitor*, November 18, 1958. PI [43;14]. MoMA Archives, NY.
38. William Rubin, "Month in Review," *Arts Magazine* (November 1958): 39. PI [43;45-46]. MoMA Archives, NY.
39. James Thrall Soby, letter to François Arp, January 5, 1959. MoMA Exhs., 631.6. MoMA Archives, NY.
40. Carola Giedion-Welcker, letter to James Thrall Soby, January 14, 1959. MoMA Exhs., 631.4. MoMA Archives, NY.
41. James Thrall Soby, letter to Monroe Wheeler, May 7, 1969. Bates Lowry Papers, I.27.e. MoMA Archives, NY.
42. This collection is now part of the Metropolitan Museum of Art's holdings.
43. René d'Harnoncourt, letter to Nelson Rockefeller, May 28, 1962. MMAA, AR.1999.1.40(6).
44. Robert Goldwater, press release, Museum of Primitive Art, March 1, 1968. MMAA, AR.1999.1.40(5).

45. John Canaday, "Art: Sculptures of Rodin," *The New York Times*, May 1, 1963.
46. "Art: Before Your Very Eyes," *Time* 81, no. 19 (May 10, 1963): 86.
47. Albert Elsen, "Rodin Rediscovered," *Art International* 7, no. 7 (September 25, 1963). PI [24;427]. MoMA Archives, NY.
48. René d'Harnoncourt, quoted in Richard F. Shepard, "Placing Picassos Required Art, Too," *The New York Times*, October 19, 1967.
49. David Shirey, "Picasso's Hidden Treasure," *Newsweek* 70, no. 16 (October 16, 1967): 110.
50. Wall label text, n.d. RDH, VIII.51. MoMA Archives, NY.
51. René d'Harnoncourt, radio interview by Ruth Bowman, "Views of Art," WNYC, October 23, 1967. Transcripts, 8. MoMA Archives, New York.
52. Shepard, "Placing Picassos Required Art, Too."
53. René d'Harnoncourt, letter to Grace Mayer, n.d. RDH, IV.297. MoMA Archives, NY.
54. Alfred Barr, letter to Henry Kahnweiler, November 8, 1967. MoMA Exhs., 841.6. MoMA Archives, NY.
55. Grace Mayer, letter to d'Harnoncourt, October 29, 1967. RDH, IV.297. MoMA Archives, NY.

René d'Harnoncourt: A Life

1. *René d'Harnoncourt, 1901–1968: A Tribute, October 8, 1968, Sculpture Garden, The Museum of Modern Art* (New York: The Museum of Modern Art, 1968), 1.
2. For the most definitive primary sources on d'Harnoncourt's biography, see transcript of interview of d'Harnoncourt by Geoffrey Hellman, n.d., The Geoffrey T. Hellman Papers; MSS 050; box 13; folder 21; Fales Library and Special Collections, New York University Libraries; Reminiscences of René d'Harnoncourt (1968), *Carnegie Corporation project*, Columbia University Center for Oral History Archives, Rare Book & Manuscript Library, Columbia University in the City of New York; and Geoffrey T. Hellman, "Profiles: Imperturbable Noble," *The New Yorker* 36, no. 12 (May 7, 1960): 67–111.
3. Reminiscences of René d'Harnoncourt, 29.
4. *The Reopening of the Mexican and Central American Hall, February 25, 1944, The American Museum of Natural History* (New York: The American Museum of Natural History, 1944), 23.
5. The citation included the following: "A versatile painter and creative craftsman, acclaimed as a writer both for your children's stories and for your scholarly work on the art of the Indians, today as Director of the Museum of Modern Art you seem to thrive on the hazardous occupation of running a museum in the no man's land of contemporary art." Typescript, "Museum of Modern Art Staff Biography," n.d. The Geoffrey T. Hellman Papers; MSS 050; box 13; folder 21; Fales Library and Special Collections, New York University Libraries; and Reminiscences of René d'Harnoncourt.

Photography Credits

All images and original documents are sourced from The Museum of Modern Art Archives unless otherwise specified and have been scanned courtesy of the Museum's Department of Imaging and Visual Resources. In these notes, the following abbreviations have been used for collections from the MoMA Archives:

PA   Photographic Archive
A&P   Artists and Personalities
RDH   René d'Harnoncourt Papers

Front cover: PA, A&P. Photographer: John Vachon for *LOOK* magazine.
Back cover: RDH, IX.A.7.
Endpapers (front): RDH, IX.A.60.
Frontispiece: PA.
Pg. 6: PA. Photographer: Albert Fenn.
Pg. 9: RDH, X.E.15.
Pg. 10: PA. Photographer: William Leftwich.
Pg. 11: PA, A&P. Photographer: Rollie McKenna. © Rosalie Thorne McKenna Foundation
Pg. 12: Carl Zigrosser Papers, Kislak Center for Special Collections, Rare Books and Manuscripts, University of Pennsylvania.
Pg. 13, both images: RDH, X.E.23.
Pg. 14: RDH, X.A.1.
Pg. 15: Tina Modotti, *René d'Harnoncourt Puppet.* The Museum of Fine Arts, Houston, Museum purchase funded by Marion and Joe Mundy in honor of Rachel Muncy, 96.563.
Pg. 16, top: Manuel Álvarez Bravo, *René d'Harnoncourt.* The Museum of Modern Art, New York. Gift of René d'Harnoncourt. © 2018 Estate of Manuel Álvarez Bravo / Artists Rights Society (ARS), New York / ADAGP, Paris; bottom: Digital reproduction from hand-colored photographs in the Morrow Family Papers by Jim Gipe, 2002. From the Morrow Family Papers, Sophia Smith Collection, Smith College (Northampton, Massachusetts).
Pg. 17: Collection of Joseph J. Rishel, Philadelphia.
Pg. 18, top: RDH, X.A.17; bottom: RDH.
Pg. 19, top: RDH, X.A.15; bottom: RDH, X.A.12.
Pg. 20–21: RDH, IX.A.39.
Pg. 22: RDH, IX.A.108.
Pg. 23: clockwise from top left: RDH, IX.A.26; RDH, IX.A.5; RDH, IX.A.18; RDH, IX.A.18; RDH, IX.A.18; RDH, IX.A.14.
Pg. 24: RDH, IX.A.10.
Pg. 25: RDH, IX.A.9.

Pg. 27: RDH, IX.C.5.
Pg. 28: RDH, IX.C.11.
Pg. 29, top: RDH, X.B.6; bottom: PA.
Pg. 30: PA. Photographer: Albert Fenn.
Pg. 31: RDH, IX.A.54.
Pg. 32: RDH, IX.A.108.
Pg. 33: RDH, IX.A.108.
Pg. 34: RDH, IX.A.33.
Pg. 35: RDH, IX.A.10.
Pg. 37: Alan Blackburn Papers, Album 1.
Pg. 38–39: RDH, IX.A.60.
Pg. 40: RDH, IX.A.114.
Pg. 41: RDH, IX.A.31.
Pg. 43: PA, A&P.
Pg. 44, left: RDH, X.A.5. © Maria Elena Rico Covarrubias; right: The Metropolitan Museum of Art, The Michael C. Rockfeller Memorial Collection, Bequest of Nelson A. Rockefeller, 1979 (1979.206.1939). © The Metropolitan Museum of Art. Image Source: Art Resource, NY.
Pg. 45, top left: MoMA Library, © Maria Elena Rico Covarrubias; top right: RDH, IX.A.9; bottom: Courtesy of the Frick Art Reference Library. © Maria Elena Rico Covarrubias.
Pg. 46: MoMA Library.
Pg. 47: RDH, IX.A.6.
Pg. 48: RDH, IX.A.6.
Pg. 49, top: Folder 2981, Box 250, Series 200R, RG 1.1, Projects, FA386, Rockefeller Foundation records (RF), Rockefeller Archive Center (RAC). Courtesy of Rockefeller Archive Center; bottom: RDH, IX.A.115.
Pg. 50: RDH, IX.A.114.
Pg. 51: RDH, IX.A.114.
Pg. 52: MoMA Library.
Pg. 53: PA, A&P. Photographer: John Vachon for LOOK Magazine.
Pg. 54: PA. Photographer: Ezra Stoller. © Ezra Stoller/Esto.
Pg. 55, top: RDH, IX.A.114; bottom: PA. Photographer: Soichi Sunami.
Pg. 56, top: RDH, IX.A.114. bottom: PA. Photographer: George Cserna.
Pg. 57: Folder 2981, Box 250, Series 200R, RG 1.1, Projects, FA386, RF, RAC. Courtesy of Rockefeller Archive Center.
Pg. 59: RDH, VIII.51.
Pg. 60: RDH, IX.A.15.
Pg. 61: RDH, IX.A.40.
Pg. 62: PA.
Pg. 63: PA. Photographer: Soichi Sunami.
Pg. 64: PA. Photographer: Peter Juley.

Pg. 65, top: The New York Public Library. © 2018 Artists Rights Society (ARS), New York / VG Bild-Kunst, Bonn; bottom: PA. Photographer: Soichi Sunami.
Pg. 66, top: PA. Photographer: Samuel H. Gottscho; bottom: PA. Photographer: Albert Fenn.
Pg. 67: Photographer: Berenice Abbott. © 2017 Austrian Frederick and Lillian Kiesler Private Foundation, Vienna. © Berenice Abbott/Masters Collection/ Getty Images.
Pg. 68: PA. Photographer: Eliot Elisofon. © Eliot Elisofon/The LIFE Picture Collection/Getty Images.
Pg. 69, left: Edward Steichen Archive, VIII.7. Photographer: Paul Berg. © Paul Berg/St. Louis Dispatch/Polaris Images; right: RDH, X.C.5.34. From *The New York Times*, June 27, 1968 © 2018 *The New York Times*.
Pg. 70–71: RDH, IX.A.17.
Pg. 73, top: RDH, IX.C.3; bottom: RDH, IX.C.8.
Pg. 74, top: RDH, IX.C.3; bottom: © The Metropolitan Museum of Art. Image Source: Art Resource, NY.
Pg. 75: © The Metropolitan Museum of Art. Image Source: Art Resource, NY.
Pg. 76: Library of Congress, Prints & Photographs Division, WPA Poster Collection, LC-USZC2-936.
Pg. 77, both images: PA.
Pg. 78: PA.
Pg. 79, top: PA. Photographer: Eliot Elisofon; bottom: PA.
Pg. 80, both images: PA.
Pg. 81: PA.
Pg. 82, left: RDH, IX.A.33; right: RDH, IX.A.18.
Pg. 83: RDH, IX.A.12.
Pg. 84, clockwise from top left: RDH, IX.A.6; RDH, IX.A.40; RDH, IX.A.40; RDH, IX.A.6.
Pg. 85, left: RDH, IX.A.7; right: RDH, IX.A.6.
Pg. 86: RDH, IX.A.7.
Pg. 87, top left: RDH, IX.A.41; top right: RDH, IX.A.42; bottom: RDH, IX.A.6.
Pg. 88, top: PA. Photographer: Soichi Sunami; bottom: RDH, IX.A.6.
Pg. 89, top: PA. Photographer: Soichi Sunami; bottom: RDH, IX.A.41.
Pg. 91: PA. Photographer: Soichi Sunami
Pg. 92: RDH, IX.A.51.
Pg. 93, both images: RDH, IX.A.51.
Pg. 94, both images: PA. Photographer: Soichi Sunami.

Pg. 95, top: RDH, IX.A.51; bottom: PA.
Photographer: Soichi Sunami.
Pg. 96: RDH, IX.A.55.
Pg. 97: PA. Photographer: Soichi Sunami.
Pg. 98, both images: RDH, IX.A.56.
Pg. 99: RDH, IX.A.54.
Pg. 100: RDH, IX.A.53.
Pg. 101, top: PA. Photographer: Soichi Sunami;
bottom: RDH, IX.A.56.
Pg. 102: RDH, IX.A.60.
Pg. 103: PA. Photographer: Soichi Sunami.
Pg. 104: PA. Photographer: Soichi Sunami.
Pg. 105: RDH, IX.A.60.
Pg. 106: RDH, IX.A.60.
Pg. 107: RDH, IX.A.60.
Pg. 108–9: RDH, IX.A.62.
Pg. 109: PA. Photographer: Homer Page.
Pg. 111: PA. Photographer: Soichi Sunami.
Pg. 112, all three drawings: RDH, IX.A.65.
Pg. 113: RDH, IX.A.64.
Pg. 114: RDH, IX.A.64.
Pg. 115: PA. Photographer: Soichi Sunami.
Pg. 116, top: The Museum of Modern Art
Exhibition Records, 423.1; bottom:
RDH, IX.A.64.
Pg. 117, top: PA. Photographer: Soichi Sunami;
bottom: RDH, IX.A.64.
Pg. 119: PA. Photographer: Alexandre Georges.
Pg. 120: RDH, VIII.45.
Pg. 121: PA. Photographer: Soichi Sunami.
Pg. 122: RDH, IX.A.70.
Pg. 123, clockwise from top left: RDH, IX.A.68;
RDH, IX.A.69; RDH, IX.A.69; RDH, IX.A.68.
Pg. 124: PA. Photographer: Alexandre Georges.
Pg. 125: RDH, IX.A.68.
Pg. 126: PA. Photographer: Soichi Sunami.
Pg. 127, left: RDH, IX.A.69; right: PA.
Photographer: Soichi Sunami.
Pg. 129: RDH, IX.A.81.
Pg. 130, top: PA. Photographer: Allyn Baum;
bottom: RDH, IX.A.81.

Pg. 131, both images: PA. Photographer:
Allyn Baum.
Pg. 132: RDH, IX.A.82.
Pg. 133: RDH, IX.A.82.
Pg. 134: RDH, IX.A.83.
Pg. 135, top: PA. Photographer: Soichi
Sunami; bottom: RDH, IX.A.82.
Pg. 136 and 137: PA. Photographer:
Soichi Sunami.
Pg. 138–41: PA. Photographer: Ezra Stoller.
© Ezra Stoller/Esto.
Pg. 142: RDH, IX.A.102.
Pg. 143: PA. Photographer: George Barrows
Pg. 144, top: PA. Photographer: George
Barrows; bottom: RDH, IX.A.102.
Pg. 145, top: RDH, IX.A.102; bottom
(both images): PA. Photographer:
George Barrows.
Pg. 147, top: RDH, IX.A.114; bottom: PA.
Photographer: George Cserna.
Pg. 148: RDH, IX.A.108.
Pg. 149, top: PA. Photographer: Dan Budnik;
bottom: RDH, IX.A.114.
Pg. 150: RDH, IX.A.108.
Pg. 150–51: PA. Photographer:
George Cserna.
Pg. 152, top: RDH, IX.A.108 (both drawings);
bottom: PA.
Pg. 153: PA. Photographer: George Cserna.
Pg. 154–55: PA. Photographer: George Cserna.
Pg. 156: RDH, X.C.5.35. Photographer:
Sidney Waintrob. © David Stekert of Budd
Studio 2018.
Pg. 158, top: RDH, X.A.11.a; bottom: RDH.
Pg. 160: PA, A&P. Photographer: John Vachon
for *LOOK* magazine.
Pg. 162: PA. Photographer: Dan Budnik.
Pg. 163: Department of Public Information
Records, II.C.85.
Endpapers (back): RDH, IX.A.55.

Major support is provided by The Contemporary Arts Council of The Museum of Modern Art, and by The Museum of Modern Art's Research and Scholarly Publications endowment established through the generosity of The Andrew W. Mellon Foundation, the Edward John Noble Foundation, Mr. and Mrs. Perry R. Bass, and the National Endowment for the Humanities' Challenge Grant Program.

Produced by the Department of Publications
The Museum of Modern Art, New York

Christopher Hudson, Publisher
Don McMahon, Editorial Director
Marc Sapir, Production Director

Edited by Madeleine Compagnon
Designed by Miko McGinty and Rita Jules
Production by Matthew Pimm
Printed and bound by Pristone Pte. Ltd.,
    Singapore
This book is typeset in Theinhardt
The paper is 140gsm Magno Natural

Published by The Museum of Modern Art
11 West 53 Street, New York,
New York 10019-5497
www.moma.org

Distributed in the United States and Canada by ARTBOOK | D.A.P.
155 Sixth Avenue, New York, New York 10013
www.artbook.com

Distributed outside the United States and Canada by Thames & Hudson Ltd.
181a High Holborn, London WC1V 7QX
www.thamesandhudson.com

Library of Congress Control Number:
2018948227
ISBN: 978-1-63345-050-9

Cover: René d'Harnoncourt during the installation of the exhibition *Modern Art in Your Life*, 1949

Back cover: preparatory vista of the exhibition *Arts of the South Seas*, 1946

Frontispiece: René d'Harnoncourt with a small wooden sculpture shown in *Arts of the South Seas*, c. 1946

Endpapers: front, floorplan of the exhibition *Timeless Aspects of Modern Art*, 1948; back, vista of the exhibition *Elie Nadelman*, 1948

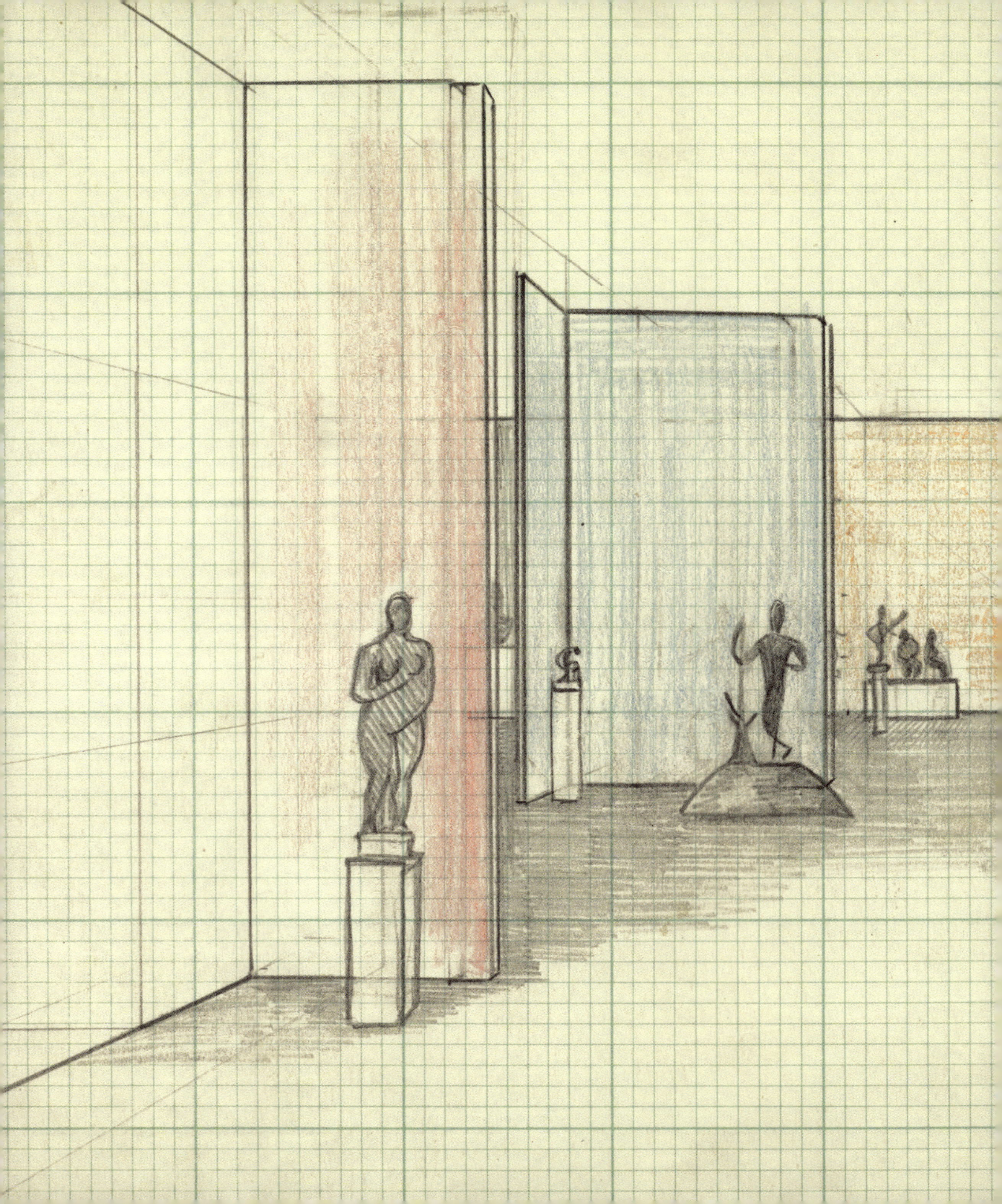